PROVIDENCE & PRAYER

How Does God Work in the World?

TERRANCE TIESSEN

InterVarsity Press
Downers Grove, Illinois

InterVarsity Press
P.O. Box 1400, Downers Grove, IL 60515
World Wide Web: www.ivpress.com
E-mail: mail@ivpress.com

InterVarsity Press® is the book-publishing division of InterVarsity Christian Fellowship/USA®, a student movement active on campus at hundreds of universities, colleges and schools of nursing in the United States of America, and a member movement of the International Fellowship of Evangelical Students. For information about local and regional activities, write Public Relations Dept., InterVarsity Christian Fellowship/USA, 6400 Schroeder Rd., P.O. Box 7895, Madison, WI 53707-7895.

Scripture quotations, unless otherwise noted, are from the New Revised Standard Version of the Bible, *copyright 1989 by the Division of Christian Education of the National Council of the Churches of Christ in the USA. Used by permission. All rights reserved.*

Cover photographs: Terry Vine/Tony Stone Images

ISBN 0-8308-1578-3

Printed in the United States of America ∞

Library of Congress Cataloging-in-Publication Data

Tiessen, Terrance L., 1944-
  Providence & prayer: how does God work in the world?/Terrance Tiessen.
    p. cm.
  Includes bibliographical references.
  ISBN 0-8308-1578-3 (pbk.: alk. paper)
    1. Providence and government of God. 2. Prayer—Christianity.   I. Title: Providence and prayer.   II. Title.
BT135.T54 2000
231'.5—dc21
                                                                                    00-026316

19	18	17	16	15	14	13	12	11	10	9	8	7	6	5	4	3	2	1
15	14	13	12	11	10	09	08	07	06	05	04	03	02	01	00			

To my parents,
Fred and Ella Tiessen,
who first taught me to pray
to the God who takes care of me and all his creatures.

CONTENTS

Acknowledgments

Most of the research and writing of the first draft of this book was done during a sabbatical from Providence Theological Seminary, and I am grateful to the school's administrators for giving me that time, without which a project of this size could not be done. My research was greatly facilitated by the assistance of a number of libraries in Oxford: the Bodleian, the Theology Faculty and Wycliffe Hall, which graciously gave me space to work as a visiting scholar throughout my time in Oxford. My wife, Gail, has been patient throughout the lengthy process, particularly through the times along the way when I have thought out loud about these complex issues. Her listening ear has been an important part of the process by which I have worked through my assessment of the various models of providence and prayer that already exist and have formulated my own.

A class of seminary students gave me an additional opportunity to hear myself think and to get some response as they worked through my manuscript in a seminar dealing with the theology of revelation and of God. Two people reviewed my earlier draft at the request of InterVarsity Press, and I am grateful for their helpful comments and further stimulus. I do not know the identity of the one who substantially agreed with me, but the other was John Sanders, whose own work on the doctrine of providence is now the definitive published statement of the openness model. John's model is very different from mine, but I consider it a highly coherent presentation, given the different stance that he takes on a few key issues. I do not expect to convince John of the greater merits of my own proposal, but it has been helpful to think through his challenge to it. He has given me permission to identify him when I interact with his comments, but I have tried to be sensitive to his observation that these were not made with quite the same precision that he uses when writing for publication.

Speaking of publication, I am grateful to my IVP editor, Dan Reid, for having seen merit in my work and given it a careful reading. He offered very helpful suggestions for its improvement, particularly in regard to ways in which the rather difficult material can be made more useful to readers who are interested in the subject but who have not read widely in the theological and philosophical literature that uses terms that are not part of the average person's vocabulary. Needless to say, there are limits to what anyone else can do with a manuscript written by another person, and so I take responsibility for any shortcomings even while I express gratitude to these who have helped bring the work to its final stage.

Each day that I entered the Bodleian Library, I was greeted by the motto on the glass doors at the entrance, *Dominus illuminatio mea.* That the Lord would enlighten me has been my constant prayer as I have wrestled with these complex issues in an effort to understand the ways of God in the world and the role that he has given to us in prayer. I am grateful for all the help that God has given me. Although I have been very conscious of his assistance at many points, there are doubtless even more ways in which God has provided than even I realize. I identify with Paul's observation: "Now we see in a mirror, dimly, but then we will see face to face. Now I know only in part; then I will know fully, even as I have been fully known" (1 Cor 13:12). It is my prayer that God will use this book to lead others further in their knowledge of God and his ways and of God's will concerning our participation in his work by prayer.

Abbreviations

AJTP	*American Journal of Theology and Philosophy*
APQ	*American Philosophical Quarterly*
CBQ	*Catholic Biblical Quarterly*
CC	*Christian Century*
CD	*Church Dogmatics*
CH	*Church History*
Col	*Colloquim*
CSR	*Christian Scholar's Review*
CTJ	*Calvin Theological Journal*
CTNSB	*Bulletin of the Center for Theology and the Natural Sciences*
EvQ	*Evangelical Quarterly*
ExpTim	*The Expository Times*
FP	*Faith and Philosophy*
HBT	*Horizons in Biblical Theology*
HTR	*Harvard Theological Review*
HUCA	*Hebrew Union College Annual*
IJPR	*International Journal for Philosophy and Religion*
JETS	*Journal of the Evangelical Theological Society*
JR	*Journal of Religion*
JRHealth	*Journal of Religion and Health*
MQR	*The Mennonite Quarterly Review*
Ph	*Philosophy*
PhRev	*Philosophical Review*
RefRev	*Reformed Review*
RelS	*Religious Studies*
RevExp	*Review and Expositor*
SCB	*Science and Christian Belief*
ST	*The Summa Theologica*
TDNT	*Theological Dictionary of the New Testament*
TToday	*Theology Today*
VC	*Vigiliae Christianae*
VE	*Vox Evangelica*
WesleyTJ	*Wesley Theological Journal*
WTJ	*Westminster Theological Journal*

1

Introduction

At a church breakfast on an Easter morning in Oxford, people sitting at our table asked what I was doing on my sabbatical. When I told them about my work on this book, we naturally got talking about prayer. Two people at the table told me of how they regularly pray for parking spaces when they go into London, where parking spots are very difficult to find, and how God provides them. I asked one of them what God would have to do to answer her prayer, and she looked a bit stunned. "I don't know," she said. "Do you think I need to pray?"

My answer was and still is yes. We *should* define our understanding concerning the nature of God's action in the world and pray accordingly. In fact, my desire to research and write this book grew out of my discovery that the way my students prayed was often not consistent with the doctrine of providence that they confessed. They often ask God to do things that he cannot do, given the way he has chosen to relate to the world that he has created, as they understand the situation. Actually, the inconsistency in the theology of my students gets even more complicated. I teach a survey of systematic theology in two semesters. One of the subjects we study in the first semester is the providence of God, that is, God's care for and action in the world that he has created. In the second semester the subject of salvation is on the agenda. At the conclusion of each of the major sections of theology I ask my students to write a personal confession of faith: their own detailed doctrinal statement. I am regularly fascinated (and a bit frustrated) to find a conflict between the truth that students confess regarding providence and their beliefs regarding salvation.

Usually when inconsistency occurs between statements of faith formulated by my students, it is because they have a model of *providence* that understands God to be very much in control of the details of their lives but a model of *salvation* that assumes that the outcome rests with the "free choice" of individuals. I recall, for instance, a day when some students had a car accident on their way to the school's day of prayer. The injured students were prayed for frequently during that day, and almost always the prayers indicated a belief that God had been completely in control when the accident occurred. It would not have happened if God had not "permitted" it to do so. From my experience in class, I knew that most (or all) of those who prayed would have confessed a doctrine of meticulous providence that was consistent with their prayer. However, when they speak about salvation, their model of the respective roles of God and human beings is different than when they speak of providence. Yet their practice of prayer in regard to salvation is often more consistent with their doctrine of providence than with their doctrine of salvation. This incoherence within their theological framework and between that theoretical framework and their practice of prayer troubles me.

In my context students tend to believe that Christ died for everyone and that the final population of heaven is determined by human decisions. They affirm this because of a strong, frequently intuited, commitment to radical human freedom. They believe in what is often called "libertarian freedom," which may be simply defined as the power to have chosen to do something other than what one actually chose to do in a particular situation. (The glossary at the back of the book should be helpful when you encounter terms like this and have forgotten how they were defined.) But when these students pray for the unsaved, they frequently assume that God can do things to bring about the salvation of people, which it is not possible for God to do if those people have the sort of freedom that these intercessors believe to be the case.

As a systematic theologian, I have a keen interest in coherence. I believe that people's beliefs should be internally consistent (i.e., that they should agree with themselves!) and that their actions should be consistent with their theology. To facilitate this coherence or consistency I did this study and wrote this book. I have set out to identify some of the common ways in which God's involvement in the world has been understood and to discern what sort of petitionary prayer is appropriate to each of these concepts or models of providence. The focus of this work is, therefore, on the providence of God and prayer, particularly petitionary prayer. I will speak of God's involvement in the world generally, in nature, history and the details of our lives, rather than focusing on the more specific aspect of salvation. It is my hope, however, that this discussion will help readers to clarify their general understanding of God's relationship to the world and his action in it, and then to be consistent in regard to all areas of God's work, including the very important work of salvation. Of course, the two are often related. When listening to people's testimony regarding the process by which they came to faith in Christ, we often hear references to minor events in their lives in which they believe God was involved as part of his drawing them to himself.

The Doctrine of Providence

It would be unwise to give too detailed a definition of providence at this point, since the nature of God's providence varies somewhat from one model to another. On the other hand, we need to have an idea of what we are looking for in searching for models of divine providence. In general terms we will think of providence as God's activity of preserving and governing the whole of creation.

Issues Arising in a Study of Providence

In 1963 Langdon Gilkey noted "the curious fact that today this concept of Providence is notable mainly in its absence from theological discussion."[1] He found this surprising because both Reformation and liberal theologians possessed "carefully elaborated and very significant conceptions of Providence," and because "the question most frequently asked in contemporary theological discussion—What is the meaning, if any, of history?—might seem to call for an equally strong view of God's providential rule over historical events."[2]

From Gilkey's perspective the doctrine of providence was secure in natural theology from Francis Bacon in the seventeenth century through the mid-nineteenth century,[3] since everything in nature was seen as designed for a purpose, particularly for the good of humanity. But, he suggests, the Darwinian hypothesis demolished this view by portraying the fittingness of things as self-explanatory, rather than attributing it to an external designer, since real causes were viewed as random, impersonal and mechanical. Charles Cashdollar notes that by the late nineteenth and early twentieth century, "For all intents and purposes the orthodox theory of divine providence was dead in academic circles. With it was buried the debate over its practical implications." It is no longer discussed in theological journals after the 1890s.[4] However, Gilkey observes that the doctrine soon recovered, as some sort of aim or purpose was identified in the progress that was being assumed. Therefore, post-Darwinian theology was once more "Providence-centred."[5] The fundamental concept of progress was rendered "unintelligible and meaningless" by the two world wars, and Gilkey then notes a "universal feeling that *no* purpose, direction, or meaning of any sort could be seen in the general passage of historical events."[6]

In the years following the second world war, Gilkey found passing references to providence, a recognition that God rules general events in some way and can bring good out of evil. But "of all the major classical doctrines of theology, Providence is the single one which has not been reinterpreted and revitalized by contemporary theology but which has, on the contrary, been generally ignored and in some cases even repudiated."[7] As recently as May 1999 a reviewer of works on history observed: "Once, the word *providence* efficiently communicated the idea that God loved us, ruled time to its minute details, and was himself a historical agent. That time is gone, however, and the word has rusted up through misuse beyond utility."[8]

Gilkey's challenge to develop a doctrine of providence has since been taken up by a number of theologians whose work we will meet in the chapters that follow, including Gilkey himself.[9] Both theologians and philosophers of religion have given much attention to the thorny issues that arise when we attempt to understand God's action in the world. It is hoped that the term *providence* can once more become useful.

Among the questions to which answers have been attempted and that will be a large part of our quest in this book are the following: What is the nature of divine causation? Should we even talk of God as a "cause" and, if not, what sort of language is appropriate to describe the nature of the divine involvement in the natural world and human history? What is the nature of God's omnipotence? No Christian theologian denies that God is omnipotent, but there is no consensus as to what that means in the practical terms of God's acts in the world.

In particular, how is God's omnipotence affected by his creation of other agents with intentions and actions of their own? How free, then, are these respective agents, God and his creatures, and how is *freedom* to be defined? Is it possible for both God and human beings to be "free," or are restraints placed upon one by the other? If God has given humans freedom to be agents in the world, what does this do to his own omnipotence? Alternately, if God's omnipotence makes him able to achieve his will on all occasions, then what is the nature of human "freedom"? The ancient question of the relationship between "divine sovereignty" and "human freedom" comes quickly to our attention when we speak of God's providence. Does God take risks, or does he have everything so completely within his control that no risk is entailed?

The matter is further complicated by the role God's knowledge plays in his providence, particularly his knowledge of the future. Once again, no Christian theologian denies that God is "omniscient." But assuming that God knows everything, how are we to understand what can be known? Is the future "some thing" to be known, or does it in fact not exist until it "comes to be" as the present? If the future is, by definition, unknowable, then the omniscience of God is in no way limited if he does not know the future, but is that the case? Of special significance, related to the issues of freedom, can the future acts of free agents be foreknown? Does foreknowledge "cause" or necessitate events? If they are foreknown, are they certain and, if so, then in what sense are they free? But what is the relationship of an eternal God to time? Is God temporal, a being about whom we can say that he knows events *before* they happen? Or is his eternity timeless, so that *pre*science or *fore*knowledge are just metaphorical ways of speaking of God's knowledge that actually say nothing about the relationship of what God knows "eternally" to what happens "in time"?

The issues are certainly "mind-boggling." Some who have an interest in prayer and in understanding how it "works" and how they should pray, may already be getting disturbed or even annoyed at the complexity of the discussion. Are these not philosophical questions that the Bible does not answer? Why not just interpret the Scriptures and answer the questions of God's acts and the effect of our requests upon his intentions and deeds from the Bible? I am an evangelical, an heir of the Protestant Reformation, and so I believe that the Bible is our "only rule of faith and practice." On the other hand, a look at the history of theology at the time of the Reformation and in the years that followed quickly alerts us to a sometimes puzzling fact. The Scriptures speak plainly on the core matters of the Christian faith stated in the Apostles' Creed and confessed by Christians of all branches of the Christian Church. Beyond those basic truths that we all affirm, disagreements concerning Scripture arise quickly. The questions we have just raised immediately throw us into the deep end regarding the first affirmation of the Creed: "I believe in God the Father Almighty, Creator of heaven and earth." What does "almighty" mean when affirmed concerning God? And what does God do as Creator? Did he create the world, with all its "natural laws," able to sustain itself and run indefinitely, like a well-made clock, without further intervention? Or is he continually "creating" what exists and occurs in the world, or just *how* is he now involved? Does God act only in general ways through the order he has established, or does he act "specially," meeting particular needs of individuals or groups in ways the normal course of his activity would not do? Are all such actions to be considered miraculous or is a miracle an extraordinary form of divine action, even given the category of special providence?

The difficulty we confront when we begin to talk about God and his action in the world is that we may find ourselves affirming statements derived from Scripture that are logically incoherent. They contradict one another—or at least they appear to do so. People commonly speak of God's sovereign control of all the events of their lives but then speak of themselves and others as acting freely and responsibly. They speak of God's comprehensive, eternal foreknowledge of the future, but they also speak and act as though we can now do something to affect that future. Not everyone agrees whether or not these are consistent ways of speaking, and we must give the matter the attention necessary either to demonstrate their coherence or to revise our statements. We may discover that Scripture did not say what we earlier thought it had said. We may reach points where we simply affirm mystery and live as though two things are both true even though we cannot logically see how that could be so. I admit that God is beyond our *complete* comprehension. If we fully understood him, he would not be God, or we would be too! On the other hand, I am very reluctant to give up and appeal to "mystery" too quickly. The mind-stretching philosophical and theological work is necessary if we are to practice our faith intelligently as God wishes us to do.

Petitionary Prayer

There is more to prayer than asking God for things. On the other hand, petition occupies a large part of the average person's prayer time, and when people wonder how prayer "works," it is petition that they are gener-ally contemplating. We wonder what we can ask God to do? Can we ask him to heal the sick, to provide good weather (rain or sun, or protection from a hurricane headed toward us), to favorably influence a prospective employer to whom we have sent an application, to assure that someone we love is not injured in a plane crash that we know has occurred? Peti-tionary prayer includes requests both for ourselves and for others (interces-sion), and this raises its own set of particular questions about human wills and God's goodness. If God wills what is good for people, why would he not wish (or be able) to do something that is good for others unless we asked him to? Even given their ability to reject God's good intentions for them, why does God wait for others to intercede before trying to help them? When we come to God in prayer, we inevitably wonder why we should make requests, if God already knows what we need and wills to give us what is good for us. Do we pray simply to acknowledge our dependence upon God or to prepare ourselves to receive with a proper attitude what he is going to give us anyway, or does God actually do some things in response to prayer that he would not otherwise do? How do we know what to pray for? Is prayer more effective depending on the number of people who make a particular request and, if so, why? The issues of providence, God's power, God's knowledge and the comprehensiveness of his will, all have an impact on our practice of petitionary prayer.

We could profitably pursue the same questions with regard to praise, but our focus is deliberately on petition. To some extent, however, this also offers perspectives on thanksgiving. There should be a consistency be-tween the things we believe we can ask God for and the things for which we thank him. Much of what we conclude about God's nature and action as it grounds our petitions will therefore also inform our prayers of thanks-giving.

Reflection on our practice may reveal strange inconsistencies in this regard, however, as happened in the revision of the Church of England's prayer book. In 1928 the revision of the *Book of Common Prayer* included a prayer for seasonable weather. By contrast, the *Alternate Service Book* of 1980 could only offer "a retrospective harvest collect expressing hearty thanks 'for your fatherly goodness and care in giving us the fruits of the earth in their season.'"[10] Observing this change, John Polkinghorne aptly notes that it seems peculiar to thank God "for what we have not had the confidence to ask for beforehand," but that "there is this deeply felt religious need to give thanks."[11]

How we understand God's action in the world will determine how and when and why and for what we pray. It will also inform us about when thanksgiving is in order and to whom. It is my prayer that this book will assist others in developing their own understanding of God and his action, and that it will encourage habits of prayer consistent with their own doctrine of providence. Whether and how God might answer such a prayer is itself the subject matter of this book!

Theological Models

What is a theological model? I will often refer to "models of providence and prayer," and so a word should be said about what we mean by *model*. Frederick Ferré has defined a model as "that which provides epistemological vividness or immediacy to a theory by offering as an interpretation of the abstract or unfamiliar theory-structure something that both fits the logical form of the theory and is well known."[12] In somewhat similar terms, Sallie McFague suggests that "a model is a metaphor with 'staying power.' A model is a metaphor that has gained sufficient stability and scope so as to present a pattern for relatively comprehensive and coherent explanation."[13] Ferré suggests that "a model simplifies the data at hand 'to a form in which the mind can grasp them.'"[14]

The nature of God's action as it relates to human action, and particularly to our prayer, is an immense and complex subject. Theologians study God's revelation and attempt to represent the truth about these important matters in a coherent way that enables others to grasp it. We could speak of each of the alternative understandings that we will present as theories. They do theorize concerning the action of God and the role of prayer. But each of these theological positions pulls together a number of theories (about causation, time, knowledge, freedom, power, agency, etc.) and forms a coherent representation that we are calling a model. Ferré suggests that theological theories cannot be developed without reference to the metaphysical model with which theology works.[15] We might argue that the conceptualization of God's providence includes so much about God and the nature of reality that it could be considered our metaphysical model. We will not make so large a claim, however, and suggest rather that these models also function as theories within the picture that constitutes our metaphysical model. They are part of the larger picture that constitutes our overarching concept of reality. The work we do in sharpening our understanding on this very important matter will contribute significantly to the development of that big picture, the "key theological model."[16]

Having asserted earlier that we believe it to be possible and worthwhile to construct a conceptual model of God's providence and our prayer, we do well to remind ourselves of Ferré's warning. There is some risk involved in the development of models that attempt to present coherently the various aspects of truth concerning a subject such as divine providence and human prayer. Models permit simplification "by requiring their users to 'see the phenomena only through a medium.'"[17] A model is not the same as what it models: it "filters the acts." None of these models, including my own proposal, is adequate to fully represent the transcendent God in whom we live and move and have our being and who acts in our world, in us, and along with us. Yet while being aware of the limitations of our theological formulations, we affirm their necessity and their value. It is with such warnings in mind that Paul Helm has argued that our theological reflection produces models rather than theories of God's relationship to his creation. We must not draw false inferences from the data that our models summarize. Unlike the enquiries of the natural sciences, "the resulting doctrine is not capable of answering our 'how?' questions" or our "why" questions. We know *that* God willed it but not *why*.[18]

How do we construct our theological model? In a sense this book is itself a case study in the way that a given theological position is developed so that it has inner coherence and fits within one's overall theology. We who are theological heirs of the Protestant Reformation frequently insist that Scripture is our sole authority, that we do theology *sola Scriptura*. Of course, it is never quite so simple in the actual doing of theology. The Reformers also asserted the perspicacity or clarity of Scripture, and we might expect therefore that Christian (or at least Protestant) theologians would be agreed about what Scripture teaches. In fact, as this book demonstrates, there are wide and very significant differences of opinion about what is the truth about many subjects, including the nature and extent of God's action in the world and of our corresponding responsibility.

Wesleyan theologians frequently speak of a quadrilateral in the construction of statements of Christian belief and practice. Scripture has a uniquely authoritative position, but it is complemented by three other factors: reason, tradition and experience. We encounter the complex interplay of these factors when we begin to formulate a biblical understanding of God's providence. We cannot simply read a theology of divine providence off the biblical page, although the teaching of Scripture is unique in its authoritative role. But, we cannot avoid philosophical questions concerning God's relationship to time, the possibility of knowledge of the future (actual and possible) and the nature of freedom (both God's and ours). Our system of theology—that is, our coherent formulation of the truth concerning God and his relationships to the world—will be no better than our biblical exegesis. But it will also depend upon good philosophy, the valid use of the principles of rationality, a knowledge of the thinking of great and godly minds who have gone before us in the history of the church and careful reflection upon our own experience in the world.

The models presented in this book do not differ from one another because they use different Scriptures as their authority. But they reach a different understanding of the teaching of Scripture through a complex process that includes all of the factors we have mentioned. Theological models differ because they assume the truth of different philosophical theories, because they disagree about the rules of rational coherence or even the possibility and value of it in speaking about God, because the experience of the proponents of these models is only comprehensible on these terms, and possibly because of the "location" of the proponents both historically and ecclesiastically.

It will also become apparent as we work our way toward a personal understanding of God and his work in the world that this cannot be achieved through analysis of a few key passages of Scripture. Each of the models has particular texts that capture the essence or shape of the model. But arguing the merits of these particular texts against another collection of texts is rarely fruitful. In my experience in doing theology and helping others to do it, I have found that one arrives at one's own understanding or model of God and his work in the world through a general impression drawn from the entire text of Scripture. Each model finds texts in Scripture that appear to pose a difficulty to the model. These cannot simply be dismissed, but they are read within the framework that emerges from the overall thrust of the biblical narrative. Admittedly, once one has become convinced of a particular overall framework in the biblical narrative (a "system" of theology), it is very difficult to see texts in a way that would call for radical revision of the overall model. This is a truth that postmodernist theologians have emphasized, although they tend to overstate it to the point of relativism. However, I do not assume that there is no value in examining alternate theological models and reevaluating our own. Periodi-

cally I have had little paradigm shifts in areas of my own theology—
"eureka" moments when the shape of truth on a particular topic suddenly
looks different than it did before. I am not permanently committed to my
own model of providence and prayer against all objections or alternate
proposals. It is the way the truth of Scripture looks to me now, and I wel-
come opportunities to dialogue with others for whom the reading of the
narrative of Scripture produces a different framework of understanding the
big picture.

At times this whole project may seem too complex, and readers will be
tempted toward agnosticism ("we simply cannot know how God acts in the
world"), to despair ("this is beyond me") or to dismissal of the theological
project ("I simply believe the Bible; I don't do theology"). None of these
routes is fruitful. We need to pray, we want to pray, and because we want
to pray effectively, we need to struggle through to an understanding of
God's action in the world that will ground our practice of prayer and all
other aspects of our life. All of us live according to a model of the world
that includes God and everything else (often called a "worldview"). Sometimes we operate on different models at different times, and this causes
confusion in our lives and in the perception of others who are watching us
and possibly learning from us.

The Scope and Plan of This Study

This is primarily a book about the doctrine of providence. In treatises on
providence, three practical issues generally emerge: prayer, miracles and
the existence of evil. About the third I plan to say nothing specifically. Of
course, the models of providence that will be presented here will all have
ramifications for our understanding of evil in the world cared for by a good
and powerful God. But we will not spell out those implications. Nor are
miracles a major point of attention, though they will come into the picture
more often because our understanding of God's miraculous work (the
mention of which makes many modern theologians nervous) will inform
our prayer in situations where we need God to act in special ways, outside
of his normal ways of acting, in order to address our need.

The literature on prayer is immense, including many books about how
to pray in order to get answers to prayer. People want to know how to be
successful when they pray. This is not primarily a book about how to pray
effectively, but it builds a foundation for addressing that critical issue. It
comes at the matter from a different perspective than books about prayer

usually do. We will not provide a list of the conditions of answered prayer or the hindrances to it. Our focus is narrower but more fundamental. Most books on prayer recognize faith as an important element in prayer that succeeds, but what are we to believe when we bring our requests to God? What is God able to do and what can we expect him to do? It would obviously be futile for us to be asking God to do things that he *cannot* do because they are impossible in the nature of things as God has constituted them. It would likewise not be reasonable to ask God to do what he *will* not do because of limitations prescribed by his nature or established by his will. Yet many of the prayers Christians commonly pray are ruled out by some of the models of providence at which we will look. On the other hand, it is possible that some of us pray too timidly because we do not adequately understand the way God works in his creation. Such unnecessary timidity also needs to be corrected.

This is not an encyclopedia of models of providence. There are, no doubt, other ways in which God's action has been explained by Christian theologians. There are also many others who have written about providence and prayer whose positions illustrate or slightly modify the models we have chosen. I have identified what I take to be the models that are major contenders for the acceptance of Christian people or which have been seriously proposed by Christian theologians. Within these models I have attempted to develop the views of key representative figures whose work gives us an understanding of the model and its implications. To avoid overly lengthy footnotes, I have resisted the temptation to identify all the authors I have encountered who represent a particular point. In many instances, more references could be cited than have been. Readers are sure to find that some of their favorite theologians do not appear. This will give them an opportunity, however, to look once more at those whose work they particularly appreciate to see where they fall within this spectrum of models and how their work offers helpful critique of the various perspectives here presented.

In the first section of the book we will look at major alternatives regarding the understanding of God's providence and see how each of these affects the practice of petitionary prayer. In the second section I will make a proposal describing my own understanding of the teaching of Scripture concerning God's providence and our prayer requests.

In presenting the models that I have identified for study, I will move from the one that perceives the least involvement of God in the details of history to the one that puts the outcome of events most strongly in the hands of God. Therefore, they could be considered on a spectrum that correlates divine and human agency, with the first model giving maximum effect to human agency and the last giving least significance to the action of humans within history. A distinction is sometimes made between "risk" and "no-risk" models of providence, depending on whether God has taken a personal risk in creating other personal beings and giving them the ability to choose and act within the world that he created. Of the ten models presented in part one, the first six are models of "risk providence," but the extent of the risk diminishes as we proceed from one model to the next. The last four models, and my own proposal, are forms of "no-risk providence," but they too differ in regard to the extent and manner of God's control of the details of history.

I have chosen a simple handle to identify each model. I will use either a term that captures its emphasis or that is commonly used by its proponents, or the name of a key representative of the model with whom the model is frequently associated. This risks oversimplification, but I have followed this course in order to facilitate cross-reference to the various models without having to use a lengthy description of the one to which we refer.

Each of the models in the first part will be presented without critical comment except where representatives of one model critique another in arguing for the plausibility of their own. I will describe the positions as fairly as I can and allow readers to do their own assessment of the merits and shortcomings of each one. In the second part I will not attempt a critique of each of the other models. I will make a positive presentation of my own model, indicating points at which it rejects and points at which it incorporates features that have earlier been proposed. My own model is not completely original or innovative. I would be suspicious of it if it were. But it is different from any I have encountered in my reading, by virtue of the particular way in which it puts together an understanding of agency, freedom, time, knowledge and power to formulate a model of God's providence and a practice of prayer.

I have joked about writing a book in which I present a variety of options and then give the "right answer." It is funny because it sounds presumptuous. On the other hand, it is obvious that I do see my own proposal as the one that fulfills the demands of Scripture, experience and reason most satisfactorily. Readers will have to determine whether they share this judgment. I look forward to growth in my own understanding through interaction with thoughtful readers of this book. Even for me, this is not expected to be the last word on the subject. Given the great complexity of this subject, I sympathize with Ian Barbour's experience that "one never finishes a book—one simply abandons it eventually."[19] But this is how the matter looks to me right now, and I hope that the time spent spelling out my own view and the perspectives of many others will aid readers to refine their own theology and improve their own spiritual practice.

A Case Study: Fred Henderson's Kidnapped Son

Fred Henderson was thankful that it was Wednesday when he received the distressing phone call from the office of the mission with whom his son worked.[20] There was a church prayer meeting that night, and Fred keenly felt the need of the prayers of others in the congregation. He had been informed by the director of the mission that his son Richard was one of three missionaries who had been abducted that day by a group of men who were now demanding ransom and seeking political concessions before the missionaries would be released. The mission had made it a policy never to pay ransom, in order to protect their missionaries who would otherwise be placed at constant risk. Mission leaders were attempting to negotiate with the captors, but this particular group had a reputation for being ruthless, so the situation did not look good. The larger conflict between the rebels and the government was especially difficult for the mission to address.

That evening Fred described the situation of Richard and the two other missionaries to the group gathered for prayer. As you will soon discover, the people at the meeting were remarkably diverse in their theological perspectives, and this was evident as they prayed for Richard and his colleagues. At the end of each model, I have introduced a member of Fred's congregation who holds that particular model of providence and have constructed the type of petition that they could appropriately pray, given their understanding of God's relationship to and action in the world.

How to Read This Book

The subject of providence is very complex, particularly because of the philosophical questions it raises. I am aware that this is a difficult book for this reason. In order to help you grasp the various models, the differences between them, and their distinctive approach to the issues of providence and prayer, I have provided a few helps along the way.

Each model begins with a brief *synopsis*. This will orient you to the general shape of the model before you head into the details. Near the back of the book you will find a *glossary*. I have tried to define technical terms the first time you meet them in this book, but you may not remember those definitions when you encounter a new term again. If you read a term and are not sure of its meaning, the glossary will be your best place to go first.

You have just read the *case study* of the abduction of Richard Henderson and his colleagues. At the conclusion of each model a member of Fred's church will reflect on this situation from within the framework of the model of providence just presented. This will include memories of discussion with other members of the church who hold different models. The person will also think about the situation in regard to the prayer that would be appropriate and will offer a prayer. An interesting way to get started on this book would be to proceed through the models now, simply reading the case study at the end of each model. It would quickly familiarize you with the gradual modifications being made as features of the model change. You should also find these case studies a helpful review of the main points of each model when you have completed the reading of the more nuanced and carefully reasoned presentation that makes up the bulk of each chapter.

Finally, I draw your attention to the *chart* that appears as an appendix. It lays out the position taken by each model on a number of critical issues. This should make a very helpful point of reference as you try to recall what a previous model did with a particular issue. Examining the chart, you will also be able to see the features that change as the models move along the spectrum of increasing degrees of divine control. On the chart I have placed my own *middle knowledge Calvinist proposal* to the left of the *Calvinist model* to reflect its appropriate position on the spectrum. In the arrangement of the text, however, it comes last, as a new proposal.

Part 1

Ten Models of
Providence & Prayer

2

The Semi-Deist Model

I N THE SEMI-DEIST MODEL OF PROVIDENCE, GOD HAS CREATED A WORLD THAT IS *governed by laws of physical and moral order. He has created intelligent, libertarianly free and morally responsible creatures, and he sustains their existence. They are expected to act wisely, in accordance with the rules of the established order. God will not intervene to protect people from either their own improper behavior or from that of others. If he were to do so on behalf of some people, he would be responsible for allowing others to experience evil without his intervention. This is a charge against which semi-deists wish to protect God. The model does not consider God inactive; it simply asserts that the entire history of the universe as it unfolds is one big act on God's part. Within that act of God, his creatures operate, and they bear complete responsibility for their actions.*

Semi-deists recognize that petitionary prayer to God is a common and perhaps natural practice of human beings. Indeed, Jesus himself taught us to address petitions to God. They urge us, however, to interpret the language of petition differently than is commonly done. When we make requests to God, we are not asking him to intervene in our particular situation and change either events or people. We are acknowledging God's existence, and we are expressing our intention to be actively engaged in deeds that will further the general harmony of the world and its people, thereby doing the "will" of God. Praying individually and corporately are ways of strengthening our own resolution to be constructively engaged in solving the problems of the world that have arisen from behavior contrary to the divinely established order.

Where was God when Richard Henderson was abducted and what can he be expected or asked to do now that it has happened? In our first model we meet theologians who doubt that God was or will be involved in the situation. They come to this conclusion because of the difficulties we face if we assume that God is directly involved in the details of our daily lives and the progress of human history.

If God Is Praised for the Good Things That Happen, He Must Be Blamed for the Bad Ones

An American airliner was hijacked to Beirut by Shiite Muslims, and all but one of the people taken hostage came away from the incident safely. After their liberation the pilot spoke for the hostages and expressed thankfulness for the way the Lord had taken good care of them. Maurice Wiles finds this kind of response "a source of profound embarrassment to many a reflective Christian," and he asks, "Where was [God's] care for the hostages when one of them was murdered and his corpse thrown out on to the tarmac?"[1] Wiles further recalls that "a service of thanksgiving was held in St. Paul's to mark the ending of the Falklands War; but there was no agreement about what it was appropriate to thank God for."[2] The service caused Wiles to wonder whether God had taken the British side in war. It is on moral grounds, rather than scientific ones, that Wiles feels compelled to believe that God's providential involvement in the ongoing history of the world is severely limited. His concern has been neatly summed up in the following conundrum: "If God can influence the course of events, then a God who is willing to cure colds and provide parking spaces but is not willing to prevent Auschwitz and Hiroshima is morally repugnant. Since Hiroshima and Auschwitz did occur, one must infer that God cannot (or has a policy never to) influence the course of worldly events."[3] If God prevented a person from boarding a plane that later crashes, by having them infected with measles or tying them up in a traffic jam, "might not a more infectious strain or an even solider logjam of cars have saved others as well? Or if only one were to be prevented from reaching the plane in time, why not the pilot so that the plane could not fly at all? One person's providence is another person's downfall."[4]

Deism

The model that we are considering in this chapter has sometimes been called "deistic," in reference to a theology that was common in the seventeenth and eighteenth century.[5] Deism is often portrayed by the mechanistic image of God as a watchmaker who makes the cosmos with all its "pieces" along with the laws that govern their operation, winds it up and then lets it run without further interference. This is a model of God's work that has virtually no concept of providence, as we have described it. It pictures God as one who "creates individual things with causal efficacy such that they produce events in the world apart from any divine causal action except the conservation of the individual 'natural agents' in existence."[6] Under the influence of Newtonian physics a model of God as divine Mechanic became common.[7] In a survey of cosmic religiosity at the end of the twentieth century, Georges De Schrijver notes that "the 17th-Century clockwork model is slowly being replaced by the paradigm of the world as a living organism."[8] De Schrijver suggests that "the present landscape of cosmology is populated mainly by neo-deists and neo-spinozists."

On the "neo-deist" front, an interesting analysis is offered by Stephen Bilynskyj.[9] He develops a taxonomy of three views of God's causal relationship to "second causes," that is, to agents other than God that also have a role in bringing about a particular event. The first view excludes any genuine causality within the created world; God is the only one acting, and he alone brings about all that happens so that the apparent agency of others is an illusion. In the second view, which Bilynskyj identifies as the deistic one, second causes are included but in a manner that raises doubts about the legitimacy of calling God a "cause" of any particular effect. The third perspective views God and the creature as working together (concurrence) in a "joint causality." Bilynskyj's preference is this third option, which he discusses in reference to the work of Thomas Aquinas and Luis de Molina, whose perspectives will come up later in our study, in the Thomist and Molinist models. Bilynskyj defines concurrence as "a general decision on God's part to conserve the world moment by moment *along with* all the changes in its arrangement produced by the causal activity of things in the world."[10] In this way both God and the creature can be called causes in any particular event, but it is the creature that determines the specific outcome, while God provides the creature with what it needs to bring about what it does. Bilynskyj contends that his account of God's "moment by moment participation" in the operation of the world through this "general decision to sustain the world's existence in each new arrangement as it is produced" is "not simply a return to the Deistic view." However, he is obviously not sure that his denial is persuasive, for he adds: "Perhaps my account simply reduces concurrence to a refinement of the Deistic view, but if that is the case, it is nonetheless a needed refinement and a corrective to the Deistic view as usually stated."[11]

We are now in a situation where theologians are reluctant to accept the designation "Deist," but as De Schrijver notes, there is a continuing appeal in the position that absolves God of the effects occurring in our history. In this chapter we will look more closely at the models proposed by two theologians of our own time who present us with descriptions of divine providence that greatly minimize the detailed action of God in human affairs: Gordon Kaufman and Maurice Wiles. Out of respect for their own denial that their theology is deistic but in recognition of the way in which it is perceived by others, I have designated this model "semi-deistic."

Gordon Kaufman: The Whole of Human History Is God's "Master-Act," But Not Everything That Happens Along the Way Is a Sub-Act of God

Gordon Kaufman observes that the concept "act of God" is "central to the biblical understanding of God and his relation to the world (Ex 15:11; Ps 40:5; 107:21; 145:4; Col 1:13)."[12] Echoing the assessment of Langdon Gilkey, Kaufman notes, however, that "the notion of a God who continuously performs deliberate acts in and upon his world, and in and through man's history, has become very problematical for most moderns." This is because we have learned to "conceive nature as an impersonal order or structure."[13] The opponents of miracles appear to have won the day, and few theologians are now "disposed to explain the occurrence of particular events by referring them directly to God's intervention in the natural order."[14] Although many might still grant that miracles are possible in principle, "it is clear that both their practical decisions and actions and their theological theories are controlled by the assumption of the fundamental autonomy of natural order." The result is that talk of a God who "continuously *acts* in and upon nature as its Lord" has become "uncomfortable and difficult" for many.

Some have conceded autonomy to nature but continue to affirm that God acts in human history, but their proposal strikes Kaufman as shallow and untenable. On the one hand, "no one conceives or experiences 'history' in this kind of sharp isolation from 'nature.' All historical events take place within the context of natural process and order and involve the movements and reordering of physical bodies and material objects of many sorts."[15] In Kaufman's view, "it will not do to speak of God as the agent who made it possible for the Israelites to escape from the Egyptians, if one regards it as simply a fortunate coincidence that a strong east wind was blowing at just the right time to dry up the sea of reeds. The biblical writer's view is coherent and compelling precisely because he is able to say that '*the LORD* drove the sea back by a strong east wind' (Ex 14:21)."[16]

Even if a sharp division could be made between nature and history, it would not solve the fundamental problem. Writing in the late 1960s Kaufman found it not surprising that people were asserting that "God is dead." Since agents are experienced and known in and through their acts, if we do not perceive events as genuinely acts of the transcendent God, "the Agent himself has faded away for us into little more than a word inherited from our past." Kaufman identifies three options in our response to the challenge confronted by a doctrine of divine providence. We can grant that "God is dead" and that life can be understood in humanistic and naturalistic ways. We can follow Paul Tillich's route and "reinterpret the notion of God in such a manner that the conception of agent is no longer implied." Or we can reexamine the notion of "act," and this is the approach Kaufman himself pursues.[17]

Kaufman defines an act as "a particular and generally a very specific event brought about by an agent." It is "activity bound together and given a distinct order and structure by the intention of an agent to realize a goal." Viewed in this way, an "act involves an element of creativity not characteristic of lower forms of life than man."[18] It is the accumulation of such creative acts that brings into being what we know as the historical order or as culture. By this definition an act of God would be a deed that God performs, that is, "an event which did not simply 'happen,' but which was what it was because God did it."[19] Kaufman considers this the biblical conception.

Currently both belief and unbelief in the reality of God's acts arise from the shared assumption that an act of God is a "particular miraculous event which God directly causes." Kaufman is convinced that the impasse will not be resolved as long as that conception persists.[20] Modern scientific and historical understanding commonly "presupposes the interrelation and interconnection of all events in an unbroken web." In spite of indeterminacy at the atomic level and "genuine creativity and self-determination on the human level," it is possible to make statistical descriptions that are usually quite precise."[21] It is in this context that the traditional notion of an "act of God" presents a difficulty. It "seems to refer to events which have their source or cause directly or immediately in the divine will and action rather than in the context of preceding and coincident finite events."[22] This makes the events unintelligible to us, and so it is meaningless to talk about such acts.

To break the conceptual logjam, Kaufman proposes that our "customary interpretation of particular relatively restricted events—the crossing of the Red Sea, the dispersing of the hosts of Sennacherib, the virgin birth or resurrection of Jesus—as particular acts of God is too simple." The problem is that "it overlooks the significance of the relation of 'simple acts' to 'master acts.'"[23] Simple acts are "constituent phases of a complex act." They are always secondary and derivative because they are not performed for their own end but as a step toward the master end. It is the "master act" that renders a piece of activity intelligible. Thus the act of a carpenter driving nails is meaningless, but putting boards together to construct a house has meaning. Analogically, when we speak of the "act of God," we should refer first to the "master act," that is, *the whole course of history,* from its initiation in God's creative activity to its consummation when God ultimately achieves his purposes."[24] God plans "the end from the beginning" (Is 46:10), and he orders his activity through history to the ultimate goal, the final establishment of the kingdom (Mt 25:34). This was epitomized in the appearance of Jesus, who was destined before the foundation of the world (1 Pet 1:20) and brought into history "as a foretaste or anticipation of the final glorious consummation."[25]

On this model God's act is "not a new event that suddenly and without adequate prior conditions rips inexplicably into the fabric of experience, a notion consistent neither within itself nor with the regularity and order which experience must have if it is to be cognizable." Rather, it is the source of the overarching order itself. It is this divine master act "that gives the world the structure which it has and gives natural and historical processes their direction."[26] If we speak of God's act in this way, contends Kaufman, we do not threaten the unity and order of the world as a whole. Such an act, however, is "intrinsically temporal: it is the ordering of a succession of events toward an end."[27]

The particular and more limited acts commonly attributed to God must not be regarded, on this model, as "more or less spur-of-the-moment decisions in which God does something in history in quite unexpected and inexplicable fashion: they should be understood (quite consistently with the eschatological orientation of much biblical, and all New Testament, thought) as functions of and subordinate steps toward God's ultimate goal."[28] This means that not all acts are subacts of God. It is only those events that move creation further toward the realization of God's purposes that are subacts of God. Finite agents may act contrary to God's purposes and acts, as is evident in the case of Jesus, but "the temporal movement of the whole, including the particular developments of our individual lives, is under God's providential care."[29]

The minimal role that God plays in the ongoing process of human history in Kaufman's scheme causes Benjamin Wirt Farley to wonder "just how free God is to 'act' within it," because Kaufman places so much emphasis on "the unbrokenness of the historical and natural nexus, once the process is begun."[30] Farley asks, "Does he [God] actually do anything following an initial act?" It appears to Farley that "simply to divide one continuous act into subacts does not clarify God's specific involvement in or with each subact. If anything," Farley suggests, "God seems to come across more as the *Master Planner* than as the *Master Actor.*"[31] Both God and the human agent appear "subject to a degree of determinism that makes it difficult for either party to 'transcend' the nexus."[32]

God Does Not Act in Response to Our Petitions

The subordinate acts of God are "governed largely by his overarching purposes and ultimate objectives, not simply by the immediate needs or the prayerful pleas of his children," in Kaufman's model. "There is no God who 'walks with me and talks with me' in close interpersonal communion, giving his full attention to my complaints, miraculously extracting me from difficulties into which I have gotten myself by invading nature and history with *ad hoc* rescue operations from on high." Kaufman thinks that "Christian piety has too long been nurtured largely on those psalms and other biblical materials which portray God as a kind of genie who will extricate the faithful from the difficulties into which they fall; it is this erratic and fickle God who cannot be reconciled with the modern understanding of the order in nature and history."[33]

So then, should we conclude that petitionary prayer for God to act in specific instances, such as the abduction of Richard Henderson and his colleagues, is ruled out by Kaufman's model? He does suggest that we, "both as species and individuals, have a place within those purposes, and *certain of his sub-acts are responsive to our acts*" (emphasis supplied). However, the proposal leads me to believe that our own acts to which God is responding do not significantly include petitions for his aid since his master act seems to rule out precisely those particular responses that would constitute acts done in answer to prayer, which would not otherwise have been done. Kaufman believes that "the place we have is [God's] to determine and assign, not our own; at the very most our lives are but almost infinitesimal constituents in his all-comprehending act, and his responsiveness to the particularities of our activity must be understood as a function and phase of his master act ordering all human and cosmic history."[34]

Maurice Wiles: God Does Not Intervene

Maurice Wiles cites Kaufman's "master act" conception as largely compatible with his own proposal.[35] He describes God as a Creator who has chosen to create a world of free beings who have "a measure of independent power over against himself."[36] We are agents who are capable of effective and responsible action, and we contribute to what happens in our world. Thus when we speak of the action of God, our primary reference should be to its "relation to the world as a whole rather than to particular occurrences within it."[37] We should think of the world as one act that includes the process that is still going on. The only act we must affirm to be God's is the "continuing creation" of the universe. Although it is a complex act, it is still a single act. The master act may be made up of subacts, but Wiles does not follow Kaufman in speaking of God as performing *any* of the subacts that contribute to God's one act of creating our world.[38]

God has a purpose, but it is very general because it must take account of our own actions as they occur. Consequently, when we express confidence in God's ultimate triumph in the world where evil is now so much a part of our experience, "we are not affirming that some fixed target will be reached, let alone that it will be reached by some predetermined date. It is a genuinely unknown future of which we are speaking."[39] We have seen God's love expressed in Christ and are confident that, in spite of the risk God has taken in creating the world, "eventually we will be able to say, as we know we cannot say now, that what *is* is God's will."[40] The work of creation will not come to an end until that will is fulfilled.

Reflecting upon the biblical account of God's action in history, Wiles wonders how we can "continue to affirm some such version of the Christian story, without having to re-introduce an unacceptable notion of God the absolute controller?"[41] Many of the events described in Scripture as being God's providential activity were brought about through the agency of pagan empires and emperors such as Cyrus, who was God's shepherd to carry out God's purpose, although he did not know God (Is 44:28; 45:4). This raises the question of the link between God and Cyrus. If there were a "hidden manipulation of Cyrus's deliberative processes," then we would have "the all-controlling God who does not respect the freedom of the world he has created."[42] Since this is unacceptable to Wiles, he suggests that we must use "general statements about the kind of world God has created" rather than make claims about "particular, specifiable acts of God in history."[43]

In the crucifixion of Jesus we find "the archetypal example of a conflict between the purposes of God and the self-interest of men and women."[44] But we must not think of the event as involving divine providence "in the sense of a specific divine foreseeing and overruling of events."[45] The significant pattern of links between the life of Christ and what led up to it is apparent to us after the event. They have the character of "retroevidence." But "any prophetic foreseeing of the future can be accounted for by insight into human nature, giving rise by extrapolation to true vision of how things may be in the future." When understood in this way, "no particular divine action is required to account for this aspect of the providential direction of history."[46]

Wiles argues that the self-limitation of God must include the possibility of direct divine intervention but that this direct action has been "sparingly and strangely used."[47] If God does act in direct ways, in miraculous fashion, it strikes Wiles as strange that no miraculous intervention prevented Auschwitz or Hiroshima. Alongside those events the miracles acclaimed in traditional Christian faith seem "trivial by comparison."[48] We are not able to reconstruct the nature of the original happenings that first gave rise to the tradition that these were miracles, but Wiles suggests that whatever was at work, there "does not depend on the reality of miracle as a form of direct divine action."[49] Indeed, in a recent article Wiles contends that miracles "should have no place in Christian theology."[50]

Considering the process by which people come to faith in Christ, Wiles acknowledges that there are many factors impinging on our decision that were not our own doing. These include "the gradual pressure of circumstance, the sudden challenge of an unexpected moment of personal crisis, or the attractive presentation of the gospel by friend or preacher." Rather than considering these to be "particular or discrete acts of God," however, Wiles identifies them as "characteristic aspects of a world that in its totality constitutes God's action."[51] As was true with purported miracles, conversion stories are retrospective. They speak of "God's active preparation, call and guidance of the person's life," but they read their stories "forward instead of retrospectively." When this is done, "there is no escape from arbitrary election, implausible disposition of external circumstance and unacceptable manipulation of internal life." We speak this way about God's action because

> our lives are a part of God's personal act in the bringing into existence of the world, a world which includes as a paramount part of its purpose the self-dedication of human lives such as those of a Paul or an Augustine. It is precisely in them that God's act finds part of its fulfilment, not because there are separate distinguishable divine initiatives in relation to them or to particular aspects of them but because the emergence of such lives is what God's one act deliberately seeks to make possible.[52]

The life of Jesus is presented in the New Testament in terms of direct and personal providence, but this too should be understood as retrospective interpretation of experience. This was the way in which the early Christians made "cosmic and personal sense of the life of Jesus and its significance for the world and for them."[53] Neither the incarnation nor the resurrection should, therefore, be treated as unique instances of providential act or miracle. Wiles notes that David Brown has been led to a "wholeheartedly interventionist account of God" precisely by his reflection on these events in the life of Jesus.[54] Brown asserts that if we do not endorse an interventionist view, "then the very idea of an Incarnation will inevitably seem such a startling exception to the uniform pattern of God's relation to the world as to be, quite literally, incredible."[55] Christ's experience would have no analogy to our own and would therefore have no relevance to us.

Wiles resists the conclusions to which Brown has been led and prefers to draw an analogy between the earlier description of God's work in the life of Paul and God's action in Jesus. "Talk of God's call of Paul before his birth was not to be understood literally as implying some particular act of antenatal preparation or even foreknowledge on the part of God" but as a "retrospective way of affirming how completely the service of God through mission to the Gentiles had been determinative of Paul's active life." In the case of Jesus, "it would be appropriate to understand in a similar way talk of his preexistence or of his being sent into the world or of the Spirit's overshadowing agency in the arrangement of his birth." We could see these "not as particular divine acts ensuring the birth of the particular person, Jesus, but rather as a retrospective way of expressing the totality of his commitment to and fulfilment of the will of God for the world."[56]

This approach to the incarnation is judged by Wiles to be more widely acceptable than a similar treatment of the resurrection of Jesus would be. But he dare not concede that even the resurrection was a direct act of divine intervention. "One action of so distinctively different a kind would be sufficient to call in question the claim that the absence of divine intervention in relation to so many evils and disasters in the world is because such direct action is logically incompatible with the kind of world that God has chosen to create."[57] Wiles therefore avers that the historical, physical evidence (for example, the empty tomb) is indecisive and that a physical resurrection is not necessary theologically because "the survival of death is not related to what happens to the body of the person who has died."[58] Faith in the vindication of Jesus and the conviction that Jesus lives in the presence of God need not, therefore, have been "derived from some special action of God in the form of supernaturally given appearances of Jesus."[59]

The most likely candidates for special divine action, the incarnation and resurrection of Jesus, have thus been viewed within, not as distinct from, the model of "the whole continuing creation of the world as God's one act, an act in which he allows radical freedom to his human creation." Having demonstrated to his satisfaction that these events fit within his model, Wiles confidently asserts that there are no "particular divinely initiated acts within the developing history of the world. God's act, like many human acts, is complex." We may rightly speak of particular acts as "specially significant aspects of the divine activity, but not as specific identifiable acts of God."[60]

In the model of God's action that Wiles has proposed, he excludes four kinds of happening or action from what we may legitimately describe as God's action. First among these are the "patterns according to which the physical world operates and which are known to us (in so far as they are known) through the study of the natural sciences."[61] We observe an amazing potential for these patterns to give rise to human life and consciousness, and this "derives from the fact they owe their existence to God's one act of creation," but even in the stages of emergence of new forms of life, they should not be thought of as acts of God in a distinguishable sense.

The second category of happenings not to be called God's act are "happenings where the normal patterns of observed behaviour do not appear to operate," that is, events that might commonly be called miraculous. There are no exceptional cases that must be attributed to God, though it may not be until a later time (if ever) that we are able to understand how they fit in with the "statistically determined regularities of observed behaviour."[62]

Third, we must exclude from God's act the "actions by human agents, who have no conscious intention to further any believed purpose of God, but which do in fact achieve results that Christians believe to be of great significance for the furtherance of that divine purpose."[63] There is no way to intelligibly relate the intention of God and the human deed, which would justify our calling it an act of God.

Finally, God's act does not include the actions of human agents "who freely intend to further the purposes of God, seek God's grace to enable them to do so, and do in fact achieve their intended goal."[64] Although Wiles speaks of God's action as "continuing creation," given the many restrictions that Wiles has placed on God's action, Timothy Gorringe seems justified in deeming this description "illegitimate as none of the 'subacts' which follow the master act of creation can properly be ascribed to God."[65]

Prayer Is a Means of Increasing Our Awareness That God Is Present with Us, but We Do Not Expect God to Act in Response

The last type of action Maurice Wiles has prohibited us from describing as God's action is one that he recognizes as "most immediately involved in the life of prayer and worship."[66] To a friend who has "stood by me and encouraged me to make my own choice" I may say, "It's all thanks to you! It's all your doing!" This is a "proper use of language in the context of the expression of gratitude" but it "would be misleading if taken literally as a straightforward account of the genesis of my action." It can be a helpful analogy, however, because "so much religious language has its place in a context of thanksgiving."

We can expect problems regarding the relation of prayer to God's action, Wiles contends, "as long as we approach them in terms of the particular occasion of prayer alone, without giving serious attention to the 'complex ancestry' of that occasion."[67] In spite of the promise of Jesus recorded in Matthew 21:22 we recognize that some requests are inappropriate. Origen, for instance, recognized that it would be improper to ask for the sun to be shifted back to its spring-time place during the heat of summer.[68] We may not request "special divine modification of the physical ordering of the world."

S. G. Hall has frequently encountered the proposal that we should not pray against the perils of bad weather, drought, flood, storm and pestilence but should pray instead for the generosity that we need in order to respond to such adversities.[69] The rationale for such a suggestion is that we cannot expect God to "change the course of events because some people asked him." Similarly, Michael Goulder has argued that "the deflection of an Exocet missile and the deflection of Mrs. Thatcher's judgment would involve equally crude forms of divine intervention," and so both should be abandoned.[70] However, both Hall and Goulder object to prayers for psychological change because they assume that such change involves physical change in the brain circuits and is, therefore, actually a prayer for the same kind of divine intervention as that which is being rejected.

Wiles agrees with Hall and Goulder that prayers for God's grace do not avoid the problem created by petitionary prayer for God to act within the world in order to remedy its problems, but his reasons for rejecting such prayers are different than theirs. "The person who prays for strength may learn that his previous efforts were a hindrance to achievement," Wiles suggests. "But he might have learnt the same lesson to relax and not to strive too hard in a non-religious context; what is involved may be more properly seen not as the replacement of human activity by divine, but rather as the substitution of a more appropriate form of human acting."[71]

> We may picture our prayers as giving rise to knowledge not otherwise accessible to us or as providing strength beyond the limits of our normal psychological capacity. Such pictures spring naturally enough out of the obvious human analogies. A friend enlightens us on issues that fall within the competence of his or her experience but lie outside our own; or he adds his strength to ours and enables us to achieve some feat that we could not have done single-handed.[72]

But Wiles thinks that this picture is too close an analogy to human relationships and that the situation is more complex than this, even in human relationships. We need a broader account, in Wiles's view.

> Prayers to God have their place within a continuing story, and just because they are prayers to *God* they cannot be adequately understood in isolation

from that full story, however immediate or precise the language in which they are expressed. That story is the story of God's action in the creation of the world. The mysterious phenomenon of human consciousness has arisen in it not by chance, but as a result of the intention that constitutes the world God's act. The capacity to attain, however incompletely, some awareness of that intention is a part of what it is to have been created free beings in God's image. Such recognition, and very partial realization, of God's purpose as the world has seen in the past have been primarily forwarded by those who have used their God-given potential to open themselves to and identify their own goals with what they have grasped of the will of God.[73]

God's intention does not only find expression "spasmodically in the lives of saints occurring at scattered points in human history." It is also expressed institutionally in a Christian vision of the world, "particularly as enshrined in the sacraments of the church," although that is a very incomplete expression. God's action in the world is such that it makes possible "the emergence, both individually and corporately, of a genuinely free human recognition and response to what is God's intention in the creation of the world." It is with this that we associate ourselves in prayer and worship. "Indeed our association of ourselves with it is not merely a means towards its furtherance in other aspects of life (though it is that), but is also itself a part of the fulfilment of that purpose."[74]

Behind our particular experience of grace is "God as the ultimate source of the conditions in which our lives are set; the availability of an awareness of his purpose of love as a source of guidance for our lives; the ways in which that love, having been apprehended and responded to in the past, is accessible to us now in such forms as the writings of the saints and the sacraments of the church." When we come to times of prayer for God's grace, our characters have already been developed in specific ways, "ways partly determined by the extent to which we have opened ourselves to God's grace in the past."[75]

Wiles recognizes that this may seem an unsatisfying description because it portrays prayer "as a means of bringing our lives into relation not so much to God as to some generalized conception of God's will for the world." This ought not to be so, if we remember that God's action was the creation of a world of genuinely free human beings.

> God's purpose is no pre-packaged blueprint to which men and women must conform or be broken. Our human actions affect the way the world develops for good and ill. It is God's will that they should. So God's will for the world

can properly be spoken of not only in the generalized form that characterizes his one fundamental act of creation; it can also be spoken of in more precise and changing ways that take account of how the world now is as a result both of human achievements and of human sin. But what that more particular will of God is at any time is something that we have to discover; it is not directly given and we need to exercise great caution in any claim to know what it is.[76]

God's will allows us freedom "to choose between various ways in which our potentialities may be developed and used." It is always "open to change in the light of past choices and actions both our own and others.'"[77] When we pray, therefore, we are not merely trying to discover what God's will might be for us. We are seeking, rather, to increase our awareness of the fact that the God whose will we are seeking is present with us. This awareness of God's presence is like our awareness of the presence of a human friend that prompts us to say, "It was all thanks to you! It was all your doing!" We need no particular, identifiable initiative on God's part to give his presence this significance. Wiles believes, therefore, that "what seems at first to be a depersonalizing interpretation, because it leaves no place for a specific divine initiative, turns out in the end to have precisely the opposite effect." He suggests that "it not only avoids the age-old difficulties inherent in ideas of election—why this person is called and not that, why this prayer is answered and not that," but "it can also claim to offer a more deeply personal and thereby a more deeply religious account of grace as a whole."[78]

When we pray, we use language suggesting particular, individual, divine actions in response to our requests. This is a language that we have inherited, though it has been differently understood in different times and places. But, says Wiles, when we pray "Give us this day our daily bread,"

> we are not asking for a supply of manna that would increase the unemployment rate among bakers. Nor are we asking God to influence the mind of the secretary of the Bakers, Food and Allied Workers' Union against the option of calling for a strike. What we are doing, surely, is acknowledging the givenness of the world, with its remarkable physical balance which has made possible the emergence of human life and the conditions to sustain it. But with that acknowledgment goes also the recognition that it is human creativity that has learnt and is still in process of learning how best to use those conditions for the growing of the corn and that it is co-operative human labour that is needed to turn it into bread. Moreover the inclusive "us" reminds us that if

the prayer is to be fulfilled for Ethiopian children, as well as those in the Western world, there will have to be a development of managerial skills and a radical reordering of priorities that are a challenge both to our creativity and to our values. . . . It appears to be asking for God to do something quite specific now, but that is not how we understand it.[79]

Such an account of prayer can scarcely be called "petitionary." It appears that, given Wiles's model of divine providence, we are called to lives of constructive and beneficial action but not to a ministry of petitionary prayer—personal or intercessory. When we use the traditional language of petition, we should understand that language as an expression of our recognition of God's role as the one who has acted and still acts in the continuing act of creation. It is not really a request that God act now, in some way distinct from his one continuously creative act, in a way that would appear to the human observer as a divine intervention.

John Polkinghorne remarks that Wiles's view "has all the detachment of deism" and suggests that "God is in danger of becoming no more than the abstract ground of possibility, an Absentee Landlord indeed, who provides the property but leaves it to the tenants to make of it what they can."[80] But Richard Sturch more precisely identifies the position represented by Wiles as "continuism" rather than deism because "the deists' starting-point was a great confidence in the human intellect's power to understand God without the need of such superstitious ideas as revelation."[81] The modern continuists (among whom he also includes Rudolf Bultmann) are not so sure of themselves. "Many of them are clear that God is not only the creator but the sustainer of the universe, and not all the old deists realised this."[82] Wiles himself notes that "deism is widely regarded as no different from atheism, as far as religious practice or religious viability is concerned."[83] He has attempted to show that this is not true of his own position, and readers can judge how well he has succeeded.

Tom Harpur: Prayer for Healing Works Because It Behaves Like Other Natural Energies and Forces in the Cosmos, not Because God Heals in Response to Our Petition

When a group of Christians gathers for prayer, and opportunity is given for people to share their needs for intercession, I am often struck by the preponderance of requests related to illness. It is when people become sick that they frequently find themselves in a situation beyond their own solution and naturally turn to God for help, as do their friends, on their behalf.

In this century spiritual healing in answer to prayer or through the ministry of someone who reputedly has a gift of healing has become highly controversial within the church. This accounts for the interest shown in the subject by Tom Harpur, a Canadian religion reporter who was formerly a clergyman. In *The Uncommon Touch: An Investigation of Spiritual Healing*,[84] Harpur reports on a variety of experiments and experiences that have led him to believe that there is a psychic dimension to health and that prayer has a role in the restoration of health when it has been lost. His own account of the function of prayer is distinctly deistic and fits very much within the model described above.

Harpur defines prayer as "a conversation with God," or as he prefers to put it, "a tuning into or turning of one's inner eye towards the very Source and Ground of all Being."[85] He is even willing to accept part of the nonbeliever's argument that prayer helps mainly oneself. This is not because it is merely auto-suggestion but because "God doesn't need our prayers." Harpur is uncomfortable with what he observes in churches, where prayer is often made for those who are sick. In his opinion, "prayer thus becomes a form of special pleading, a pious attempt to twist the arm of the Ultimate Power. There is an assumption here that God plays favourites, that those who know the right prayers or who manage the correct amount of fervour or faith will succeed where the great masses who are sick around the globe lack this special kind of health-care insurance and so are on their own."[86]

From the research that he has presented in his book Harpur develops what he considers a "much more sensible approach." He asks us to "suppose for a moment that there are natural laws governing the way prayer works, that it behaves in exactly the way other energies and forces in the cosmos do; that is, according to the laws of its own nature and the nature of those aspects of reality it affects most directly." We might suppose further that "there is energy released by the act of praying and that this energy is akin to other unseen or unheard energies." This suggestion is related to his argument earlier in the book that "the kind of subtle energy kindled or directed by a healer's mind, through his hands or sometimes at a distance, does have verifiable, biophysical effects." It seems quite possible and indeed probable to Harpur that "a similar mechanism is involved in praying." In visualizing the sick person becoming whole in body and soul, "by the act of linking with God through prayer, we may well be directing a flow of high-intensity healing energy towards the person who is ill or injured. This flow, in turn, has the capacity to boost or kick-start the person's innate capacity for self-healing."[87]

Harpur believes that all of life comes ultimately from God and that this truth is not diminished by an acknowledgment of "the fact that it operates according to immutable laws."[88] So then

> if one of two people with similar diseases requested prayer, as well as pray-
> ing for him- or herself, while the other would have none of this, it would not
> be a case of asking God to play favourites. If one patient refuses all drugs
> while another benefits from whatever the doctors prescribe, nobody would
> dream of calling it favouritism if the first did poorly while the second recov-
> ered quickly. . . . In the same way, availing oneself of prayer energy while
> getting the best in medical care is really a matter of bringing to bear all avail-
> able resources, seen and unseen.[89]

At San Francisco General Hospital, Dr. Randolph Byrd did a double-blind control experiment with 393 coronary care patients. Of these, 192 were prayed for by home-care groups, and the other 201 were not. Dr. Larry Dossey describes Byrd's methods as "the most rigid that can be used in clinical studies in medicine, meaning that it was a randomized, prospective, double-blind experiment in which neither the patients, nurses, nor doctors knew which group the patients were in."[90] Byrd recruited both Roman Catholic and Protestant groups from across the United States to pray for the members of the first group. The prayer groups were given the patients' names with a little information about their condition and were asked to pray for them daily. They were given no instructions on how to carry this out. Byrd explains that each person praying interceded for many different patients, with the result that each person in the experiment had between five and seven people praying for him or her.

After ten months

> the prayed-for patients differed from the others in several striking ways: they
> were five times less likely than the control group to need antibiotics (three
> compared with 16); they were three times less likely to develop pulmonary
> edema, a condition where the lungs fill with fluid as the heart fails to pump
> strongly enough (6 compared with 18); none of them needed endotracheal
> intubation (an artificial airway inserted into the throat and attached to a
> mechanical ventilator), while twelve in the control group had to have ventila-
> tory support; and fewer patients in the prayed-for group died during the
> study, although the divergence here was not statistically significant.[91]

The distance of the people from their patients varied considerably but seemed to make no difference. Harpur concludes "that if there is a subtle energy involved in prayer it is quite different from understood energetic forces, which grow predictably and inexorably weaker as they travel from the source."

It is not our purpose to assess the experimental evidence for the effectiveness of prayer in regard to healing. What Harpur does not mention is that "while patients who received prayer did better in six specific areas of care, there still remained twenty other areas for which no differences were found," and "some of those prayed for did not do well at all."[92] In another study of the experimental evidence for the effect of prayer on physical health, Paul Duckro and Philip Magaletta conclude that "for the present, there is simply not enough experimental evidence on the direct effect of prayer on physical health to move either side from its *a priori* views."[93]

Our interest is in the explanation offered by Harpur, which shares the deistic conception of God's involvement only through the establishment of an orderly system of laws. Healing takes place through prayer not because of divine "intervention" in the natural process but because prayer is an instrument for promoting health through action in keeping with those laws. Harpur is convinced that

> trust and confidence in a loving God who has made us, who sustains us, and who heals us can constitute a potent factor in the self-healing process. But God 'who sends the rain upon the just and the unjust alike' does not play favourites. Atheists or agnostics who believe in the power of their minds and bodies to recover health or who, to use Einstein's words, believe that the universe can be trusted, are employing a God-given force whether they acknowledge it or not. To the extent that anyone makes use of the underlying spiritual and physical laws by which the cosmos works and heals itself, the same healing resources are available to all. Thus, what I am really saying, in conclusion, is that spiritual or non-medical healing is available to all of us, whether we believe in a particular religion or in none. Antibiotics don't ask what denomination or faith we belong to before going to work. Neither does true spiritual healing. It's simply a part of the way the universe runs.

The Case Study

On the evening that Fred Henderson received the news about his son Richard's abduction, he shared the situation with others at his church prayer meeting, among whom was Millie Dennis. People in Fred's church often used to say that they could not understand why Millie Dennis went to prayer meeting at all. Apparently she did not believe that praying for things actually brings about any changes in the concrete situation. She came to this conviction out of a deep concern to protect God's goodness in the face of suffering and evil in the world. It bothered her profoundly when people attributed to God the deliverance of one individual from a dangerous situation when others in the same situation were *not* delivered. It seemed to her that this made God accountable for the tragedy that occurred to the others. If God could rescue one person, as many of her fellow Christians thought he had, why did he not rescue them all? Millie believed sincerely in God, but she believed that God had created an orderly universe, placed people in it and then allowed them to exercise their God-given freedom in morally responsible ways. He had given them the intelligence they needed to gain an understanding of the physical and moral order that God established and he expected them to act wisely in harmony with those "laws" of nature.

In spite of the puzzlement experienced by her fellow church members, Millie attended prayer meeting regularly because she enjoyed getting together with fellow Christians, and besides, she found that praying about things helped to strengthen her resolution to be an agent for change in the world. She was well known by members of the congregation for her strong confidence in the significance of human action. She believed that God sustained the existence of everything in the world and maintained the laws according to which those things operated. Consequently, she felt a keen responsibility to be active in working toward the good of everyone through wise cooperation with the natural order. As Millie heard Fred describe the predicament of Richard and his colleagues, she did not expect God to intervene on Richard's behalf. She did not even expect God to make a special effort to encourage and strengthen Richard or to comfort Fred and others who were distressed about the abduction of the missionaries. It was clear to Millie that the need facing this congregation was to assess the situation clearly, to gather all relevant information about the factors surrounding the abduction and to discover what avenues of communication and influence existed by which the abductors might be convinced to release the missionaries. One way of getting the group focused on this task was to pray together about it, thereby committing themselves corporately to get involved in action to free Richard and his friends.

Millie was the first to pray. "Dear God, you are the Creator of this world and all who are in it. We acknowledge your wisdom and love in constituting things as they are, given the limitations that you have placed upon yourself by generously creating human beings and giving us freedom to act within your master act. We ourselves desire to act in ways that are consistent with your own good purposes, but this is not true of everyone, and it is certainly not true of those who have abducted Richard and his two fellow missionaries. We express our confidence that in the end of all things, your purposes will be accomplished, but we do not know when that will be true. In the meantime we know that Richard and his colleagues are committed to serving you, and we too shall do what we can to bring good out of this evil and to further your benevolent purposes for the world. In the name of Jesus, whose life so well modeled what you wish us to be, Amen."

3

The Process Model

I N THE PROCESS MODEL, GOD HAS TWO "POLES" OR ASPECTS IN HIS BEING, AND *he is quite unlike the God of classical Christian theology. From the perspective of process theologians, the God of classical theism is too distant (or overly transcendent) and insufficiently affected by other beings. In the process model, God has an abstract (or primordial) and a concrete (or consequent) pole or aspect, and he is therefore a being that is in process. His being is not fully actualized; it is becoming. In his abstract pole, God has a fixed character. But in his concrete pole, God is very much subject to influences outside of himself. He takes these up into himself and responds to them, so that he is in constant interaction with everything else. This does not reduce God to the level of other things or beings, but it puts him in a reciprocal relationship with them. He influences them and attempts to persuade them to become something better, but they also contribute to the total experience of God. In terms of God's providential action in the world, this means that God is continually at work in every situation. In love, he is attempting to move all things and persons in a direction that is their own greatest good. However, God is limited in his ability to achieve this because other entities have the power to resist his persuasions, and he will never be coercive. Evils occur that are contrary to God's will but which he was unable to prevent because of the freedom of other wills active in the situation. However, God does not despair in such instances, he works with the new situation that has come about through the activity of all the entities involved and makes continual new efforts to persuade things in the direction of good.*

It is the belief of proponents of the process model that their model of providence gives significance to the action of beings other than God. We humans genuinely affect the outcome of things, and we contribute to the determination of the future that actually comes to be. We can resist God's efforts to bring about the greatest good of all creatures, but we can also cooperate with him. We can respond positively to his persuasion so that we ourselves move toward the greatest good for ourselves, but we can also become helpers to God in achieving that good in the experience of other entities. Prayer is one of the means by which we get involved with God and cooperate with him in his own purposes. We open ourselves up to his activity in our lives, and we make ourselves available to him for his action in the experience of other beings also.

The problem of evil is a critical issue for theologies of providence. In the previous chapter we saw how it provided an important starting point for the semi-deist or noninterventionist model proposed by Maurice Wiles. If God is not causatively involved in the details of our daily existence—saving one hostage and allowing another to be murdered, giving strength to one person but not to another, preventing or permitting a holocaust—then we need not justify his actions on the occasions of human suffering. But other theologians have been convinced that God is more intimately related to us and more actively involved in the history of the world and in the individual lives of his creatures while still not being responsible for the evils that occur. To conceptualize how God can be intimately related to the events of our experience without controlling these occurrences in a manner that impinges on the freedom of the creatures is the goal of process theologians. Amidst the very fragmented theological scene in the latter half of this century, process theology continues to arouse significant enthusiasm among British and American theologians in particular. With its roots in the philosophy of Alfred North Whitehead, it is an understanding of God and his action that speaks a very different language than the tradition to which most Christians are accustomed through their reading of the Bible and their congregational patterns of worship. Yet it undoubtedly has made an impact on the work of many nonprocess theologians, and it is worth our effort to attempt an understanding of the model that it presents. Readers who have not previously been exposed to process theology will probably find this the most difficult model in the book to understand, but it is worth the effort.

The Classical Notion of God Has Significant Problems

In their introduction to process theology, John Cobb and David Griffin identify two problems in the classical notion of God. It is interesting that these problems parallel the primary starting points that we have encountered in the theologies of divine action proposed by Kaufman and Wiles. Indeed, Cobb and Griffin cite deism as a manifestation of the difficulty inherent in the classical doctrine of God.[1] They are, therefore, sympathetic to the concerns identified in our previous chapter, but they offer a different solution.

The classical notion is described as the view that God is active in all events as the primary cause, though he usually works through secondary causes and on occasion acts directly in miracle.[2] The first complaint against that model reminds us of the concern expressed by Maurice Wiles. The classical notion "raises serious doubt that the creative activity of God can be understood as *love,* since it creates an enormous problem of evil by implying that *every* event in the world is *totally* caused by God, with or without the use of natural causes."[3] On a similar note, Norman Pittenger objects that the doctrine of providence has been "reduced either to God's providing comfort for those who happen to please him or his arranging," as G. K. Chesterton once suggested, "that banana-skins shall be placed conveniently, so that a man whom God likes can slip and fall on one of them, thus sparing himself from entering a bus which a few minutes later will plunge down a decline and bring death to all the passengers."[4]

In the second problem identified by Cobb and Griffin we hear an echo of Gordon Kaufman's concern from the semi-deist model.

> Since the Renaissance and Enlightenment, the belief has grown that there are no events which happen without natural causes. Accordingly, the notion of "acts of God" has lost all unambiguous referents. Every event termed an act of God was said also, from another perspective, to be totally explainable in terms of natural causation. This rendered the notion of "act of God" of doubtful meaning. If an event can be totally explained in terms of natural forces, i.e., if these provide a "sufficient cause" for it, what justification is there for introducing the idea of "another perspective"? This seems like special pleading in order to retain a vacuous idea.[5]

When theologians speak of something as a "sufficient cause," they are saying that this cause is adequate to account for the effect that came about.

Whatever other causes may actually have been involved, the event would have occurred even if this had been the only cause at work in the situation. It is possible, however, that a particular cause may be sufficient to produce a given effect, but it may not be "necessary," that is, other causes could just as well have produced the same effect. If, however, a particular effect could not occur without a particular cause, then that cause is described as a "necessary cause." Keeping these definitions in mind we see that Cobb and Griffin are arguing that there is no need to speak of God acting in a particular situation if other causes would be sufficient to explain the event even without any involvement by God.

To a great extent, Cobb and Griffin suggest, twentieth century theology has been "a return to the idea of the double perspective." Karl Barth complained about the traditional understanding because it ignored the complete graciousness of God's universal causation,[6] but formally Barth deemed the principle of primary and secondary causation to be correct.[7]

Rudolf Bultmann is also perceived as continuing to take a double perspective, presupposing the epistemology of Immanuel Kant.[8]

> From the objectifying perspective of science and ordinary life, all events are linked together in a chain of cause and effect, which means that "there remains no room for God's working".[9] In fact, the essence of myth, which makes it objectionable, is that it affirms the interruption of the natural course of affairs by attributing a natural effect to a supernatural cause.[10] But from the perspective of faith, the believer can in the moment confess that an event is "nevertheless" an act of God.[11] The believer affirms a paradoxical identity between a divine act and a fully natural event.

By contrast with both the classical notion and revisions of that notion by major theologians in the early part of this century, Cobb and Griffin are convinced that "process theology provides a way of recovering the conviction that God acts creatively in the world and of understanding this creative activity as the expression of divine *love* for the world."[12]

God Has Two Poles or Aspects in His Being

Cobb and Griffin consider the biblical record "ambivalent on the question of whether God is in complete control of the world," and they find much indication in the Bible that divine providence is not all-determining.[13] It was the interpretation of God as perfect, in terms derived from Greek philosophy, that led Christian theology away from those aspects of the biblical witness, "thereby making creaturely freedom *vis-à-vis* God merely apparent."[14] By contrast, the God of process theology is responsive to the world and is essentially related to it. Actuality (the world as it comes to be) is partially *self*-creative, and future events are therefore not yet determinate. Consequently, even perfect knowledge cannot know the future, and God does not totally control the world. Whatever influence God exercises upon the world is persuasive, not coercive. Charles Hartshorne recommends that we begin with a definition of *perfection* as worshipfulness. "A God worthy of worship must be worthy of admiration, respect and love without limit—an ideal for human imitation." But this is not true of a God whose power is active and never passive, who is completely immutable and independent.[15]

To express this responsive involvement of God in the events of unfolding cosmic history, process theologians speak of "dipolar theism," by contrast with traditional theism and its doctrine of divine simplicity, that is, the teaching that God is totally integrated and without any "parts." Alfred North Whitehead spoke of the two poles of God's being as his primordial and his consequent natures. Charles Hartshorne, who was one of the first to incorporate Whitehead's philosophical concept into a more consciously Christian theology, defined the two poles or aspects of God's being as his "abstract essence" and his "concrete actuality." We might think of these two poles as corresponding to the transcendence and immanence of God. "The abstract essence is eternal, absolute, independent and unchangeable," and it includes the "attributes of deity which characterize divine existence at every moment."[16] Of this pole or aspect, for instance, we can say that God is omniscient, that is, "in every moment of the divine life God knows everything which is knowable at the time."[17]

In his concrete actuality (which is identical to Whitehead's consequent nature), God is "temporal, relative, dependent and constantly changing." God's concrete knowledge is dependent on the decisions made by the worldly actualities. In this pole God's life has moments in which he comes to know new happenings in the world, which only then become knowable and which were consequently not foreseen. But God's relationship to the world is not just one of growing knowledge through observation. He has "a sympathetic feeling with the worldly beings, all of whom have feelings."[18] As a result, God's emotional state is also dependent on the happenings in the world. The kind of knowledge God has includes "genuine contingency and unpredictability." He shares "in that processive quality which 'everlastingness' inevitably possesses."[19]

New Occurrences Come into Being Through A Convergence of Factors That Include the Past and the Subjective Aim of Agents in the Present, Including God

Process theology assumes that reality is dynamic rather than static. It stands in the heritage of Heraclitus rather than Parmenides. The world is "an inter-related society of occasions."[20] These occasions cannot be isolated from one another and considered in themselves alone. "Into each of the given occasions, there enter past events as well as the surrounding and accompanying pressures of other occasions." To these are added the "lure of the future."[21] We therefore live in and "are confronted by a richly inter-connected, inter-related, inter-penetrative series of events."[22]

What is commonly spoken of as causal efficacy must be understood in this context of interrelated occasions. Causation "is to be taken as another word for describing the way in which given occasions are brought to a focus and in which they make their impact upon those to whom they are presented."[23] We have particular experiences rather than others that we could possibly have because of the converging process that brings this occasion rather than a different one into being.

> What in an older kind of philosophy would have been called the chain-of-cause-and-effect is here seen as being very much richer; it is a congeries of occasions, events, pressures, movements, routes, which come to focus at this or that point, and which for their explanation require some principle that has brought and still is bringing each of them, rather than some other possible occurrence, into this particular concrete moment of what we commonly style "existence."[24]

Within the process that is made up of this series of occasions, there is always a "subjective aim" at work. The aim has a directive quality, being the "goal or end toward which a given process moves," but it "must also be seen as in some sense immanently at work in that process moving it towards its goal or end or actualization."[25] We ought not to think that each set of occasions is conscious of the aim that is before it, and from which it derives its distinctive identity, in the way that humans experience consciousness. An acorn, for instance, is not "aware of the 'aim' which keeps it moving towards its proper development into an oak tree." Nevertheless, "what does keep it moving towards its proper development is the given subjective aim which is proper to the acorn. And so, in appropriate measure and of course with vast differences at each level, throughout the cosmos."[26]

God is not the only agent in creation, but nothing comes to pass without his activity. He "provides the ultimate efficient cause which turns mere possibility into sheer actuality."[27] He is also the "the final *end* of all that comes to pass" because it is for the fulfillment of his purpose (or the satisfaction of his subjective aim, to use Whiteheadian language) that the process goes on, with both consistency and novelty. God is the "sufficient *ultimate* explanation of what occurs," even of evil occasions, though God is not "responsible for them."[28] Although this divine activity is working in, through, by and under creaturely occasions, it is largely unrecognizable as the work of God.[29]

God himself has a subjective aim, as does every entity in the process, all of which are "dynamic, inter-related, inter-penetrative" of one another. Indeed, it is this subjective aim that constitutes the identity of entities as they develop through the continuous succession of occasions and are themselves each a society of occasions. In other words, the God who is active in nature and human history, which are dynamic processes, is himself dynamic and processive.[30] As Whitehead said in his Gifford lectures, "God is not to be treated as an exception to all metaphysical principles to save their collapse. He is their chief exemplification."[31] Since the world is in dynamic movement, so is God, ceaselessly adapting himself to novel possibilities. Becoming, rather than being, is the major emphasis in the process approach to God's being and action. Aseity (complete self-sufficiency) is not a value, just as it would not be within human relationships. "A man who is utterly self-contained and whose chief ambition is to be 'self-existent' and hence to exist without dependence upon relationships of any sort, is a man whom we regard as an unpleasant if not vicious specimen of the race."[32] This is not to deny the consistency of God's subjective aim or purpose of self-realization in all his relationships, which constitutes God's self-identity. God is always the same in that regard. But at the same time God is continuously adapting so that his being is richly concrete and not just abstract.[33]

This dynamic view of reality, including God, is seen by Norman Pittenger to be characteristic of the biblical writers, for whom

> creation is a directed movement in which novelty occurs, in which the unexpected may and indeed often does happen, and in which great ends are in process of achievement. A view of the world which regards it as a finished product has little relation to the world as the Bible sees it; while a world that is nothing but a complicated mechanism, like a machine which grinds along

engaged in nothing but repeating standard patterns of behaviour, is not the world of movement and change of which the Scriptures speak. The Bible tells us of a *faithful* God whose purpose is unchanging; hence whatever he does will be consistent with his ultimate objective, while the created world will not be the scene of irrelevant and meaningless intrusions. But with all his faithfulness God is living and active, and the creation is not a "finished" world, much less a dead and inert substance. Granted once again that the biblical witness is in highly pictorial terms and that its "science" is outmoded, the fact yet remains that the biblical witness always recognized the possibility of novel as well as significant developments.[34]

As primordial, abstract and eternal, we may say that God "'contains' all that might ever be." Of these possibilities, certain specific occasions come to be, and God is the metaphysical explanation of this "concrete world, with its emergent order and value." He is "the 'principle of concretion' who by his 'decision' has established the good which is in the order of things as it is."[35] What comes to be, in this way, creates new possibilities for what may happen afterward. The future is based upon the past in that "what has happened and what does happen determines, in a general way, what is *to* happen." It all enters into the decisions that God makes for the establishment of further actualities. In God's concrete nature, he too is affected by what occurs in the created order, "for what happens enters into his life and influences his 'decision' by providing new possibilities for his further activity." God is always "the chief principle of explanation for such concrete emergents of the good—in all its variety—as do in fact appear," but God himself is "enriched" by his satisfaction in what happens and by his provision of possibilities of future action by that which has occurred."[36]

Norman Pittenger sees this process perspective as a mean between the absentee God of deism and the pantheistic God. It tends toward pan*en*theism. Everything that is not divine is in God who is "the circumambient reality operative in and through, while also more than, all that is not himself; or conversely all which is not God has its existence within his operation and nature."[37]

God Works in the World Through the Persuasive Action
of His Creative Love, Which Is Often Rejected

Granted that God is intimately involved in all that comes to be, he does not wholly control finite actualities, and this is especially because God only exercises persuasive and not coercive power. "Persuasive power operates more indirectly, for it is effective in determining the outcome only to the extent that the process appropriates and reaffirms for itself the aims envisioned in the persuasion."[38] To exercise coercive power would restrict creaturely freedom, diminish the reality of the world and hence impoverish divine experience. "Creaturely freedom is all important, for without it God is deprived of the one thing the world can provide which God alone cannot have: a genuine social existence." Instead of "angelic marionettes who merely echo his thought as further extensions of his own being, God has elected to enter into dialogue with sinful, yet free," people.[39] God's relatedness to each occasion does not restrict the occasion's freedom. By confronting the world with unrealized opportunities, God "opens up a space for freedom and self-creativity." Yet even in its operation to persuade rather than to control, God's power is "finally the most effective power in reality."[40] God himself is genuinely free, but in deciding to create he has limited his freedom to act by the conditions established by those creatures. In interacting with the creaturely world, God "may receive an 'amen' which opens up for him new possibilities and novel opportunities of action, or from it he may receive a 'no' which denies him those particular possibilities and opportunities." In such a case God must find "other ways, more subtle perhaps, in which his intended purpose may find its fulfilment."[41]

Like a husbandman in the vineyard of the world, God fosters and nurtures its continuous evolutionary growth "throughout all ages; he is the companion and friend who inspires us to achieve the very best that is within us." He creates "by persuading the world to create itself."[42] God offers the "lure" that evokes from each occasion the movement toward satisfaction of its subjective aim. He "draws out, elicits, provides data for, and is himself enriched by, the new occasions as they occur."[43] This relationship between God and the world is the only one that could grant the world the ontological independence inherent in its own activity. It allows God to be creative without resulting in a situation that is either deterministic or purely by chance.[44] This is, of course, risky for God. He continually directs the creation toward its own good, but his persuasive power is only effective if creatures affirm that good for themselves. God has taken that risk because he has faith in us, and it is "up to us to respond in faith to him."[45]

It is in this risk-taking commitment to influence others only by persuasion that God is seen to be essentially loving. He pours himself out for others, takes into himself all that is made available to him and absorbs the evil that is there so that he can distill something good out of it. All this he does

not for self-aggrandizement but for the benefit of those to whom he is intimately related. "God is love because he is infinitely related; he is love
because he enters into and participates in his creation; he is love,
supremely, because he absorbs error, maladjustment, evil, everything that
is ugly and unharmonious, and is able to bring about genuine and novel
occasions of goodness by the use of material which seems so unpromising
and hopeless."[46] Through his persuasive luring (also called the "initial aim")
God tenderly moves creatures toward self-decisions that can bring about
greater good. He "works toward the appearance of a realm in which his
own satisfaction of aim in a realm of love becomes also the satisfaction of
the creaturely aim and a sharing in love, as the creation moves forward
towards richer life."[47]

Process theology is sometimes accused of denying the personal nature
of God, but Pittenger insists that God is profoundly personal in the sense
that he has awareness and self-awareness, because he has a capacity to
communicate or enter into active-reactive relationships. He has freedom of
action within limits of consistency and possibility.[48] Charles Hartshorne
argues that "a personal God is one who has social relations, really has
them, and thus is constituted by relationships and hence is relative—in a
sense not provided for by the traditional doctrine of a divine Substance
wholly nonrelative toward the world, though allegedly containing loving
relations between the 'persons' of the Trinity."[49]

Interestingly, it is human beings whose "personality" is still judged to be
in process. God is "personal in the highest conceivable degree," but human
beings are only "on the way to becoming personal." By freely responding
to God's influence we proceed along the way to genuine personhood, but
when we respond negatively to "the initiating love which is God himself in
action in his world," we elect to become less personal than we might and
could be.[50] But, the cosmic Lover does not let us go. In the long run "every
creature will be held captive to the Lover-God. And he will be held captive
by no coercive measures applied in thus securing his acceptance but by his
own entirely glad and free response." We are, by creation, intended lovers,
called to be "co-creators" with God in a dependent way since God is the
one who initiates and supports us by "grace."[51] God does not "use" people
by "pushing them about and treating them as if they were manikins, without regard for their own freedom and integrity." God uses us by our own
"glad and entirely free consent" and it is when we are open to such "use"
that we are truly and deeply ourselves.[52] In Christ we see perfect humanity,

utter faith in God, utter obedience and love in action.[53]

In this personal, deeply related existence, the succession of time is real to God. "He is not above and outside all temporality, in an eternity which negates succession." Temporality is a "reflection of his own dynamic life," and it also enters into his own reality. *"What happens matters to God.* And it matters to him in more than a superficial sense, as if he simply observed and knew in an external way what was going on in the world." What happens in the world is "a genuine manifestation of the living process which is his own nature." It makes a difference to God because "it makes possible the novelty of adaptation, the emergence of new actualities, and the appearance of real possibilities, which otherwise would not be available to him." History and historical occurrences in time, are "real to him, for him, and in him."[54] The past is made up of events that have occurred, the present is the occasion that is now occurring, but the future is radically different because it contains no occasions. The present is influenced by the past and will influence the future. In Whitehead's terminology, future occasions "prehend" or "feel" previous ones.[55] Time is linear, not cyclical, and every moment is new and unrepeatable. Yet "every moment is a now, which in this sense is timeless."[56] The past does not completely determine the present. In each new moment of experience, "an entity creatively synthesizes the multiple data or stimuli presented by the past into a new emergent whole in act of self-creation. Both freedom and determination are in this manner accounted for."[57]

In the conception of classical theism, God is the cause and the world is his effect. There could be no world without God, but God would still be God without the world. This is not so in process theism. Since creative activity in love is God's very heart, "he cannot be the *God he is,* and hence not really God, unless there is a world in which his creativity is expressed and which itself is an expression of that creativity, and unless he is 'affected' by that world and what happens in it."[58] "God is the divine Eros urging the world to new heights of enjoyment."[59] But the desire to be self-expressive is universal. In each self-creative experience, an occasion does not aim only at its own private enjoyment but aims to contribute also to the enjoyment of others.

Providence Is God's Loving Work, Luring Us to What Is Good Without Determining the Outcome

Pittenger proposes that providence is "largely a *prospective* matter," having to do with what Whitehead called the "satisfaction of subjective aim."[60]

Providence is God's calling us to *"become* a son of God 'in Christ.'" It is suggested that 2 Timothy 1:12 is a key passage, for its expression of trust in God's providence for his children.[61] God does not remove difficulties from our lives or save us from pain, any more than he did in the case of his Son Jesus Christ. But he offers us the "assurance of faith that enables each man to say, 'I am his, and he is mine, forever.' Nothing other than this, nothing less or more than this, is the meaning of providence."[62] In short, providence is God's way of relating to us.

Charles Hartshorne wrote that "providence can reasonably be conceived, not as a simple alternative to chance, its mere negation or prevention, but only as a channelling of chance between banks less than infinitely close together."[63] This is because "every event is the joint product of lawful causes, self creation and God's influence."[64] Although "the definiteness of an event is almost entirely provided by its antecedents, which completely determine a well-defined and usually narrow range of alternatives," it is the event itself that finally decides upon a single outcome. It is neither the previous causes nor God that reduces the potentialities to an actual occurrence.[65] It is precisely because God's providential working is by persuasion, not coercion, that room is left to the creature for alternatives.

Miracles Are Instances of Particularly Intensive Influence by God That Create Wonder in Those Who Observe Them

The above description of God's intimate, interpenetrative involvement in the becoming that is taking place within cosmic history, clearly indicates that it is impossible, within a process theological perspective, to speak of God as "intruding" or "intervening" in the world. God is everywhere at work, and always here. Yet "there may be 'fuller' or 'deeper' or 'richer' instances of the divine operation in this or that particular area or aspect of nature and history." These occasions are indicative of the total structure and dynamic of God's operation. "Hence they may be seen as possessing a peculiar importance for our interpretation of its meaning."[66] God can "intensify" his work in a given place "without contradicting or suspending or violating or interfering with the regularities which give a relatively settled ordering to the world."[67]

Defining the three terms the New Testament uses for "miracle," Pittenger suggests:

A "sign" is the manifestation, in an actual concrete instance, of God's nature and purpose. The occurrence is meant to bring home, to this or that person or group of persons, who God is and what God is "up to" in respect to his human children. A "power" is the release of the divine energy, gracious as it always is, in this or that special situation, so that those present or affected by it can experience God's working and in consequence be strengthened and empowered more adequately to fulfil his intention for them. A "wonder" (and this is the closest to the conventional understanding of "miracle", yet with subtle differences) is an event which is so extraordinary and unexpected that it awakens awe and wonder in the beholder, making him say (as Professor A. E. Taylor once put it, in an admirable contemporary phrase), "Oh, my God!!" The "Oh" expresses the shock of wonder which the occurrence arouses; the "my God" expresses the realisation that in this happening, whatever it may be, it is *God* who is at work.[68]

In short, notes Pittenger, miracle is God's special providence with reference to humanity.

Prayer Affects God, Who Receives Our Request into His Own Decision Concerning His Next Action, and It Affects the Outcome by Opening Up God's Possibilities for Influence in the World

John Cobb has defined *prayer* as "a means of adjustment—adjustment of the individual to situations in the world and especially to the larger purposes of God." He proposes that the purpose of spiritual discipline "must be to align ourselves with the direction in which God is already drawing us."[69] But Phillip Cooley finds no place in Cobb's work for "prayer as the request for, and expectation of, divine intervention."[70] David Basinger observes that most process theologians affirm the importance of prayer and argue for petitionary prayer, but he contends that "there is no basis for retaining the concept of efficacious petitionary prayer within the process system."[71] This is because God cannot act unilaterally to bring about a state of affairs either in the moral or in the natural realm.

Marjorie Suchocki, on the other hand, argues that intercessory prayer is useful in the life of the one praying. We "have raised to the conscious level new thoughts about the object of our petitions. And since, according to process thought, our decisions are always conditioned by our past, this new consciousness will necessarily have some effect on our present and future."[72] Suchocki suggests that if I pray for my aunt, it "may trigger a desire to call or visit or send a note." The act of praying for my aunt changes the "set of experiences which God takes into consideration when determining which possibilities to present to us." For example, God could now attempt to lure me to visit my aunt, since I have generated conscious thoughts of her.[73] Furthermore, I will have expanded God's possibilities for interaction with the one prayed for. God might now lure my aunt to invite me to visit. Intercession changes things for the one prayed for because my aunt's world also now includes my prayers.

Norman Pittenger is another process theologian who has sought to find a place for petitionary prayer within a process theological framework. Based on his observation of common Christian practice, Pittenger contends that petition "has been taken out of its rightful context and exalted in such a way that it was not entirely a parody when a friend remarked, 'Prayer is bringing to God's attention what he has overlooked and so insisting upon getting one's way with him that he can only grant one's requests.'"[74] Pittenger himself does believe, however, that our prayers make a difference to God "not only in his awareness of them but in the activity which is his true nature. What we do towards him, in thought and word and deed and *a fortiori* in our praying, counts in the working out of his purpose of good; what is more, it counts for *him* and, I dare to say, *in* him as well."[75] Prayer is not a "purely human enterprise, in which nothing really happens from God" toward us. There is a relationship between God and humans that involves a giving and receiving on both sides.[76]

It is the concrete pole of God's dipolar existence that makes it possible for us to influence divine decisions. Charles Hartshorne suggests that when we speak of God as supremely sensitive, we "say that in his rule he allots to us a privilege of participation in governing which goes infinitely beyond a mere ballot. It means that with every decision, however secret, that takes place in our minds, we are casting a vote which will surely be taken account of and will surely procure effects in the divine decisions."[77] There is mutuality and reciprocity in the influence that God and humans have on one another. God receives the world as an object of awareness into his own life and experience. The manner in which God integrates that experience is his self-determination, which further influences the world by becoming a datum of experience universally. "The creatures then receive this datum and decide how they will integrate it. Their response in turn contributes to the divine life. The degree of divine influence depends entirely upon the response of the one being influenced."[78]

The basic point of prayer, as Pittenger understands it, is to unite two desires so that our desire may be fulfilled in God and God's desire be fulfilled in us. "God wills for man that which in its truest intentionality is also man's will—to realise his personality, to be fulfilled, to become truly the son of God. Man wills that God's will should be done; and he wills this not abstractly, as if from the sidelines cheering on those who are engaged in the struggle, but by giving himself utterly for that doing."[79]

This is a relationship that affects both partners. "Since God *is* love, the supreme cosmic Lover, to look at him with attention and to think upon him in concentration will bring about in those who engage in the practice a conformity of their 'minds'—we should rather say, their whole 'becoming' personalities—to God." In this way we are started on our way to be lovers. We are strengthened and increased in our capacity as lovers. This has "by-products in tranquility of soul, inner peace, sense of assurance and increase in understanding."[80] On the other hand, God is also "changed," precisely in that "through his relationship with the world he is given further opportunities to create greater good and to implement such good as is already there." These particular opportunities, in these ways, "would not be available to him without the consentient acceptance which the world can give to him."[81] God is, therefore, also "'enriched' in his own life." This is not to say that he becomes more God but that his experience is aug-mented.

The effect of prayer, however, is not confined to its impact on the divine and human partners; things happen in the world as a result of prayer. In this regard, Pittenger's model of providence leads to a quite different con-ception than classical theology has offered. Readers should evaluate Pit-tenger's negative assessment of the classical position in the light of the models that I will describe in later chapters. Nevertheless, it is on the basis of that assessment that Pittenger justifies his alternative proposal, a process model of prayer. In his view, classical theology assumes that God, in his timelessness, knows what we will ask for. Consequently, "those desires or askings have already been taken into account. What is overlooked is that prayer, in this way of seeing things, becomes merely a formal exercise without any effective significance."[82] What results, "after a long series of such steps, will be a world in which nothing new ever happens because the God who is its 'logical explanation' *himself* does nothing. No praying Christian," argues Pittenger, "can think like this."[83] He observes that Aquinas did pray but judges him to be a "double-man," with one half of him being a "devout prayerful Christian whose religion was nourished on biblical images and deep communion with the God who was for him living and active and affected by prayer" and the other half being a "philosophi-cal theologian whose theoretical description of God contradicted what in his heart of hearts he both believed and practised."[84]

In Pittenger's model of providence, God does not have everything all laid out beforehand. "*Of course* he knows in his wisdom all *relevant* possibilities, but in this picture he is not said to know all actually *chosen* possibilities," because these are contingent and "their contingency is as real to God as it is to us." In God's inexhaustible love he "has the resources which will enable him to deal with any particular contingency; but those resources can only be put to work, so to say, when the contingency has occurred." Thus when earnest prayer is made to God for some person or situation, "God *then* 'takes account of it.'" In God's ongoing activity in the world, because of the relationship he always has with that world, God receives and then uses the good desires and urgent requests we offer to him.

The way situations develop in the world is affected by our human activity, including our prayer. Were this not so, petitionary and intercessory prayer would be "absurd and irrelevant." The world is not a finished product. "There is absolutely no reason whatsoever for thinking that the created order is not patient of pressures upon it, workings within it, and influences operative through it, which can and do produce fresh and unexpected events."[85] Given the contingency of human choices, we can speak of "the openness of God to receive all decisions into himself and to use them for the accomplishment of his purposes, and with that openness the joy which is his as these occasions are made available to him." We do not determine which of our desires or requests God implements. He does what is "in accordance with his will," but this is "not some arbitrary fiat which bears no relationship to the fulfilment of his creatures; his will is *precisely* that fulfilment," and this is especially true where humans are concerned. Consequently, we may say that "God takes account of *all* desires and requests, but he implements them only insofar as they contribute to accomplishment of his purpose of love in its widest sharing."[86]

Our petition and intercession need "purification or disinfection." This is achieved by "balancing human praying with constant 'recollection' of God as Love, meditating upon him as Love, and contemplating him as Love." When we approach prayer from this perspective, "the sort of petitions and intercessions we feel impelled to make will have a very different character."[87] Our own desire will become increasingly "one with God's passionate desire for good; our requests will be 'according to his will,' so far as we can glimpse that will in its details."[88]

The Case Study

At the seminary in town, a few years ago a guest lecturer had done a series on process theology. A number of people went to hear it. They found it fairly heavy going because it was a very different way of thinking about reality, but Mark Peterson had latched on to the position with great enthusiasm. At first it seemed terribly philosophical, but it did answer some of his serious questions about why there was so much evil and suffering in the world, so he decided that the lecturer was right: this was a metaphysic that provided a helpful framework for the biblical narrative about God. He liked the vision of God patiently persuading all aspects of creation toward their own fulfilment in spite of the fact that there was often resistance to his influence.

When Mark heard Fred's account of the abduction, he was immediately comforted to know that Richard and the others were not alone in that jungle with their captors. God was very much at work there as he was everywhere. Mark knew that God was not happy with what had occurred. God would have been making persuasive efforts in the consciousness of the guerrillas, trying to deter them from their plans to kidnap the missionaries as he saw this intention develop. God would also have been at work on the political leaders in the situation. He knew that the rebels were not evil at the core of their being. They were responsible members in their families and leaders in the tribal structure. But all their peaceful efforts to obtain justice from the government had been unsuccessful, and they had gradually moved on to increasingly aggressive forms of protest, which had culminated in armed rebellion. The missionaries actually had sympathy for the cause of these tribal people among whom they worked, but they strove to maintain political distance and to focus on their work of evangelism and church development. The rebels had no animosity toward the missionaries themselves, but they hoped that abducting these foreigners would gain international attention to their cause. Obviously the leaders of the government had been decidedly resistant to God's loving persuasion and the frustrated rebels had also not responded to efforts that God made to lead them to nonviolent means of protest.

As Mark contemplated the situation, he assumed that God was cognizant of all of the details and that God was already at work to bring good out of the evil that had developed. He could even see prospects for God's program to be advanced by the presence of the missionary captives in the camp of the guerrillas, and he hoped that the rebels would succeed in generating international pressure upon the government to institute a more just situation for the tribal people. He could see ways in which the whole situation could prove to be beneficial to the work of the missionaries and the church. Mark believed that God did not need to be invited into the situation by the believers gathered in prayer. He was there, and he was already doing his utmost, in the circumstances, to bring about the greatest good for all concerned, without having any foreknowledge of how well his efforts would succeed. On the other hand, Mark did believe that prayer was a meaningful and helpful ministry on their part. It would open them up personally to God's persuasion in their own lives, thus making them more useful to God for whatever action he might wish to have them do toward a remedy of the complex evil in the situation. This expression of reliance upon God and of desire for good in the particular context provided God with an additional "occasion" that he could receive into his own ongoing development, consider in his own decision-making and use in the next moves that he would make in the world. Prayer was not the only thing that these Christians could do, but it was one valuable way that they could seek to discover and to cooperate with God in his purposes for the world.

Mark prayed: "Loving God, we know that you have good purposes for all of your creation, as you draw us toward the full realization of what is good for us. We are deeply comforted in the knowledge that you are active in, with and through all occasions in this world. Consequently, we know that you are present with Richard Henderson and his colleagues just as you are here with us. We pray that Richard and his friends may experience peace and confidence in their own knowledge that you are active in their situation. We ask that their own responsiveness to your loving influence in their lives may itself be a means by which your love may affect those who have abducted them.

"We know, dear God, that you are also active in the lives of those who captured Richard. They are obviously men who have been rejecting the influences by which you have been ceaselessly luring them toward fuller personhood. They are not living according to your will, but we are not without hope in this situation. On many occasions your love has effectively transformed the evil intent of rebellious human hearts, and we have experienced that tender work in our own lives. It is now our prayer that your love will continue to tug at the hearts of these men even in their current rejection of it, and that they might be led to act justly and compassionately in this situation and indeed to turn themselves toward you for the future of their lives. We believe that our own prayers and those of Richard and his fellow missionaries will open a way for your love to work, bringing good out of this evil, including the establishment of greater justice for the tribal people. In that hope, we make ourselves available to you as instruments of your purpose to achieve the good of all your creatures. In the name of Jesus, whose own life inspires us to costly obedience, Amen."

4

The Openness Model (1)

T HE OPENNESS MODEL GETS ITS NAME FROM THE PROPOSITION THAT GOD IS *open to his creatures, to whom he has given libertarian freedom, and that the future is open because it will be brought about to a large degree by the decisions those creatures make. God is omnipotent, but he has freely limited his own ability to control every event within creation by giving libertarian freedom to moral creatures, human and spiritual. God is personal in his relationships with these creatures, and so he is affected by them as well as having an effect upon them. There were risks in creating this kind of world, but God decided that it was better to have a world in which free creatures love and obey him than to have one in which he could guarantee that his own will would always be done. God is faithful to himself and unchanging in his moral nature, but he is not absolutely immutable, as though he had formed a comprehensive plan for his creation, in eternity, and was now working out all the details of that plan, in the time and space that he created.*

God is omniscient, knowing all that can be known, but this does not include the future acts of free creatures. Consequently, the future is genuinely open, even for God. Although he knows the immense range of possibilities and has amazing powers of prediction because of his knowledge of all things past and present, he cannot know what will actually happen in the

*future until it happens, if the event is conditioned on decisions made by free
creatures.*

*God has good purposes for his creation, and he is working toward these
goals through continual interaction with all of his creatures. Along the way,
many things will take place that God did not want to happen, but in the end
his purposes will be achieved. Yet this will come about without his coercing
his free moral creatures along the way. His ways of influence are varied
and his power is great and he has reserved to himself the right to intervene
forcefully when it is absolutely necessary to the achievement of his goal.
However, this is a rare and unnecessary course of action for God because of
his great knowledge and power.*

*Because God has given his creatures significant freedom and has willed
to have a responsive relationship with them, he is open to their requests in
prayer. Although no creature's petition can change God's final purpose,
God's own intentions for specific events along the way are subject to revision. There are many things that he will do for the good of his creatures,
whether or not anyone prays, but there are also things that he will not do
unless he is asked to do them. There are specific goods that people will not
have if they do not ask for them and specific evils that will occur if the
prayers of God's people are not offered for their prevention. This does not
mean that everyone, even every obedient believer, gets what she asks for.
God is free, as his creatures are, and may choose a better course than is suggested by us. But petitionary prayer has a real effect on the way things turn
out and even on the actions that God takes to influence those outcomes.*

When we think of God's action in the world, we are immediately confronted with the existence of other agents and are forced to consider the
relationship between the divine and created agents. God was not the only
one at work when the abductors burst in upon Richard and his fellow missionaries. What, then, is the relative contribution of divine and created
agents to the events that occur? In the semi-deistic model, God has greatly
limited his own ongoing agency in events so that human agents, working
within the boundaries established by the created natural order, are the
"causes" of most of the events of human history.[1] The process model postulates greater continuing divine activity through the deed of luring creatures
toward their good. But again, it is primarily the decision of the creatures in
responding to or rejecting the divine influence that determines the outcome.

From at least the time of Augustine, there have been teachers within the

Christian church who perceived of God's control as comprehensive and determinative of all that happens. We will meet their perspectives at a later point in the book. Proponents of God's comprehensive control also affirm human freedom as necessary to moral responsibility, but they define that freedom as volitional. So long as people act willingly, without external coercion, they are deemed to be free and hence responsible for their actions. This is called a "compatibilist" position because it contends that human freedom is compatible with divine predetermination.

In recent decades numerous theologians and philosophers of religion have articulated their rejection of this model of the God who controls all things and is sovereign in a comprehensive way. The primary objection stems from a conviction that such a view of God negates human freedom because genuine or significant freedom is understood to be libertarian. The volitional or noncoercive understanding of freedom is considered inadequate, indeed illusory, by these objectors. Not all of these theologians and philosophers are agreed on the definition of libertarian freedom, but it is commonly assumed to include the power of contrary choice. If people are unable, at the time of acting, to do otherwise than they do, regardless of the reasons for that inability, their action is judged not to be free.[2] This is sometimes called "contracausal freedom," but we shall primarily use the term libertarian. From this definition of human freedom arises a model of God's power and action that significantly restricts what he is able to do in order to give space to the wills and acts of the creatures to whom he has given freedom as agents within creation. It is also widely assumed that libertarianly free acts cannot be known ahead of time, and consequently this model of providence also denies comprehensive divine knowledge of the future. Not all proponents of this model identify their own position with the term "the openness model," but the name has been widely used, particularly in evangelical circles, since the publication of *The Openness of God: A Biblical Challenge to the Traditional Understanding of God.*[3]

William Hasker provides a rationale for the term *openness* to describe this model: "God is open to us his creatures, to the world he has made, and to the future."[4] The model now being described has been identified as *free will theism*[5] or as "neotheism."[6] However, it is best to view the openness model as a particular form of the broader theological framework described as "free will theism," which attempts to affirm both libertarian human freedom and God's sovereignty in the world. David Basinger has concluded that free will theism is compatible with different views regarding the nature of God's knowledge.[7] God might have only present knowledge, might have simple foreknowledge or have middle knowledge (knowledge of counterfactuals, that is, what a person *would* do if the circumstances were different.) The distinctive feature of the openness model, within the range of free will theisms, is its commitment to God's knowledge as including only the past and the present comprehensively, on the conviction that the future acts of libertarianly free people cannot be known until those people have decided on their action and done it.

An additional motivation for most representatives of this model of the "openness of God" is to protect God from the charge of being responsible for human suffering and evil in the world. Here there is a starting point shared with proponents of the first two models. There is a common perception that particularly the theodicy of a model that gives God comprehensive control is inadequate in the face of the human experience of evil. Given the focus of this book, I will not devote attention to the implications of this model of providence for evil, but it is useful to keep it in mind as the model of providence is spelled out.

Obviously not all of those who accept the basic premises of this model formulate their conception in exactly the same way. A book could be written on the range of submodels within the general model being described here. I shall try to delineate basic points that are widely affirmed by those who hold the general model, while giving some indication along the way of the different nuances in the approaches taken by various late twentieth-century theologians. Not everyone mentioned below would concur entirely with all the perspectives put together here, but I believe that all of them would accept the big picture that emerges from this exposition. Theologians and Christian philosophers whose work figures prominently in the following exposition have devoted books to the subject or to significant aspects of it. They are Peter Baelz, Gregory Boyd, Vincent Brümmer, John Polkinghorne, Richard Rice, John Sanders[8] and Keith Ward. The contributions of a few others will be mentioned in passing. More space has been given to this model than some of the others because of its relative newness on the theological scene and because its challenge to the more classical view is gaining such wide attention.

God Is Responsive to His Creatures and Has Limited His Own Control in Order to Give Them Libertarian Freedom

God's self-restraint. Marcel Sarot observes that it is only in this century that the concept of divine self-limitation has become widely accepted in Christian theology. He identifies four motives for this change: (1) it results from a view of Christ's experiences as affecting the divine nature; (2) it follows from an understanding of the creation of the universe as an act of divine self-limitation; (3) it is a way of dealing with evil; and (4) it derives from the belief that God is love and that love makes room for the beloved and is vulnerable in relationship.[9] After the destruction of the second temple, Jews found consolation in "the self-limitation, the sadness, suffering and lamentation of God."[10] It is an idea that continues to be important in the wake of the Holocaust. In the words of Hans Jonas: "Not because he chose not to, but because he *could* not intervene did he fail to intervene . . . God . . . has divested himself of any power to interfere with the physical course of things; and . . . responds to the impact on his being by worldly events, not 'with a mighty hand and outstretched arm,' . . . but with the mutely insistent appeal of his unfulfilled goal."[11] Although theologians often speak of "divine self-limitation," Sarot considers it an unfortunate choice of term and prefers to speak of God's self-restraint. God remains in control, but he chooses not to intervene.[12] Keith Ward likewise argues that "there is a sense in which God can limit his own power, for instance, by creating free beings which have the power of autonomous decision, which God is unable to control as long as that freedom remains." But he describes this as "simply a limitation of the exercise of power, not on its possession." God always and necessarily possesses the power to control beings totally, but he may choose not to exercise that power. Only in that sense should we speak of God as "self-limiting."[13]

Peter Baelz invites us to "rethink our ideas of God's power in accordance with the way in which that power was expressed in the life of Jesus."[14] We should think of it as the power of love. Love requires freedom, "but letting go, respecting otherness, does not involve ceasing to care. Love continues to desire and to seek the good of the beloved. It longs and works for the wonder of a renewed and deeper relationship." God wills his creation to be free and so he "withdraws a space from the world in order to let it be itself." God gives to the world "a real measure of independence. But he does not cease to care for his world. And he does not cease to work in and for his world. He comes. He calls. He shares. He gives and forgives. He creates and re-creates."[15] Since love creates in and for freedom, we might say that God creates the world by "persuading it to create itself." This involves experiment and risk, the potential for both triumph and disaster, but it is necessary because the loving Creator seeks and awaits the creature's own response. Even boundless love is, by its very nature, self-limiting. Consequently, there are many things that God cannot do, though he would like to, yet we know that "God is already doing all that Love can do."[16] So our trust is not grounded in God's power but in his love. Recalling the rarity of miracles, in light of horrors like the Holocaust, Polkinghorne comments that "if God were a God who simply interferes at will within his creation, the charge against him would be unanswerable." It is not clear, however, that God is to be blamed for not overruling the wickedness of humankind "if his action is self-limited by a consistent respect for the freedom of his creation (so that he works only with the actual openness of its process) and also by his own utter reliability (so that he excludes the shortcuts of magic)."[17]

Vincent Brümmer is another one who posits that God's control is limited and "his freedom to realize his purposes is dependent on the co-operation" of humans. But Brümmer denies that this is a "limitation or a dependence which is imposed on God from outside."[18] God has freely chosen this as one of "the necessary corollaries of the sort of universe he has freely decided to create." God made himself "vulnerable to our independent action."[19]

As Peter Baelz analyzes the situation, two results follow from our granting a limited independence to the world of nature and history. First, it is "no longer necessary to ascribe unusual and often destructive events to the immediate working of God. Earthquakes occur because of natural processes" and are not "the acts of a God who intervenes in the normal course of affairs to express his displeasure and to punish the sinful." By the same token we must admit that unusual and beneficial events are also the result of natural processes. "If a prolonged drought is to be understood as a natural occurrence and not a divine visitation, so too is the coming of the rain which ends the drought." Both the onset of the cancer and its unforeseen remission are to be explained in natural terms. The recognition of an order in nature enables us to say that ills are not sent by God but also "prompts us to say that blessings are none of his bounty either."[20] Polkinghorne likewise accepts this as the consequence of the "free-will defence" for dealing with the incidence of moral evil when applied to the whole of creation in a "free-process defence."[21] God "allows the physical world to be itself," which leads "not only to the evolution of systems of increasing complexity, but also to the evolution of systems imperfectly formed and malfunctioning." God neither expressly wills the growth of a cancer nor the act of a murderer, "but he allows both to happen." It is the "open flexibility of the world's process" that "affords the means by which the universe explores its own potentiality, humankind exercises its will, and God interacts with his creation."[22]

The second result of attributing a measure of relative independence to creation, according to Baelz, is that we can still "see the *whole* process of nature and the *whole* course of history as, in some sense, the work of God." God is the transcendent 'cause' of all finite being who has made and sustains things as they are, including the natural processes in the midst of which humans struggle "to establish a properly human form of life." But Baelz finds deism ultimately unsatisfactory because it gives us no positive assurance of the goodness of God and does not inspire worship. It makes God too impersonal and makes the language of God's help irrelevant.[23] John Polkinghorne suggests that "the recently gained understanding of the distinction between physical systems which exhibit being and those which exhibit becoming may be seen as a pale reflection of the theological dialectic of God's transcendence and God's immanence—consequences, respectively, of divine reliability and of the loving gift of freedom by the Creator."[24]

Keith Ward accepts Whitehead's postulation that God is a dipolar being but contends that "Whitehead's God does not truly interact with the world."[25] The creating is done by the many occasions that constitute the process of reality. "The cosmic tyrant, against whom Whitehead so strongly protests, has become the cosmic sponge, absorbing all experiences, but contributing nothing except an abstract array of eternal possibilities for the creative multiplicity of the world."[26] Ward does not want God to be a "monarchical tyrant, determining by his omnipotent will everything that happens," presumably his perception of the Thomist and Calvinist models. Nor does he want God to be "the remote designer of 'the machine of the universe', leaving it to its own concerns" (cf. the semi-deist model). But he also does not want God to be the "helpless experient" of all the universe's feelings, a "fellow-sufferer who never himself appears to act" (cf. the process model). Ward's alternate proposal, shared by many others in this model, is of a finite world that is "given the sort of autonomy and importance Whitehead wants," but with God "related to it more positively than he seems to allow." God must "ultimately control the universe fully, guiding it to its unique and proper fulfilment, in finally conscious relation to himself."[27]

Divine risk-taking and chance. Although some might perceive such self-limitation as putting God's realization of his purposes in jeopardy, Brümmer encourages us not to underestimate God's "ability to respond adequately to whatever we in our sinful defiance might do to oppose the realization of his intentions."[28] God knows all future possibilities and probabilities, and "his creative resources are also infinite so that he is always able to respond creatively to whatever we might decide to do." If we refuse to cooperate with God in realizing one plan, "our non-cooperation is instrumental in making a new plan possible. Thus, if we refuse to be his *agents,* we become his *instruments.*"[29] Likewise, Peter Baelz notes our "real, though limited, power to direct the immediate course of events," but he argues that "the apprehension of God's being and activity includes the faith that his purposes cannot ultimately be frustrated. . . . God's purposes may be delayed by human disobedience, but they cannot finally be thwarted."[30] Somewhat less absolute in his declaration that God cannot be defeated, but still confident, Timothy Gorringe says, "Because God is gracious even he cannot be certain that refusal will not be final—but we hope in his hope. It is hope in that hope which is finally the only possible response to the question of whether God may be defeated."[31]

While admitting that God does not have total control because God accepts "the precariousness necessary in his enterprise of giving freedom to creation," Polkinghorne asserts that "what is beyond control is not beyond total redemption."[32] Richard Rice also grants that "on the individual level, God's designs are often thwarted." Yet, though God will not achieve his ultimate objectives for every human being, he will achieve them for human life.[33] In Clark Pinnock's words, God's sovereignty "is not the all-determining kind but is an omnicompetent kind."[34] It is not that God is impotent, claims Hendrikus Berkhof, who does not deny God's omnipotence. But he is "defenceless," not as one who is unable to exercise power actively but as one who has chosen this special way to make his power felt.[35] Although God allows himself to be "limited and resisted by the freedom" of the partner he created, "all of salvation history guarantees that ultimately he will not lose his grip on the world and will not rest until he has—no, not conquered and subjugated but—led his human opponent to the true freedom of the sons of God. In his association with the world he is so great that he can remain present in it when he is cast out, and active when he is resisted."[36]

Those who are prepared to admit that God takes real risks are more likely to grant a role to chance in the eventual outcomes. David Bartholomew, for instance, argues that "chance was God's idea" and that it is used by God "to ensure the variety, resilience and freedom necessary to achieve his purposes."[37] By "chance" Bartholomew means that a situation exists "in which there is more than one possible outcome for an event, and where one cannot predict, with certainty, which outcome will occur."[38] In many cases this is not because the events are intrinsically unpredictable but because we are ignorant of all the factors. Many accidents, for instance, are not foreseen, but they could have been. Likewise for things like the toss of a coin or the roll of the dice: when these random processes are observed in the aggregate, there is pattern and regularity that allows for prediction. But at the atomic level there is no apparent causal explanation, and the same is true of human choice, if behaviorism is to be avoided. Divine providence is likewise viewed as chancy in light of its unpredictability.[39]

What makes this risky for God is that chance happenings are part of God's overall plan, but "events occur which do not express his direct intentions." For example, events resulting from free human decision may be contrary to God's will.[40] Free creatures are able to interfere with natural processes and thwart the Creator's intention. Nevertheless, chance is viewed as offering advantages that could possibly not be otherwise attained, such as creativity and the generation of curiosity. God is concerned with the macro-effects, and "the uncertainty at the micro-level provides the built-in flexibility needed to make the system adaptive and responsive."[41] The use of the lot to determine the divine will (cf. Lev 16:9; Josh 18:10; 1 Sam 14:41; Jon 1:7; Acts 1:26) might appear to indicate belief that God determined it, but Bartholomew considers Ecclesiastes 9:1-3, 11 a declaration otherwise. Although the New Testament views God as concerned about everything (e.g., Mt 10:29-31), "not all happenings are his deliberate acts though all provide opportunities for his real nature to be revealed."[42] Chance, which is largely neutral, may "determine what God in his providence is called upon to do, but it does not constrain his power to do it."[43]

God's openness to change. One of the goals of the "open view of God" is to "restore some important biblical metaphors to the prominence they deserve in our thinking about God, in particular metaphors such as divine suffering and divine repentance."[44] This reading of Scripture finds a God who makes plans but occasionally changes his mind or repents as factors arise that make it impossible for God to realize his intentions and necessary to reformulate his plans in response to the changes.[45]

Keith Ward rejects the classical (Anselmian) argument that God cannot be changed by anything other than himself. "Omnipotence is limited by love; but there is no imperfection about that. The ultimate fact remains that God, the ground of omnipotent love, cannot be destroyed or corrupted, but it is essential to his being love that he can be changed and affected by what his own power permits to be."[46] The next temporal segment of the world will partially be determined by the free acts of creatures. God will respond to those free acts, moment by moment, and hence "in a strictly limited sense, God can be changed from without."[47] The key is to drop "the incoherent notion of metaphysical perfection as the actual possession of the maximal degree of every possible property" and to replace it with the notion of "evaluative perfection, of what is preferable to possess."[48] Then it can be seen that most changes in God bring about a state neither better nor worse than the previous one. Of course, his evaluative perfections are changeless.

Proponents of this model reject the view that God has a will that is fixed from eternity and is immutable. As Vincent Brümmer describes the problem, "All temporal events would be inevitable since their occurrence would be predetermined from eternity by the immutable will of God." In such a universe, he argues, "No events could have the two-way contingency necessary in order to be objects of impetratory petition. In the end we would have to accept the proposition put to Origen by his friend Ambrose: 'If all things come to pass by the will of God, and his counsels are fixed, and none of the things he wills can be changed, prayer is vain.'"[49] (*Impetratory* is not a commonly used word. It can mean the same thing as *petitionary,* simply a request. As Brümmer uses the term here, it has a stronger meaning, namely, prayer that obtains what it requests *because of* the request. It is in this stronger sense that I will use the term throughout the book.) It appears to Brümmer that, if everything was determined by God in eternity, God would not be the sort of being to whom petitions could be meaningfully addressed because he could not react to what we do or feel or ask. We could not say that God did something because we asked him to. In certain respects, God is immutable, particularly in that "we can trust him to remain *faithful* to his character."[50] It is precisely this faithfulness that is the ground of our trust in bringing to God our desires in prayer. But in other respects God is able to change, as in instances where he responds to contingent events and human actions. From this perspective, real change took place in God's will because Hezekiah prayed when Isaiah told him that he would not recover from his illness. Hezekiah's request had a real effect on God's intentions and changed them.

It is not that God has no intentions for the world, but his "plan" is not fixed and invariable. God's "purpose must be implemented in a dynamic historical context," and so his "plans must be sufficiently comprehensive and flexible to include a variety of possible courses of action."[51] God had a plan in view of the possibility of sin, and he implemented it when sin became an actuality. He had planned for every possible development, and he will ultimately achieve his objectives for humankind because he is capable of working for good in every situation.[52] Paul's oft-quoted words in Romans 8:28 assure us that "God is always at work for good. He seeks to make the best of things in every human life. But the fact remains that He can do more for those who respond to His creative power than for those who resist it."[53] Providence is, therefore, to be understood as God's creative response to things as they happen.[54]

Divine repentance. According to the biblical account, human repentance can avert God's judgment and apostasy can incur it (Jer 33:10-16). Terence Fretheim argues that divine repentance is "not something unusual in the Old Testament understanding of God" but that "the language of repentance is part and parcel of a much broader range of language used to speak of God." It "has to do with divine affectability by the creation. The God who repents is also a God who is provoked to anger, who rejoices over the creation, who responds to prayer."[55] Richard Rice observes that God is described as rejecting something that he had already done (Gen 6:6; 1 Sam 15:35), and something that he had promised to do (Jon 3:10).[56] He repented in response to the intercession of Moses and changed his intention to destroy the nation (Ex 32:12-14).[57] In response to the pleas of Abraham, he "reconsidered his plans" concerning Sodom (Gen 18), indicating that they are still "open to revision" after he has formulated them. Abraham's pleading for Sodom and Gomorrah (Gen 18), says Polkinghorne, "is not a charade about an already determined future."[58] In 2 Samuel 7:15-16 there is an unconditional promise of perpetuity, but in 1 Kings 2:1-4 David urges Solomon to walk faithfully so that the promise will be fulfilled, and Solomon later restates the condition, himself (1 Kings 8:25). This is taken to be an indication that God attached conditions that were not spelled out at first.

God repents precisely because he is God (Joel 2:13; Jon 4:2), because he is a compassionate and gracious God, slow to anger, abounding in love and forgiving wickedness (Ex 34:6-7). Over against two passages indicating that God does not repent (Num 23:19; 1 Sam 15:29), we find about forty that say he does. The negative statements should be understood as affirmations of his truthfulness, while his promises not to repent presuppose that he could if he chose to. When God pledges himself unconditionally to a course of action, the possibility of repentance is foreclosed, but otherwise it is open. The Old Testament references to God's emotional responses ought not to be taken as anthropopathisms of the same order as the anthropomorphic references to body parts. They are what distinguishes God from the false gods and from human beings. They portray the "inner life of God."[59] It is because God's fundamental desire is for life, not death, that "God hopes to be able to reverse himself."[60]

God Experiences Time and Does Not Know the Future Acts of Libertarianly Free Creatures

The temporality of God. God's relationship to time is obviously a critical matter in regard to his action within human history. The proponents of this model are committed to God's temporality in some significant sense. In his *Monologion* Anselm had argued from God's immutability to his timelessness. Were God to change, he either would have been or will no longer be perfect. God must, therefore, be immutable. But "since 'time is merely the numbering of before and after in change,'[61] what cannot change cannot be in time."[62] We have already seen the grounds on which divine immutability has been challenged. Keith Ward further argues that "temporality is a necessary property of God."[63] God creates the space-time in which we exist, but he possesses temporality as an uncreated property that is the "condition of his uniquely originative creativity." We cannot fully comprehend how divine time relates to human time, "but we must certainly think of God, as he is in relation to us as contemporary with every present. To that extent, we must think of the Divine time as running in parallel with human time." This is the only way that God can "hear and respond to prayer or act causally to produce new effects in the world."[64] We can say that God is temporal because we can only speak of him as he exists in relation to us. Whatever eternity means, it cannot contradict the truth that God is temporally related to us as creatures.

God is temporal in that "he does some things before he does others, and, in changing, he projects his being along one continuous temporal path."[65] But in another sense we should speak of God as multi-temporal because "God can create different universes, different space-time systems, which cannot be spatially or temporally related to one another." God relates himself to each system, so that he exists simultaneously with each event in each system, but the different time sequences are not temporally relatable to each other. Even from God's point of view, it would not make sense to say that the events in one universe exist before or after the events in another.

While including all time, therefore, God also transcends it. "All past-time is perfectly preserved in him; all possibilities are fully known by him and the future goal of creation is assured by his omnipotence and immutable love."[66] Time is not a force independent of God that moves God unwillingly along its path. Nor is the future "an abyss of arbitrary freedom or chaos of non-being." God is in control at each moment.[67]

Boethius offered a perspective of time that has solved the problem of determinism resulting from foreknowledge for many who adopt his proposal or a modified version of it (cf. the Thomist model in chapter nine). God exists outside of time and sees all events simultaneously like a spectator on a mountaintop who is able to see the full length of a caravan passing by on the road at the foot of the mountain. God therefore sees everything as it occurs, not beforehand, and its contingency is not excluded. If things occurred differently, God would see them differently but no foreknowledge would thereby be falsified. Brümmer, and many others holding the openness model, consider the approach flawed because it describes time as if it were space. But "while time is the relation between events which occur one *after* the other, space is the relation between objects which exist *next* to each other." In Brümmer's opinion, "it is a serious category mistake to reduce the former to the latter as happens when *consecutive* events known by God from his point of view 'beyond' time are taken to be related to each other like the objects *next* to each other in the valley as perceived by the lofty spectator on the mountain top."[68]

> The most damaging way in which this analogy breaks down is the following. If the lofty spectator on the mountain should perceive two spatially distinct objects in the valley simultaneously, they do not thereby become the same object. But if God were to experience two moments in time simultaneously, they would have to *be* simultaneous and thus be the same moment! The view that God 'sees' all moments in time simultaneously entails that all time is reduced to one moment. Our experience of temporal succession would then

be an illusion. But if there is no real temporal succession there would be no real *change* either, and impetratory prayer for things to happen would become meaningless. In any case, if God is 'beyond' time then he could not be the kind of being who could have a temporal relation with the world and with human persons. He would not be a personal agent who could respond to what happens in the world. In this way, too, impetratory prayer would become meaningless.[69]

Brümmer does not deny that God is eternal, but he understands this "in the sense of having no beginning or end, being God 'from age to age everlasting' (Ps 90:2)." Richard Swinburne agrees. God "exists throughout all periods of time." This does not make him "time's prisoner, for the reason that although God and time exist together—God is a temporal being—those aspects of time which seem so threatening to his sovereignty only occur through his own voluntary choice. To the extent to which he is time's prisoner, he has chosen to be so. It is God, not time, who calls the shots."[70]

The unknowability of the future. If God infallibly foreknew every event and human action, it is argued, impetratory prayer would be meaningless. In the words of Vincent Brümmer, "No event could take place differently from the way it in fact does, and no human agent could act differently from the way it in fact does, for that would falsify God's infallible foreknowledge, which would be logically impossible."[71] If the everlasting God had always possessed infallible knowledge of all future events in history, "then it would have to be foreknowledge, and we are back with the problem of determinism."[72] It is the conviction of John Lucas that a view of providence in which God foreknows and foreordains the details of the future course of events, though widely held, "is un-Christian. Apart from leaving no room for human freedom, it poses the problem of evil in irresoluble form, and subverts the moral teaching of Jesus."[73]

Richard Swinburne also complains that foreknowledge is impossible because it affirms backward causation, in that the actions of agents cause God's earlier beliefs. "We act freely and God's beliefs are as they are because of how we have acted."[74] Since God is necessarily and eternally perfectly free, he must be ignorant even of his own future actions "except in so far as his perfect goodness constrains him to act in certain ways."[75] God's omniscience concerns the past, which is causally unaffectable, and his omnipotence concerns the future, which is causally affectable. If God's omniscience included knowledge of his own future actions, he would no longer be free.[76] Furthermore, according to David Bartholomew, God's ignorance of the future in detail is a consequence of the role of chance within the world as he has made it.[77]

The denial of divine foreknowledge is not deemed to be a rejection of divine omniscience. God knows everything that can be known, but this does not include the future, which contains various alternative possibilities, any one of which could be actualized.[78] Through God's intimate knowledge of all human beings, he knows "the precise range of alternatives available to every individual."[79] God could have created a deterministic universe in which he knew the one possible course that future events would take. But, "we all know from personal experience that this is not the sort of universe which he has in fact created." Rather, God has created a world with an open future in which various possibilities could be actualized; a world, therefore, where events have two-way contingency and human beings are personal agents who are able freely to decide which of the possibilities presented to them they will realize." Given God's decision to create this sort of world, "he has limited his own possibilities for knowing beforehand which future potentialities will become actual."[80]

Polkinghorne likewise argues that it is only possible to talk about a timeless God's knowledge of the future in a totally deterministic universe "where Laplace's calculator can retrodict the past and predict the future from the dynamic circumstances of the present, so that effectively the distinction between past, present and future is abolished."[81] In such a view, the world is a world of being but not of becoming, but this is not the world of experience where the past is closed and the future open, nor is it the world of modern science. The future is not already formed ahead of us precisely because it is, in part, our creation. Consequently, even an omniscient God cannot know the unformed future with certainty. He may have "highly informed conjectures about its possible shape" and may have prepared plans for all eventualities, but in his actual experience and knowledge "he must be open to the consequences of the exercise of human free will and the evolution of cosmic free process."[82] God will not be caught by surprise nor find himself at a loss in new situations because of his sovereignty, but he does have to respond to each new occasion that arises without having known for certain what would happen beforehand.

Similarly, Keith Ward argues that "an omniscient being, if it is temporal, can know for certain whatever in the future it determines, to the extent that it determines it but not absolutely everything. If this is a limitation on omniscience, it is logically unavoidable, for any temporal being,"[83] and Ward argues that God is a temporal being. Brümmer therefore claims that God knows all the possibilities in the future, and he knows the relative probability of each of them being realized. God knows all of our intentions and he knows the relative probability that we will not change our minds. God also knows his own intentions, and these "he will most certainly realize, whatever we might decide to do or not to do."[84] Consequently, Richard Rice is convinced that either in the case of absolute foreknowledge or perfect anticipation, "God's response to the course of events in the creaturely world will appear to be exactly right," but he sees a great difference between the two situations in terms of creaturely freedom.[85]

Ward reasons that God's not knowing what cannot be known, namely, the future decisions of self-determining beings, does not detract from God's maximal knowledge or cause him to be either ignorant or misled. God's control, even of the unforeseen future, is not limited by his lack of knowledge. It is guaranteed by his omnipotence, and this is not threatened by the nonexistence of the future.[86]

Salvation, election and foreknowledge. Although God "planned seemingly mundane things in advance, such as the building of a reservoir in Jerusalem (Is 22:11), most of what he planned related to the history of salvation."[87] Among Arminians and other non-Augustinians it has been common to assert that God's election of individuals to salvation was based upon his foreknowledge of their faith. That is a perspective that will not hold, however, if God cannot foreknow those future, libertarianly free decisions that are made when people hear the gospel.[88] This makes the concept of corporate election a natural fit in the openness model of divine providence. Accordingly, Richard Rice asserts that the existence of a plan for human salvation as early as creation "may indicate only that God was aware that sin was a distinct possibility with man's creation, rather than a future actuality, and that He was fully prepared to meet the situation should it arise."[89] The success of Christ's mission was not, therefore, a foregone conclusion. It was "achieved during the actual course of His earthly life." The temptation of Jesus was real (Mt 4:1-11; Lk 4:1-13; Heb 4:15), and his victory was too. The death of Jesus was the fulfillment of a plan established far in advance (Acts 2:23; 1 Pet 1:20), but Jesus "came to full acceptance of his Father's will through a process of intense spiritual struggle."[90] Acts 2:23 and 4:28, which appear to speak of the events leading to the death of Christ as implementing a long-standing plan of God, should be read as indicating God's ability to "so modify the implementation of His plan to developing circumstances that any decision somehow contributes, even though it may be inherently opposed to His will."[91]

Biblical references to people as objects of God's foreknowledge or predestination are "typically concerned with corporate election. They do not refer to personal salvation."[92] In preferring Jacob to Esau, God was calling their descendants, and the "call had to do not with their individual destinies but with that of the people whom they represented." What was true of Israel, a body of people set apart to be a light to the other nations (Is 42:6; 49:6), is also true of the church. New Testament references to God's foreknowledge and predestination "have to do with the nature and purpose of the church as a whole, especially in its relation to Christ. These terms do not imply that God knew from eternity the personal identity of all who will eventually be saved."[93] It is possible for individuals to fail and fall away, as the frequent admonitions and exhortations to watchfulness indicate. "But the destiny of the church as a whole is assured." Certainly, individuals are also called to service by God's prior intention, as was the case with Jeremiah (Jer 1:5). But Rice sees nothing in the biblical narrative to contradict the idea that Jeremiah could have rejected the call.[94]

Even in regard to salvation, God's plans are not always fulfilled. He wants everyone to repent (2 Pet 3:9), and he wants everyone to be saved (1 Tim 2:4; cf. Tit 2:11), but "God's will does not guarantee the outcome that he desires."[95] He did everything that he could to ensure the prosperity of his chosen people, but he was bitterly disappointed (Is 5:7).[96]

The nature of predictive prophecy. Rejection of foreknowledge may seem to be contradictory to the phenomenon of biblical prophecy, but Ward reasons that the biblical predictions "rarely, if ever, prophesy exactly what is to happen. On the contrary, they are often provisional and very inexact in detail, and they need to be sensitively interpreted to make them into prophecies at all."[97] As an example he cites the "transference of prophecies about David's successor as king, in 2 Samuel 7 . . . to a far Messianic future. Jews and Christians still disagree about whether that prophecy has been fulfilled, and, if so, how."[98] When Polkinghorne hears Isaiah speak about God's telling of new things before they happen (Is 42:9), his sense is that this is because God is bringing them about "not because he has spied them lying waiting in the future."[99]

Richard Rice argues that the fundamental purpose of prophecy is "to reveal the will of personal Being, declaring His intentions to accomplish certain things."[100] Three kinds of prophecy may be distinguished.

1. There are prophecies designed to "express God's knowledge of what will occur in the future as the inevitable consequence of factors already present." An example is found in Jeremiah 37:6-10, where Jeremiah is given a message for the king of Judah to tell him that Pharaoh's army will not be a persistent ally and that the Chaldeans will return and raze the city. This may also be the case in Daniel 2, where the demise of one nation and the rise of another one are predicted. It may explain the situation regarding Pharaoh, whose character was so rigid that his actions were entirely predictable.[101]

2. Some prophecies "express God's own intentions to act in a certain way." Cases in point are Isaiah 46:9-11 and 48:3. An outstanding example would be the return of Christ, which will occur "no matter what course human history takes in the meantime (Heb 10:35-37)." Rice suggests that we are not able to calculate the relation in a given prophecy between these two factors, God's foresight and his intention. As John Sanders puts it, "The future is partly open or indefinite and partly closed or definite. Which is which depends solely on God's sovereign choices."[102]

3. A third group of prophecies "express God's intention to act in a certain way if a particular course of action obtains or if people behave a certain way." These are often called "conditional prophecies," and Jonah's message to Nineveh is frequently placed in this category, even by those who believe that God has comprehensive knowledge of the actual events of the future. Jeremiah 18:7-10 is a classic statement of God's principle of working, in this regard. If he predicts destruction of a nation, but it turns from its evil, he will change his mind. But if he declares an intention to build a nation and it does evil, he will change his mind about the good that he had intended. Conditional prophecy is intended to evoke a response, not to provide information about the future. Rice suggests that it has a new integrity, however, if God cannot foresee the future. Within this model, we assume that God was genuinely intending to destroy Nineveh but that he decided not to when their repentance was evident. Proponents of the "open God" extend the application of this traditional category by asserting that many fulfilled prophecies were also conditional. A clear instance of this is seen in Jeremiah 38:17-18, where Zedekiah is told that both his life and the city will be spared if he surrenders to the officials of Babylon but that both will be destroyed if he does not surrender. In other instances, however, the conditional nature of prophecies is not apparent to us pre-

cisely because the unstated conditions were fulfilled. Of Cyrus, for instance, Rice asserts that if Cyrus had refused to repatriate the Jews, "we would no doubt interpret Isaiah's prediction as a conditional prophecy."[103]

William Hasker recognizes the importance of the objections to the explanation of predictive prophecy in the openness model. Critics have frequently focused on this issue as a major flaw in the theory that God does not have comprehensive knowledge of the future. In response to these criticisms Hasker argues that "any problem about prophecy that may exist for the open view applies also to simple foreknowledge and divine timelessness."[104] This is because "the giving of a prophecy is just as much an action as the causing of a plague, and can have effects that are equally great; indeed, the prophets were inspired to speak as they did precisely in order to cause their hearers to act in ways they otherwise would not have."[105] Hasker therefore concludes that the only ways to escape the problem claimed by critics of the openness model is to move to the Molinist or Calvinist models. The other models treated in this study, which assert libertarian freedom but also claim that God has foreknowledge or comprehensive atemporal knowledge, face the same challenge that is directed to the openness model, despite the fact that this criticism is being raised by theologians who work within one of those models. Similarly, John Sanders posits that "the only way of avoiding an omniscient God who takes risks," in the sense affirmed in the openness model, "is to uphold divine foreordination of all things."[106] Sanders therefore concludes that "the key issue is not the type of knowledge an omniscient deity has [whether simple foreknowledge or present knowledge] but the type of sovereignty an omniscient God decides to exercise."[107]

From the biblical teaching regarding divine repentance, Terence Fretheim deduces that "the future is genuinely open, . . . not blocked out in advance." God does not have "an unchangeable will with regard to every matter the prophets ever discussed concerning the future." In order to accomplish his "unchangeable salvific will" God can "cut off a prophetic word altogether." He will change his ways in order to accomplish his purposes.[108] As John Lucas puts it, "The clear picture is of a God who can change His mind, and is prepared to make prophecies, issued in His name and on His explicit commands, come false."[109]

The predictions that Judas would betray Jesus (Mt 26:20-25; Mk 14:18-21; Lk 22:21-23; Jn 13:18) and that Peter would deny him (Mt 26:34; Mk 14:30; Lk 22:34; Jn 13:38) may have been warnings of the spiritual danger they were in. Analogously, a teacher might tell a student, "You are going to fail this semester." This may not be an infallible prediction but an exhortation designed to avert the disaster while there is still time. Then again, Jesus may have known them both so well that he knew that, at that point in time, these actions were inevitable.[110]

As to Jesus' prediction of betrayal by Judas (Jn 6:70-71), it is deemed possible that this was a conditional prophecy, though one for which the condition was ultimately fulfilled. Judas' behavior, it is suggested, may not have been the only way in which Psalm 41:9 could be fulfilled.[111] Michael Langford suggested that "given the nature of Jesus, it was certain, humanly speaking, that someone would eventually betray him." It became evident to a sensitive observer that Judas would be the one. This was not a certainty, but it was highly probable. Langford notes that only John, among the Gospel writers, says that Jesus knew from the beginning. Langford concludes that either John was wrong or Jesus' knowledge was of the highly probable, rather than the infallible, kind.[112] The behavior of God's creatures is not always predictable, even by God. Thus he tells Jeremiah: "I thought, 'After she [Israel] has done all this she will return to me'; but she did not return" (Jer 3:7; cf. also 3:19, 20).[113]

5

The Openness Model (2)

Within His Self-Determined Limits, God Is Continuously and Impartially Active in the World for Good, Although He Cannot Ensure That His Desires Are Fulfilled in Every Instance

Proponents of the openness model, while giving a relative independence to libertarianly free human beings, do not intend to eliminate thereby the possibility of divine action. John Polkinghorne, for instance, asks why we should deny to God the radical freedom that he has allowed to human creation.[1] In other words, all the agents in the world are libertarianly free, and this includes God. Obviously none of them can therefore be free to act completely alone, but all of them act freely within the bounds established by the existence of other free agents.

Divine agency and human freedom. Agents are the originators of actions in the sense that their free decisions to perform those actions are necessary conditions for their occurrence. The actions would not have happened had the agents not intended them. The acts were done by the agents rather than happening to them. But an agent's decision is "never a *sufficient* condition for his own action,"[2] that is, the decision alone is inadequate to bring about the action. Furthermore, we cannot bring about the sufficient conditions for someone else's action, though we can bring about some of the necessary conditions. Within these givens Vincent Brümmer argues that "God realizes his will through the actions of human agents, by (*a*) arranging their factual circumstances in such a way that they are *enabled* to do what he wills; and (*b*) inspiring them by his Spirit in order that they might be *motivated* to do his will."[3] God does not, in this way, deny the freedom and responsibility of the human agent through whose action he realizes his will. But if the human agent decides not to do God's will, it is not done. "Double agency is a matter of co-operation between two agents and not of one agent using the other as a tool."[4]

Sometimes we speak of the whole set of necessary conditions as the "cause." At other times we may identify as the cause the most significant factor in bringing about the effect. "Thus the believer will always give God the credit for his own conversion or spiritual successes: If it were not for the fact that God enabled me and inspired me to do it, I would never have done it. Therefore, to him be all praise and thanksgiving!" In giving God credit as "*the* cause" of our own action, however, we do not, of course, deny that we performed it ourselves and of our "own free will."[5] An inconsistency arises only if we ascribe primary responsibility to both agents.

Given that "God can intervene to prevent any particular event occurring," says Brümmer, "no event is possible unless God allows it to occur. Divine agency is therefore part of the complete cause of *every* event, and in this sense his agency is not finite like that of human persons."[6] But God never allows his agency to be the complete cause of any event. "His agency is one of the necessary conditions for every event, but not the only one, since he has decided to allow for secondary causes to co-operate with him in what he does." These other agents are independent originators "with whom God has decided to share his power." Of course, the independence is bestowed by God, and so it could be taken back, but the price for this would be a deterministic universe in which divine agency is the complete cause of all events and this is not the universe that God wanted to bring about.[7]

In language reminiscent of the process theologians, Peter Baelz urges us to "think less of God's compelling the world to do what he wants and more of his persuading and enabling it of its own free will to do what he wants."[8] It is not clear to Baelz what this might mean at the subhuman level of atoms and organisms, but at the human level "it means that God acts through the re-direction of our thoughts and desires." Therefore, what occurs in the world is "not a case of *either* God *or* man" but rather "of God in, through and together with" us. How we respond to God is determined freely by us but "in so far as our thoughts and desires are being re-directed by our recognition of God's declared love for us, they are God's own gracious gift to us." Consequently, God's active involvement in our lives respects and enhances our freedom, rather than destroying it.[9]

God acts in the world by making himself present in it, says Baelz. The response that occurs is our own, but its beginning and end, and the "very possibility of its happening at all, lie with God."[10] We can only know directly the movement of our own hearts and minds. "We have no equally direct access to the action of God." Yet we have reason for believing that the promptings of our own hearts are a response to God's Spirit within us. "In Paul's paradoxical but persuasive affirmation: 'I live; yet not I, but Christ lives in me' (Gal 2:20)."[11] Even on the human level, then, we "can never offer an altogether convincing proof" that the hidden hand of God, working in love, has had any effect at all. We are right to expect that the working of God's love will make a real difference in the way that the world goes, "but we should not expect to be able to detect it by scientific observation. It will work with nature rather than against. It will evoke from nature what nature has it in herself potentially to become."[12]

John Polkinghorne draws an analogy between God's action in the world and our own action. We are a psychosomatic unity "with the material and mental as complementary poles" of our nature. In that way we are able to "participate in a noetic world of ideas and purposes, as well as being able to act within the physical world." This avoids Cartesian dualism by "appeal to the complementary linkage of the material and mental as aspects of the world in different degrees of organizational complexity and flexibility." It is here that Polkinghorne finds "a promising location for the causal joints by which both we and God interact with the universe."[13] We both exercise "the holistic power to influence, respectively, our bodies and the world by means of causal joints hidden within the unpredictability of process." There are differences, however, between human and divine participation in the world, and these go beyond the "contrast of scale between the limited and the Unlimited." Most important of these is that *"we* are constituted by our physical bodies and so are in thrall to them. . . . God, on the other hand, is not constituted by the cosmos, even in part of his nature, and so he is never in thrall to it."[14]

Polkinghorne doubts, however, "whether God interacts principally with the world by scrabbling around at its sub-atomic roots."[15] More fruitful for our conceptualization of God's providential activity in the world is "a most

surprising discovery of twentieth century science" that there are "systems
which are so exquisitely sensitive to circumstance that the smallest distur-
bance will produce large and ever-growing changes in their behaviour."
This reality dawned on Ed Lorenz when he was trying to model the behavior of the earth's weather systems and found that "the smallest variation in
the input to his equations produced exponentially-large deviations in the
behaviour of his solutions."[16] This phenomenon is called the "butterfly
effect" because "a butterfly stirring the air with its wings in the African jungle today will have consequences for the storm systems over London in
three weeks time." The unpredictability that results in such systems has
been described as "chaos theory."[17]

Given these factors in the current theories in physics, Polkinghorne postulates that God may "interact with his creation through 'information input'
into its open physical processes." This is, then, a world in which "the God
who holds it in being has not left himself so impotent that he cannot continuously and consistently interact within cosmic history." It is to such a
God that Polkinghorne believes a scientist can "pray with complete integrity."[18] David Bartholomew, in his discussion of chance, views the action of
divine providence in similar fashion as coming "top-down" rather than
functioning from the bottom up at the subatomic level (as William Pollard
proposes.)[19] God's action is primarily "at the springs of creative thought in
the human mind. The provision of guidance, inspiration or whatever one
calls the power which enables a man to rise above himself and brings new
things into being, would then be an obvious expression of God's involvement."[20] Special providence is thus evident in "all the great works of science, art and literature." God may influence human decisions or even
thwart decisions contrary to his ultimate purposes. Bartholomew argues,
therefore, that "we are more likely to see the mind of God at work in the
unpredictability of free human beings than in the unpredictability of subatomic particles."[21] God works by influence and persuasion rather than
control and power, thereby preserving human freedom.

In the semi-deist model, Maurice Wiles had cited as one of his difficult
cases for providence the giving of thanks for victory in war. He asked
whether God takes sides, and the model of God's action that Wiles develops provides a negative answer. Keith Ward, on the other hand, with a
greater openness to God's action in the world, answers that God does take
sides and that he is on the side of justice and right.[22] We may be ignorant of
which side that is, but that is where we should look for God's action, and

when we think we have discerned the way of justice and right, we are in a position to give thanks for God's act. Disasters will happen as part of the nature of the world, and God cannot eliminate them all. "But he can save some from disaster, and when he does, one main reason is that such action is designed to bring as many people as possible, now and in the future, nearer to God."[23] In the present structure it is not possible for God to allocate reward and punishment with strict fairness. Consequently, we must not conclude that God directly wills everything that happens to people.

As to Maurice Wiles's assessment that it is "morally and spiritually unacceptable" for us to attribute to God the saving of one hostage and not another, Ward proffers that it is better that God help some people, even when he cannot help them all.[24] We may assume that an omniscient mind has "good reasons for particular forms of help, directed to particular persons." Although it is impossible for us to know the factors involved, "we may say that the factors will usually be factors inherent in the total situation, rather than properties" of the particular individuals. God will consider "the way the historical process may be affected by his action" and, though he cannot save everyone, "he is actively present in every situation; and at some points that presence may open the possibility of providential deliverance."[25]

Ward does not want to portray God as able to help or heal everyone but choosing to help only a few people, apparently at random. He suggests, rather, "that God is constantly working in the world to increase knowledge and love, and that, as one enters into active loving response to God, God can purposively shape the events of life to enable them to conform more closely to his will."[26] We cannot discern the details of God's actions, but we "may believe that he is at work, as a constant causal influence, interacting" with us, "helping to shape the course" of our lives, and to make them vehicles of his purposes. This will be especially true as we "enter into the interactive form of personal relationship with God which we call prayer. In providential action, God works to turn all things to final good. In prayer, he shapes causal processes in response to human requests."[27]

Miracles and special providence. Peter Baelz grants that there may occasionally be miracles which "go against the grain of the world," and that we will not fully understand how or why God works them, though we accept them as the "expression, albeit uncharacteristic and unfathomable, of boundless Love."[28] Vincent Brümmer also argues that "violations of the natural order," if they occur, "must of necessity be very rare" or the very notion of a natural order would be rendered nonsense.[29] "Thus, if answers to prayer are only possible in the form of miracles which violate the natural order, then very few petitionary prayers would ever be answered." Most petitions are for "ordinary events which are believed to be possible within the natural order."[30] An example would be David's ceasing to pray when his child died (2 Sam 12:15-23). Of course the Humean notion of miracle as "violation of a law" is itself unsatisfactory. Ward prefers to characterize miracles as events "beyond the possibility of physical law-like explanation," to avoid the connotation of arbitrary interference.[31] On rare occasions, he suggests, "material objects may transcend their natural powers so as to become awe-inspiring sacraments and vehicles of the Divine. They will thus be, not mere anomalies in an autonomous nature, but epiphanies of the spirit, showing the underlying nature and the final destiny and purpose of the material order."[32] When this happens the physical is not contradicted; it is "perfected beyond its normal temporal state by becoming transparent to the eternal."[33] In similar terms Polkinghorne describes miracles as "transparent moments in which the Kingdom is found to be manifestly present."[34]

The recognition of unusual acts of God poses a further problem, namely, "Could events that occur according to the laws of nature count as answers to prayer?" In speaking of answers to our petitions we assume that they were necessary conditions to the occurrence of the event: had we not prayed, it would not have happened. But if natural causes are a sufficient condition for the event, then it is difficult to see how our prayer could be deemed necessary. Thus either an event is due to natural causes or it is due to our prayer, but neither alternative is satisfactory to the believer. This dilemma only arises, however, if we assume that events are necessarily determined in their causes, but Brümmer rejects that assumption. To accept it would involve natural determinism that excludes not only God's performance of contingent acts within the natural order but also all free human agency. It rests on a scientifically obsolete view that presupposes the mechanist and determinist theories associated with Laplace. Assuming the validity of the quantum theory "according to which the laws of nature are not deterministic but statistical," we cannot infallibly predict the weather, for instance, but we can make statistical forecasts of probable trends.[35]

Brümmer argues that there is a "fundamental indeterminism" in the universe. "The complete set of causal conditions *sufficient* to bring about any event will always include some conditions which are subject to chance since there are not sufficient conditions to determine them. It follows that no event can be predicted with absolute certainty because there will always be some of the necessary conditions for its occurrence which remain unpredictable in principle."[36] Consequently, we are able to perform free acts in the world and to bring about contingent changes in what happens. We do this by bringing about conditions necessary for these events that would otherwise be subject to chance. For God to act need not, therefore, be miraculous intervention, anymore than it is for us. The contingency of an event is not excluded by its scientific predictability, and the fact that an event can be explained in terms of natural causes does not exclude the possibility that it could have resulted from divine agency in answer to prayer. God could thus "perform contingent acts *by means of* the natural order and not in violation of it."[37]

Keith Ward is less committal about the nature of the universe, reasoning that we cannot yet be certain whether the perceived indeterminacy is real or is only a matter of our ignorance.[38] We cannot, therefore, be certain where and how God acts to cause physical changes in the universe. Even if God acts constantly in the world, we could not likely discern with certainty where God acts. But we can accept that states come about "not sufficiently explained by the operation of physical causes alone."[39] This supposition contradicts no canons of scientific thought. If God acts in the world, "science is incompetent to explain those acts for they will be unique; they will not form part of a system of physical forces, and the causing intentions cannot be measured and correlated with physical forces."[40]

Ward proposes that "critical junctions can exist in the physical world, which can bring about large changes by small determinants of otherwise random probabilistic changes."[41] As an example, he cites the case of a metal ball balanced at the top of an elliptically curved wire. If it rolls in one direction, it will break a diaphragm releasing poison gas, in another it is innocuous. Only a tiny force is needed to send it one way or the other. "Such junctions will only exist at certain points of the physical world, and this may be one constraint on Divine action within the parameters of normal physics. Such determining action will be in principle undetectable, since it always could have happened by chance."[42] Ward doubts that God directly chooses every outcome of physical processes, since we need "a structure which will permit Divine determination on some, but not all, occasions, and which will cause some occasions to be more conducive to Divine determination than others." Modern physics suggests such a physical structure, but we dare not take it to be the final word.

What makes it possible to speak of miracles, and the reason that they are by definition unusual actions by God, is that "God can determine just so many outcomes as leave the general probability laws of nature intact; and he is likely to determine those which have a focal structuring position within an integral structure—a key position in an unstable dynamical system far from equilibrium—which will maximize novel patterns or consequences for good within the system as a whole."[43]

Brümmer and Polkinghorne make a distinction between (1) "miraculous events which appear to violate the laws of nature," that is, which have a "radically unexpected character," and (2) those that are the "co-incidence" of two states of affairs, both of which can be naturally explained, which coincide in a felicitous way. The resurrection of Jesus is an example of the first category. Of the latter sort, Brümmer instances a friend who walks into the room with just the kind of help I need at the moment, or the engine driver who faints, causing the train to stop within inches of a man on the railway line, whom the driver did not see.[44] Polkinghorne describes these "arranged coincidences" as "causal chains, lawfully propagating in the world, whose impingement upon each other can produce a situation of apparent significance."[45] These are brought about by the "sensitive openness of the world's process." They are acts of providence that those who experience them understandably call "miraculous" because of their unique significance.[46] In neither case, however, can we expect that unbelievers will be convinced by the believer's claim that a miracle has occurred. As Ward admits, they are "not clear and indisputable proofs of God and his purpose. But, for those who live in relation to God, they clarify the nature of his activity in the world, being particular paradigms of his action and purpose for all humanity."[47] Their purpose is not primarily the relief of suffering but the revelation and effecting of God's purpose in history. Thus "when a miracle is claimed to occur in a context of prayer and attention to God, when it seems to disclose the Divine presence and purpose in a startling yet illuminating way, and when it can intelligibly be interpreted as effecting that purpose in particular historical events, then the believer in God is wholly justified in accepting its occurrence as a miracle, if it is testified to by reliable and honest witnesses."[48]

Since miracles are unusual, and since they do not benefit everyone equally, they imply a certain partiality on God's part. It is on this account that some have been nervous about conceding the possibility that God may act in special providential ways distinct from his regular providential working. By contrast, John Polkinghorne argues that "total impartiality would be total impersonality—which is not to say that a personal God has to have favourites, but that he will treat particular people in particular ways." Without special providence, Polkinghorne suggests, the idea of a personal God is emptied of content. He concedes, therefore, that Vernon "White [a representative of the Calvinist model] is right to protest that 'If God's purposive activity for the world is uniform and undifferentiated (except through creaturely response) then it is liable to be impersonal, amoral and relatively impotent.'"[49] With respect to the concerns voiced by Maurice Wiles, however, Polkinghorne grants that our doctrine of providence must account both for the people who are saved from danger and for those who are not.[50] On the one hand, if we evoke special providence too glibly, we may trivialize God's action in the world. On the other hand, if we reject all such particular action we reduce "God to the role of an impotent spectator."[51] In an appreciative response to Polkinghorne's proposal of a free-will (and free-process) theodicy, Nancey Murphy argues that "a God who acts sometimes is better than one who maintains a strict policy of restraint." Assuming that "there must be many occasions where there is *moral* room for God to maneuver," she suggests, however, that these acts are likely to be of a trivial sort. "That is, God's action is not as likely to be restrained in small matters as in significant ones by 'sufficient reasons' which (we must presume) deter the wholesale destruction of evil." Contrary to Wiles's claim that there are greater moral objections against a God involved in the world than against one who only does one great creative act, Murphy argues that "the triviality of many claims for miraculous helps is not an objection to the theory of God's action, but rather turns out to be just what we should expect if there are any grounds for the arguments of theodicy."[52]

God Is at War with Rebellious Spiritual Beings Who Are Also Libertarianly Free and Therefore Able to Thwart God's Desires on Some Occasions

Most of the presentations of the openness model have focused on the role of human agents within a world in which God has voluntarily limited his own control by giving them libertarian freedom without giving up his own purposes or his involvement in the world as he works to achieve them. An important new dimension to the providential working of God in the world has been introduced by Gregory Boyd, who has focused his own attention on the role of the nonhuman rational and moral creatures within God's creation and providence.[53] Boyd works within the basic framework of the openness model as I have described it, but he is particularly interested in the way in which God's control of the world is limited by the activity of rebellious spiritual creatures, Satan and his demons.

Boyd believes that the basic biblical understanding of the cosmos is a "warfare worldview." In this perspective "the good and evil, fortunate or unfortunate, aspects of life are to be interpreted largely as the result of good and evil, friendly or hostile, spirits warring against each other and against us."[54] By contrast, with "the myopic nature of the Enlightenment Western worldview," this conviction concerning the reality of spiritual conflict is a nearly universally shared intuition.[55] The truth attested by both the Old Testament and the varied mythologies found around the world is "that God's good creation has in fact been seized by hostile, evil, cosmic forces that are seeking to destroy God's beneficent plan for the cosmos." God is waging war against these forces and has secured their overthrow through Jesus Christ. The church is "a decisive means by which this final overthrow is to be carried out."[56]

As was true of the semi-deists, Boyd's quest for a new model of providence is significantly stimulated by the need to address the reality of evil in the world. He posits that the "classical-philosophical theistic tradition" has rightly assumed that God is perfectly loving and good but wrongly assumed "that divine omnipotence entails meticulous control."[57] By contrast, his own "warfare worldview" works on "the assumption that divine goodness does not completely control or in any sense will evil; rather, good and evil are at war with one another." This means, of course, that God does not now have "exhaustive, meticulous control over the world." Rather, "God must work with, and battle against, other created beings. While none of these beings can ever match God's own power, each has some degree of genuine influence within the cosmos."[58] It is Boyd's conviction that this perspective will generate less theologizing *about* evil and more war *against* it. Particular evils "flow from the wills of creatures," and we need not speculate about a divine purpose for them, but we should revolt against them.[59]

It is not only the Thomist or Calvinist models that Boyd finds objectionable. Like other theologians of the openness model, he believes that Arminian theologians have generally not carried through their understanding of the nature of creaturely freedom to its logical and biblical conclusion. They have continued to affirm God's immutability, timelessness,

impassibility and other attributes derived "more from Hellenistic philosophy than from the Bible, and they render genuine freedom on the part of
created beings impossible."[60] What particularly locates Boyd's proposal
within the openness model rather than the church dominion model, with
which it also has affinities, is his belief that God does not have "exhaustive,
detailed knowledge of what shall occur in the future." This is deemed to be
necessary to a consistent affirmation of self-determining human freedom.[61]
Where Boyd goes beyond both classical Arminian theology and the work
of most openness theologians is in his conviction that angelic freedom has
not been given sufficient attention in their formation of a theodicy and his
intensive effort to remedy this perceived deficiency.

Petitionary Prayer Has an Influence on God and on His Decisions and Is Therefore an Effective Contributor to the Outcome When God Works Because We Asked Him To

Proponents of this model of providence are generally convinced that petitionary prayer is given a role in determining the actual outcome of events
more actively and more genuinely than is true of the "classical notion" of
providence, with its God who has complete and detailed control. As representative of the function of prayer in that model, Keith Ward cites Thomas Aquinas. Aquinas said, "We do not pray in order to change the decree
of divine providence, rather we pray in order to acquire by petitionary
prayer what God has determined would be obtained by our prayers."[62]
Ward grants that there is a sense in which our prayers have real effects,
within this model, "for God has always decreed that they should have."
But Ward remains suspicious that "in such a case, our prayers are not
really freely made, and God does not really respond to them in new and
creative ways."[63] In Ward's own model, by contrast, "creation is a continuous series of acts, leaving open new possibilities, often in response to free
human actions. Thus in principle prayers could affect Divine action." Ward
consequently sees prayer as an extension of human freedom. "We are not
only free to perform certain acts, thus bringing about states of affairs by
our choice, but we are also free to ask God to bring about some states of
affairs, and thus bring them about by our requests." God is not obligated
to do what we ask him, and he may not do so either because our requests
are outside the bounds of what is suitable in the system or because it
would be harmful. On the other hand, "God may permit some outcomes
that he would otherwise determine himself to be modified or directed by

human choices, in the form of requests made to him in the context of worship."[64]

In the passage quoted above, Aquinas also wrote, "We must pray, not in order to inform God of our needs and desires, but in order to remind ourselves that in these matters we need divine assistance." Once more Ward questions whether this is adequate. John 15:15 speaks of our asking, not just our desiring. We have a duty to pray for others, and God will bring certain goods to people only if they are prayed for.[65] Ward is further convinced that "prayer will always make a difference to the world. It will sometimes make precisely the difference we desire. For it is part of the way in which God decrees that his creative and redemptive action in the world should be given a particular shape and form."[66] Asserting that prayer can make the future different (Mt 7:7; Jas 4:2), Clark Pinnock insists that "God actually accepts the influence of our prayers in making up his mind. . . . Future events are not predetermined and fixed. If you believe that prayer changes things," says Pinnock, "my whole position is established. If you do not believe it does, you are far from biblical religion."[67]

Vincent Brümmer identifies two presuppositions in impetratory prayer, that is, prayer "aimed at getting things by praying for them."[68] First, we suppose that the things prayed for have a "two-way contingency," that is to say, "it is neither impossible nor inevitable that God should bring them about."[69] Second, we assume that the "prayer itself is a necessary but not a sufficient condition for God's doing what is asked." In other words, we believe that God does "what he is asked *because* he is asked." The petition itself is therefore "a *condition* for God's doing what he is requested. On the other hand, however, it is not a *sufficient* condition making it inevitable for God to comply with the request."[70] If God inevitably answered our requests, he would not be a rational agent who acts from free choice. Therefore, we can say that the petition is not the *cause* of God's response but that it is the *reason* for his response. It is necessary in that, had we *not* prayed, God would not have done what he did.[71]

Hendrikus Berkhof suggests that where prayer is neglected in systematic theological works, "it could be a sign (though this is not absolutely certain) that either man's freedom or God's power is underrated." It is his own conviction that "the first is the case in predestinarian-marked Reformed Scholasticism, the second in nineteenth century modernism and twentieth century Existentialism."[72] The proponents of the "open God" who accomplishes his ultimate purposes in a world where his creatures have been given a measure of independence believe that their own theology of prayer strikes the proper balance between God's power and human freedom. In the perspectives on petitionary prayer that are described below, it will become apparent that not all who have made a commitment to divine self-limitation because of libertarian human freedom are equally convinced that petitionary prayer effects changes in the world, but usually they are. A range of applications of the openness model of providence developed above is possible when one comes to prayer.

Prayer is a means of accepting God's will and sharing his desires. John Lucas suggests that we should better our wants by "coming to want the things that God wants us to want," and that we can ask God what that is. So questions are appropriate prayers, as well as requests.[73] The concern expressed by Keith Ward that prayer should have an effect on outcomes seems not to be shared by John Boykin. He applies this model of providence in a theology of prayer that gives minimal place to petition in effecting change. He contends that, while God occasionally gets involved in special circumstances with special people, we should not assume that this is his normal way of working. Most of the time, things happen by human decision.[74] It is his "fervent hope" that the perspective he offers "will make us think twice before saying such nonsense as, 'God was so gracious in arranging for me to get this job,' or 'I guess this tragedy was just God's will.'"[75] God's normal way of working is the Holy Spirit changing us personally, making us better believers. It is not that God does not care "what you do for a living or a hobby, only that He is not in the business of developing your secular skills, much less of conducting your secular affairs on your behalf."[76] For God to force us to go along with him would be "psychic rape," but "planting ideas in your head and emotions in your heart is certainly fair game. Advertisers plant ideas constantly. So do professors."[77] The difference lies in the means God uses for planting these ideas and the content of his inspirations. Once planted, however, God's inspirations must compete for our attention and cooperation on the same basis as the other ideas in our heads. We choose between them.

Boykin suggests that if we recognize these realities about God's way of working, we will pray more avidly and more candidly, not that we will stop praying. "God delights in our prayers, but prayer is primarily for our own benefit, not God's." He knows what we need and want, but "prayer is the process of aligning our will, our attitudes, and our perspective with His." Praying should make us willing to be the answer to our own prayers: "So

we would pass from praying, 'Send someone,' to saying 'I'll volunteer.'"
Therefore, the purpose of prayer is "not to talk God into things or to
change our circumstances, but to change *us*." Although it is acceptable to
pray about our circumstances, we do so as "a way of facing up to them
frankly, reevaluating them, getting new ideas about how to deal with them,
changing our attitude about them, and drawing on the strength God is in us
to cope." It is good to "lay our trouble at the Lord's feet" but not so that he
can solve our problems for us. "God is not Santa Claus. When we lay our
troubles at His feet, we can begin to put them in perspective. We can begin
to remember that *He*—and not our problems—is our master."[78] Boykin's
position actually seems to be something of an anomaly. In its echoes of
statements quoted from Aquinas by Keith Ward, and in its emphasis on resignation to God's mastership, it sounds as though it belongs within a more
deterministic model. On the other hand, it is included here because it demonstrates one way in which an emphasis on the contribution of human
agency to the outcome of events, and on the element of chance, can lead to
a denigration of petitionary prayer as a means by which God's action is
affected. In other words, active petitionary prayer may be threatened from
both ends of the spectrum in the efforts to find the proper balance between
God's control and human freedom. The semi-deist model maximized
human agency in the world, in order to absolve God of complicity in evil,
but this eliminated petitionary prayer as a means to affect the future. At the
other end of the spectrum, the fatalist model also eliminates the usefulness
of petition because God's control is so absolute as to make human action
meaningless. All of the models in between those two are committed to the
usefulness of petitionary prayer and are trying to find a ground for it in the
proper balance between God's providential control and the agency that he
has given to creatures.

In his 1966 Hulsean Lectures, Peter Baelz addressed the issues
brought to our attention by a consideration of prayer and providence.[79]
He posits that God has chosen to complete his creative purposes
through and with human beings, and prayer is "a discipline in which
man seeks to learn what is the divine will for him here and now in his
present situation." We cannot expect to hear an "inner voice instructing"
us what to do but must deliberate and decide "in reflection on the eternal purposes of God revealed in Christ and nourished by faith in God's
secret activity" within us.[80] In prayer we bring to God our desires for the
good that we think will better our lives and the lives of others. We are

prepared both to work and to pray for these goods.[81]

Hendrikus Berkhof suggests that even the most superstitious who came to Jesus asking for bread or healing were answered. But "in fellowship with him they learned to ask for *more* than they had begun with and to ask differently: no longer only from the standpoint of their own needs but much more from the perspective of God's purposes of which their cares were a part."[82] The disciples, in particular, learned this new way of asking "in a hard training school." But even Jesus, their master, was not spared the training school. His agonizing prayer in Gethsemane—"yet, not what I want, but what you want" (Mk 14:36)—was not simply "an acquiescence in the unavoidable that is going to happen. It is a real prayer, of the same nature as the third petition in the Lord's Prayer. Jesus asks of God that his own will and desires be made subordinate to the great goal in which he is of one mind with the Father."[83]

Christians working within the model that attributes to God a knowledge of the future, as well as a specific plan for it, characteristically pray for divine guidance. Richard Rice addresses this matter from within the model of the God for whom the future is open. God has neither middle knowledge nor simple foreknowledge, but he can often predict with great accuracy what will happen. Nevertheless, since things may not turn out as even God anticipates and given the impact that human decisions have on the outcomes, divine guidance is best sought for the present rather than the future.[84]

Since God has a general will but not a detailed plan, we do not have to worry about whether we are "in the will of God" in a sense other than moral; hence extrabiblical guidance regarding our daily decisions is of less critical importance than is assumed by those who think that God has a specific will for the future. Furthermore, we need not chastise ourselves when we make a bad decision, as judged by its consequences. We may well have made the best decision, even from God's perspective, at the time, but then had it turn out differently than any of us expected. We should not simply assume that it was not God's will and rebuke ourselves, but we should also not continue in a situation that is a mistake at the present time on the assumption that it is God's will since he let it happen.[85] Since most events come as a result of human decisions, open or closed doors are not a good means of discerning God's will, and we should be proactive in situations rather than resign ourselves to them.[86] Whereas process theists understand God to be working in continuous persuasion, usually at a subconscious level, the openness model posits that God may break through with specific conscious guidance, but it will not happen necessarily.[87]

Petitionary prayer is a means of fostering relationship. Our fundamental need, claims H. D. McDonald, is not for things but for God himself. It may be a specific need that takes us to prayer, but "real prayer issues in a deeper communion with God, in whom the soul finds abiding satisfaction." The prodigal son went home because he was hungry, "but in the end, the restored fellowship was more important to him than the prepared feast."[88] Keith Ward views petitionary prayer as "part of establishing a fully personal relationship with God, of asking him to act to realize particular goods, and thus of responsibly using our God-given capacity to channel responsive Divine action in particular ways."[89] Vincent Brümmer has particularly focused on the relationship-building function of prayer. He posits that all forms of prayer "affect the *relation* between God and the person who prays and therefore have a *real* effect on both." God is a "personal agent who is capable of *real* responses to contingent events and to the free acts which humans perform, as well as to the requests which they address to him."[90] In prayer we neither inform God of something he does not know nor remind ourselves of something we might tend to forget. But we acknowledge our personal dependence on God in a way that enables God to give us what he could not have given us without that acknowledgment.[91]

Most of the time, suggests Brümmer, God fulfills our needs and desires without our asking, but if he did this all the time, our relationship with him would not be personal. "Without our requests God can *bring about* what we need, but he cannot *give* us anything in a personal sense."[92] Our petitions create the conditions necessary for God to be able to give us as persons what we need or desire.

Keith Ward agrees that a significant function of petitionary prayer is the fostering of a closer relationship with God. If God responds to our requests just because we make them, it shows his love for us.[93] It will "allow a proper degree of creaturely autonomy to influence what will happen next," and it will "strengthen the relationship of obedient love to God, by inviting creatures to trust and depend upon God for the fulfilment of at least some of their desires." By allowing himself to be influenced by our requests, "God shows himself not to be an all-determining tyrant, but a co-operating power for good." On the other hand, by "requiring that these are requests and not in any sense commands (attempting to cause Divine response with magical efficacy) God ensures that his own distinctness and sovereign power remain unmistakable." Consequently, it is precisely in petitionary prayer that we have the deepest form of personal relationship with God. "Far from petition being an irrational attempt to change the mind of an omnipotent God, it is the supreme power of that fully personal relationship with God which is the truest form of human existence."[94]

Working within his Reformed context, Hendrikus Berkhof conceives of a covenant relationship between God and humans that has a "two-directional actuality." Repentant people accept God's acquittal and acknowledge his authority over their lives. God becomes their goal, and so they submit their thoughts and plans to those of God. But they also become God's goal and are made a part of his thoughts and plans. "One who gives priority to the petition, 'Hallowed be thy name,' may later also pray for bread and for protection against temptations. God takes the side of those who take his side. And it is an integral feature of this covenant that he stands up much more for us than we for him."[95] Prayer is "a primary and explicit expression of the covenant relationship," which is why it can be dealt with under so many different headings in the work of theology.[96]

Intercession may also be understood according to the relational character of prayer. Once more, we need not assume that prayer is aimed to stimulate either the petitioner or God. But we must take into account "the *mediate* nature of divine agency."[97] In intercession we ask God to act on behalf of the person or cause for whom we intercede, and we make ourselves available "as a secondary cause through whom God could act in answering the prayer."[98] God answers prayer both by "bringing about contingent events within the order of nature and by enabling and motivating human agents to realize his intentions."[99] In intercession we are cooperating with the will of God, which is at work in and through our relationships with one another. Both God and the petitioner are involved in realizing what is being asked. This means that we cannot use intercession as a way of evading our duties and getting God to do them instead. It also implies that "corporate prayer is more effective than individual prayer, not because it brings more pressure to bear on God but because it enlists more people in the realization of God's will."[100] We are entitled to pray for the success of whatever we can sincerely relate to the work of God in the world, which makes the will of God the criterion for our requests.

Prayer is training in recognizing God's actions. On Vincent Brümmer's account, God's agency can only be seen in the agency of secondary causes, either natural or human. This makes it difficult to know when a particular event is an act of God in answer to prayer and when it is merely the effect of natural causes or human agency. We cannot simply read this conclusion off the empirical facts. It is "not a matter of perception, but of interpretation with the 'eye of faith,'" an interpretation that we make in conjunction with a prior belief in the Creator.[101] The same is true in the case of apparent miracles in answer to prayer. "Without faith we cannot experience something as a miracle."[102] This does not, however, make prayer just a "*monologue* in which the petitioner utters a request, and then interprets whatever happens as a reply to his request."

Peter Baelz also grants that empirical evidence for answered prayer is difficult to produce because prayer does not work mechanically. It must be set in the context of an all-embracing relationship between people and God. There we affirm that "within the particularity of this context, at this particular juncture of events here and now, this particular prayer is a significant factor in shaping what follows after."[103] This is not a magical formula but is one moment "in the total response of the human creature to his creator, a moment which, perhaps, removes a condition restricting the fuller expression of the divine will." From that perspective the occurrence is seen as "an instance of God's providential activity, a sign of the furthering of his purposes."[104] The real ground for the conviction will lie in what we believe about the character of God and his relation to the world.

Petitionary prayer has an important function in training us "to recognize God's actions by looking at the world through the eyes of faith."[105] When we petition God, we expect an answer. This expectation causes us to be "on the look-out for God's response" and thus sharpens our ability to recognize the answer when it comes. As A. Alhonsaari puts it: "When praying, the believer is . . . repeatedly making himself see the world in a certain way in which everyday experiences are fitted into what he thinks is the proper reality; he is repeatedly bending his emotional life and his behaviour to conform to this reality."[106] By praying for things to happen believers become "able to recognize the providential action of God."[107]

Prayer is assigning value to things. John Polkinghorne gives credit to John Lucas[108] for the suggestion that when we pray, we are called upon to commit ourselves to what it is we really want. In so doing we assign value to it. "Such an assignment will be taken seriously by God, though it is not, of course, an over-riding obligation upon him, as if he were some heavenly Father Christmas." The principle is observed in the encounter of Jesus with the blind man, in Mark 10:46-52. The Lord asked him what he wanted, although it was perfectly clear that he wanted his sight. He had to commit himself to ask for it, before he was healed. "In a similar way, we have to say what it is we really wish for."[109]

Petition is beneficial because it fosters gratitude. John Lucas makes the suggestion that petition is good because, although God sends rain on the unjust as well as the just, those who have requested it in prayer receive it as a token of God's goodness and hence experience gratitude.[110] This is not the only reason for petition, however, or the concept of answered prayer would be thoroughly illusory. Lucas contends that it is right for Christians to ascribe their successes to God. What is wrong is to suggest "that God's activity here is taking the form of a special intervention in order to right the course of events for the benefit of some persons rather than others."[111] The appropriateness of thankfulness for the good that we experience lies in God's "securing generally beneficent conditions for our existence, and in there being certain tendencies in natural phenomena and human affairs that work to our advantage."[112]

Prayer is a form of cooperation with God to get things done. The primary desire of Christians when they make requests of God is that their prayers will result in obtaining what they want. We want to know whether and how God works to make things happen because we pray, which would not otherwise have happened. This is "impetratory" prayer, in the strong sense of the term, and proponents of the openness model are convinced that their understanding of providence offers the best framework for the understanding of petitionary prayer. In fact, John Sanders contends that "divine foreordination of all things [as in the Thomist, Barthian or Calvinist models] would rule out any divine response to our prayers," and those models must therefore be rejected.[113]

Sanders doubts that it makes sense within models of specific sovereignty or meticulous providence to say that God "responds" to prayer or that he does something because we requested him to. From Sanders's perspective, "for a God of specific sovereignty to 'respond' means simply that God decided first to have someone pray for a particular request after which God would do what was requested."[114] But this is not what we normally mean by "responding" and Sanders is committed to the relationality of God that entails genuine response. Therefore, Sanders finds it difficult to see how non-risk views of providence can make sense of James's statement that "you do not have, because you do not ask" (Jas 4:2). "If the God of specific sovereignty wanted you to have it, then he would ensure that you asked for it. If God's will is never thwarted in any detail, then we can never fail to receive something from God *because* we failed to ask for it."[115]

In the risk model that the openness model propounds, God is believed to be genuinely responsive to us so that he does things precisely because he was asked to do so. He removed plagues at the request of Moses (Ex 8:13, 31) and later changed his mind about destroying the people because Moses interceded for them (Ex 32:10-14). When Hezekiah asked God to allow him to live longer than God had predicted he would, through Isaiah, God sent Isaiah back to tell him that God had changed his mind and would grant his request (2 Kings 20:1-6). To John Sanders these are illustrations of the truth of James 4:2: "If Moses and Hezekiah had not prayed to God about these matters, biblical history would have been different."[116] Because of the personal relationship we have with God, our prayers make a difference to him, and he chooses to make himself dependent on us for some things. Thus our prayers have an effect on how things turn out in the world because they have an effect on God himself. One of the reasons that the future is partly open is "because God elects not to decide everything apart from our input. Biblical characters prayed boldly because they believed their prayers could change things—even God's mind. They understood that they were working with God to determine the future."[117] In our relationship with God we may "participate with him in determining" which of the possibilities open to him he will take. He "takes our desires into account," but he may also get us to "change our minds and pursue a course of action that we did not initially think best."[118] Prayer is therefore a dialogue with God that affects both parties and changes the situation.

The argument is sometimes made that a good God would give us what is best for us whether or not we asked for it. Of this suggestion H. D. McDonald comments that it may indeed be that God does give his best possible to everyone without prayer because God makes the sun rise on both the evil and the good. "But the best possible that God, as faithful Creator, assures without prayer to every man may not be the best possible which could come to any man if he really prayed." If God met our needs without prayer, we would live in an "imaginary independence."[119]

In contemplating the manner of God's direction of history, Timothy Gorringe draws an analogy between God and a theater director. "God works without script and without plan but with . . . a profound understanding of theatre and the profoundest understanding of the play. The theme of the play is love, and the realization of love."[120] Like the good director, God must be able to "impose his will," as seen in the Joseph story, for instance, but he must do this without resorting to force or manipulation. He therefore does it through a process of mutual exploration between himself as director and the actors. Prayer is the dialogue between the two, and "because this is a real dialogue there must be an element of genuine surprise for God as well as for the creature."[121] God has given us prayer "as a way of sharing in the fashioning of the world. Once human beings learn to pray the future is fashioned between God and the creature together. Human asking becomes 'a movement in the cycle which goes out from God and returns to God,'" that is to say, in the outworking of providence.[122]

It is commonly stated by proponents of this model of providence that in prayer we are not informing God of what he does not know (cf. Mt 6:32), nor are we expecting to persuade God simply because we ask him. Yet the fulfillment of God's purpose "may itself be conditional upon our approaching him in prayer and what is ultimately for the best itself be dependent upon our praying."[123] We may give the divine love an opportunity through our prayer to "realize possibilities which only in this way it can actualize." It might be necessary to "go on praying in the faith and hope that this is so, even though we cannot yet explain how it is so. In prayer we refuse to accept as ultimate what appear to be the fixed conditions of the world because we believe that these conditions are not ultimate." Though they have "a temporary validity within the purpose of God," they are "in the end subordinate to his love."[124]

The context in which we pray is a world that has "an ordered but open reality" in which both God and humans participate. It cannot be a "device for by-passing the reality and order of the world."[125] John Polkinghorne therefore argues that we ought not to pray for alterations in the motion of the solar systems because this is "fixed by divine transcendent reliability."[126] However, prayer for rain is not "ruled out of court" because here "small triggers could generate large effects." The immanent action of God lies "hidden in those complexes whose precarious balance makes them unsusceptible to prediction."[127]

Although there are limitations placed upon us and our prayer by the stability of the world, since we are participants in the formation of the emerging reality, we may only pray for the world as we are willing to be transformed ourselves. Only when we are willing to work for a new world may we pray for the coming of the kingdom. "Prayer and work are two aspects of a single response."[128] In prayer our spirits meet God's Spirit, and we respond to God's care and concern for the world. "The faithful worshipper becomes the hopeful fellow-worker."[129] Given the role of God in the world described above, we must not expect that, as a result of our prayer, "the world will now behave as if it were subject to a powerful and external manipulation." But we should expect that through our response to the Spirit of God "things will look different and, with new possibilities arising, will become different. . . . If prayer can move mountains it is because Love can move mountains, the love of God kindling a fire of love" within human hearts.[130]

Just how it is that our prayer helps God do what he wishes to do is not easy to say. Baelz posits that "it may be the case that the natural world is more complex and more open than we ordinarily assume, and that the network of causal connections is less restricted than we imagine."[131] If this should be the case, then our prayer may bring into play "a wider causality than usual," which "becomes available for the service of Love." Baelz speculates that "there may be links and connections between human beings at the psychological, and even at the unconscious, as well as at the physical level." Although he judges the evidence for telepathy to be uncertain, he considers it "at least sufficiently impressive to be taken seriously." If the connections he has been surmising do, in fact, exist, "then what we can 'do' for others in response to the gentle but insistent pressure of the divine love is not restricted to our ordinary physical actions." These deeds will sometimes be the fruits of prayer and will flow from the decisions we make as a consequence of our prayers. But beyond these direct actions Baelz postulates that we "may also be 'doing' something for others in the very act of prayer itself. We may be making resources available for them which stem directly from our praying and which they are able to use themselves." While this is not a proof that God has intervened and answered our prayer, "if the telepathic link is the expression of the union between divine and human love, then it may properly be called the fruit of prayer."[132]

Polkinghorne pictures the future as one in which both God and we have room for maneuver in its formation. He suggests that "when we pray, we are offering our room for manoeuvre to be taken by God and used by him together with his room for manoeuvre, to the greatest possible effect."[133] We produce a situation like laser light, which is effective because "the waves making up the light are all in step. All the crests come together and add up and all the troughs come together and add down, to the maximum effect."

Similarly, "divine and human coherence in prayer is genuinely instrumental; it can make things possible which would not be so if we and God were at cross-purposes." Herein lies the rationale for valuing corporate prayer. It "is not because there are more fists beating on the heavenly door, but because there are more wills to be aligned with the divine will."[134] We notice a similarity between Polkinghorne's description of the manner in which our prayers give God room to work and the description provided by process theologians. Not surprisingly, Polkinghorne has described his own proposal as "a kind of demythologization of process thought, with panpsychism replaced here by informational interaction, and a consequent possibility of effective divine action instead of mere pleading."[135]

We have earlier noted the agreement of David Bartholomew with the sort of "top-down" form of divine providential activity that is here observed in Polkinghorne. Given that God has created a world in which accidents are bound to happen, and distress and suffering are inevitable, God's work in the world is primarily in the realm of the mind. Consequently, this is the direction in which most petitions must be aimed. Even the request for daily bread is not expected to be met apart from means, and many of these are personal. It is this factor that makes it virtually impossible for us to demonstrate divine causality when prayer is supposedly answered.[136]

Keith Ward has noted that there is a widely held view that prayer does not effect change in the world objectively but that it empowers the one who prays to do God's will more effectively. This prompts him to ask: "But if we can ask God to help and strengthen us, why should we not ask God to help others, since that is the ultimate focus of our concern in any case? If he can empower us in response to our prayers, so he could help others by modifying the conditions which surround them, in response to our prayers."[137] Ward argues that it "it is not sensible to complain that, if I fail to pull my neighbour out of a ditch when I could easily do so, God is responsible for leaving him there. It is no more sensible to complain that, if I fail to pray for my neighbour when I could easily do so, God is responsible for not doing what my prayer might have effected."[138] As Ward imagines the situation, "when we show love by praying for others, we may open up channels of healing that God can use; creatures and creator can cooperate in making the world more transparent to Divine influence."[139]

The Case Study

A young university student often came to prayer meeting. Oliver Dueck had been a cause of concern to the youth leaders during his last years in high school. Jerry Walls, his Sunday school teacher, had been particularly anxious as Oliver had so many questions about God and his ways of working in the world. Mr. Walls was a Calvinist, and he was troubled when Oliver described God as just a puppet master, pulling the strings so that everyone in the world did what he wanted them to. But that was how the teacher's perspective sounded to Oliver. So Mr. Walls was much relieved when Oliver came home for Christmas after his first semester at university and reported that he had become involved in a Christian student group and made friends with strong believers. On the other hand, Oliver had encountered and accepted some ideas that still made his teacher rather nervous. Oliver no longer challenged God's control because he had come to understand God's relationship to people quite differently. "God is responsive," he said. "He doesn't control everything that happens because he has given people freedom to make decisions. He doesn't always know what they will decide ahead of time, either. But he is powerful, and he is able to adapt to each new situation and keep working for good." It sounded rather strange to Mr. Walls, but at least Oliver seemed firm in his trust in God.

Within the congregation Oliver had occasionally been involved in discussion with both Millie (semi-deist) and Mark (process). He agreed with Millie that there was a serious problem if God was so completely in control in the world that his will was always done, as Mr. Walls believed. Terrible tragedies occurred every day, and if these were God's will, then God himself is guilty of evil, and this could not be the case. But in addressing this problem, Millie had made God much too distant and uninvolved to fit with Oliver's reading of the Bible. Oliver had become increasingly aware of God as a personal being who had created other personal beings because he wanted to have a relationship with them. But relationships involve give and take; they require interaction and a measure of interdependence. If God always gets his own way in the relationship and we simply do his will, then it is really not a very satisfying fellowship for either God or for us. Millie's God seemed to have no relationship at all, and the God of Mr. Walls was a dictator, not one with whom we can have intimate fellowship. Not that God and his creatures are on exactly the same level. Being God, he is sovereign, and he could have done anything he wanted. He could have made creatures who always do his will if he had wanted to, but Scripture indicates that he did not do that. He wanted his creatures to love him voluntarily and to obey him when they were free not to do so if they chose.

In personal relationships like this, of course, there is a risk, and on this point Oliver was agreed with Millie and Mark. Having given his creatures the freedom to disobey, God had given up his ability to have everything happen just the way he wanted it to. By contrast with Millie, it seemed to Oliver that Mark's God was at least continuously involved in the world. Mark's God was certainly vulnerable, as the God of the biblical narrative seemed to Oliver to be. But the process model portrayed God as too dependent on the creatures to satisfy Oliver. God himself was as much in process as we are, and he too is becoming. Not that his becomingness was completely open; there was an antecedent or primordial aspect of God's being that included his moral nature so that there was no risk that God might become evil in the process of interaction with his creatures. But from Oliver's perspective the process model that Mark worked with was too dependent on Whitehead's philosophy and not sufficiently based in the biblical narrative.

Oliver did like the way Mark perceived of God's effort to achieve his good purposes in the world through persuasion but not coercion. The Calvinist view of God's control seemed so coercive, and human freedom looked to be an illusion. Oliver was convinced that real freedom means that we have at least two choices in most situations, and there is nothing, either inside of us or outside of us, which predetermines which of those choices we will make. It is precisely at that moment of deciding that we are free.

Oliver was aware that the aspect of his current theological understanding that gave Mr. Walls most concern was Oliver's belief that God did not know the future in all its details. But this was not a limitation on the knowledge of God, whom Oliver believed to be omniscient. It was just that neither God nor anyone else could know what decision a person would make until that person had made the decision. The decision did not exist until that time and so was not "there" to be known. Oliver had encountered the response that God can know these decisions that are future to us because they are not future to him, since he does not experience time as we do. That seemed to work for many theologians through the centuries but Oliver now believed that it was a concept based more on Greek philosophical ideas than on the biblical narrative. It was all part of a package in which God is unchanging and without emotions, but this seemed so alien to the picture of God that Oliver got from the Bible. There he met a God who gets angry, who repents, who changes his mind because people ask him to, who rejoices and who is genuinely involved in reciprocal relationships with the creatures he made for fellowship with himself. Consequently, Oliver had concluded that God must experience events in sequence and be able to respond and change his own decisions while always remaining faithful to his moral character as God.

Thinking about Richard Henderson and his fellow missionaries, Oliver knew that God would not be happy with the way the guerrillas had abducted them and that God would want to bring good out of this for everyone involved. Although God knew the guerrillas better than anyone else could, perhaps including themselves, he could not have known that they were going to abduct the missionaries until they actually did so. However, this would not have caught God by surprise because he knew the immense range of things that could possibly happen, and he knew of things that could be done in all of those possible scenarios. What he did not know was which of those particular possibilities would be actualized yesterday. Nor could God predict just how it was all going to turn out because many of the variables were not in his control. There were so many people involved who could affect the outcome—the guerrillas, the missionaries, the politicians, other members of the tribe and so on. Each of these people was free to make choices, and the complex combination of these human decisions and of God's influence or direct action would ultimately determine the future.

Oliver did not believe, however, that God was powerless in the situation. God could intervene dramatically with an angel, as he had done with the apostle Peter, or with an earthquake as he did for Paul and Silas. But Oliver rather doubted that these were likely options in the current situation. God's normal way of working in the world was less dramatic. Given that God had not intervened in a spectacular way to prevent the Holocaust, or to protect the many Christians experiencing serious persecution around the world even at that time, it seemed unlikely that he would now do so for the sake of three missionaries and their circle of family and friends. God usually chose to work within the structures of the physical universe as he had set them up and to influence people through the persuasions of his Spirit. Of course, these persuasions could be resisted, and so God could not guarantee the outcome without taking back the freedom he had given, and this he would not do.

Oliver did believe that he and his friends gathered in church that evening could make a difference and that prayer was one way of doing this. Because of the special personal relationship that exists between God and his followers, God was deeply interested in their concerns and in their requests. He might even take a different direction than he had at first intended, simply because of the earnest entreaties of his children. So for Oliver this was not simply an exercise in submission to the will of God or a form of therapy to make them all feel better. The future was still not determined, God could act in noncoercive ways to influence that future, and he would be responsive to the prayers of his people in making his own decisions about what he would do to bring good out of evil.

Oliver stood up and prayed: "Loving Father, we know that you are a powerful God but that even you are not able to do everything that you would like to do because you have chosen to involve us in significant ways in the world. You want us to love you and to serve you willingly. We are frightened right now because we realize that Richard and his friends are in grave danger. The men who have taken them don't care about their lives; they only want to get the benefits they need for their own cause. We have no guarantees that things will turn out well for Richard. They did not turn out perfectly for your own Son when he was nailed to a cross as an innocent man, although you made that great evil the means of immense good. Things have not turned out well for many of your children. On the other hand, we can also think of times when those who followed you have been in danger and have come through it. We know that evil wins sometimes, Lord, even though you do not want it to. You can bring good out of evil, in the long run, but that does not negate the seriousness of the evil itself. On the other hand, we believe that it makes a difference when we pray, that there are ways in which you will work because we have prayed, which you would not otherwise have worked. And so we are serious now about our request that you act in this situation.

"We are assuming, Lord, that the best thing for the missionaries would be to escape unharmed, and so we are praying that you will do what you can to bring that about. We don't fully understand the ways in which you work. We know that you can dramatically change the hearts and minds of their captors. We also know that you can give Richard and the other missionaries a keen eye for ways in which they can convince the men to let them go or even to escape. We know that you could even do something supernaturally miraculous, but we know that doesn't happen often, and we aren't sure what the limits are in that regard. However you choose to do it, Father, we are asking you to protect them and to rescue them.

"In all of this, Lord, we realize that what is most important is the relationship that Richard and his friends, and also their abductors, have with you. I ask that the missionaries will be very conscious of your presence with them and that their captors will experience in them a strength and peace and love that is unusual but attractive. It would be wonderful if this troubling experience could be a means by which your Spirit could work in grace in the lives of those who are currently living in ignorance or rebellion against you. Help us too, Father, to think of things we could be doing to help in this situation. We ask these things because you have invited us to bring our requests to you, and we give you praise for your own love and goodness even when things go differently than you want them to. In Jesus' name, Amen."

6

The Church Dominion Model

THE CHURCH DOMINION MODEL BELIEVES THAT GOD IS IMMENSELY POWER-*ful and is able to accomplish his will in the world but that he has chosen to restrict his special action to those things for which the church prays. He has done this in order that prayer might be a training ground in dominion for the church. In the beginning, God gave dominion over the earth to human beings. They relinquished it to Satan, who then became legally the prince of this world. Through the perfectly obedient life of the incarnate Word and his voluntary death, the legal claim of Satan was annulled. Those who trust in Jesus Christ as their Savior are the people of God who will ultimately exercise dominion over the renewed creation. In order to prepare them for that rule, God has made the petitions of the church the range of his special and redemptive activity in the world. He will not act unless believers ask him to do so. When they petition according to his purpose for the world, he answers powerfully. Indeed, they can even change his mind about the particular way in which he would accomplish his will.*

The church dominion model is represented in popularly written works on prayer rather than in scholarly treatises on providence, but these books have been printed (and presumably read) in large numbers, and they offer a distinctive proposal that should not be ignored among our models of providence and prayer. The proponents of this model have certainly not come to their theology of prayer by the route that was taken in the openness model. However, the two proposals have a point of contact in that both models believe that God limits his own control. They differ about the reason for this. Whereas the openness model emphasizes God's self-restraint in giving his creatures libertarian freedom, the church dominion model argues that God's primary purpose is to develop the administrative or ruling skills of the church. This model attributes a decisive role to the church within God's providential ordering of the creation, and this provides for a distinctive theology of prayer. Representatives of the church dominion model are Brother Andrew, Paul Billheimer and Watchman Nee. Although none of them refers to the thought of any of the others, there is a remarkable similarity in the general tenor of their understanding of providence and prayer.

Fatalism Is a Dangerous Error in the Church

Brother Andrew, also known as "God's smuggler" for his ministry of delivering Bibles to closed countries, is concerned about the crippling effect of fatalism on the prayer ministry of the church. He recalls hearing two women discuss a hostage taking by Middle Eastern terrorists. One of them said, "I feel sorry for those poor men and their families, but really, this is God's problem not ours. We have to remember that He has already decided how their stories are going to turn out."[1] It was the conviction of these women that "*nothing* happens outside" God's will. Andrew considers this an example of the Christian fatalism that is a "false doctrine that has infected the thinking of an alarming number of Christians in our time."[2] Moreover, it is an error to which even some of the greatest heroes in the Bible succumbed occasionally (cf. Job 1:21: "the LORD gave, and the LORD has taken away"). Job's words were "uttered in absolute ignorance" that "God and Satan were using his body as a battleground. Job couldn't see that Satan was counting on fatalism as his most potent weapon."[3]

To counter this dangerous passivity Andrew proposes that God's action in the world is genuinely dependent on the prayers of his people. He is convinced that "unless we shake off our fatalistic apathy and use the power God makes available to us through prayer, the blood of many on this planet will be on our hands. We are responsible!"[4] Fatalism is, in Andrew's view, "a paralyzing disease that has invaded the Body of Christ with disastrous consequences. It infects its victims with complacency and apathy that immobilize their will to resist evil while eroding their determination to accomplish the great work of Christ."[5] On the other hand, if we "discern when God's mind is open to change" and if we "believe He is waiting for our prayers in order to defeat the enemy, then all prospects for a conventional life will be gone forever." We will "take up the sword of the Spirit and perform great exploits for God, fulfilling His eternal purpose in ways nobody else can."[6]

God Has Limited His Control in the World
by Giving Us a Measure of Independence

Like theologians in the first three models we have studied, Andrew believes that in endowing us with the "ability to make independent choices" God has "in a sense restricted His own omnipotence by allowing us to say yes or no to His will."[7] He "has given us the privilege of choosing how our lives (and our world) will turn out," and he has not already decided how this story will develop. He has plans for the world, and he has not taken his hands off it, so we are not in "ultimate control over God" as though he had put us in charge of everything. He is still sovereign, but his "plans for us are not chiseled in concrete. Only His character and nature are unchanging; His decisions are not!" Even if God has made plans to do something, suggests Andrew, God is "always ready to listen to our side of the story," and "He is open to changing those plans under the right conditions."[8] This is something that Moses understood when he interceded for the people of Israel (Ex 32:10, 11, 14).

Watchman Nee finds many passages in the Gospels that "affirm that God has subjected Himself to limitations." He could not do a mighty work in Nazareth (Mk 6:5), and the people in Jerusalem would not come to him (Mt 23:37).[9] "The water of divine deliverance depends upon the provision of human ditches."[10] God has determined not to accomplish his purpose without the cooperation of human wills. "Whereas in the eternities God was absolute, here in time He has chosen, instead of compelling His creatures, to limit His own omnipotence to their free choice. Man has been given power to make way for, or to obstruct, the power of God." He subjected himself to this limitation because he knew that it would result in the triumph of divine love in the eternal future.[11]

God Has Given to the Church the Task of Dominion over the Earth

According to Paul Billheimer, the universe was created "to provide a suitable habitation for the human race." And the human race was created for just one purpose: "to provide an eternal companion for the Son."[12] At creation, humans were "given rulership of the earth, kingship of its life, and the control and mastery of its forces" (Gen 1:26). This was a "bona fide grant"; it was God's to do with as he wished, and he did not give the earth to humans "with certain strings attached."[13] Tragically, the first humans then gave the dominion to Satan who became "the legal and actual ruler of this world," the god of this world, the prince of this world and the prince of the power of the air.[14] The only way that God could legally recover this dominion for humans was through a human being, the original trustee of the earth. But because humans had now become enslaved to Satan, they were incapable of freeing themselves. "A man had to be found upon whom Satan had no claim or control in order to head a movement for swinging the world back to its original allegiance. This man had to be able to remove Satan's legal claim to the earth before it could be restored to its original rulership." He also had to be "a member of the trustee group" who was "absolutely perfect in order not to furnish Satan with any legal claim upon him."[15]

When Satan brought Jesus to the cross but failed to incite him to rebellion against the Father, Satan "became the murderer of an innocent victim upon whom he had no claim; he therefore became subject, in the court of universal justice, to the death penalty."[16] This is believed to be the point of Hebrews 2:14. All of the legal claims that Satan secured upon earth and humanity through the fall of Adam have now been canceled. "Since the cross, he has absolutely no right at all upon any one or any thing. It means that all the power which he exercises now he exercises solely by deception and bluff" (cf. Mt 28:18).[17]

The legal victory achieved at Calvary must be enforced, and the enforcement has been placed in the hands of the church, which is Christ's body upon the earth (Mt 16:18, 19; Lk 10:17-19; implied in Mt 28:18-19). "The body with hands and feet is the vehicle which carries out the commands of the head. If the body fails to respond, the will of the head becomes a dead letter."[18] Brother Andrew posits that "many events we call 'natural disasters' are really satanic attacks. Storms, earthquakes, floods, forest fires—all of these could be (but are not always) the devil's attempts to kill a certain project or a person of value to God's Kingdom. We must be ready to pray against the evil forces when such disasters occur."[19] He recounts an occasion when he was preaching in South Africa and a great storm suddenly arose. The noise on the tin-roof was deafening, and the wind was approaching hurricane level and threatening to tear off the roof. Andrew stopped speaking since no one could hear him. He then prayed and rebuked the storm and "within a few seconds the wind stopped," and they continued with their meeting." Such incidents are reportedly commonplace for him.[20]

Billheimer argues that "the church, and only the church, is the key to and explanation of history"; this is the only aim of creation. "From before the foundation of the world until the dawn of eternal ages God has been working toward one grand event, one supreme end—the glorious wedding of His Son, the Marriage Supper of the Lamb" (Lk 12:32; Rev 3:21).[21] The Messiah came for just one purpose, "to give birth to his church and thus to obtain his bride." The church, which was later to become the bride of Christ, is "the central object and goal not only of history but of all that God has been doing in all realms from all eternity" (Rev 21:9).[22]

Christ has "deputized the church" to implement his administration (Mt 16:18-19; 18:18; Lk 10:19; Jn 20:21-23).[23] God is able to work in the world and could presumably do so on his own initiative, but his primary purpose is to develop the church, preparing it for its end as the bride. He has thus limited his own initiative in acting in the world, in order to maximize the training of church members and thereby to fulfill his primary intention for human history. Billheimer says nothing about the general providence of God, his caring for all creatures and his preservation of creation. Presumably these are things God does without having to be asked by the church. Where the church exercises administration would appear to be in the area often called special providence, the specific acts of God to protect, strengthen, heal, influence minds and so forth.

In similar terms Andrew writes that "those of us who know God are elevated to a stunning position" within the world because of the fact that God has given humans a measure of independence. "We become God's partners and collaborators in writing the story of mankind. Not only that, but we are empowered to challenge the powers of evil that have been at war with God since the beginning of time." Through our own faith and our prayers we can "lift the world off its hinges—if only we *will*."[24] In making himself "susceptible to our influence" God has "given us 'the keys of the kingdom' (Mt 16:19)—the power to change human history for the better" (cf. Jn 14:12-14).[25] We need not take life as it comes; "we can have an earth-shaking impact on our world because God's mind and heart are open to us and His power is available to us. It's no wonder God gets exasperated when He sees how reluctant we are to use the power of prayer" (cf. Is 42:22-23).[26]

Watchman Nee takes the same approach, arguing that Jesus has entrusted to us, the church, the use of the authority in Jesus' name. In his last discourse Jesus instructed his disciples three times to ask in his name (Jn 14:13-14; 15:16; 16:23-26). The power of this name operates in three directions: (1) in preaching to salvation (Lk 24:47; Acts 4:10-12; 10:43; 1 Cor 6:11), (2) in spiritual warfare—binding and subjection (Mk 16:17; Lk 10:17-19; Acts 16:18), and (3) in asking God through prayer.[27] "Jesus is now exalted in heaven, and all His work of saving men, speaking to their hearts, and working for them miracles of His grace, is done through the medium of His servants as they act *in His name.* Thus the Church's work is His work. The name of Jesus is in fact God's greatest legacy to her, for where such a self-committal of God is really operative, He himself takes responsibility for what is done in that name." It is God's *desire* to commit himself in this way, "for He has allowed Himself no other means for completing His task."[28] However, we can only use his name with authority when we live in union with him. God's eternal purpose is the sovereign rule of Christ, "but as with the kingdom of Solomon, so now, there is first a period of spiritual warfare represented by the reign of David. God is seeking those who will cooperate with Him today in that preparatory warfare." It must be done in God's power and for his glory.[29] Speaking reverently, Nee nonetheless posits that the church is "to restore to God His own omnipotence." It is the church's task "to secure for God the release of His power into the world, by bringing it to bear on evil situations in the realm of the spirit, for their overthrow."[30]

Prayer Is the School in Which the Church Learns to Exercise Human Dominion

The reason for God's establishment of his prayer program, as Billheimer understands things, was "to *give us training for overcoming* in preparation for rulership. God is using it as an apprenticeship. He did not devise prayer as merely his unique way of getting things done. In his plan, prayer has only one purpose—to give us exercise in overcoming."[31] God has the "power to accomplish all his other purposes without our cooperation in prayer." But this is the only means by which he can train us for rulership. This is why "he does nothing in the realm of human redemption except through prayer. He has tied all of his activity and accomplishment to prayer." In getting answers to prayer, then, the crucial factor "is not primarily spiritual superiority but simply the boldness, courage and faith to pray regardless of our sense of unworthiness." We go to God because he is worthy, not because we are (cf. Heb 4:15-16).[32] And this is the reason that prayer must be in the name of Jesus, not in our own name.[33]

Scripture does not give us a clear description of the duties of God's people in the millennial kingdom, but "it is clear that the administration of the great King's will, overseeing of all parts of his vast, eternal realm, will certainly be included." It is in preparation for this "unique and distinguished function" that God ordained the plan of prayer. By this means the bride enters "into personal encounter and conflict with Satan and his hierarchy, overcoming their opposition to God and his kingdom." It is not that God needs our assistance in overcoming Satan but that he wants "to give the church exercise and practice in overcoming." A necessary prerequisite to rulership in Christ is the character we acquire in overcoming, so prayer is "God's master plan for producing overcomers for the throne. It is "purely, totally and entirely *on-the-job-training*."[34] This training "for co-sovereignty with Christ over his universal empire" is thus gained by the church through "practising in her prayer closets the enforcement of heaven's decisions in mundane affairs." Here we "learn the art of spiritual warfare, of overcoming evil forces" in preparation for our assumption of the throne.[35] This is the reason that God has "bound himself to the church's prayers."

In Ezekiel 22:30-31, when God looks for an intercessor, it is not because he needs help but for the sake of his people. God could have incarcerated Satan immediately but he is using Satan to train the future corulers (Lk 10:19; Rev 3:21-22).[36] When God gives us a burden for prayer, we know that he is already at work to accomplish it, and this strengthens our confidence.[37] We are not influencing God by our prayers, he is completely sovereign. When he decides on a course of action in the world, he looks for someone upon whose heart he could place a burden, someone who will cooperate with him by voicing his own purpose and desire. Even though God has inspired the prayer, he does not act until he has found someone to verbalize the request, at least in spirit. That petition "galvanizes heaven into operation," which is why the claim is made that "God regulates the world by prayer."[38]

Prayer Is the Church's Means of Dominion

Having deputized the church to implement his administration, God has committed himself to work in response to their prayer. His authority is "inoperative apart from prayer" (cf. Ezek 22:30-31),[39] Billheimer asserts, and God will not override the church to whom he has given this responsibility as part of the training program for ruling.[40] As a case in point, God wills the salvation of all, and he has made provision for this, but "salvation is limited wholly and entirely by the intercession, or lack of it, of the church. Those for whom the church travails are saved. All others are lost" (cf. Jn 20:22-23).[41]

Clearly, the failure of some to believe and be saved does not lie in a divine self-restraint that is required by the libertarian freedom of creatures, nor does it lie in an intrinsic inability of God to move persuasively in human minds and spirits. "The Holy Spirit has the power to so enlighten the mind, awaken the spirit, and move the emotions of a man that he will find it easier to yield than to continue his rebellion."[42] So why does God not do this? It is not, as the Calvinist model would propose, because God has his own reasons for choosing the particular individuals to whom such gracious enlightenment is given. It is, rather, because "God will not go over the head of His church even to save a soul without her cooperation. If she will not intercede, the Holy Spirit, by His own choice, cannot do His office work of convicting and persuading." Consequently, "the Spirit can and will woo" and he "can and will persuade any soul who has not crossed the deadline, for whom the Church travails."[43] As both Brother Andrew and Watchman Nee understand Matthew 16:19, Jesus taught that what we bind on earth will be bound in heaven, and likewise what we loose.[44] On earth today God's power is as great as the church's prayers—no greater.[45]

Prayer According to God's Will Is Always Effective

If we are convinced that our prayer concern is truly from God, the answer to our petition is never in doubt. God is all-powerful, and he answers all prayer that is offered in his name, so we need only persist. If we do not give up, we can be assured that a positive answer will be obtained.[46] The point of the persistence is not that God must be persuaded to do something for which he has urged us to pray; the delay is a part of God's training of us in overcoming Satan. So God only allows Satan to resist us "as long as it serves his purpose for our growth, development and maturity." As soon as we have learned the new lesson in overcoming that God is teaching us, he "will take care of Satan."[47] Watchman Nee comments on the church's experience in China that "if there is ground for doubt whether our work is of God, then sure enough we find God is reluctant to answer prayer in relation to it. But when it is wholly of Him, He will commit Himself in wonderful ways."[48] God's will comes on earth by a union between the created will and the Uncreated Will, "seeking the displacement of the rebellious will of the devil." God will not act alone against that rebellious will. "He awaits our prayers."[49]

In the proposal by Watchman Nee, the will of God is the starting point, but we are the ones who voice God's will. "And if we do not voice it, it will not be done. Our prayers thus lay the track down which God's power can come. Like some mighty locomotive, His power is irresistible, but it cannot reach us without rails." If the church ceases to pray, "God ceases to work, for without their prayer He will do nothing. It is they who bring heaven's power to the place of need."[50] The church cannot increase God's power, but she can limit it. "She cannot make Him do what He does not will to do, but she can hinder that which He does will. There are many things that He would bind and loose in heaven—things which hinder to be bound, things of spiritual value to be loosed—but movement on earth must precede movement in heaven, and God always waits for His Church to move."[51] There are many things accumulated in heaven that have not yet found an outlet on earth because the church has not yet prayed.[52]

The reason that God restrains his own freedom in action is that if he were to take things out of the church's hands, to go over her head, as it were, it would sabotage the training program. But "if she will not pray, God will not act, because this would abort his purpose of bringing his church to her full potential as co-sovereign."[53] It is analogous to a situation in which checks require two signatures. At Calvary God signed the checks in his own blood, but "no promise is made good until a redeemed man enters the throne room of the universe and, by prayer and faith, writes his name beside God's. Then, and not until then, are the cheque's resources released." Or again, analogy could be drawn to a safety deposit box with two key holders: the keeper and the owner. The box cannot be opened without both keys. God holds the "key by which decisions governing earthly affairs are made; but we hold the key by which these decisions are implemented."[54] So the praying church "is actually deciding the course of human events. Some day we shall discover that prayer is the most important factor in shaping the course of human history."[55]

In a similar vein Brother Andrew posits a distinction between the prayer ministry of Jesus and our own work in prayer. We are the ones who must intercede for the salvation of our family members, our neighbors, our coworkers, our nation and the world. "If we don't intercede for that poor widow we know about in some forgotten village in a remote part of the globe—then *there's nobody else to do it*. Jesus won't do it. He is not praying for the world; He's praying for *us,* so that *we* will do what He has commanded (Jn 17:9). It's *our* job to pray for and go into all the world (Mk 16:15)."[56] Though God will not do everything we ask of him, the Holy Spirit will help us to see the situation from his perspective so that we can understand why not. In the meantime we should be persistent until we have an answer.[57]

Prayer Is a Means of Changing God's Mind

Brother Andrew contends that "the people who change God's mind are the people who know two things about Him—His character and His will."[58] Moses understood that God is "reasonable, merciful and true to His word," and so he felt free to intercede that God would change his mind and spare the people whom he had intended to destroy (Ex 32:14). Once more, in Exodus 34, Moses appeals to God's character, and "God responds instantly by giving Moses everything he asks, and much more," and so he gives the Israelites another chance, which they do not deserve.[59] When we begin to know God better and to understand his plans for the world, we can follow scriptural guidelines and "learn to pray in ways that are consistent with His loving, holy purposes and will, we become involved in carrying out—and sometimes changing—God's plans. This is, in fact, the way we glorify Him and become true participants in His creative work."[60]

From 1 Kings 17—18 we can conclude that Elijah knew God and that he also "knew two things: God wanted him to pray for rain and God would not have changed His mind about the drought—that is, ended it—had Elijah not prayed."[61] Even though Elijah knew God's will, "it still needed intensive intercession for God to implement His plan." It is those who are close to God who can change His mind.[62] As our intimacy with God grows, we gain a clearer understanding of his will. Andrew contends, however, that we ought never to pray "If it is your will," because this is an insult to God. The account of Jesus' prayer in Gethsemane (Mt 26:39, 42) may appear contrary to this statement, but Andrew understands Jesus to have been asking not to die prematurely (cf. Mt 26:38; Lk 22:44). His prayer was heard and he was strengthened (Heb 5:7).[63]

Andrew illustrates this point by relating a personal experience in Moscow when he and a companion were unloading Bibles. As they did so, a man was watching them, but this was not unusual. However, on this occasion the Holy Spirit gave Andrew a sense that the situation was dangerous, and he immediately began to pray, at which point the man walked away. Andrew suspected that the man had gone to report to the KGB, and so Andrew and his companion prayed that God would divert him in some way so that they could safely make their delivery. Those Bibles were delivered without incident, and Andrew has no idea what happened, but he reports being "certain that unless [God] had revealed to me the danger we were in and unless we had prayed, we would have ended up being questioned by the KGB that day." God's warning was his way of offering them "the chance to participate in the execution of His will by asking Him to change the outcome of the situation." If they had not prayed, and if they had been arrested, God would have brought good out of it, but, he says, "I am convinced that in this case, we were able to do that which God *most* wanted us to do—deliver our Bibles—because we understood what He was telling us and acted upon that information by praying. This kind of revelation gives us extraordinary opportunities to work hand in hand with God."[64]

Andrew notes that God does not usually reveal himself to him in that way. Direction usually comes through "a combination of spiritual insight gained over many years of friendship" with God and what Andrew calls "circumstantial evidence."[65] It is important to Andrew, though, that we not pray out of a desire to change God's mind or to "tell him what to do" but from a longing to know him better as our Friend and Father. "Opportunities to change God's mind are only one result of that relationship."[66] Consequently, we must not approach a means such as fasting as a way of "getting God's ear when He seems silent." That is rather like a child who holds his breath until he turns blue. "It becomes another legalistic exercise, another way to earn merit badges to prove how spiritual and self-disciplined we are," and God will not respond to it.[67]

The Case Study

When people in Fred Henderson's congregation had a need for which they wanted prayer, Sandra Buxton was usually the first person they called. A couple of years before this time she had been confined to bed with illness for a few weeks. One day during that time she had been watching television when a man spoke about prayer and described how God was training the church to rule in his kingdom by means of a program of prayer: God had chosen not to act in the world unless the church asked him to do so. It sounded strange to Sandra, but a book was offered to listeners who would write in and so she did. The book convinced her that there was truth in this teaching, and she soon developed a reputation as someone who was keenly interested in praying for things that she discerned to be important in the overcoming of evil in the world. She had enlisted some other women who gathered with her for prayer in her home on a regular basis.

As Sandra listened to Fred describing what had happened to Richard that day, she was intent on discerning what God could be wanting in the situation. She was keenly aware that Satan would want to disrupt the work of the missionaries, but she was puzzled that God had not protected them, given the regular prayer for their safety and their ministry that she and others in their church had offered. It occurred to her that God might actually have a good purpose for the abduction of the missionaries. However, since she did not know specifically that this was so, she assumed that God wanted the missionaries free. But God could not simply do what he wanted in this situation, not because of any intrinsic lack of ability but because he had chosen to give dominion of the earth to human beings.

Sandra believed that in the garden of Eden Adam and Eve had surrendered their dominion to Satan, and it was he who now ruled as the prince of this world. However, God had sent the Son to break the legal claim of Satan to dominion and to reestablish the rightful human rule in the church that Christ established as his own body and bride. Ultimately, it was God's intention that his people, the church, should rule once more over a pristine creation. To prepare them for that reign he had chosen to limit his special operation in the world to the things for which the church prayed. Prayer was the training ground for the church's rule, and God was willing to reveal to his people what he wanted to do in the world. However, he had committed himself to act only when they asked him to do what he willed. The vice-regency that God had entrusted to his redeemed people was so extensive that he was even prepared to take a different course of action than he would otherwise have chosen, if they fervently asked him to do so, provided that it was consistent with his overall purposes for the good of creation.

Sandra was firmly convinced that the believers gathered together that evening could affect the situation where Richard was being held captive. God was powerful in his ability to move people and change circumstances. He was simply waiting to be asked by his children who understood his purposes in the world and who wanted to see those purposes achieved. With this in mind, Sandra prayed.

"Dear Father, the sad story that Fred has told us reminds us once more that we are involved in a fierce spiritual struggle. The missionaries have been trying to bring the good news concerning Jesus to people who are in bondage to sin and Satan. Satan is doing all that he can to keep that deliverance from taking place. Now he has acted boldly through these men who have taken the missionaries captive. As we are gathered together this evening, dear Lord, we have a strong confidence that you are going to deliver Richard and his colleagues and bring good things for your kingdom out of this event. I am sure of this because I sense that there is so strong a spirit of prayerful concern in this meeting tonight. We are strongly united in our belief that it is your will that Satan should not triumph in his attempts to hinder the spread of the gospel. We know, O Lord, that you are powerful. There are ways in which you could act in this situation that we cannot even imagine. So we will not tell you what should be done. We simply ask you to act, to respond to our fervent prayers, and to show yourself mighty in this visible spiritual conflict. We will keep praying until we have overcome the evil one in prayer, and we give you glory that he is already conclusively defeated by Jesus at the cross and that you are simply delaying his ultimate destruction in order to involve us in your training program to exercise dominion in your name. We pray these requests in the powerful name of Jesus and look forward to giving you the glory for the victory won. Amen."

7

The Redemptive Intervention Model

OF THE MODELS WE HAVE EXAMINED THUS FAR, THE REDEMPTIVE INTER-
*vention model is closest to the openness model. Both of them believe that God
has given his creatures libertarian freedom and that this has limited the
extent of his own action in the world. But the redemptive intervention model
attributes to God slightly greater control of the outcome of events in the
world, even when those events are brought about through the will and
action of free creatures. This is because he has comprehensive knowledge of
the actual future, something that was denied by the openness model. The
redemptive intervention model does not believe that God knows possible
futures, but he does know the actual future, and thus he has been able to
plan his own action with that knowledge in mind. In one of the representa-
tions of this model, God's knowledge of the future is deemed possible because
God himself is timeless, but this is not the rationale in our other chosen representative who believes that God experiences the duration of time. Nevertheless, both of the theologians whose work is grouped under this model
believe in God's comprehensive foreknowledge.*

*Although God has chosen to limit his action in the world on account of
his gift of creaturely freedom, the redemptive intervention model emphasizes
that this is not a threat to the accomplishment of God's general purpose for*

the world. When necessary God can and does act decisively, supernaturally or miraculously in order to keep his program of redemption going. However, because of God's comprehensive foreknowledge, achievement of his overall redemptive program does not require frequent special intervention. This model complains that the Calvinist model, with its conviction of God's comprehensive decree and his persistent activity in the world, has generalized too widely from the biblical portrayal of God's action in history. It is granted that God was intentionally involved in the sale of Joseph into Egyptian slavery, along with Joseph's brothers whose intentions were rather different than God's. But Joseph's was a special case because it was an important step in the redemptive program through Israel. The same is not true in most of the incidents in the lives of most people, even of God's servants, throughout history.

Petitionary prayer is believed to be efficacious. Things do happen because we pray. This is not because God has given us the prerogative to determine his action (church dominion, see chapter six) but because of God's foreknowledge. He has known our petitions, and he has factored them into his own plan. Of course, this fact has to be located within the general limitations stated above in regard to the range of God's interventive action in the world.

In the openness model, God limits his own control in order to give creatures freedom of a libertarian kind. In that model, God is not completely unable to act in the world to effectuate his purposes, but he rarely does so apart from a work of persuasion in the minds of human agents. It was assumed that, by definition, decisions freely made cannot be foreknown. Were they to be known with certainty ahead of time, then no genuinely free decision would be possible. Through the years there have been many who wished to preserve a large measure of human freedom but who were also committed to the possibility of divine foreknowledge and who gave more latitude to God's action than is now true in the openness model. Among recent works by theologians who affirm divine self-restraint but still retain a commitment to divine foreknowledge, two will serve as representative in this chapter: Bruce Reichenbach and Jack Cottrell.

Bruce Reichenbach: God Is Temporal and Knows the Future but Limits His Own Power to Give Freedom to His Creatures

Human freedom and divine power. Bruce Reichenbach defines human freedom as contracausal and noncoerced. For an act to be free the person must have been able to do otherwise and must not have been compelled by causes, either external or internal. It is not that there are no influences on a person who makes decisions to act, but these do not *determine* the choice or action. On the other hand, a person's choices are neither arbitrary nor of chance since reasons can be given for them.[1] Evidence that humans have this sort of freedom is found in the universal, introspective sense that we have choices when we act. It is further argued that moral accountability for people's actions requires that they "must have been able to have acted differently."[2]

In granting significant freedom to his subjects the sovereign God makes it possible for his authority and will to be resisted. He is not to be analogized to the author of a novel whose creatures have no freedom but act strictly as the author determines.[3] That God should limit himself in creating free creatures is not considered to be inconsistent with his omnipotence. On the other hand, he does sometimes limit human freedom, as is seen in the case of Peter's jailer. This is the sort of limitation that a parent places on a two year old by closing the door to keep her in. However, to remove morally significant freedom totally would be dehumanizing.[4]

God's experience of time. Like the theologians of the openness model, Reichenbach believes that God is in time experiencing duration or time-sequencing. "Productive actions are necessarily time-bound and sequential. There is a time prior to the causal event when the person had not acted to produce and there is a subsequent time when he acts to produce the effect. Otherwise one cannot act for the production of the effect at a given time." But God is productive. "He reveals himself and his will sequentially (Eph 3:1-12); he became incarnate at the right time (Gal 4:4); he remembers or forgives sins (Ps 25:7; 79:8; 86:5; Lk 11:4); he once considered us sinners, but now he does not (Rom 5:8-9)."[5] God is immutable in his nature, but he is constantly changing in his relations with creatures.[6]

God's knowledge of the future. Unlike the openness model, Reichenbach believes that God has foreknowledge. Paul speaks of God's foreknowledge (Rom 8:29) and of his choosing people *before* the foundation of the world (Eph 1:4).[7] God's knowledge is either concurrent or prior, depending on his relationship to the time of an event. To the proposal that foreknowledge and freedom are incompatible, Reichenbach responds that the order of knowledge must not be confused with the order of causes. God knows the event because it occurs, and the occurrence of the event cannot be made dependent on God's knowledge of it. "What God knows about the acts of a person is relationally dependent on what the person who is the object of that knowledge does." We have the power, therefore, "to act so that the past is what it is, that is, that God truly believes something about the present."[8] (This seems to be a form of retroactive causation such as Swinburne rejected as implausible [in the openness model].)

In a response to Reichenbach's proposal Clark Pinnock, who works within the openness model, considers Reichenbach's only problem to be that he clings to a divine omniscience that includes the future. Pinnock therefore agrees with John Feinberg (of the Calvinist model) that foreknowledge is as determining as is predetermination.[9] But Reichenbach does not think that foreknowledge is the issue. God can foreknow an event, and that event can be either determined by him or undetermined. What makes predictive prophecy possible, however, is that God foreknows the future events themselves.[10] In Reichenbach's opinion Pinnock is wrong to assume that what has not yet occurred cannot be known in advance. An example would be an eclipse that has not yet occurred but which astronomers know in advance will occur. Pinnock is therefore deemed not to have "established his claim that one cannot know future actions of free persons."[11]

Although God knows the actual future, Reichenbach does not believe that God has middle knowledge, that is, knowledge of what *would* happen in circumstances that never actually exist. God knows what free persons choose, but he "does not know what free persons would choose were conditions different from what they are or about the choices which would be made by possible but never-existing individuals."[12] In asserting that the future can be known Reichenbach thus agrees with determinists and with proponents of middle knowledge, but he disagrees with the libertarians of the openness model. However, he does not agree with the Molinist model, that God knows what would happen if the situation were different. God only knows ahead of time what is *actually* going to happen. This is because counterfactual conditions of free will are not true, but they would have to be if they are part of God's knowledge.[13] (By "counterfactuals" philosophers mean events that do not in fact occur but which could occur if the circumstances were different.) Reichenbach's rejection of middle knowledge is an important part of his rejection of complete divine control as that is presented by John Feinberg, representing the Calvinist model. Reichenbach observes that "Feinberg must assert that all persons ultimately and noncoercively can be persuaded to God's perspective (as found in his decrees), and that as omniscient, God would know what would be persuasive in those cases where the person would dissent." This is problematic precisely because it presupposes God's knowledge of counterfactual conditions of free will, which Reichenbach considers impossible.[14]

The operation of divine providence. The providence of God is defined as God's "wisdom revealed in his plans and purposes by which he directs us to that which is good for us" and as his power "by which he attempts to realize these purposes by his actions in the cosmos and, more especially, in the affairs of humanity." God has purposes for the cosmos (Eph 1:10). He also has purposes for individuals: that they be saved (2 Pet 3:9), that they be conformed to Christ's image (Rom 8:29), that he might show his grace in kindness (Eph 2:7), that Jeremiah be a prophet (Jer 1:5-9), that Saul be an apostle to the Gentiles (Acts 9:15-16), that Peter feed the flock (Jn 21:15-17). Additionally, God has purposes for groups, such as to bring the Gentiles into joint heirship with Israel (Eph 2). In order to realize his purposes, God acts in specific ways. For different roles he calls Abraham (Gen 12:1-3) and Pharaoh (Ex 9:16). He uses Nebuchadnezzar and the Babylonians to punish Judah and then raises up Cyrus to restore them (Is 44:28). He works through Christ to redeem people and to destroy the works of the devil (1 Jn 3:8).[15]

Most often God realizes his intentions through persuasion "which is most consistent with human freedom and with the moral and spiritual development it makes possible." His purposes "do not include every detail of human existence," and even those general or exceptional plans of a specific nature are sometimes frustrated, as is seen for example in his purpose of universal salvation.[16] In such instances, God then adopts different plans to realize his ultimate purpose, which is the unification of the cosmos under Christ. However, this is not an ad hoc adaptation, as was the case in the openness model. "There is an eternality about his purposes based on his omniscience" (Acts 2:23; Eph 3:8-11).[17] Those who believe in God's comprehensive control often appeal to Ephesians 1:11, but Reichenbach sees an ambiguity in Paul's statement. He wonders, does it teach that "God does or works out *everything* in conformity with his purposes" or that "*everything* God does he does in conformity with his purposes?" He judges the grammar to be not decisive either way. For example, of the statement "John does everything very slowly," we are unsure whether the point is that John does everything but does it slowly or whether he does slowly everything that he does, although not doing everything.[18]

Jack Cottrell: God Restrains Himself but Maintains Active Direction of a Limited Number of Events Important to the Salvation-Historical Purpose

The nature of human freedom. A free act is one that is "performed without there being any *necessary* condition or cause." This means that a person does not act freely, even if she does what she wants, if what she wants is predetermined. However, the power of contrary choice need not be arbitrary, capricious or random. "Desires, motives, influences, and circumstances are all important factors in the distribution of preferences. One does not choose in a vacuum." On the other hand, we are not helpless in the face of circumstances nor slaves to our own desires and motives. "Sometimes a person chooses the more difficult course; sometimes he goes against his deepest desires and opts for duty; sometimes after much persuasion he may reverse his decision. As long as there is this possibility, there is freedom."[19] Within God's general providence, God permits human beings to make their own decisions and to "forge their own ways in the historical process."[20]

Determinists consider the will free if it acts voluntarily, but Cottrell finds this insufficient because God determines the desires, motives or circumstances, according to the scheme of determinists. Humans are free to do what they want, and God sees to it that they do what he wants. This is a "farcical use of the term *freedom*," in Cottrell's view.[21]

The limited scope and purpose of God's rule. Like Reichenbach, Jack Cottrell is committed to a model of divine providence that includes libertarian human freedom but does not exclude divine foreknowledge. His is a proposal that offers a strong view of divine freedom and initiative in history without making God determinative of all that happens. Cottrell's thesis is that "God is not only active in the world, but is active in *all* the world, in *everything* that happens (though not necessarily in the same way): the known and the unknown, the familiar and the mysterious, the trivial and the spectacular, the minute and the majestic, the sad and the joyful, the painful and the pleasant, the good and the evil."[22] So comprehensive is this list of what is included within God's activity that one might expect Cottrell's work to be included in the Thomist or the Calvinist model. What makes that inappropriate is his firm rejection of "theistic determinism" because it strikes him as teaching that even when God works through so-called secondary causes, he is the only originator of the action. This position is unacceptable because (1) it negates genuine human freedom (defined as contra-causal); (2) it robs humans of dignity and moral responsibility; (3) it fosters resignation, inactivity and quietism; (4) it makes God responsible for evil; and (5) it makes it difficult to distinguish good from evil.[23]

Cottrell considers Calvin illogical when he denies that God is the author of evil even though he determines all things,[24] and he accuses G. C. Berkouwer of simple "semantic quibbling" because he refuses to call the Reformed position determinism. Cottrell asserts that "if all events take place as the result of the causal influence of an overruling force, so that it was impossible for these events to have happened any other way, this is determinism whether the force is personal or impersonal, free or bound, arbitrary or purposeful."[25]

In Cottrell's model, God has given up omnicausality, both in nature and in human history. He lets creatures use their wills and minds in self-determination and does not intervene "unless his special providential purposes call for it."[26] God maintains his sovereignty because he maintains the right and the power to intervene if his purposes demand it, but he does not usually do this. He is also sovereign because it is a self-limitation, not of his being but only of his actions.[27] "True sovereignty consists in absolute control, but absolute control does not require causation, predetermination, or foreordination of all things." Free creatures are allowed to go their way unless there is a reason to intervene. God is free to bestow limited freedom or relative independence on his creatures.[28] As Lord of all, God is not necessarily the cause of all. Though there are many things that he does cause (the lot to fall on Jonah, the Red Sea to part, the raising of a dead person, etc.), he does not directly cause everything after creation.[29]

What leads determinists to a belief in total divine causation is the denial that a sovereign God can react to anything the creature does. Cottrell is prepared to speak of the divine decree but not of a decree that is unconditional. He posits that there is a divine permission of both good and evil, a point for which he commends Karl Barth[30] but which many determinists are reluctant to make.[31] Although an unconditional nonreactive decree includes secondary causes, Cottrell questions their genuineness. "The term *cause* is meaningful when applied to persons only when the second cause operates *alongside* the first cause, not when it is an *instrument* of the first cause."[32] From Cottrell's perspective the usual Reformed approach makes human causes meaningless, since they contribute nothing that has not been predetermined and fed into them. In an unconditional decree the divine will is, effectively, the sole agent in the world.[33] If human actions are free, then God must respond to them. If he cannot respond to them, he must cause them, and this is the problem of the unconditional decree.[34]

God's general purpose for the world is his own glory (Rom 11:36), and his lordship is founded on his being the Creator (Ps 24:1-2).[35] Yet he has "limited the way in which he would exercise his own authority over the world," by creating free creatures.[36] There is even a sense in which Satan, by subverting humankind, has usurped authority from both God and humans and "has now become prince or god of this world (Jn 12:31; 14:30; 2 Cor 4:4)."[37] Nevertheless, God "is able to work out his purpose for man and through men even when they are not aware of it. God's hand and God's purpose will prevail (Acts 4:28)." He controls kings and kingdoms (Dan 2:21; 5:21) and even small events like the lot (Prov 16:33).[38] Even so, people can defy and defeat God's will and desire for them, though they cannot defeat his plan for creation and the "purposes of redemption that he is working out in history."[39]

Everything was directed to the goal of preparing for the coming of Christ. What is most important in considering the scope and purpose of God's providential activity is that his dealings with Old Testament Israel were unique because of the purpose he had for the nation. We have no reason "to think that in some other part of the world at that time, such as Australia or East Asia, God was dealing with other nations in similar ways." Furthermore, "there is no reason to think that God is working with any nation or nations in the Christian era, including today, as he worked with Israel and her neighbors in Old Testament times."[40] Specific promises such as are found in 2 Chronicles 7:14 (a promise of material blessing, good weather and crops, if God's people repent and seek his face) cannot be generalized to apply to nations today. It was for "my people," namely Old Testament Israel, which had a role of preparing for the coming of Jesus. But "not even modern-day Israel as a political nation nor even the Jews as a race are equivalent to Old Testament Israel," and Jews are no longer distinguished from Gentiles (Gal 3:28; Eph 2:11-14).[41] In reading a passage like 1 Chronicles 17:21-22, which says that God made Israel his people "forever," it must be remembered that *olam* frequently means "age-lasting" (e.g., Ex 28:43; 29:28; 30:21; 31:16-17; 40:15; Lev 16:29, 31; 1 Kings 8:13; 1 Chron 15:2; 23:13). The successor to Israel is the church that needs providence of a different kind, "spiritual providence" such as the opening of doors for the gospel (2 Cor 2:12; Col 4:3; 1 Thess 2:18; 3:10-11).[42]

The role of divine foreknowledge. Like Bruce Reichenbach, Cottrell has proposed a model of God's self-restraint in providence out of respect for the freedom he has given his creatures, but he believes that God still has foreknowledge. Indeed, for Cottrell, God's true foreknowledge is based in the divine decree, yet it does not render human actions certain. God knows the choices people will make, and he can therefore "make his own plans accordingly, fitting his purposes around these foreknown decisions and actions." As a case in point, Acts 2:23 indicates that God had predetermined that Jesus would die as a propitiation for sin. However, the manner in which that came about was according to God's foreknowledge of situations and human choices.[43]

As Creator, God has "full and simultaneous knowledge of every detail of the visible and invisible creation from its beginning to its end." I take from this statement that Cottrell shares the classical view of God's eternity as timeless (cf. the Thomist and Calvinist models), contrary to the process and openness models, which assume that God experiences duration. God's foreknowledge is essential to his providential control. It is how he stays in control of free beings making free choices.[44] His "knowledge of future contingencies is what enables him to bestow a relative independence upon his creation. It enables him to create beings with free will without surrendering his sovereignty in the least." God maintains control through his foreknowledge of human free choices. He is not taken by surprise and is able "to work out his purposes in spite of and by means of these foreknown choices."[45]

God's knowledge of the future gives him "the genuine option of either permitting or preventing men's planned choices, and prevention is the ultimate in control" (cf. Jas 4:13-15). God has the power of veto over our plans (e.g., in Lk 12:19-20; cf. Prov 19:21). God can also plan his own responses and use of human choices in eternity, before those human decisions are made.[46] Cottrell claims that he does not believe in "mediate knowledge," a position Reichenbach also explicitly rejected as incoherent. However, I find this very difficult to understand in view of the situation Cottrell has described. His depiction of God's prospective planning would seem to indicate middle knowledge. To speak of God preventing an action is to assume that there is an action that would have occurred had God not prevented it, hence of a "counter-factual" action. God appears to know what would happen if he did not intervene and then to decide when he will introduce a factor into the situation that will change the outcome while not coercing the agents.

Lewis Sperry Chafer argued that God could not look into the future and find out what people were going to do because that would make him dependent on his creatures. His foreknowledge therefore had to rest on his decree.[47] Consequently, this becomes foreknowledge of what God will do rather than of what creatures will do. From Cottrell's perspective that makes God the only real agent. On the other hand, Cottrell agrees with Reichenbach, against the openness model, that foreknowledge does not *make* acts certain, it "only means that they *are* certain." God has infallible foreknowledge of the future as it will come about by the decisions of the agents involved at that time.[48] Yet this does not make God "dependent upon the world" as determinists assume.[49]

God's rule in nature. Cottrell asserts that with a "general providence" God rules over all (Ps 103:19), he preserves nature, and he operates in its normal processes, such as evaporation (Job 36:27-28; Ps 135:6-7) and rain (Ps 65:9-10; 104:13; 147:8).[50] Everything is the work of God (Job 38—39) and he has complete and detailed knowledge of the phenomena of nature (Job 39:1-3; Ps 50:11; 147:4; Mt 10:29-30; Lk 12:6-7). His relationship to nature is intimate, since he cares tenderly for creation (Deut 11:12; Job 38:25-27; Ps 104).[51] In order to give second causes a legitimate role, Cottrell believes, the classic concept of concurrence "will have to be rejected or at least modified considerably." He suggests that it is better to think of a relative independence for nature and the forces working within it, not that they are independent in their being, but in their actions.[52] In his sovereignty God permits things to happen "in accordance with their created abilities without his interfering with them." These are mainly aspects of God's general providence. He permits things not because he is weak and could not stop them but because he chooses to. This is a physical rather than a moral permission; he permits it in that he does not prevent it.[53]

There are three senses in which the phenomena of nature may be deemed God's works. God is the Creator of the whole system with its uniform processes. He is the one who preserves them in existence, and he "exercises a constant and intimate control over everything that happens."[54] In the infinity of God's knowledge, Heisenberg's indeterminacy principle no longer holds because God "*can* discern at the same time both the speed and the location of an atomic particle—indeed, of *all* atomic particles!"[55]

Cottrell acknowledges that sin has had a corrupting effect on creation (Rom 8:20-22). Satan further manipulates nature, sometimes with God's permission (cf. Job 1:19; 2:7; 2 Thess 2:9). "If God is the sole cause, or even the concurrent cause, of every natural process, it is very difficult to assimilate this data into the total picture. But if nature has been given a relative independence, it is more easily understood how it could be corrupted by sin and perverted by Satan."[56] Yet of every event in the natural world it can be said that God could have prevented it if he wished.[57]

God's purposes in special providence. Moral creatures have the same relative independence that nature has. Yet God remains in control and "can intervene via special providence whenever he chooses, in ways consistent with the free will given to his creatures."[58] God can act on natural laws and influence human decisions "so as to cause results that would not have occurred without the intervention but which are still within the possibilities of natural law itself and which do not violate the integrity of free will." God can even arrange seemingly chance meetings to further his purposes, as in the case of the traders who happened along as Joseph's brothers were deciding what to do with him (Gen 37:25-28).[59] To achieve God's purposes now, the providence needed by the church is primarily that which leads to acceptance of the gospel. In order to open hearts (Acts 16:14) God may use special providences such as accidents, sickness, close calls, particular songs or sermons, but these are not irresistible (Acts 7:51). The necessary understanding of the word of God may come about through a sharpening of the mind or through means such as a providential meeting of someone who is able to assist.[60]

The general principle that there is a special providence for God's people is asserted in both Testaments (2 Chron 15:2; 16:9; Ps 5:12; Rom 8:28; Phil 4:19).[61] But there is a change in application from Israel to the church. In the Old Testament, providence was tied closely to the physical prosperity of Israel. Now it is mainly protection from spiritual enemies or spiritual prosperity and wholeness. In the Old Testament there were many promises of protection and deliverance, but application now is mainly with regard to spiritual enemies (Mt 6:13; 12:29; 1 Cor 10:13; 2 Tim 4:18; 2 Pet 2:9; 1 Jn 4:4), and persecution is to be expected (Mt 5:10; 10:16-24; Jn 16:33; 2 Tim 3:12; 1 Pet 4:13).[62] Although God may permit some to prosper so that they can exercise the gift of giving (Rom 12:8), our prayer should be for daily bread (Mt 6:11), and our goal should be contentment (Phil 4:11-12). On the other hand, God has promised the necessities of life (Mt 6:26-30; 2 Cor 9:8-15; Phil 4:19).[63] "God can and often does answer prayers for healing by exercising his special providence on our behalf. And we believe that he will do so, unless there is an overriding purpose that is served by the sickness itself." By contrast, spiritual healing is guaranteed (Ezek 36:26; Rom 6:3-4; 8:11; Eph 2:5; Tit 3:5).[64]

Correction is also a part of God's purpose in special providence (Heb 12:3-11) and could be through God's control of the weather (Job 37:11-13) or through sickness (1 Cor 11:30). God can work through natural law to bring about his purposes, for example, in the casting of a lot (Prov 16:33), which is mostly a matter of muscular movements that God can control. Witness the lot that fell on Jonah (1:7). Another instance is seen in the warnings of Deuteronomy 28:38-39, which were fulfilled with the locusts (Joel 1:4; Amos 4:9). This may have been "by granting the species extraordinary reproductive success, or by causing an imbalance in the food chain in their favor. Also with slight effort God could arrange for a ram to be caught in a thicket at just the right time (Gen 22:13), or for a lion to be at a certain road just as a certain prophet was going that way (1 Kings 13:26)."[65]

In the Old Testament God is seen to be ceaselessly at work, able to accomplish his purposes even by "hardening the heart" of various people (Ex 10:1, 20; 14:17; Deut 2:30; Josh 11:20).[66] God acted in giving blessing for various reasons: to reward faithful living, in the cases of Obed-edom (2 Sam 6:11), Solomon (1 Kings 3:14) or the whole nation (Deut 11:13-15; 28:1-14). Sometimes it was in response to repentance (Jer 29:10, 14; Joel 2:23-26) or just because it furthered his purposes for individuals like Joseph (Gen 39:2-3) and Nehemiah (Neh 2:8, 18, 20). God also acted to punish (1 Sam 2:25; 4:11; 25:38; 2 Sam 7:14; 12:17-18; 21:1; 1 Kings 13:26; Prov 3:11-12; Jer 3:3; 5:5-19, 29; Lam 3:33, 37-40; Amos 4:4-11; Hag 1:6-11).[67]

Once the Fall occurred (foreknown but not purposed), redemption has become the key point of reference for God's purposive or decretive will (Lk 22:42; Jn 4:34; 5:30; Gal 1:4; Heb 2:9; 10:7 [Ps 40:6-8]). Most of the other things at this level lead to or follow from redemption, including the choice of Abraham (Heb 6:17), Jacob (Rom 9:11), David (Acts 13:36) and others (Rom 9:18-19). This is the context of Ephesians 1:11 where the statement "[God] accomplishes all things" must be understood within the context of redemption. The point of reference is the establishment of the church as a body uniting Jews and Gentiles under one head (cf. Acts 22:14; Col 1:27). Included within this "decretive" will of God is his purpose to glorify all those whom he foreknew would believe (Rom 8:29).[68] What distinguishes Cottrell's position on the decretive will from that of the Calvinist, then, is that it does not include everything. There are many areas where God has desires unfulfilled because of the freedom he has given to human beings.

These unfulfilled desires are not part of the decree or purpose, as they are in a Calvinist model.[69] Included in this large unpurposed category are all those things that God permits. God permits them in the sense that he neither desires nor purposes them, and many of these things would be contrary to his desires, that is, sinful (cf. Acts 18:21; 21:14; Rom 1:10; 15:32; 1 Cor 4:19; Jas 4:13-15; 1 Pet 3:17; 4:19).

God's Means of Special Providence

Direct control. Sometimes God used direct control to achieve his purposes. This is seen in the cases of Balaam (Num 24:1ff.), Saul (1 Sam 19:24) and the languages given at Pentecost (Acts 2:4ff.).[70] God may do with the human will what he does with nature in miracle. On rare occasions he may deem it "necessary directly to cause someone's will to come to a particular decision." He can do this because creaturely independence is relative, not absolute. Examples would be the hardening of hearts, the moving of rulers to make political decisions and the stirring up of Cyrus.[71] What we must not do is generalize to the assumption that this is the way God works with every decision of every will. Though Proverbs 16:1 (the answer of the tongue being from the Lord) is illustrated in Balaam's case, this is not a general rule. If God simply allows us to go ahead and say what we planned to say, most of the time, "then the answer of the tongue is still 'from the Lord' in the sense that he permitted us to say it."

Similarly, Proverbs 21:1 states that God can turn the king's heart, but he does not necessarily do so all the time. "We cannot assume that *every* decision of *every* king is directly controlled by God." Once again it is important to remember that the situation of Israel was unique.[72] Death is God's ultimate form of control, and he applies it if he chooses.[73]

Having created free beings, it is God's right to give them commands.[74] However, it would be contrary to God's purposes to move the will directly in order to save a person, though it is "not impossible that he would do so to serve his subordinate purposes." God does not *purpose* to save every one, in the strict sense, "otherwise he would effect a universal salvation because his purposes cannot be thwarted." But he does "*desire* that all should be saved, of course (Mt 18:14; 1 Tim 2:4; 2 Pet 3:9)." In regard to salvation, "his *purpose* is that those who freely accept his grace and lordship will be saved (Mt 23:37; Rom 10:9-13; Rev 22:17)."[75]

Indirect control. Most of the time we can understand situations by reference to God's indirect control, by which is meant "any influence that God can bring to bear upon the will that lies outside the will itself." The means of this influence include laws of nature, God's word in Scripture, appeals to reason, persuasion in preaching, inner checks and restraints, outward circumstances, closed doors and open doors.[76] God raised up Pharaoh and Moses without violating their free will, and he may also have stirred up Cyrus through external means, such as a mention to him of the prophecy of Isaiah 44:28 and 45:1.

Jeremiah and Ezekiel predicted that God would give his people a new heart (Jer 24:7; 32:39-40; Ezek 11:19-20; 36:26-27) after their return from Babylon. "Just as the reports of the exodus event struck fear into the hearts of Israel's enemies, so may the great deliverance of the restoration have melted the hearts of God's people to fear and serve him." There is possibly also some prophetic application to the New Testament people. We do not understand mental states such as thoughts and memories, but these are indicative of how God can "put certain thoughts into our minds," which is something we also attribute to Satan in instances of temptation. This is not in the category of new revelation, it is simply "the manipulation, if you will, of the normal processes of thinking. Once the thoughts or memories are present in the mind, they become occasions for making decisions of one kind or another. These decisions are ours to make, but they may be influenced by the thoughts."[77] God could fix thoughts in us that excite or calm our passions, encourage us to bold action or check us by fears. Possibly there was an instance of this with Reuben, who may have thought of the pain to his father and urged the brothers not to kill Joseph. Or God may have put into his mind the idea of selling Joseph to the traders "who just 'happened' to come along at that time" (Gen 37:26-27).[78]

Perhaps the hardening of Pharaoh's heart was on this order also. God may have given him thoughts of "what a great loss of free labor it would be to lose these Israelites, or what a laughing-stock we will be when other nations hear how a bunch of slaves had their way with us." Or again, we might consider the decisions of Jeroboam (1 Kings 12:15), the king of Assyria (Ezra 6:22) and Artaxerxes (Ezra 7:27) or the opening of Lydia's heart (Acts 16:14) "influencing her to respond to Paul's preaching of her own free choice."[79] These are all "indirect influences which leave the actual decision to the individual."

In the case of salvation, which might be considered the most significant instance of special providence given the purpose described above, the principal influence is the word of God (Rom 10:17). In Acts 18:27 the coming to faith of the disciples "through grace" is probably a reference to the preaching of "the word of his grace" (Acts 14:3; cf. 20:24). Again in Matthew 15:13, every plant that is not planted by the Father will be rooted up, but these are planted by the seed of the word (Lk 8:11-15). And in John 6:44, no one comes to the Father unless drawn, but in John 12:32 Jesus says that if he is lifted up, he will draw all people to himself.[80]

In Romans 9—11 the focus is identified as choice for service rather than for salvation. The question Paul addresses is whether God is breaking his covenant promise. In reply Paul says that God can choose or reject anyone he wishes to serve him. Since Israel was chosen as a nation for the service of preparation, to reject them for that role is not to exclude them from salvation. They had actually accomplished their purpose and were, therefore, due to be set aside anyway (9:5; cf. Eph 1—2). God was patient with them in their idolatry but eventually destroyed them ("vessels of wrath prepared for destruction"), having made way for vessels of mercy, the church. "Temporal dissolution of the Jews as God's exclusive people was both planned and deserved." Moreover, it was not the *whole* nation that was being rejected, only those who refused to believe. Any individual Jews who are rejected are rejected because of their unbelief, not because of an arbitrary decision on God's part. Hardening as a nation is judicial confirmation of their stubbornness and does not preclude any individual Jew from being saved.[81] Choice for service was therefore God's sovereign decision, but salvation was an individual choice.

These are all instances of *special* providence within the salvation historical purpose of God, and therefore we ought not to generalize from them. It is also important to note that God's indirect means are also not irresistible. God's chastisements sometimes did not produce the desired effect (Amos 4:6-11; Hag 1:2ff.). Yet, because of his foreknowledge, God can still work out his purposes.[82]

Through sin and evil. In achieving his purposes by providential means, God is even able to use sin and evil to good ends. He hardens hearts (Rom 9:18), including those of Pharaoh (Ex 10:20, 27; 11:10; 14:8; cf. Rom 9:17), of King Sihon (Deut 2:30ff.; Josh 11:20) and of Israel (Is 63:17; Lam 3:65; Rom 11:7, 25). He sends an evil spirit (Judg 9:23; 1 Sam 16:14; 18:10 ff.; 19:9ff.; 1 Kings 22:19-22; 2 Kings 19:7). He worked through Joseph's brothers (Gen 45:8; 50:20) and turned the Egyptians against Israel (Ps 105:25). Samson's sinful desire was "of the Lord" (Judg 14:1-4; cf. 2 Sam 12:11-12; 16:21-22), as was David's numbering of Israel (2 Sam 24:1) and the evil of

Rehoboam (1 Kings 11:9-11; 12:15), which was divine punishment on Solomon and the idolatrous nation. He made the people eat their children (Jer 19:9) and predestined the crucifixion of Jesus (Acts 2:23; 4:27-28). He deceived people (2 Sam 17:14; 1 Kings 22:22-23; Jn 12:39-40; 2 Thess 2:11) and raised up nations against other nations (1 Chron 5:26; 2 Chron 21:16; Is 10:6; Amos 6:14; Hab 1:6).[83]

Miracles. In the Bible miracles were not done primarily to meet the needs of God's people, but that is what often resulted. They are signs. Hence they are unusual and exceptional, and they are generally grouped in "revelatory clusters." The "signs" confirm the revelation they accompany. They were usually done for a redemptive purpose. This is not because of deficiencies in creation for which God had to compensate, but some of them addressed areas where restoration was needed because of sin.[84]

Cottrell has no objection to the statement that a miracle violates natural law. That is what makes them "miraculous." However, we must recognize that nature is less easily described than we thought prior to Einstein. Therefore, a miracle is defined as "an event which occurs outside the knowledge and control of natural law *as available to the miracle worker,* and which occurs purposefully within a context where it is intended to function as a sign."[85] Miracles do not violate the principle of cause and effect, and they do not violate nature as such. Science is possible precisely because miracles are exceptional, and the "laws" remain in effect and do not have to be revised on their account. Nor is the recognition of God's providence in miracles a devaluation of his providential involvement in the normal order.[86] In a different situation the event might even have been possible naturally, but in that context it was not. Whether we can explain it at a later time or not is irrelevant; the issue is the time and place at which it was done. While we may become capable of developing an antigravity device that enables water-walking, the important thing is that such a device was not available to Peter and Jesus.[87]

Cottrell distinguishes between special providence and miracle. Answers to prayer are generally a matter of special providence. God intervenes, but he usually does so through natural means. We discern the hand of God at work, but it lacks the demonstrative "sign" element. On the other hand, some things are miraculous but are not instances of special providence. Examples would be revelation, the inspiration of Scripture, the incarnation, the atonement, regeneration, the work of the indwelling Spirit and the operation of ordinary spiritual gifts.[88]

Foreknown Petitions Influenced God When He Formed His Plan
So That Some Things Happen Only *Because* We Pray

Scripture makes it clear that God does act in answer to petitionary prayer. For instance, in the Old Testament he is portrayed as giving blessings in answer to prayer, as in the cases of Hannah (1 Sam 1:5-20) and Hezekiah (Is 38:1-5).[89] "God can and often does answer prayers for healing by exercising his special providence on our behalf."[90] The key to the problems raised in people's minds by petition is found by Cottrell in divine foreknowledge. God has "known from eternity" every prayer that people would freely offer. "Thus, in his own eternal and unchangeable decisions about everything he would and would not do in the course of this world's history, he was able to decide which prayers he would answer and which he would not answer, from the very beginning." Consequently, God does not need "to change his plans in response to our petitions."[91] Here we see how crucial the difference is between this model of providence and the openness model on the matter of divine foreknowledge. In that model we saw a God who does not know the future but who has a general plan that he keeps adapting as he goes along, depending on the decisions humans make. Here we have a God who knows the future in detail and who has factored into his sovereign control the prayers that people will offer. Lest this sound like the Augustinian models in chapters nine through eleven (Thomist, Barthian and Calvinist), it is important to remember that the plan or purpose of God is much less comprehensive in Cottrell's model.

"Answers to prayer are prearranged according to foreknowledge, just as faithful believers are predestined to glory according to foreknowledge." Consequently, we can pray for God to act in a situation that has previously occurred as "long as we do not already know the actual outcome of that event." Since God sees our prayers from all eternity, "he can take account of that prayer even if it occurs historically after the thing prayed for."[92] Because of God's foreknowledge, prayer does influence him. He decides to do certain things just because of our prayers. Thus they have "a real effect on the course of nature and history." Cottrell suggests that only determinists would have a problem with this because, in their view, God cannot react or respond to anything. They understand the injunctions to prayer within the framework of God's ordaining the means as well as the ends. "The prayer originates from God in the same way that the answer does."[93] But this approach is only necessary on the assumption of unconditionality, which has been rejected in Cottrell's model. By contrast, it is his conviction that "there may be times when our prayers are the *only* reason why something happens the way it does."[94]

Miraculous intervention is not deemed necessary for answered prayer. God can work "within natural law." As A. H. Strong put it, God can work "by new combinations of natural forces . . . so that effects are produced which these same forces left to themselves would never have accomplished."[95] Foreknowledge makes this easier because God "can begin to modify the natural processes even before the prayers are offered in anticipation of them." A miracle is unnecessary if God can answer by means of special providence.[96]

First John 5:14 promises an answer to prayer that is "according to his will." The passage is talking about prayer according to the *purposive* will of God. If prayer is in keeping with God's purpose, he will answer it, otherwise he will not. An example would be David's unanswered prayer for his baby (2 Sam 12:18), since God purposed to punish David.[97]

The Case Study

Tom Stransky had not grown up in the church but had become a Christian while he was a university student. He found the situation rather confusing at first as he came to realize that there was considerable diversity of opinion regarding the nature of God's action in the world and the role of prayer. He had been introduced to Christ by a campus minister who believed that everything that happened had all been included in God's plan, which was made before the world began. Tom had a tough time figuring out why there was any point in praying if this were true, even though the people who believed it were committed to the importance of prayer. When a friend loaned him a book about the "openness of God," he was attracted to parts of it, but he had a difficult time believing that God did not know the future. Eventually he found a position that seemed to offer the best of both worlds. It depicted a God who was sovereign and who knew the future but who did not purpose or cause everything that happened because he left many things to come about as free human agents decided them. Sometimes God would intervene but only when it was necessary to the accomplishment of his grand purpose for salvation in the world.

Tom and Oliver (openness model) shared a great deal in their perspective on God's action in the world as it applied to the situation of Richard Henderson and the abducted missionaries. They both believed that God has limited his range of control within the world because he wants to give humans and spirit beings a significant degree of freedom. Both of them believed that this meant libertarian freedom, the ability to choose to do at least one thing other than what a person does choose in a given situation. Neither of them were comfortable, however, with the positions taken by either Millie (semi-deism) or Mark (process). In Millie's position God was far too uninvolved, and in Mark's understanding God was, in a sense, *too* thoroughly involved, so that he was a being still growing and becoming just as we are, although in a much more influential position.

The key difference between the models of Tom (redemptive intervention) and Oliver (openness) was that Tom believed that God knew the actual future, whereas Oliver did not think it was possible for God to know things that had yet to be made reality by the unpredictable decisions of free creatures, human and spiritual. Tom thought that the Bible was very clear in its statement that God knows the future, but he also differed from Oliver in his understanding of God's relationship to time. Oliver believed that God personally experiences events in sequence (the duration of time) so that his knowledge of events that are future to us is also a knowledge of events future to him, at the time of his knowing them. But Tom believed that God does not experience time at all, and so his knowledge of what is future in our experience is simultaneous with those events in God's own experience. While Tom believed that God knew the actual future (from our perspective), he agreed with Oliver that God did not know possible futures, things that would have happened if particular circumstances had been different.

As Tom thought about the situation of the captured missionaries, it gave him comfort to know that this was not a surprise to God. He had foreseen that the guerrillas would abduct the missionaries, hold them hostage and seek political concessions as a condition for their release. There were things that God could have done to protect them. He could have used angels as he had done with Elijah. He could have inspired fear in the hearts of the abductors or prompted the missionaries to act in a way that would have put them out of danger. However, these special interventions of God in the unfolding human history were generally reserved for times when the overall program of God for his creation required it. Tom was prepared to admit that he was not always able to discern when a seemingly minor incident had great significance in the large picture. But in this particular situation he considered it unlikely that the deliverance of three missionaries was critical to the accomplishment of God's larger purpose. Many other Christians had been martyred in the past without divine intervention. Tom was confident, however, that even if God did not intervene to save the captives, there were ways in which he could bring good out of their situation, even if it included their death at the hands of their abductors. On previous occasions the story of missionary martyrs had stirred the hearts of many other Christians to get involved in God's program of world evangelism and had even resulted in significant conversion to Christian faith among the people responsible for the missionaries' death.

Tom had always appreciated the strong confidence with which Sandra (church dominion) prayed. She seemed so sure that we can get God to do things in the world simply because we ask him to. In fact, she believed that God has limited his own working in the world not primarily out of respect for the freedom he has given us but because he intends humans to have dominion in the world. She felt God is training us for that goal by giving us the power to determine what he does in the establishment of his own rule by the range of our petition, provided that we are praying for things consistent with his purpose. Much as Tom coveted Sandra's confidence of success in prayer, he had a more limited view of the church's ability to elicit God's intervention in the world. For Tom, it was important to accept the limitation God has placed upon himself in creating free beings and giving them significant freedom. On the other hand, God's knowledge of the future has enabled him to maintain significant overall control of the progress of human history. Furthermore, if Tom prays tonight for God to act in the needy missionary situation, God will have known ahead of time that he would do so. Tom does not now have to change God's mind about what he is going to do (as Sandra thinks we can) because God has decided in his eternal now what he is going to do, having taken into account Tom's prayer. This does not mean that Tom's prayer is useless because it does not change what God was going to do or cause him to act in a different way. It means that Tom's prayer is an important part of what God took into account in his own decisions regarding his action in Richard Henderson's situation.

Tom prayed, "Gracious Father, nothing that has happened today has taken you by surprise. You knew that these men were going to abduct Richard and his colleagues, and you could have prevented it from happening, if you had chosen to. This does not mean that you wanted it to happen or that you purposed it, but at least we are confident that things are not out of your control. Lord, we believe that what we pray is important because you do hear and respond to our requests, having known those requests in your timeless eternity. Tonight we are agreed together that we would like to see these three missionaries released. We would also love to see some good come out of all this. It would be wonderful if the contact with these captors should lead to an opportunity to share with them the good news concerning Jesus. Please give them sensitive hearts, Lord, and open up their spiritual eyes to see the truth. I pray also for Fred that you will comfort him now and encourage him with the knowledge that you are sovereign in this situation and that you are able to protect Richard and to bring good out of this evil. We ask these things in the name of Jesus, Amen."

8

The Molinist Model

THE CRITICAL NEW FACTOR INTRODUCED BY THE MOLINIST MODEL TO THE *consideration of God's action in the world is God's knowledge of what would happen in all possible situations. God knows the actual future that will come to be (unlike the openness model), and he also knows all possible futures that could be if circumstances were different (unlike both the openness and the redemptive intervention models). Once more, it is assumed that God's intelligent creatures have libertarian freedom. But this is deemed to be a fairly minimal self-limitation on God's part because of his middle knowledge, that is, his knowledge of possible or hypothetical future events. The history that actually unfolds in the world is the result of the free action of all of the agents involved, both of the creatures and of God. Events are occurring because libertarianly free agents decide and act to bring them about. But these free creatures act and interact within a complex of events, and the whole complex that is human history has been chosen by God as the world that he willed to actualize.*

Along with the Calvinist model, the Molinist model proposes that everything that occurs is part of God's eternal plan. But in the Calvinist model, as we shall see in chapter eleven, each particular event in human history is brought about because God chooses that it should happen just the way it does. By contrast, the Molinist model posits that the whole complex of events is chosen by God, but the individual events are chosen by the libertarianly free agents involved. The history of the world is made by all of the actors in it, but God chooses which of all the possible histories will be actualized. This is possible because of different logical moments in God's knowledge. There are some things that God knows will happen simply because their coming to be is entailed or determined by the past. This is God's "natural knowledge." There are things that God knows could happen if particular circumstances existed prior to and at the moment of the events in question. This is called God's "middle knowledge," because it comes logically between his natural and his free knowledge. The third logical moment of God's knowledge, his "free knowledge," is the sum total of the actual events of history that God knows because he freely chooses that, from among all the possible histories of the world, he will actualize this particular one.

In the Molinist model, petitionary prayer has a definite effect upon the future that actually comes to be. It is impossible to change the future, just as it is impossible to change the past. But the past was brought about by the action of free agents, and so will the future be. Free creatures have the power to act now in ways that will bring about a future that would be different than it would have been if they had now acted differently. Thus the future that will come to be as a result of a human petition offered now, to which God responds with his own action, would be different than the future that would have come to be if that petition and God's response had never occurred. Prayer, therefore, "changes things."

In succeeding chapters we will meet the work of theologians who believe that God has complete control of all that happens in the world, even though the creatures who act within it are morally responsible and free. Many of them will define a free act as one done according to the agent's own desire and without external coercion. In all the models that we have encountered thus far in the book, freedom has been defined in libertarian or indeterminist terms, as the power of contrary choice. This has led to different overall perspectives that, nevertheless, all share the conviction that there are things happening in the world not caused by God in any sense. The degree to which he controls within that limit has varied between those models. Before we get to the model of God as omnicausal, there is one more model that needs to be examined. It attributes libertarian freedom to human agents but does so within a framework that also places everything that happens within God's control and by his decision. This is accomplished through God's middle knowledge, a knowledge of future contingencies, that is, of things that could happen, although many of them will not actually do so. Like the redemptive intervention model, this one asserts that God has foreknowledge. Like the other preceding models, it also affirms libertarian human freedom. Like the Thomist model (of the next chapter), however, it believes that everything that occurs in the world is part of the divine predetermination. Holding these two features together, libertarian freedom and divine determination, is the balancing act that middle knowledge attempts and which makes it a fascinating model for the consideration of anyone who is struggling to reconcile these factors.[1]

The concept of middle knowledge is often associated with the name of a Spanish Jesuit, Luis de Molina (1535-1600), on which account the theory is frequently called Molinism. It is generally conceded that Molina coined the phrase,[2] though not the concept. Thomas P. Flint has contended that "*any* orthodox Christian will have only two genuine choices when it comes to providence: a view that is more or less Molinist, or a view that is more or less Thomist." He argues this because, outside of Roman Catholic theology, to a very large extent, differences between Molinism and Thomism "map onto differences" between Arminians and mainline Calvinists.[3] From the perspective of the models that I am expounding in this work, Flint's categorization is overly simple, but it does bring to our attention the extent to which we are here involved in a discussion that has occupied both Catholic and Protestant theologians for centuries without consensus being achieved. (As a broader category, Arminianism would include the openness, the church dominion and the redemptive intervention models, as well as Protestant expressions of the Molinist model, which I now present.) It also affirms a datum of my own experience, that there is a great theological watershed between those who view God as the comprehensively governing being in all creaturely events and those who give a measure of independence to humans that leaves some events outside of God's control. Historically, it is a watershed that was defined in the initial responses to the work of Augustine and that is perpetually brought to light anew in the theological heirs of Augustine and of his Pelagian or semi-Pelagian opponents.

In developing this model, I will not focus attention specifically on the work of Molina because the middle knowledge perspective that he argued has a number of prolific representatives today. One of their number, William Craig, contends that middle knowledge is "but a name for an old and established doctrine."[4] He cites Augustine as an early example who "sought to explain the death of an infant on the grounds that God knew that were he to become an adult, he would fall away from the faith and be lost; or again, God did not allow the gospel to reach certain persons because He knew that even if it had, they would not have believed."[5]

God's Comprehensive Foreknowledge Does Not Eliminate the Libertarian Freedom of His Creatures, but Their Freedom Limits God's Own Control to Some Extent

Characteristically, proponents of middle knowledge have been committed to a libertarian (indeterminist) understanding of human freedom,[6] just as all the other models to this point have been. A major point of contention between these positions is whether precognition negates libertarian freedom. The openness model argues that it does. From the perspective of the Molinist theologians and philosophers, it does not. Precognition does not entail determinism. As William Craig puts it, "The future is predeterminate in that future propositions have a determinate truth value, but that does not mean that the future is predetermined." Only the latter notion involves the idea of causation. Craig cites C. D. Broad's assertion that "there is not the least inconsistency in saying that a certain event *e*, which happened at t_1, was already completely predeterminate at *t* but was not then completely predetermined."[7]

As long as a person's "free act is logically prior to the truth value of propositions about it, the chronological priority of the propositions' being true or being truly asserted is irrelevant to the issue of what is within one's power."[8] In other words, the statement about an event is a true proposition because the event is actual or real. The statement is true *because* the event really happens. It does not matter whether the statement concerning the event as a fact is made before the event or afterwards. The agents who brought about the event had the power to do so even if a true factual statement about their action had been made prior to the act itself. This does not mean that we have the power to change the future, but it means that we have the power to act in such a way that the future would be different, if we did so. "So long as we can act such that, were we to act in that way, the past would have been different, no threat to human freedom can raise its head."[9] A critical error in the argument of fatalists is "a confusion between the counterfactual dependence of a state of affairs on some future state of affairs and the logically impossible feat of changing the past."[10] More will be said about this matter of causation regarding the future and the past in the discussion of foreknowledge that follows shortly.

As was the case in models previously presented, this one entails some limitation on God's power by virtue of the libertarian freedom given to his creatures. God cannot actualize just any world he pleases. Within the range of possible worlds there is a "subset of worlds which are *feasible* or *realizable* by God," given his middle knowledge of true counterfactuals of freedom (i.e., of things which free beings *would* do in certain hypothetical situations but which they never actually do). This restriction does not impugn God's omnipotence "since it is a matter of logical necessity that God cannot actualize worlds corresponding to a false counterfactual of human freedom." Therefore, middle knowledge does not limit God's omnipotence, but it "does reveal restrictions on what God can actualize as a consequence of purely logical considerations." This is not a negation of God's universal causality, and the limits it places on divine omnipotence are purely logical.[11]

Commenting on Don Carson's collection of texts indicating God's foreordination of everything,[12] William Lane Craig pronounces Carson's conclusion "overdrawn."[13] Craig's own concern is to forestall any suggestion that all divine foreknowledge is based on his determining. Consequently, he welcomes Carson's identification of texts that indicate a great measure of human freedom and moral agency.[14] Passages speaking of God's repenting (Gen 6:6; 1 Sam 15:11, 35) underscore "that God's sovereignty is not a blind force acting irrespective of human actions, but is contingent in certain cases upon human decisions."[15] Our thoughts and future sinful acts are among events that God foreknows but does not determine.

God Has Three Kinds of Knowledge

A major tenet of Molinist theologies is that God has three different types or "logical moments" of knowledge. It is important not to assume that there is a chronological relationship or temporal succession between these. God has known what he knows from eternity. The relationship is logical "in that His knowledge of certain propositions is conditionally or explanatorily prior to His knowledge of certain other propositions."[16]

The first of these types may be called God's *natural* knowledge, which is unconditioned. God knows all necessary truths, such as laws of logic or the fact that $2 + 2 = 4$. These do not depend on God's will but are known by virtue of his nature. This category includes a knowledge of all possibilities, of "all the possible individuals he could create, all the possible circumstances he could place them in, all their possible actions and reactions, and all the possible worlds or orders which he could create."[17] It is a knowledge that is essential; without it God would not be God.

A second form of divine knowledge may be designated his *free* knowledge. This is God's knowledge of the actual world he has created and it includes his foreknowledge of everything that will happen. This knowledge follows God's decision to create the world and, therefore, God's control over which statements are true and which are false is part of this type of knowledge.[18] Included in this "stage" is God's knowledge of his own actions that he has decided to do through consideration of the information that is gained in God's third kind of knowledge, which is logically the middle "moment."

God's natural knowledge is necessary, and his free knowledge is dependent on his will. Counterfactuals of human freedom are not part of either category.[19] In between these two, logically, though not chronologically, lies God's *middle* knowledge, which includes his knowledge of counterfactuals of human freedom. Here God knows what every possible creature *would* do in particular circumstances. He knows whether Peter would deny Christ three times in certain circumstances or what he would freely choose. Knowing this, God might have decided not to place Peter in those circumstances or perhaps not even to create him. God's middle knowledge identifies the limited "range of possible worlds" that God could create, given the free choices that creatures would make in those worlds. God freely decided to create this particular world based on what he knew in his middle knowledge. As a result, his free knowledge is his knowledge of his own will, of that which will be because he chose to let it be.[20]

God Has Comprehensive Knowledge of the Present and the Past

William Lane Craig cites the biblical witness to God's comprehensive knowledge of the present. God observes everything going on in creation (Job 28:24), knows the number and nature of the stars (Job 38:31-33; Ps 147:4; Is 40:26), sees the fall of a sparrow, has a count of the hairs on our head (Mt 10:29-30), and he understands all that he observes (Job 28:12-27; 38—41). He is acquainted with all the events of human lives (Job 24:23; 31:4; 34:21; Ps 33:13-15; 119:168; Jer 16:17; 32:19; cf. 2 Chron 16:9; Ps 14:2), discerns human thoughts (Jer 17:9-10), and looks upon human hearts (1 Sam 16:7), which are "the center of the human personality in all its spiritual, intellectual, emotional, and ethical aspects." God knows all our plans and thoughts (1 Kings 8:39; 1 Chron 28:9; Lk 16:15; Acts 1:24; 15:8; Rom 8:27; 1 Cor 4:5; Heb 4:12-13; 1 Jn 3:19-20).[21] "Since every moment of the past was present and God knows all things happening in the present, the only way in which his knowledge of the past might be incomplete would be for him to forget something."[22]

God Knows the Actual Future Completely

The logical possibility of foreknowledge. William Lane Craig argues that tenseless statements are always either true or false, and a tenseless statement that is true at all is always true. (As a tenseless statement we might use the example "Peter *deny* Jesus three times." It is a statement of fact, but it gives no indication of the temporal relationship of that fact to the statement about it. By contrast, "Peter denied," "Peter denies" or "Peter will deny" are all tensed statements, in that they indicate the temporal relationship of the event to the speaker's statement.) Since God always knows the truth of all tenseless statements, he foreknows the future.[23] (He knew, in other words, that "Peter will deny Jesus" was a true statement one hundred years before it happened, just as the statement "Peter denied Jesus" is true now.) In order to affirm divine foreknowledge, we do not have to be able to explain how God has it, we only need to prove that it is not impossible.[24]

Those who deny divine foreknowledge have argued that this is not a limitation of God's omniscience, since the future does not exist and is, consequently, not there to be known. It is sometimes asserted that, since the future does not exist, there is nothing for statements about it to correspond with or fail to correspond with, and hence future-tense statements are neither true nor false. Craig argues that this is a misunderstanding of truth as correspondence, which does *not* mean that the things or events referred to must exist. This would only be true in the case of true present-tense statements. With true statements in other tenses, the thing or event described need not exist. Of things in the past, it is only necessary that they *have* existed and, of things in the future, it is only necessary that they *will* exist. This is a sense in which the past and future are parallel. For example, if it rains on April 13, "it rained yesterday" (said on April 14) is as true as "it will rain tomorrow" was on April 12.[25]

In the openness model we saw that divine foreknowledge was rejected in order to preserve libertarian human freedom. The common assumption among representatives of that model was that if a future act is known for certain, the agent of that act is not free to do otherwise than it was previously known she would do. Since middle knowledge theologians are committed to both divine foreknowledge and libertarian freedom, this is an important issue. In the philosophical literature on the issue of the compatibility or incompatibility of freedom and future certainty, Nelson Pike's case of Jones mowing his lawn is now a classic.[26] Pike contended that, if God foreknew, eighty years ago, that Jones was going to mow his lawn this Saturday, then Jones is not free to do otherwise. If he did not mow his lawn on Saturday when God foreknew that he would, he would make a truth known by God to be untrue, which is an impossibility. Hence, Jones is not free to do otherwise, by virtue of God's foreknowledge. Pike is cognizant of the attempt to avoid theological fatalism by positing God's timelessness, but he does not accept its validity, preferring to deny God's essential omniscience. From the perspective of divine timelessness, God "simply 'sees' and believes whatever Jones is doing, and Jones has the power to perform an action other than that which he is performing so that God's belief would be other than what it in fact is."[27]

In an approach representative of proponents of middle knowledge (and hence of foreknowledge), Craig counters that "Jones has the power to act in a different way, and if he *were* to act in that way, God *would have* believed differently." It is only certain that Jones will mow his lawn, not that he must.[28] Jones is free either to mow or not to mow his lawn, and whatever he does God will foreknow. This is not to say (contra Swinburne's statement cited previously) that Jones's action *causes* God's foreknowledge. When we say that God foreknows *because* Jones mows, it is a logical, not a causal, relation that is described. "God's foreknowledge is *chronologically* prior to Jones's mowing the lawn but Jones's mowing the lawn is *logically* prior to God's foreknowledge. Jones's mowing is the ground; God's foreknowledge is its logical consequent." The reason God foreknows that Jones will mow the lawn is because Jones will mow the lawn. God's foreknowledge does not determine what Jones does, and divine foreknowledge and human freedom are, therefore, not mutually exclusive.[29] The logical order, that events occur before they are known, "does not mean that there was a *time* at which certain events occurred without God's knowing about them. The priority here is purely logical, not temporal."[30] Craig rejects the proposal of Pike that divine foreknowledge necessitates the events foreknown in a way that would not be true of human foreknowledge. The infallibility of the knower's beliefs is not the point at issue, it is that the belief about Jones's future action is, in fact, knowledge.[31]

It is true that both the past and the future are unchangeable, but the future is causally open whereas the past is causally closed. Consequently, no conclusions for the possibility of foreknowledge can be drawn from the unchangeability of the past. Backward causation is ontologically impossible, but that is not a problem because the relationship between God's foreknowledge and the future is not causal, it is logical. "Future events do not retroactively cause the thoughts in God's mind. Rather, future-tense statements about future events are true or false depending on how things will turn out." Since God is omniscient, he "has the essential attribute of knowing all true future-tense statements." As a result, he foreknows the future, even though it is entirely nonexistent. "Foreknowledge thus does not require or imply backward causation."[32]

The critical distinction that must be kept clear is between *changing* past or future events and *causing* past or future events. "To change a past or future event would be to bring it about either that an event which actually did occur did not in fact occur or that an event which actually will occur will not in fact occur." On the other hand, "to cause a past or future event would be either to produce an event via an exercise of efficient causality such that the occurrence of the event precedes temporally the exercise of that causal power or to produce an event via an exercise of efficient causality such that the occurrence of the event succeeds temporally the exercise of that causal power." By these definitions, "to cause the past or future does not imply changing the past or future, since one causes what has been or will be."[33] Thus neither the past nor the future can be changed. That would be a logical contradiction, requiring that which has happened or will happen be made not to have happened or to happen. Nor can the past be caused from the present moment, because it is actual. The future, however, as potential, is still open to causation (though not change) in the present moment. This is not to say that the future is caused at a temporal distance. "Causation is simultaneous," but "the things which exercise causal influence endure through time and so impinge on each other in new relationships." We cause the future, and we do so freely. This "accounts for our intuition of the future's contingency, which is misexpressed in the notion that we can change the future. Since our actions have a causal effect on the future and determine which causally contingent branch or course of events will be actual, the unalterability of the future does not entail fatalism in any significant sense."[34]

The basis of divine foreknowledge may be described either in empiricist

or rationalist terms. The empiricist approach interprets God's foreknowledge on the model of perception. The rationalist approach, on the other
hand, is conceptual and asserts that "God innately knows only and all true
statements. Since true future-tense statements are included among them,
God foreknows the future." Craig notes that "the implicit assumption of the
perceptual model underlies virtually all contemporary denials of the possibility of divine foreknowledge of free acts," and he therefore prefers the
rationalist approach.[35] Since these propositions exist only in the divine
mind, "they are immediately present to God and known by Him to be true
or false."[36]

Biblical evidence of divine foreknowledge. A point of contention between models we have recently surveyed is God's knowledge of the future.
Craig argues that divine foreknowledge "seems to underlie the biblical
scheme of history," which is "not an unpredictably unfolding sequence of
events plunging haphazardly without purpose or direction." God is
depicted as one who knows the future and who is directing "the course of
world history toward his foreseen ends" (Is 44:6-8; 46:9-10; Eph 1:10; 3:9-
11; cf. 2 Tim 1:9-10; 1 Pet 1:20).[37] Significant events of history occur in fulfillment of prophetic predictions, and true prophets were evident from their
success in foretelling the future (Deut 18:22).[38] Indeed, Isaiah indicates that
God's knowledge of the future is a decisive test in distinguishing him from
false gods (Is 41:21-24; 44:6-8; 46:9-10).[39]

The Old Testament consistently represents God as one who foreknows
the future and can disclose it to prophets. Specifically, Abraham was foretold about four hundred years of captivity and the exodus (Gen 15:13-14).
Joseph asked God for power to interpret dreams that presaged the future
(Gen 40:8) and then accurately predicted the restoration of the butler, the
execution of the baker, and seven years of plenty and famine. An unnamed
prophet predicted the birth of Josiah and the destruction of pagan religious
practices in Israel, and he gave a sign of the authenticity of his prediction
that was fulfilled (1 Kings 13:2-3). Another prophet foretold the imminent
death of a prophet (1 Kings 13:20-24). Elisha predicted the death of the
king of Syria and the terrible reign of his successor (2 Kings 8:7-15), and
Amos and Hosea both foresaw and warned of the fall of the Northern
Kingdom. Similarly, Isaiah, Jeremiah and Ezekiel predicted the fall of the
Southern Kingdom and the destruction of Jerusalem, the Babylonian captivity, the restoration of God's people, and the subsequent doom of Assyria,
Babylon and many lesser nations. To Daniel three empires were revealed

that would succeed the Babylonian (Dan 2:36-43), along with the course of world history from the Persian Empire well into the intertestamental period (Dan 11).[40]

Jesus considered the Old Testament to be prophetic of his own life (Lk 24:25-27; cf. 24:45-47; 1 Pet 1:10-11) and was himself depicted as a prophet. He predicted the destruction of Jerusalem, signs of the end of the world and his own return as Lord (Mt 24; Mk 13; Lk 21).[41] He foretold his passion, death and resurrection (Mk 8:31; 9:31; 10:32-34), the existence of money in the mouth of a fish (Mt 17:27), and a man who would be carrying a jar (Mk 14:13-15), something usually done only by women. In the latter instance "Jesus is represented as foreknowing a free and highly singular event."[42] Jesus predicted his betrayal by Judas (Mk 14:18-20; Jn 6:64) and the denial by Peter (Mk 14:27-30). He knew Nathaniel before he saw him (Jn 1:47-50), and he knew what was in the minds of people (Jn 2:24-25).[43]

Later, prophets in the church told of events to come (Acts 11:27-28; 13:1; 15:32; 21:9-11; 1 Cor 12:28-29; 14:29, 37; Eph 4:11).[44] Indeed, "the prophet's ability to foretell the future is rooted in God's foresight or foreknowledge" (Acts 3:18; 7:52; Gal 3:8; 1 Pet 1:11).[45] Thus the handing over of Jesus was not accidental or unexpected but was "in accord with God's decided purpose and foreknowledge of what would happen" (Acts 2:23, 25, 30-31).[46] Acts 4:28 speaks of Jesus' death as foreordained to happen *(proorizō)* Craig posits that we cannot be sure from these passages "that foreknowledge is based on foreordination rather than the reverse." He asks whether God's foreordination might not "be based on his knowledge of what Herod, Pilate, and the others would do should Christ be sent." Technically, this would not be foreknowledge but middle knowledge.[47]

God foreknows future contingencies such as "the results of Nebuchadnezzar's divinations to determine his battle routes" (Ezek 21:21-23). He knows the thoughts the psalmist will have (Ps 139:1-6) "from far away." Craig takes the latter phrase to be indicative of temporal distance, a statement that "God knows the psalmist's thoughts long before he thinks them."[48]

Response to arguments from Scripture against divine foreknowledge. There are passages that appear to indicate divine ignorance about the future free reactions of his people, an ignorance that is shared by his prophets (Gen 18:20-21; Jer 26:3; 36:3; Ezek 12:3). Craig considers some of these to be "clearly anthropomorphic."[49] When the Lord appeared to Abraham, for instance, as one of three men, he spoke of "going down to see" what was happening in Sodom. Of further significance, however, is the fact that what God was "ignorant" of, in that instance, was not the future but the past and present, which God clearly knows, as is indicated even within this passage (Gen 18:12-15). Elsewhere, indications that people might repent are not an expression of ignorance "but rather an assurance to the listeners that it is not too late for them to change and avert disaster." However, in Ezekiel's case God knew that the people would not repent, but he insisted that Ezekiel proclaim the message anyway (Ezek 2:5, 7; 33:31-33; likewise, Is 48:8).[50]

On some occasions, God predicts that something will happen but then repents so that it does not (Is 38:1-5; Amos 7:1-6; Jon 3). Craig considers the most plausible interpretation of these instances to be the existence of the implicit condition "all things remaining the same." Hence, they were predictions of what would happen unless people responded properly to God. In this light, the reactions of Hezekiah, Amos and the people of Nineveh were appropriate because they did not know if the prophecy contained "conditions that made it possible to avert disaster." This was made explicit in Jeremiah's prophecy to Zedekiah (Jer 38:17-18), and the general principle is stated in Ezekiel 33:14-15.[51]

We find other biblical prophecies, however, that were not inferred from present causes and were not just forewarnings but were instances of genuine foreknowledge. Craig notes that examples of fulfilled prophecy, such as are cited above, are explained away as (1) a declaration by God of what he himself intends to bring about, (2) inferences from present causes or (3) conditional predictions of what will happen *if* something else happens. He responds that if (3) does not reduce to (1) or (2), it is evidence of middle knowledge and that the Gospel writers clearly did not interpret Jesus' predictions in terms of (2). It is true that many prophecies are based on God's intention (Is 48:3) and demonstrate God's omnipotence rather than his omniscience, but all the instances cannot be placed into type (1) because that would negate human freedom, in the form to which those who reject foreknowledge are committed to it. On the contrary, God is depicted as knowing future events that he does not directly cause, as in the prediction regarding Cyrus (Is 44:28—45:1).[52]

God Has Knowledge of Future Counterfactuals
or "Middle Knowledge"

Biblical evidence for middle knowledge. Some sixteenth-century Jesuit theologians cited 1 Samuel 23:6-13 and Matthew 11:20-24 as biblical indications of divine middle knowledge.[53] In the first case God told David what the men of Keilah would do if he entered their territory. Being told that were he to go to Keilah, they would hand him over to Saul, David did not go. In the second passage Jesus pronounced woe upon the people of Chorazin and Bethsaida because miracles had been done in their midst that would have led the people of Tyre and Sidon to repent, had the signs been done in those cities. In both of those cases, it was assumed that God demonstrated knowledge of future free acts, that is, of what people would freely do *if* particular circumstances existed. The Dominicans (Thomist model) rejected middle knowledge, and they argued instead that counterfactual knowledge is part of God's free knowledge so that there was only natural knowledge prior to God's decree.[54]

William Craig and Robert Cook both consider the two biblical passages equivocal. First Samuel 23 "could be explained on the basis of God's knowledge of the present character of Saul and the men of Keilah." Matthew 11 "is probably religious hyperbole meant to underscore the depth of the depravity of the cities in which Jesus preached." However, the inconclusiveness of specific biblical evidence is not considered to be a serious problem. Cook postulates that conditional prophecy may be viewed as indicative of middle knowledge. "God warns the people by presenting them with a genuine possible future."[55] Furthermore, in the opinion of Craig "the doctrine is so fruitful in illuminating divine prescience, providence, and predestination that it can be presumed unless there are insoluble objections to it."[56] For precisely this reason it was appropriated by Jacob Arminius, Thomas Goad and John Wesley.[57]

Support from human experience. Robert Cook has argued that "the psychical research of the past hundred years or so may be interpreted to lend weight to the possibility of middle knowledge since many of the subjects are warned by the premonition and alter their behaviour accordingly."[58] He cites the case of Susan Anthony who dreamed that she was being burned alive in her hotel room. She and her niece left the hotel immediately, and the next day it burned to the ground.[59] It is particularly significant that "what seems to have been foreseen was not the actual future but a possible one."[60]

For demonstration of the existence of foreknowledge, even among humans, Lindsay Dewar refers us to the work of the Society for Psychical Research.[61] Like Cook, in this research he finds evidence of precognition, which might be called "conditional foreknowledge" and which is not deterministic. The story is told of a Lady Z who dreamed of driving in a street near Piccadilly and of her coachman falling off the box onto his head in the road, crushing his hat. The next day, she notices the coachman leaning back as he had done in the dream, and she calls to him to stop and urges a policeman to catch him, which the policeman does, preventing the foreseen fall. Dewar cites this as a clear example of foreknowledge that is not deterministic, and he posits that "God foreknows not a single possibility—like Lady Z—but all the possibilities, and that He is able to exercise His power accordingly." This would not necessarily give God complete and detailed control over all that happens, "but we shall probably not be going too far if we believe that it will give Him sufficient influence over the course of events to prevent accidents of the 'unfortunate' type from happening to those who seek to identify their wills with His."[62]

Response to objections against middle knowledge. The philosophical objection has been made that counterfactual statements about what a person would have freely done under different circumstances cannot be true. It is argued that since these are statements about what never in fact exists but only what would exist if things were different, then "they do not correspond to reality and so cannot be true." However, Craig notes, this objection rests on the same basis as the one made against foreknowledge, as described above.[63] Consequently, the response to this objection is the same as the answer given previously: "The view of truth as correspondence requires only that such actions *would* be taken if the specified circumstances *were* to exist." What makes counterfactual statements true is what makes any statement true—correspondence. In the case of counterfactual statements there does not need to be an existent reality to which the statements correspond. They correspond to the reality that *would* exist, under other circumstances.[64]

From the theological standpoint, it is asked why God would have actualized a world in which so many are lost if he desires all people to be saved. Craig posits that "some people, no matter how much the Spirit of God worked on their hearts, no matter how favorable their upbringing, no matter how many times or ways they heard the gospel, would still refuse to bow the knee and give their lives to Christ." They would believe only if God coerced them. Therefore, God cannot be blamed for creating a world in which such people are lost.[65] To those who then question why God did not create a world in which such people do not exist, Craig replies that "it is possible that no matter what world God created, someone would be stiff-necked and refuse to believe in Christ." The more persons God creates, the more probable this becomes. It is assumed that God is not "able to create a world in which all persons freely receive Christ" but that he preferred "to create a world in which many people are saved and a few lost than to create a world in which a handful of people are saved and nobody lost."[66] S. T. Davis postulates that the existence of a group of the saved may depend upon there having been some who were lost. A given Christian may have a personal identity that depends on having been conceived with certain genes that were only available in a father who freely chooses to rebel throughout his life.[67]

There may well have been other possible worlds in which the balance would have been worse. Or it might be that a world with fewer people in hell would also have fewer in heaven. It is even possible, surmises Craig, that "all who are lost would have been lost in any world in which God actualized them." We may suppose that God "has providentially ordered things in such a way that those who are lost are those who would never have been saved in any case."[68] In regard to the unevangelized, Craig speculates that, in God's providence, he may have "so arranged the world that those who never in fact hear the gospel are persons who would not respond to it if they did hear it. God brings the gospel to all those who he knows will respond to it if they hear it."[69]

The same question that has been raised regarding the perdition of people who do not believe can be addressed to all manner of evils in the world that God has chosen to actualize. The free will defense takes account of the logical limitations placed upon God by the range of possibilities in a world of free creatures. Alvin Plantinga, another proponent of middle knowledge, applies the argument to the broader picture of evils in the world in his classic statement of the free-will defense, which appeals to the concept of "transworld depravity."

> A world containing creatures who are significantly free (and freely perform more good than evil actions) is more valuable, all else being equal, than a world containing no free creatures at all. Now God can create free creatures, but He cannot *cause* or *determine* them to do only what is right. For if He does so, then they are not significantly free after all; they do not do what is right *freely*. To create creatures capable of *moral good,* therefore, He must create creatures capable of moral evil; and He cannot give these creatures the freedom to perform evil and at the same time prevent them from doing so. As it

turned out, sadly enough, some of the free creatures God created went wrong in the exercise of their freedom; this is the source of moral evil. The fact that free creatures sometimes go wrong, however, counts neither against God's omnipotence nor against His goodness; for He could have forestalled the occurrence of moral evil only by removing the possibility of moral good.[70]

Although Craig does not think that there is conclusive biblical evidence that God has middle knowledge, he supports it by arguing that the alternative would be unacceptable. The most serious problem is that God would be unable to plan if he only has simple foreknowledge, that is, if he only knows what will actually happen but not what *would happen* if the circumstances were different. If God knew that humans would sin, for instance, there would be no way that he could act on the basis of that knowledge to keep it from happening.[71] To do so would be to change the future, which is logically impossible. In the scheme of simple foreknowledge, God has to make his plan logically prior to his precognition of the future. But if God has no middle knowledge, "then in that prior moment we must say either with the Thomists that God decrees which world to actualize and then strongly actualizes it by causing the wills of secondary agents to choose this way or that," or we must assert that "God's actualizing a world is a blind act without planning or direction or knowing of the result." The first option "makes God the author of sin, as Molina charged." The second is inconsistent with the biblical concept of creation (Prov 8:22-31).[72]

With Middle Knowledge, God Is Able to Achieve His Purposes Even Though His Creatures Act Freely

"Molina defines providence as the ordering of things to their end either directly by God Himself or mediately through secondary causes."[73] But, as the situation looks to William Craig, if God had foreknowledge but did not have middle knowledge, he "would find himself, so to speak, with knowledge of the future but without any logically prior planning of that future."[74] There would be a sense in which "what God knows in the logical moment after the decision to create must come as a total surprise to him." He finds himself "with a world and a future." Craig does not deny that this is possible, but it strikes him as "certainly peculiar," and it "diminishes the role of God's wisdom in creation."[75] Without recourse to middle knowledge, "there would be no explanation of why God finds himself with this foreknowledge rather than foreknowledge of some other eventuality. About the only answer that could be given would be, 'That's just the way it happens to be.'"[76]

Given middle knowledge, however, God is able to "bring it about that creatures will achieve his ends and purposes and that they will do so *freely*." It is assumed that "everything which happens comes to pass either by the will or by the permission of God." He wills good things directly, and he desires that we will choose to do good in whatever circumstances we find ourselves. "But he permits sin and allows creatures to do the sinful acts he knew they would do, since he wills creatures to be free." God arranges things providentially, however, so that "in the end even the sinful acts of creatures will serve to achieve his purposes." The words of Joseph to his brothers who had sold him into slavery are paradigmatic of this divine providence. What they intended for evil against Joseph, God had meant for good (Gen 50:20).[77]

Molina distinguished between God's absolute and conditional intentions for creatures. It is his absolute intention that no one should sin but that all should reach beatitude. This intention can be frustrated by free creatures. His conditional intention, however, takes account of what free creatures would do, and it cannot, therefore, be frustrated. God wisely orders which states of affairs come to be so that his purposes are achieved "despite and even through the sinful, free choices of creatures. God thus providentially arranges for everything that does happen by either willing or permitting it, and He causes everything to happen insofar as He concurs with the decisions of free creatures in producing their effects, yet He does so in such a way as to preserve freedom and contingency." Hereby, resolution of the tension between divine sovereignty and human freedom is addressed through the appeal to middle knowledge.[78]

Although God wills positively every good creaturely decision, he merely permits but does not will evil decisions. Molina put it thus:

> The *evil* acts of the created will are subject as well to divine predetermination and providence to the extent that the causes from which they emanate and the general concurrence on God's part required to elicit them are granted through divine predetermination and providence—though not in order that *these particular acts* should emanate from them, but rather in order that *other, far different, acts* might come to be, and in order that the innate freedom of the things endowed with a will might be preserved for their maximum benefit; in addition evil acts are subject to that same divine predetermination and providence to the extent that they cannot exist in particular unless God by His providence *permits them in particular* in the service of some greater good. It clearly follows from the above that all things

without exception are *individually* subject to God's will and providence, which intend certain of them *as particulars* and permit the rest *as particulars*. Thus, the leaf hanging from the tree does not fall, nor does either of the two sparrows sold for a farthing fall to the ground, nor does anything else whatever happen without God's providence and will either *intending* it *as a particular* or *permitting* it *as a particular.*[79]

Molina rejected the Thomist concept of divine concurrence in terms of *premotion,* and proposed, instead, the concept of *simultaneous* concurrences, because he considered the former position to be deterministic and incompatible with the existence of sin.[80] In what came to be known as the doctrine of premotion, Aquinas had posited that God not only supplies and preserves the power of operation in every secondary cause, he acts on them to produce their actual operations. In contingent acts of the will, God causes the will to turn itself one way or the other, but human freedom is not annulled because the will is caused to turn itself *freely*. Molina proposed instead that God acts *with,* rather than *on,* the secondary cause to produce its effect.[81] "He compares divine concurrence with secondary causes to two men pulling a boat: there are two causes cooperating to produce a single, total effect. Thus, when a man wills to produce some effect, God concurs with the man's decision by also acting to produce that effect; but He does not act on the man's will to move it to its decision."[82]

Were creatures to choose differently, as they are free to do, things would turn out differently. Then, of course, God would have possessed different middle knowledge than he does, and he "would have chosen a different providential plan to bring about his ends." Thus God will certainly achieve his ends, and it is the infallibility of his middle knowledge that makes it possible for him to do so without infringing upon the freedom of his creatures.[83]

The application of middle knowledge in the area of predestination to salvation is particularly illuminating. Scripture speaks of God's foreknowledge of the elect (Rom 8:29; 1 Pet 1:1-2). Previously we encountered the proposal that election is corporate and that God has simply foreordained that those who believe should inherit eternal life. The openness model denied that God foreknows which individuals this will entail, but the model in the divine intervention model (and Wesleyan theology generally) asserted that God elects those whom he foreknows will freely believe. The middle knowledge position is able to assert with traditional Calvinists that particular individuals are predestined to salvation. But it denies that God chose to actualize this particular world in which these individuals believe and are saved *with the specific intention of saving them as individuals.* "God simply chooses the world he wants, and whoever in that world would freely receive Christ is, by the very act of God's selection of that world, predestined."[84] Therefore, their election is both God's free decision and the consequence of their libertarianly free choice to believe. By the same token, since God gives everyone sufficient grace in all possible worlds, those who are lost have no one to blame but themselves.[85] Election is simultaneous with predestination and reprobation is not a counterpart to it. Instead it corresponds to approbation.[86]

Because God wills for everyone to be saved, he provides sufficient grace for salvation for each person. "In his middle knowledge, however, he knows who, as circumstances vary, would freely accept and who would freely reject" his gracious initiatives to draw them to himself. As a result, the act of selecting a world to be created is a sort of predestination. The persons whom God knew would respond will do so and will be saved. They are still free to reject God's grace, but, of course, if they did so, God's middle knowledge would have been different than it is. Those who are not saved are lost because they reject God's grace, which is why they are not predestined. This is their own responsibility, and the reason for their perdition does not lie in any insufficiency of God's grace. "In fact, many of the unsaved may actually receive greater divine assistance and drawing than do the saved."[87] On Molina's view we might say that it is "up to God whether we find ourselves in an order in which we are predestined, but that it is up to us whether we are predestined in the order in which we find ourselves."[88]

The great usefulness of middle knowledge is evident in the way that people appeal to the concept even though they are unfamiliar with the term. An instance of this is cited below, but Craig finds that the idea of middle knowledge is commonly called upon in discussions of the salvation of infants who die in infancy. Sometimes the assumption is made that God judges them on the basis of what they would have done *if* they had grown up. Similarly, in discussing the fate of the unevangelized, it has been suggested that "God bases his judgment on what would have happened if someone had heard the gospel. It is part of God's omniscience to know not only what will happen, but also what would happen if a different set of circumstances were to occur."[89] At the "moment" logically prior to God's free decision to create the world, the counterfactuals concerning human freedom were true. That is to say, it was then true that if particular individuals existed in particular circumstances, they would act in specific ways. That such individuals or such circumstances are never actualized is no contradiction of the truth of the counterfactual statements concerning them.

Because of His Middle Knowledge, God Is Able to Make His Provision Dependent on Freely Offered Petitions While Still Ensuring That Essential Goods Are Requested

Some people have objected to the whole concept of petitionary prayer because a good God would do the best that he could do for his creatures and would not make his doing of good dependent upon the request of his creatures. To indicate the reprehensibleness of this situation, analogy is made to parents who know what is good for their child but who withhold it because they have made the supply of these goods dependent on the child's asking. Eleonore Stump has argued against this line of thought in favor of the validity of God's doing some good only in answer to petition. She reasons that this is important to the development of our personal relationship with God.[90] (We met the same point in Vincent Brümmer's work, under the openness model.)

To Stump's argument Michael Murray and Kurt Meyers add the factor of middle knowledge. "A God who exercises providence in light of such conditional future contingents can be sure, prior to creation, that even in a world in which provision hangs on petitions, there will never be individuals who are unjustly denied provision because of lack of petition." By virtue of his middle knowledge God can "know what creatures will petition for across the possible worlds." If there is a world in which a situation exists "in which God knows that (a) the creature needs some good, the provision of which God has made dependent on the creature's petitioning for it, and (b) the creature will not petition for the good, then God will not actualize that world." By this means God "could make provision hang on freely offered creaturely petition with no risk that creatures will fail to petition for a good essential to their well-being."[91]

Murray and Meyers argue that God's situation is significantly different from that of the parents described above because the parents are ignorant of what the children will ask for, whereas God is not. Furthermore, God knows exactly how either granting or denying our petitions will add to or detract from our well-being. He knows, for example, what would overwhelm us and what would make us thankful, what would lead us to idolatry and what would make us resentful. He knows "how to distinguish those goods that should depend on the petitioner's request from those which should not."[92] As to the practice of corporate petitionary prayer, justification is found "in light of the fact that God has an overriding desire to cultivate and maintain a harmonious interdependence amongst members of the church." Since corporate prayer can contribute to this, "God can justifiably make the procurement of various (important) goods hang on believers petitioning God in this way."[93]

Middle knowledge proponents would concur with those committed to the models previously reviewed that libertarian freedom is critical to the genuine efficacy of petitionary prayer. The entire course of the particular history of our world is known to God and is indeed God's choice, as a whole, but not with a view to the predestination of every particular within that history. The actions taken by individuals within that history are the outworking of their own free decisions. God, as another free being, is able to work within the world in ways that will not negate human freedom. Consequently we are in a position to affect the future by our petitions. What is yet future to us is known by God precisely because it is the future that comes into being through free divine and human actions. For reasons described above, God has chosen to do some things only in answer to our petitions. We are able, therefore, to contribute to bringing about states of affairs that would not otherwise be realized, by successfully requesting God to act. By the same token, we can assume that some goods will not be realized if we fail to petition God for them. Prayer literally "changes things," though it obviously does not change the future, since that is a logical impossibility.

William Lane Craig notes that people often assume middle knowledge in prayer, even though they may be unaware of their assumption. They pray for guidance, for instance, on the assumption that "God knows which of two paths would be better for them to take."[94] If God had only simple foreknowledge, he would know what they were actually going to choose and what its outcome would be, but he would not be in a position to give guidance before the decision is made, based on his knowledge of what would result from each of the two possible courses of action.

On the matter of praying for something that has already occurred but about which we are ignorant, Craig denies that this is backward causation. The prayer does not effect something in the past, but God, who foreknew the prayer, has brought something about in response to the foreknown prayer. A father whose son was on a ship that has been wrecked may legitimately pray for that son's safety, provided he is unaware of his son's situation. On the basis of that foreknown petition, God may have already decided to save the son when the shipwreck occurs. Technically, "retrospective prayer (just like the truth of future-tense statements and God's foreknowledge based on them) does not involve backward causation, even if such prayer has many of the same practical consequences as does backward causation."[95] When we pray concerning the future, we are not asking God to make happen what *will* happen. We are asking "that he *will* make something happen." In the same way, when we pray about something that has happened (though we are ignorant of its outcome), we are not asking God to make something that has happened not have happened. We are "asking that at the time of the past event He should then have done" what was needed. With regard to both the past and the future, we are not asking God to do the illogical, to change the facts.[96]

Since Scripture neither encourages nor gives an example of prayer for the past, Craig leaves the issue to the individual Christian conscience. On the one hand, Jesus taught his disciples to pray in the knowledge that their heavenly Father knows what they need before they ask him (Mt 6:8). "But he did not say that God answers prayer prior to its being offered." Craig surmises that Jesus may have "had in the back of his mind the promise of Isaiah 65:24: 'Before they call I will answer, while they are yet speaking I will hear.'" In that circumstance, the answer clearly precedes the prayer, "but even so, there is no suggestion here that we should pray for the past."[97]

The Case Study

Andrew Martin is a person who likes to understand how things work, and he is frustrated when he cannot figure out how particular facts relate to one another. It seemed obvious to him that people are free in a libertarian way: they have genuine choices and are not simply acting in ways that are predetermined. He had engaged in long discussions with Oliver (openness model) about human freedom because Oliver contended that if things were known ahead of time, then they were certain and hence determined: if God knew what we were going to do before we do it, then we are not really free to choose to do otherwise. Andrew's problem was that it seemed so clear to him from Scripture that God *does* know the future and is able to predict it; indeed God had done so through his prophets. Andrew struggled with these two "facts," that we are libertarianly free but that God knows and even seems to have decided the future. Things finally came together for him when he came across a book on "middle knowledge." The author argued that God not only knows the actual future but also all possibilities. From all the possible worlds that could have been, God has chosen to actualize this particular one. In this world people act freely (in a libertarian or indeterministic sense), but the world as a whole is the one that God chose, and so he knows all about it. This brought things together in a way that made sense to Andrew.

Andrew believed that God was not taken by surprise when the missionaries were abducted. Not only had God known that this was going to happen, he had chosen to actualize the world in which it does happen. Obviously a great deal of history lay behind the day that the guerrillas decided to use the three missionaries as a political bargaining chip. But even given the complex of events that had already occurred, and given the factors at work that day, there was still a range of possible future outcomes. Things could happen in the guerrilla camp, in the missionary homes and elsewhere that would bring about a situation in which the missionaries would not be kidnapped. In addition to the many human or natural variables, God himself had a number of possibilities from which he could choose his own course of action. In fact, God could have acted differently than he had done, months or years prior to the day of the abduction and thereby have brought about a situation very different than the one that had now occurred.

There was no doubt in Andrew's mind that Richard Henderson and his colleagues were in a situation that was part of the world that God had intentionally chosen to actualize. God had not brought the situation about single-handedly. Most of the circumstances that existed were the result of human actions, and many of those actions had been sinful and hence contrary to God's moral will for his creatures. Nonetheless, God could have chosen to actualize a different world than this one, a world in which the abduction had not taken place. It comforted Andrew to know that things were in God's control, as far as the large picture was concerned. He believed that God had a good plan toward which all of this was working, even though individual events along the way were tragic and were brought about through evil and sin. Andrew was also convinced that God wanted the Christian friends of Fred Henderson to get involved in bringing good out of this situation. There were some things that they could do personally, but many things were outside of their power and could only be done by God. So petitionary prayer was one of the most important things that the believers in that congregation could do.

Andrew had discussed the matter of prayer with Oliver (openness model) and Tom (redemptive intervention model) on a number of occasions. All three of them believed that God had given humans libertarian freedom, and this meant that much of what happens in the world depends on what people decide and what they do. But the three of them disagreed about how much room God had left himself to accomplish what *he* wants in the world, and they had discovered that the critical factor in this regard was the extent of God's knowledge of the future. Oliver believed that God *could* not know the future actions of libertarianly free creatures and so he had to act and react when the creatures decided what they would do and did it. Of course, God knew what would be best, and he was continually trying to move his creatures and all of his creation toward that goal, but the creatures often chose to disregard God's persuasion and even to disobey his specific commands. Tom, on the other hand, believed that God did know the actual future but that he did not know possible futures, which could have been realized in different circumstances. Both Andrew and Oliver argued against Tom that God's simple knowledge of the future did him no good. There was nothing he could do about the actual future that he foresaw. Tom never conceded that point, but Andrew believed that this was a critical difference between his own understanding and Tom's. By having middle knowledge God had an opportunity to decide what his action would be in a particular situation and then to foresee how the situation would develop when his own action was inserted into the complex of causative factors. In Andrew's model of providence, God's decision concerning his own action was not on an ad hoc basis (as Oliver proposed), it was made ahead of time when God chose the particular world that he actualized.

As Andrew prayed, he believed that God had known that he would pray this prayer. Andrew's free act of praying had been part of the world that God chose to actualize. Because of this, God had already decided on the course of action that he would take in response to Andrew's prayer. In fact, it would not matter if an effective answer to Andrew's prayer required God to have begun acting some time ago in order for the deliverance of the missionaries to be brought about now. God had foreseen Andrew's prayer, and he could already have begun to answer it even before it is spoken.

Thus Andrew believed that his prayer for Richard and the others could bring about a change in their current situation and that it could bring about a different future than the one that would occur if he did not pray. This was not because he had the power to *change* the future but because he had the power to *bring about* a particular future through his involvement in the events leading up to it and particularly through the activity of God, who hears and responds to the prayers of his people.

Andrew prayed: "Dear Lord, I certainly agree with Tom that you have not been taken by surprise in the incident that has taken place. I am also deeply conscious, however, that your knowledge of what has happened does not constitute approval. It is within your goodness and wisdom that evils like this occur, but they are no less evil by virtue of the fact that you have permitted them. We know that the future is already certain, but we are confident that it is not fixed apart from what we and others do. We are actively a part of determining the future, and you have invited us to ask you to act in ways that appear to us to be for the good of your creation and for your glory. It is with that assurance, Lord, that I add my request to those that have already been offered. I too want to see the lives of these three missionaries spared, the lives of their abductors positively directed and good come out of this situation which has such potential for suffering and evil. Dear Father, please hear our prayers and act now to bring deliverance to your children. We pray also that you will give wisdom to those who are in direct contact with the situation, that they may act in ways you know will be productive of the best outcomes. In Jesus' name, we make these requests. Amen."

9

The Thomist Model

I
N THE THOMIST MODEL, GOD IS COMPREHENSIVELY IN CONTROL. EVERYTHING
*that happens is brought about by God as the first or primary cause, but God
acts concurrently with libertarianly free agents so that the actions of moral
creatures are the free choice of the creatures themselves. God's agency in
every event of history determines the outcome, but he usually works through
secondary, creaturely causes, and he works in such a way that the events
are genuinely contingent or dependent upon the actions of the creatures.
God is timeless, and so his own action never precedes the creature's action.
For this reason God has a comprehensive knowledge of all of history past,
present and still future, but he knows it all in his eternal "now" so that he
does not technically have "foreknowledge." It is on account of this timeless
being and knowledge of God that Thomists assert both divine control and
libertarian human freedom, both the certainty of the future and the freedom of the creatures who act to bring that future about.*

*Thomists believe that prayer is an effective contributor to the ultimate
outcome of events in history; it is genuinely "impetratory." In petitionary
prayer we ask God to act in ways we consider wise and good. Although God
knows the future eternally, this does not prevent him from responding to our
prayers. It is precisely because he knows our petitions that he is able to
include answers to our prayers within the plan for the world that he purposed in his timeless eternity.*

In the models presented to this point we have met frequent efforts to correct other models perceived as inadequate. Frequently those proposed amendments addressed some form of the general proposal included in the Thomist and the Calvinist models. This is the position that the proponents of the openness model identify as "the traditional view of God"[1] or that process theologians call "classical theism."[2] It is a perspective that might well be dubbed Augustinian because it is so obviously rooted in Augustine's thought. Representatives of this model frequently cite Augustine as one who set the course properly, although they modify his perspective in various ways. The theologians who work within this model all share a conviction that *nothing happens in the history of creation that is outside of God's sovereign providential control.* This (along with the Barthian and the Calvinist models) would therefore be called "no-risk" models, by contrast with the six models that we have examined thus far. I have chosen to start the presentation of no-risk models with the Thomist representation of this model because this is the means by which the Augustinian tradition has been mediated to so many Christians and because it probably tries the hardest to preserve a strong view of human freedom along with absolute divine sovereignty.[3]

God Is the Primary Cause of All Occurrences in History and Has Comprehensive Knowledge of Past, Present and Future

God as first cause. Thomas Aquinas held that "God is the universal cause of all being" and that God's effective action in causing things to be as they are "reaches to every created effect, so that all effects occur exactly as he intends. Since His causal efficacy is perfect and universal, and since he knows His intention fully, God knows all created things through their cause, which is God Himself."[4] Aquinas incorporated into his theology the Aristotelian concept of causes, which may be formal, efficient or final. He also made use of the "principle that antecedents imply their consequents, and above all, from the *Nichomachean Ethics,* the principle that 'prudence arranges things to an end' or, in Aristotle's words, 'all knowledge and every pursuit aims at some good.'"[5] Benjamin Farley deems this last principle "central to Aquinas's doctrine of providence, as he ultimately conceives of providence as a function of wisdom, thus subsuming it under God's knowledge. Further, since God's knowledge is part of, or one with, his being, providence is subsumed under God's being."[6]

Aquinas understood providence to be God's eternal planned disposition

of all things and divine government to be his temporal disposition and execution of what he has planned from eternity.[7] In God's simplicity both his
knowledge and his will are the cause of all things. "By one act God understands everything in his essence, and similarly by one act he wills everything in his goodness."[8] Aquinas thus asserted that God is the cause of
everything that exists but not in a way that negates the agency of other
causes. He believed in joint causality or concurrence and asserted that
"God is the cause of everything's action inasmuch as he gives everything
the power to act, preserves it in being *and applies it to action,* and inasmuch as by his power every other power acts."[9] In other words, "God
moves the natural cause to action as an instrument of his own power to
produce the effect."[10]

The difference in causal roles is that between first and second cause.
The natural effect "proceeds from God as agent, but from a second cause
as instrument." It is God's causal action that "determines the kind of event
produced."[11] God has given creatures the power to work effects, and so he
is the cause of that power. Therefore, he works through secondary causes
that act in their own right, but they act in the manner in which he ordained
them to function.[12] As primary cause, God is "in a different order from all
instrumental secondary causes."[13] God can produce effects directly, as he
does in the case of miracles, but he usually works through secondary
causes. Consequently, this is not a deterministic world that God has created
because some things are governed by necessary but others by contingent
causes.[14] In the words of Aquinas, "What the divine providence plans to
happen contingently, happens contingently."[15]

Reginald Garrigou-Lagrange sums up the witness of the Old Testament
concerning providence in three statements: (1) it is a "universal and infallible providence" that "directs all things to a good purpose"; but (2) though
providence is an evident fact, "in certain of its ways it remains absolutely
unfathomable"; and (3) its end is the manifestation of the goodness, mercy
and justice of God.[16] The twofold foundation of our hope in God is "His
providence, with its individual care of each one of the just, and His omnipotence."[17] The unfathomability of God's providence comes through most
clearly in the New Testament in regard to the mystery of salvation. Here we
have indication that God wills all to be saved (1 Tim 2:4) but also that we
have nothing that we did not receive (1 Cor 4:7), indicating a selectiveness
in the divine love.[18] In the words of Aquinas, "Since God's love is the cause
of goodness in things, no one thing would be better than another, if God

did not will a greater good for it than for the other."[19] Garrigou-Lagrange asserts that this is reconciled in "the intimate life of God," but it is an inaccessible mystery for us, "too luminous for the feeble eyes of our minds."[20]

Thomist omnicausality stated in modern language. Alan Padgett offers a statement of the Thomistic position in the language of modern science. "God is the cause (among other things) of the basic matter or energy of the universe and of any natural laws."[21] The effect of this, in Thomistic terms, is that "God is the cause of the distinct being *(esse)* which is the essence of each particular thing, at each moment of its existence."[22] Padgett suggests that today we might say that God is "the cause of the essential properties of an object 'hanging together' over time," or that "God is the cause of whatever it is that itself holds these properties together."[23] This does not make God the cause of every effect, but he is "the cause of the essential properties any object has at every episode of its existence, including its causal properties (i.e., its ability to bring about some effect)." Additionally, God is the "cause of the continuing in existence of any object." So then, God's sustaining power is "a necessary but not sufficient cause of every effect in space-time. No physical object can continue to exist apart from the exertion of some power from God." This is because no physical object can continue to exist apart from its essential properties. As Aquinas put it: "Were God to annihilate, it would not be through some action *(per aliquam actionem)* but through the cessation from action."[24] God sustains creation by a direct act in the sense that no causal sequence intervenes to bring about an immediate effect. There is no "created causal chain between the divine cause and its effect."[25]

The basic matter or energy of the universe, the natural laws operative in the universe and the being of each object are all sustained by God. If God acts indirectly, by means of a causal sequence, the elements of that sequence will themselves have to be created and sustained by a direct act of God. Consequently, we can assert that "the power of God is directly involved in any causal sequence in our universe," and no time duration occurs between God's act and its effect, which is true of any direct act of God.[26]

The Will of God

God's wisdom directs, God's will commands, and God's power executes.[27] Of course, God can do only what is possible, not what is logically contradictory.[28] Within those necessary limits, however, God directs all things to their ultimate good,[29] and his will is always fulfilled.[30] Everything that happens takes place under God's control and has been chosen because it contributes to the ultimate good of the creatures, namely, "to return them to himself, to unite them to himself in heaven."[31]

The antecedent and the consequent wills of God. Given that God wills universal salvation (1 Tim 2:4), an objection may be raised that God's will is not always fulfilled. A Thomist response to this objection is to distinguish between the antecedent and consequent will of God. For example, a mother may will always to have a harmonious relationship with her son, but she scolds him when he misbehaves. Her "antecedent will" is to live in harmony with her son, but when he is disobedient, she scolds him as an act of her "consequent will." God always wills what is good but "sometimes what is good absolutely considered is not good in the circumstances. In such cases God may be said to have an inclination *(velleitas)* for the good absolutely considered, but what he actually wills is what is good in the circumstances."[32]

God has an inclination or aim or yearning to save everyone, "but since some persons refuse grace and persist in sin, what God actually wills is not to save some of them."[33] In other words, "God *antecedently* wills what is good absolutely, but he *consequently* wills the good in the circumstances. God antecedently wills all persons to be saved; but he consequently wills that some not be saved."[34] What God wills in his antecedent will is what he ordains for his creatures, so far as it is within his own sole determination. "But when a created person, because of some defect he introduces into himself, hinders himself from coming to the end God ordained for him, then God's willing nonetheless to bring that person to as much good as he is capable of (given the state of his will) is God's consequent will."[35] In regard to the consequent will of God, we can say that all God's acts of will are fulfilled, but this is not true of God's antecedent will.

The divine will of good pleasure and the divine will of expression. A distinction may also be made between "the divine will of good pleasure and the divine will of expression."[36] The will of expression includes God's commands, prohibitions and counsels, and it is what we are asking for when we pray "Thy will be done."[37] God's "will of good pleasure," on the other hand, is the "interior act of God's will" upon which the future depends. We must be obedient to the expressed will of God, but trusting surrender is our appropriate response to the will of God's good pleasure, since we are "certain beforehand that it wills nothing, permits nothing, unless for the spiritual and eternal welfare of those who love God and persevere in that love."[38]

God's knowledge of all things as knowledge of himself. Thomas Flint suggests that the fundamental Thomist criticism of Molinism is the complaint that "Molinism robs God of the supreme independence and power that he as First Cause is required to possess."[39] Contingent beings and truths must be determined by God's will, otherwise God would be passive in his knowledge and would not be pure Act. The counterfactuals of creaturely freedom (things that would happen if particular circumstances obtained that are never, in fact, realized) must therefore be part of God's free knowledge. For the Thomist, *"any* possible world is such that God had the power to actualize it."[40] God fully determines which world is actual, and therefore "the passage from natural to free knowledge is accomplished immediately upon his creative act of will." Since that act of will has eternally been present in God, "he has eternally known exactly what was going to happen; that is, he possesses complete and perfect knowledge." God's providence includes foresight, and his knowledge does not grow in any significant sense as time passes. There is nothing that "does or can take a provident God by surprise."[41]

It is because God is the cause of all things that he has divine knowledge of every detail, "for obviously God knows all that He does Himself and all that He concurs in producing." In the case of sin, God *"merely permits it,* tolerates it in view of some greater good. It is through this permission that He has knowledge of it; and He sees it in its final overthrow, which in its own way will once more contribute to the manifestation of the good."[42] In one eternal instant, "God sees the entire succession of time periods," and he "sees the effects in their causes, and the means in the ends they subserve."[43]

The place of miracle within the divine omnicausality. If God is the cause of all that happens, there might appear to be a flattening out of the divine action were it not that God does not always work in the same way. This difference allows for the category of special divine action that is called *miracle.* In the thought of Aquinas, both nature and miracle are aspects of God's providence, and God's activity remains hidden in both, but each displays his power in its own way. The effects of natural things produce wonder in those who do not know the cause, as in the drawing of iron to a magnet, for example. By the same token, God's secret working in all things produces wonder in humans, but certain of those works are particularly wonder producing because they surpass the usual power of God's work in nature.[44]

Aquinas distinguished three levels of miracles. First are those that are *above* nature, "in which God induces a form into matter which nature is utterly incapable of inducing."[45] Examples are the incarnation and the glorified body. A second level, *contrary* to or *against* nature, in the individual sense, may be done by nature itself, as when the moon causes the tide to rise, against the nature of water or when a stone is thrown upward. Nature might be able to produce what is produced but not in this manner. Miracles of healing are in this category, as is the resurrection, since nature can produce life but not in a corpse. At a third level miracles are accomplished *without* nature, in any of three ways: either because (1) the processes of nature are dispensed with, as in the turning of the water into wine in Cana, or (2) God acts more copiously, as when he produced the plague of frogs, or (3) God produces at once what nature only produces by degrees, instanced in the cure of the fever of Peter's mother-in-law.

In summary, miracles surpass nature in the substance of the deed, in that which is done, or in the measure and order of what is done. In its relationship to God, universal nature has the status of particular nature. Indeed there is a sense in which God does nothing contrary to nature "because the nature of each thing is what God does in it." This was a concept Aquinas cited from Augustine.[46] However, Aquinas does not consistently speak in this manner, and it is clear that he does conceive of God as occasionally acting in a way that is outside his usual operation in nature, in a supernatural way.

Within the Divine Omnicausality God's Creatures Exercise Libertarianly Free Agency

Augustine's affirmation of human freedom. Augustine affirmed the necessity of free will because "without it, man sins either by virtue of his nature or contrary to the will of God."[47] He insisted (against Cicero) that foreknowledge is not only compatible with human freedom, it is the cause of it.[48] On the other hand, he denied that God's foreknowledge of the future is a causal condition of sin and evil. These come about because people elect them, and they will certainly come to pass but not because God's foreknowledge makes it inevitable. In his *City of God* Augustine objects to accounts of historical events that attribute these events to fortune, fate or astrological phenomena, but he also objects to Stoic hard-determinism. He deems the Stoics correct to believe that "God allows all things before they come to pass" but in error because they fail to understand "that what God allows in the moral order includes the free choices of men. Hence Augustine is willing to concede that God 'is the Cause of all causes,' but 'not of all choices.'"[49]

Furthermore, Augustine argued that divine foreknowledge does not vitiate human accountability. Rather, "our choices fall within the order of the causes which is known for certain to God and is contained in His foreknowledge—for human choices are the cause of human acts."[50] Benjamin Farley observes that Augustine's synthesis brought to an end the patristic period, for he retained the necessity of free will that his predecessors had insisted upon, but he recognized the bondage of the human will to concupiscence and ignorance in a way not characteristic of the older tradition, "stretching as far back as Hesiod's 'far-seeing son of Cronos,' which posits that God's election is based on his foreknowledge of man's free choices."[51]

Compatibilism in Thomism. Aquinas believed that God is the universal cause of all things, but he also taught that rational agents have freedom of choice. In other words, his was a compatibilist position. Although "God moves the will with necessity toward the universal good which is the natural end of the rational agent," the will is "moved toward particular goods according to the practical judgment of reason."[52] Thomists believe that "human acts are true causes," even though they "obtain certain effects in the manner determined by God."[53] The will is not moved with necessity by any finite object because the will does not only move itself to act, it also moves "all other powers of the being insofar as their acts can be apprehended. Hence the will can move the practical judgements of reason as it likes, in addition to moving itself to act." Thus the will has control not only "over *whether* it chooses (the exercise of its act), but also over *which object* it will choose (the specification of its act)."[54]

Humans are free agents in that "no created temporally antecedent causes to the free act of choice are sufficient to determine that act."[55] That is to say, what we do cannot be explained by the sum of the created and temporal causes that exist prior to our acting. We are able to choose or not to choose any finite object that we apprehend, given the full set of created causes that are exerting influence upon us. "The will determines its own act through the exercise of its own power." At the same time, however, Thomists have held that "God immediately applies each agent to each free act in a fully determinate and efficacious manner." The divine premotion, as it is called, is "prior in nature, but not in time, to the free act" and is "compatible with the agent's freely moving himself or herself to act."

Thomas Loughran thus deems Thomism to be a form of compatibilism, in contrast to the libertarian account offered by Molinism, which we presented in the previous chapter. What makes this a compatibilist position is the manner in which it factors the direct divine causality into the final outcome. Both human freedom and divine causation are asserted.[56] "God's movement of the will does not preclude the will's moving itself,"[57] but "the divine motion enables the will to move itself in virtue of the first motion, just as the craftsman who applies the ax to the wood does not preclude but enables the ax to cut, even while the craftsman cuts the wood by means of the ax."[58]

God "communicates the dignity of causality" to us by governing the lower creation through the higher.[59] However, Thomas Flint observes that "the kind of divine activity that the Thomists see as compatible with human freedom would not be deemed compatible by those with libertarian inclinations" because of their conviction that "what an agent does freely is genuinely up to the agent to do freely or refrain from doing freely; no external circumstance, no other agent, does or even can determine what I do freely."[60] From the Thomist perspective, what preserves the freedom of the human agent, given the operation of God's action, is that the "actions by which God determines our free actions are not prior to, but concurrent with those actions." For example, if someone performs a commendable action, the Thomist will insist that the action was "determined by God's bestowal of intrinsically efficacious grace." But as already noted, "such grace is generally viewed as cooperating rather than prevenient. It is present *when* one acts, but not *before* one acts; otherwise one would have the dreaded determinism of circumstances."[61]

Flint is probably correct that the Thomist picture of simultaneous divine determinism will strike the "true libertarian" as being just as destructive of human freedom as is a determinism that posits physical laws or prior states as determinative.[62] However, from the perspective of the Thomist the difference is significant. What preserves the moral quality of a person's act is that the agent's being moved by another does not prevent its being moved from within itself.[63] God's moving of the will in a general way, by sustaining its nature, or in particular ways directly through grace, does not preclude the will's moving itself as a secondary efficient cause.[64]

Self-determinism. An evangelical Thomist, Norman Geisler accordingly rejects both moral determinism and moral indeterminism in favor of moral *self-determinism*. He finds moral indeterminism incoherent because "every event has an adequate cause."[65] Moreover, he argues, it is inappropriate to draw philosophical conclusions from Heisenberg's principle of indeterminacy at the subatomic level. This is because the subatomic realm is not observable without investigator interference, and the unpredictability may be the result of our attempts to observe. Further, even at the subatomic level the principle does not state that there is no cause, only that we cannot predict where a given particle will be at a given time. It is "not the principle of uncausality but the principle of unpredictability."[66] Geisler therefore criticizes Bruce Reichenbach's proposal (redemptive interventionist model) because it underestimates the extent of God's control. "All free events," Geisler asserts, "are also determined," and Reichenbach has offered "no good reason why we should give up the strong sense of omnipotence which is at the heart of orthodox theology."[67]

On the other hand, the moral determinism "espoused by people from Jonathan Edwards to Gordon Clark" (the Calvinist model) is also considered problematic by Geisler because it makes God the efficient cause of all free choices, including evil actions, and it eliminates moral responsibility.[68] In fact, on the moral determinist scheme only God is free, since he can decide contrary to his desires, but we cannot.[69] Geisler deems the solution to be self-determinism, the reality that acts are caused by oneself. Either God's acts are not free or else our free actions, like God's, are self-determined.[70] In Geisler's view, John Feinberg's problem (within the Calvinist model) is that he confuses efficient with final causality. It is not the "reason" that brings about an action, it is the agent who can reject even the best desires or reasons.[71] It is commonly assumed in Calvinist doctrines of providence, following Jonathan Edwards, that we always act "for a reason" and so if one completely knows a person's reasons, motivations, inclinations and so on, one can predict what that person will do in a given set of circumstances. This is described as a moral determinism because the factors determining the person's action are internal. It is the person who chooses to act in this way. But Geisler, with his commitment to *self*-determinism, does not wish anything other than the person herself to be the final cause of the act she does.

It makes no sense, in the opinion of Norman Geisler, to ask the cause of the actor; "the free moral agent is the cause of free moral actions." Technically, therefore, "free will is not the efficient cause of a free act; free will is simply the power through which the agent performs the free act. The efficient cause of the free act is really the free *agent,* not the free will."[72] If it were impossible for humans to be the first causes of their own actions, then it would also be impossible for God. The question therefore reduces to whether God is the only true agent, that is to say, the only genuine person. God is able to determine the future without violating human free choice because "the interaction between sovereignty and free choice is immediate."[73] "God is the cause of the fact of freedom, and humans are the causes of the acts of freedom. God made the agent, but the agents cause the actions." Acting in time, from his timeless eternity, God's will acts on the human will directly, by his infinite power and wisdom.[74] Geisler wants to assert then that "God is determining moral actions by his knowledge of what, by unfettered free choice, we are causing to happen. In this case our actions are self-caused (that is, caused by us), even though God determinately knew (and knowingly determined) we would so choose."[75] "God-given desires, reasoning and persuasion can be conditions of a free choice. But they are not the cause. That is, they are not the sufficient causal condition of our action." If they were, then the human agent would not be the efficient cause of the action but only the instrumental cause through which God's action is exercised. In that case, any moral blame due would be directed at God.[76] Geisler charges Reichenbach with having posited a false disjunction by insisting that either a free act is caused by God's knowledge or vice versa. There is a third alternative, namely, that "God's eternal knowledge can determine that the act be caused freely. In this case God neither produces the act, nor does the act produce God's knowledge." Instead God "simply knows (eternally and determinately) what we choose to do," and the act is "both determined from the standpoint of God's knowledge and yet free from the point of view of the agent's choice."[77]

The real contingency of human actions. In the Thomist model, God provides each being with a natural inclination genuinely its own, yet one that also expresses his purposes. "He endows every creature with an intrinsic nature and a way of acting, and leaves it free to follow the goal toward which it strives." He then "acts on each level of being in accordance with its character." Where the human will is involved, "God moves it from within, inclining it toward the good, calling forth its own powers, so its free acts remain its own. Here his influence is the final causality of attraction to the good, and God's action becomes the power of love."[78]

As Aquinas understood the situation, God foresees not only effects but also causes. He foresees free causes acting freely and necessary causes act-ing necessarily.[79] God knows a person perfectly "in the intimacy of cre-ation, and because of his infallible knowledge of that being in its cause, he has an infallible knowledge of that being in its effects."[80] In spite of the fact that nothing occurs that is not part of God's providence, Thomists contend that contingency is not ruled out. Garrigou-Lagrange insists that the abso-lute universality of providence "safeguards the freedom of our actions," rather than destroying it. Indeed God actuates our liberty. "By moving vol-untary causes," God "does not deprive their actions of being voluntary, but rather He is the cause of this very thing in them."[81] This is because provi-dence extends to the free mode of our actions, which it produces in us with our cooperation; "for this free mode in our choice, this indifference dominating our desire is still within the realm of being, and nothing exists unless it be from God." In God's providential wisdom he knows "the slight-est idiosyncrasy of temperament and character, the consequences of hered-ity, the influence exerted on our actions by the emotions." His providence "penetrates into the innermost recesses of conscience, and has at its dis-posal every sort of grace to enlighten, attract, and strengthen us."[82]

There are human acts that God permits within his consequent will that are not good in themselves, but the allowance of which, in the particular circumstances, is a good thing. Not to do this "would require undermining the nature he created, and the loss of being and hence of goodness entailed by doing so is a greater loss of being than whatever loss may be incurred by the evil God permits." However, God permits an evil only if he can direct it to some good.[83]

Everything that occurs is therefore willed by God, either as part of his original plan for his creatures or as "part of his consequent will warranting as good in the circumstances something he would reject considered uncon-ditionally."[84] The reason this does not rule out contingency is that some things that happen occur contingently "because God has prepared contin-gent causes from which contingent effects eventuate," including humans with free will.[85] Consequently, not everything that happens is by imposition of God's governance.[86]

Within the boundaries of God's governance humans will their actions freely. Thus God can limit the pain that is brought about by human evildo-ers. In the story of Haman, for instance, we see that God "may permit an evildoer to will an evil and yet keep him from accomplishing the evil he wills to bring about." Haman willed the slaughter of the Jews, but the end result of the chain of events he initiated was not genocide but an enhancement of power for the Jews within a foreign nation. "Consequently, it is also clear that God does not let evildoers determine the amount of suffering in the world. As Mordecai makes clear in his message to Esther, the amount of suffering the Jews experience in Ahasuerus's kingdom is under God's control, not Haman's or Esther's."[87]

The Timelessness of God Enables Him to "Foreknow" and to Determine Creaturely Acts Without Robbing Them of Libertarianly Free Agency

In the models already examined, God's relationship to time and hence the content and nature of his foreknowledge have been very significant. Within the Thomist model it is usually asserted that God is timeless, an idea that developed early in the thought-life of the church under the influence of Middle Platonism.[88] For Thomists the concept of God's timeless eternity is the answer to many of the objections that are brought against divine providence as it is understood by those who endeavor to hold together human freedom and comprehensive divine foreknowledge within the framework of all-encompassing divine control.[89] Boethius and Aquinas viewed divine timelessness as a way of reconciling these two, though Augustine and Anselm had not done so.[90]

The development of the concept of divine timelessness. Origen taught that God is beyond our concept of time and our temporal language. In *On First Principles* he wrote: "The statements we make about the Father and the Son and the Holy Spirit must be understood as transcending all time and all ages and all eternity" (4.4.1).[91] The begetting of the Son by the Father did not take place at some time or other. In his *Enneads,* Plotinus insisted that the One was absolutely timeless, and his discussion influenced Augustine, Boethius, and through them Anselm, Thomas and the medieval tradition.[92]

Augustine asserted that God created time with the rest of creation, and he himself is therefore timeless.[93] Timeless eternity was considered essential to God's immutability. On the other hand, Alan Padgett asserts that it is not completely clear whether Augustine believed that eternity is absolutely, durationlessly, timeless or only relatively timeless.

The Roman philosopher Anicius Manlius Severinus Boethius (c. 475-525) is often referred to for a classic definition of eternity as absolutely timeless. Eternity is "the complete and perfect possession at once of an endless life."[94] Boethius was concerned about the nature of God's *fore*knowledge, which he noted is not strictly such, since God sees the future in his timeless present. In this way Boethius believed that he had resolved the apparent conflict between foreknown certainty and human freedom, which has troubled proponents of some of the models he have studied thus far. Since God lives in timeless eternity, his knowledge of our future choices is no more in conflict with our present free will than my present knowledge is in conflict with someone else's present free choice.[95]

Divine timelessness as the key to compatibilism. Drawing on this tradition, Aquinas asserted the durationless timelessness of God. In God's absolute simplicity his essence and his existence are one.[96] God is timeless "because he is changeless, and time is the measure of change."[97] As First Being, God is "Pure Act without any potentiality," and it is therefore "impossible for God to be in any way changeable."[98] Being eternal, God is interminable, without beginning or end, and he "has no succession, existing whole at once."[99] The "idea of Time follows motion," just as the "idea of Eternity follows immutability."[100] We apply words indicating different times to God "inasmuch as His eternity includes all times; not as if He Himself were altered through present, past, and future."[101]

As a consequence of God's timelessness, he does not strictly *fore*know the future, he simply knows it. All time is present to him in a simple act of perception. "The unchanging will of God determines not only the existence of his effect, but also the time of its existence."[102] God knows and wills all things in the single, eternal "moment" in which he lives. God's knowledge is not discursive because "discursive reasoning means to proceed from the known to the unknown." He sees his effects in himself as their cause, seeing other things in himself rather than in themselves.[103] He relates to factors in time as the center of a circle to the circumference. Every point on the circle is present to the center, though it may be past or future with reference to another point on the circumference. So God, in his eternity, coexists with whatever is in time and determines the temporal location of everything that exists.[104] A timeless God can act timelessly to bring about a temporal effect, so God can act within the changing circumstances of our time.[105]

Norman Geisler contends that the most Reichenbach and others who posit that God experiences the duration of time have shown is that productive actions are necessarily time-bound and sequential; "they have not shown that the producing actor must thereby also be time-bound."[106] Geisler posits that "neotheism" (his term for the openness model) is guilty of a confusion "between the eternal *Actor* (God) and his temporal *actions*."[107] But Thomism argues that the effect can be temporal (or finite) without the cause being temporal (or finite). In Geisler's view, both the process and the openness models confuse God's attributes and his acts. They therefore assume that God must be temporal in order to act in time. On the contrary, he posits, "There is nothing logically incoherent about a timeless God acting in a temporal world."[108]

God's existence in a timeless eternity does not prevent him from knowing that events which occur in time do so at a particular time. Aquinas argues that in his immutability God knows the event of Christ's birth, but he also knows the three statements, "Christ is being born," "Christ was born" and "Christ will be born," though he knows them without formulating each of them one term at a time.[109] As Gerard Hughes explains the situation, "In one simple act God knows not simply the event but the event *as time-bound*."[110] That is to say, God knows that "tensed propositions about it can be formulated, even though God does not need to formulate those propositions in order to have that knowledge. As we might put it, God's knowledge of the birth of Christ as time-bound consists in God's knowing 'At t_1 Christ's birth lies in the future,' 'At t_2 Christ's birth is present' and 'At t_3 Christ's birth is past.'"[111] To say that the whole of time is "present" to eternity is not to speak in a temporal sense but to assert that it is "immediately accessible to God's knowledge and causal activity."[112] Consequently, all time-bound events are not "simultaneously real" to God, nor are they simultaneous in time, simply because God knows them in an eternal, durationless moment. From the perspective of temporal beings like ourselves, some of them do not yet exist, and some no longer exist. An event does not exist in eternity "before" it has come about in time.[113]

Given this account of God's timelessness, God is able to know events as included within the certainty of his providence yet still contingent, that is, not uniquely determined by their natural causes. An action can be uncertain or indeterminate within the world until it takes place, yet it is determinate in the eternal decree where it has in a sense already taken place for God. God knows the events in his decree not as potentially and indeterminately contained in its contingent causes.[114] "If contingent causes genuinely contribute to the kind of effect which is produced, and do so only at a particular time, then prior to that time those effects are not determinate either, despite the fact that God 'cause' [i.e., timelessly cause] those effects in respect of their existence."[115]

God's knowledge of future contingents is not absolutely necessary because his "nature did not require him to know causally the contingents which he sees as future." But it is necessary "by supposition" because he "freely chose to make them come to be, and granted that choice, it is now necessary, because of God's immutability, that He know and will those future contingents to be."[116]

Norman Geisler argues that timelessness is necessitated in God's being by his simplicity (absolute indivisibility) and by his nonspatiality. Were God temporal, having thoughts and acting sequentially, then he would be spatial and even material, since space and time are correlative, "and if God is a space-time being, then he is subject to entropy (degeneration) as is the whole space-time universe."[117] God's predetermination is according to his foreknowledge but is not based on it. Both are one in God, as a simple and eternal being. This permits God to be totally sovereign while allowing humans to be totally free, freedom being defined as the absence of coercion so that it is not eliminated by determinism.[118]

Divine timelessness stated in modern scientific terms. Alan Padgett has presented a view he describes as "basically Thomistic, with a change from Aristotelian to modern science as a working assumption."[119] In this perspective, "God's sustaining act is a direct act which is 'Zero Time Related' to its effect." This is because "in cases of direct causation, once all the sufficient conditions are present, there will be a Zero Time Relation between the complete set of causes and the effect."[120] Thus God's sustaining work does not require temporal distance for the causation to be effected. God chose eternally "to have a temporal universe in which to live," and his choice to live a dynamic, active changing life "is the ground of the temporality of the universe." One of the ways in which God transcends time is precisely his decision to create a universe in which time would be an aspect of its nature.[121] Padgett's understanding differs from that of Thomas, in that he considers God to be temporal in himself, though he transcends our time.

God is "timeless" in the sense that his time is immeasurable, meaning that he is not in any Measured Time. Measured Time Words, therefore, would not truly apply in eternity. It could be possible, of course, for God to simply decree that a certain Measured Time would apply to his eternity. Perhaps he might do this to ease communication with his creatures. But this would be a wholly arbitrary convention, and would apply to the whole of eternity only because of the power of the divine decree, and not by anything in the nature of God's time.[122]

God is timeless in that he does not exist in any measured time and therefore not in the same measured time as we do.[123] He "exists in a 'timeless time,' which we call eternity."[124]

The Proper Christian Response to God's Providence
Is Abandonment

In most of the models presented thus far, it has been assumed that at least some events happened without divine action or in some sense outside of the divine control. In this, our first model that accepts a comprehensive, detailed divine providence, a new concept arises: abandonment to providence. Garrigou-Lagrange calls upon us to abandon ourselves to God's providence on account of his wisdom and goodness and because of four principles: (1) Everything that comes to pass has been foreseen by God from eternity and has been either willed or permitted by him. God has willed the reality and goodness in things, but he has merely permitted what is evil.[125] (2) God has not willed or permitted anything that does not contribute to the manifestation of his goodness and the glory of Christ (1 Cor 3:22-23). (3) As Paul tells us in Romans 8:28, God sees to it that everything contributes to our spiritual welfare. This includes not only the grace he bestows and the natural qualities with which he endows us but sickness and reverses as well. As Augustine said, even our sins are permitted by God to lead us to truer humility and purer love. Knowing the goodness of God's intentions, we can abandon ourselves to his providence. (4) We must be active in obeying God's "expressed will" but should abandon ourselves to the will of his "good pleasure," no matter how mysterious it may be. The future is in God's hands, and we are dependent on events that he controls, just as Joseph was when the merchants came by at exactly the right time for him to get to Egypt.[126]

When events are independent of the human will, such as in accidents or diseases, our self-abandonment should be absolute. But when suffering comes about through the injustice of others, Aquinas believes that there are occasions when action is required "either for the good of the person who injures us, to put a stop to his insolence, or to avoid the scandal such slanders and calumnies may cause." If we think it right "to offer some sort of resistance, let us put ourselves unreservedly in God's hands for the success of the steps we take." Our disapproval and reaction to acts of injustice ought to be "not because they are wounding to our self-love and pride, but because they are an offense against God, endangering the salvation of the guilty parties and of those who may be led astray by them."[127] If properly approached, these injustices may also have the benefit of detaching us "from creatures, to rid us of our inordinate affections, our pride and luke-warmness, and thus oblige us to have immediate recourse to a fervent prayer of supplication."[128]

When suffering comes about because of our own failures or weakness, we ought to distinguish the element of disorder and guilt in the situation from the "salutary humiliations" that may result. Although we must regret the wrong done to God and the harm to our soul and to our neighbor, we can accept with complete self-abandonment the beneficial humiliation (Ps 119:71-77).[129]

In the opinion of Garrigou-Lagrange, nothing should be considered a matter of chance. In small, unforeseen incidents God can providentially "upset the cunning calculations of those hostile to spiritual good." Here Joseph serves as a ready example. "Had not the Ishmaelite merchants, by chance apparently, passed by just when his brothers had decided to put him to death, he would have been left there in the cistern where they had thrown him. But it was then and not an hour later, as was ordained by God from all eternity, that the merchants arrived on the scene, and Joseph was thus sold into slavery" to be a later benefactor. Other instances of apparently chance incidents that were divinely planned, with momentous significance, include Esther, Daniel and even the birth of Jesus, whom God saved from Herod by sending an angel to warn Joseph.[130]

David Bartholomew suggests that Aquinas is an exception to the general rule among theologians, since he grants that distinctions between individuals may be by chance,[131] and since he argues that providence does not exclude chance or luck.[132] However, these comments by Aquinas need to be placed within the context of his larger commitment to divine omnicausality. Aquinas defines chance occurrences as those that are "due to the concurrence of two or more causes, through some end which was not intended ensuing from the concurrence of some cause."[133] It is with this definition in mind that Aquinas asserts that it "is not incompatible with providence that there be luck and chance in things." In fact, the order of divine providence "requires the presence of luck and chance in the world" because "it is through things happening beside the intention of the agent that things occur by chance or luck" (cf. Eccles 9:11).[134]

Intervention by "guardian angels," sent by God "to inspire some holy thought" in the minds of the just, whether they are asleep or awake, is "a

providential occurrence by no means rare in the lives of those who abandon themselves completely to God" (cf. Ps 91:10-11).[135] Of course, we must
not tempt God, but we should resign ourselves humbly into his hands
while going about our daily duties, "and those who thus abandon themselves to Him, He will protect as a mother protects her children. If He
allows persecution, often bitter persecution, to come upon them, as He did
in the case of His own Son, nevertheless He will not allow the just to lose
courage, but will sustain them in invisible ways and, if in a moment of
weakness they should fall, as Peter did, He will raise them up again and
lead them on to the haven of salvation."[136]

Petitionary Prayer Is Foreknown by God Who Factors It into His Absolute Control as One of the Secondary Causes

Prayer has a beneficial effect on the one who prays. When we pray, our attitude toward the way things turn out is improved. This is a notion that has
been expressed often in the Christian tradition, one that Vincent Brümmer
describes as the "concept of prayer as self-therapy."[137] Some have stated
this to be the sole purpose of prayer, as seen in the comment of Ceslaus
Veleck that "in so far as prayer affects anything at all, it affects ourselves,
not God. We do not pray to sway God. We pray in order to change and to
dispose ourselves so as to receive properly what God has willed to give to
us."[138] While this is not a complete description of the role of prayer in the
thought of Augustinian authors, there were occasions when this impression
was left, as was observed among proponents of the church dominion
model who argued for a more effective role for prayer as an alternative to
this therapeutic approach.

In a letter to Proba, Augustine wrote that "God does not need to have
our will made known to him—he cannot but know it—but he wishes our
desire to be exercised in prayer that we may be able to receive what he is
preparing to give."[139] Preaching on Matthew 6:8, Augustine urged listeners
and readers to "remember that He wants you to ask so that He may be able
to grant His favours to people who really do desire them; He does not wish
His gifts to be held cheap."[140] Aquinas likewise said that "we must pray, not
in order to inform God of our needs and desires, but in order to remind
ourselves that in these matters we need divine assistance."[141] Or again:
"Prayer is not offered to God in order to change his mind, but in order to
excite confidence in us. Such confidence is fostered principally by considering God's charity toward us whereby he wills our good."[142] Prayer is an

act in which "we continually acknowledge that we are subject to the divine governance," that everything we have was received from God (1 Cor 4:7).[143] Fostering this attitude is one of the great benefits of prayer.

Prayer is included in the providential order foreknown by God. The fatalist model (see chapter twelve) assumes that, if everything is firmly controlled within the providence of God, petitionary prayer is futile as a way of affecting the course of future events. That perception is continuously opposed by Thomists who argue, with Aquinas, that prayer is as much a part of the divine order as are the winds and the waves and the weather.[144] Whereas a Latin poet urged people to "cease to hope that the gods' decrees are to be changed by prayer," Richard Downey insisted that a well-instructed Catholic "prays in the sure knowledge that his prayers have been foreseen by God 'before anything was, from the beginning,' and that they have been taken into account, as it were, in the divine economy of his marvellous mercies and infinite love."[145] In the words of Reginald Garrigou-Lagrange, God's "knowledge extends not only to all that He is Himself, but also to all that He can do, to all that He actually realizes, whether by his own power exclusively as when He created in the beginning, or with and through our co-operation as when He directs us to the free performance of our everyday actions."[146] Therefore, in the "instant of eternity, God already knows all that will come to pass—all the prayers, for instance, that under His direction we shall freely offer Him later on in order to obtain the graces we need."[147]

Aquinas identified three errors regarding prayer that existed "among the ancients."[148] (1) Human affairs are not ruled by divine providence so that it is useless to pray. (Such an attitude is identified in Malachi 3:14.) (2) Everything happens by necessity, either divine or through the stars, or through the connection of causes, making prayer useless. (3) Providence is changeable and can be changed by prayer.

Prayer is one of the secondary causes that effects the divine decree. Aquinas calls for an account of prayer that neither imposes necessity on human affairs subject to divine providence nor implies changeableness of the divine disposition. He asserts that providence disposes not only effects but the causes and the order in which the effects proceed from them. This is why we do not pray to change God's disposition, but "we may impetrate that which God has disposed to be fulfilled by our prayers." It is by asking that we "may deserve to receive what Almighty God from eternity has disposed to give, as Gregory says." God wishes to bestow certain things on us at our asking, for our own good, "that we may acquire confidence in having recourse to God, and may recognize in Him the Author of our goods."[149]

Augustine, who urged prayer as a means of preparing ourselves to receive joyfully what God willed to give us, also believed that petitions should be offered because God sometimes "condescends and gives what people ask for, while declining to give to those who do not ask Him. For God has His pride and consequently will not give save to such as ask Him."[150] Augustine urges us to "ask for something really great, not as people ask who do not believe." Since "God gives money even to criminals who do not believe in Him," we will not be asking for something really great if we "ask for things which God grants even to the wicked." God gives the wicked light and rain (Mt 5:45), and we ought to ask for things that are due to rain and sun, since these are God's gifts. Yet our requests should go beyond such things to ask God that our souls might be "fat" with wisdom, as the psalmist did (Ps 63:5).[151] Yet it is also God "who puts the desire" into our hearts.[152]

Clark Pinnock argues that prayer proves that the future is open, since it assumes that it can be changed by our petitions, but Norman Geisler responds that this "confuses God's eternal vision (which is complete) with our temporal viewpoint (which is not). God has determined all things, but he has determined that prayer would be the means to accomplish some things." This does not mean that we are not free when we pray: "God knew who would freely pray when he predetermined to use prayer to achieve his ends. So it is open to us to change the world by prayer, but it will not catch God by surprise when we do."[153]

Aquinas believed that "divine providence not only disposes what effects will take place, but also the manner in which they will take place, and which actions will cause them."[154] The actions of human beings are genuine causes, but they do not change divine providence, they "obtain certain effects in the manner determined by God." Prayer functions in the same way, within the divine order. "We do not pray in order to change the decree of divine providence, rather we pray in order to acquire by petitionary prayer what God has determined would be obtained by our prayers."[155] In the constant Gospel teachings regarding the necessity of prayer, Garrigou-Lagrange finds evidence of the comprehensive extent of God's providence. God is at least as attentive to our needs as is an earthly father (Mt 7:7-11).[156]

The challenge that God's all-controlling providence brings to our understanding of the efficacy of petitionary prayer is not lost on Garrigou-Lagrange. If every period of time has been embraced in this universal providence and if God has foreseen everything, we might wonder what is the use of prayer. "How is it possible," he asks, "for us to enlighten God by our petitions, to make him alter his designs, who has said: 'I am the Lord and I change not'? (Mal 3:6)."[157] But Garrigou-Lagrange discerns the root of this fallacious objection raised by deists of the eighteenth and nineteenth century to be their "erroneous view as to the primary source of efficacy in prayer and the purpose for which it is intended."[158] He argues that a proper solution will show that (1) prayer is founded on providence, (2) it is a practical recognition of providence, and (3) it cooperates in the workings of providence.

Prayer is not a force that originates within ourselves and then compels God to alter the dispositions of his providence; the will of God is absolutely unchangeable. "Yet in this very unchangeableness the efficacy of prayer, rightly said, has its source, even as the source of a stream is to be found on the topmost heights of the mountains."[159] It was God's will that prayer should be "one of the most fruitful factors in our spiritual life, a means of obtaining the graces necessary to reach the goal of our life's journey." To imagine that God, from eternity, did not foresee and intend the prayers we address to Him in time, is as ridiculous as the "notion of a God subjecting His will to ours and so altering His designs."[160]

Prayer does not affect the divine preordination, insists Aquinas. In that sense, predestination cannot be "furthered by the prayers of the Saints. For it is not due to their prayers that anyone is predestined by God,"[161] but as to the effect of preordination, prayers are a help

> because Providence, of which Predestination is a part, does not do away with secondary causes, but so provides for effects, that the order of secondary causes falls also under Providence. So, as natural effects are provided for by God in such a way that natural causes are provided to bring about those natural effects, without which those effects would not happen; so the salvation of a person is predestined by God in such a way, that whatever helps that person towards salvation falls under the order of Predestination whether it be one's own prayers, or those of another; or other good works, and such-like, without which one would not attain to salvation. Whence, those predestined must strive to pray well and do good works; because through these means Predestination is most certainly fulfilled (cf. 2 Pet 1:10).[162]

True prayer, which is offered according to the requisite conditions, "is infallibly efficacious because God has decreed that it shall be so, and God cannot revoke what He has once decreed." God has not only foreseen and intended (or permitted, as the case may be) whatever comes about within his providential decree, he has included "the manner also in which it comes to pass, the causes that bring about the event, the means by which the end is attained." God has ordained that there should not be a harvest without the sowing of seed, nor knowledge without mental effort. Similarly, in the spiritual order God has providentially destined from eternity that prayer should be the cause by means of which certain effects are produced, particularly the attainment of the gifts of God necessary for salvation. Prayer is thus one of the causes that function within the divine providence. They are "efficacious before God," says Aquinas, "yet they do not destroy the immutable order of divine providence, because this individual request that is granted to a certain petitioner falls under the order of divine providence."[163] It is just as absurd "to say that we should not pray in order to obtain something from God, because the order of His providence is immutable," as it would be to say that "we should not walk in order to get to a place, or eat in order to be nourished."[164] The fatalistic Stoics argued that prayer was useless because the same effect would follow from the universal order whether or not prayers were offered. In the opinion of Aquinas, however, their error was that they isolated "from that universal order the wishes of those who pray."[165] If, on the other hand, "these prayers be included under that order, then certain effects will result by divine ordination by means of these prayers, just as they do by means of others causes."[166] Prayers therefore retain their power, not in changing the order of eternal control but in existing under such an order.

The Lord is like a father who has decided to grant some favor to his children, who then prompts them to ask him for it. Drawing on the story of the Samaritan woman (Jn 4:10-14), Garrigou-Lagrange suggests that Jesus first willed that she should be converted "and then gradually caused her to burst forth in heartfelt prayer; for sanctifying grace is not like a liquid that is poured into an inert vessel; it is a new life, which the adult will receive only if he desires it."[167] It is an act of worship to God when we ask him, in faith, to heal the sick or enlighten our minds in the midst of our difficulties, or to give us grace to resist temptation and persist in doing good. This reminds us that we must not seek temporal blessings for their own sake but only for their usefulness for salvation (Mt 6:33). It also explains why, on occasion, God is slow in responding "as if to see whether we shall persevere in our prayer," as in the case of the Canaanite woman (Mt 15:23, 26-28).[168]

When we come to God in prayer, we should endeavor "to wish in time what God wills for us from all eternity." Although it may seem that the divine will is submitting to our own, in reality ours is being lifted and harmonized with God's. "Instead of one, there are now two who desire these things." Of course, it is God who converts the sinner for whom we have been praying, but "we have been God's partners in the conversion. It is God who gave to the soul in tribulation that light and strength for which we have so long besought Him; yet from all eternity he decided to produce this salutary effect only with our co-operation and as the result of our intercession."[169] The significance of this is that the more closely our prayer conforms to God's intentions, the more we are cooperatively involved in his governance. Prayer is a potent force that can "obtain for us what God alone can bestow, the grace of contrition and of perfect charity, the grace also of eternal life, the very end and purpose of the divine governance, the final manifestation of its goodness."

Proponents of the models of providence reviewed thus far, with the exception of the semi-deist model, have all argued that a benefit of their model is that it provides a role for the effectiveness of prayer in bringing about different outcomes than would eventuate if prayer was not offered. Particularly important to the openness model is the fact that God does not know the future. They believe that this openness of the future makes the present, including our petitions to God, particularly significant. Since the future is not yet certain, we can act and request God to act in ways that will bring about great good. God is naturally responsive, and we can expect our prayer to have an important, though not guaranteed, effect for a better future than would otherwise materialize. The openness model believes that God can act supernaturally to bring about good in history, although it is not his usual practice to intervene in this way. However, it is precisely at this point that Norman Geisler considers the Thomist model superior because "a God who does not know for sure what any future free act will be is severely limited in his logistic ability to do things that a God who knows every decision that will be made can do."[170]

The problem of unanswered prayer. Naturally, those who pray want their requests to be granted, but Augustine encourages readers that a reason for unanswered prayer is that God will not give us what is harmful. Paul, for instance, was not heard because "it was still time for him to exercise patience" (2 Cor 12:7-9). On the other hand, the devil's request was granted when he asked to try Job (Job 1:9-12; 2:4-6). "The Apostle asks and is not heard; the devil asks and is heard. The Apostle was not heard for his perfecting's sake, the devil was heard for his damnation's sake."[171] Unanswered petitions can be accepted with greater tranquillity when we trust in the wisdom of God's will who "knows well what he is doing."[172] Parents might pray for the life of their son and be disturbed when he dies, assuming their petition to have been for a good thing. "But supposing," says Augustine, "your son *was taken away lest wickedness should alter his understanding?*" The parents might reply that their boy was a sinner and that they "wanted him to live so that he might put himself right." Augustine replies: "You wanted him to live, then, in the hope that he might improve. But supposing now that God knew that if he were to live he would only become worse? How can you know whether it were better for him to live or to die? But if you are ignorant of that then turn back to your own heart and leave God to His own plans."[173] Rather than seeking specific things that we request, we should seek God for delight of himself, as the psalmist did in Psalm 27:4. There are many things in this world for which we will ask and not be heard, but prayers for eternal life will always be heard.[174]

The Case Study

Maria Sanchez had grown up in the Philippines, where she had been educated in a Roman Catholic school run by the Dominican Order. The friars who taught the classes in Christian doctrine convinced her of the great wisdom of Thomas Aquinas and had impressed upon her a devotion to God as the one in whose control all the details of our lives lie. She believed that everything takes place within God's providence, either by his intention or by his permission. This gave her a serenity in facing the difficulties of life that did not keep her from active resistance to the evil that is contrary to God's commandments. She had a particularly strong sense that what really matters is what moves us forward in achieving the goals of God for human salvation, but she still felt free to pray for solutions to the problems of daily life, large and small.

As Maria listened to her friends praying for the situation described by Fred Henderson, she found herself in agreement with all of them on one major item. Like those who had already prayed, Maria believed that human beings are libertarianly free. She concluded that the abduction of Richard Henderson and his two colleagues had occurred by the action of people who had the ability to act differently than they had done in the situation that existed. Maria considered the future open in the sense that everyone involved (the guerrillas, the missionaries, the local and foreign diplomats, the Christians gathered in her church for prayer) had the power to contribute to the final outcome. This gave her a sense of power. The future was not determined in such a way that nothing they did could have a significant effect on how it unfolded. Even their decision to intercede for God's help was not determined. They were free to pray or not to pray, and this would impact the outcome.

Unlike Oliver (openness model), Maria believed that God knew the future. Oliver had complained to her on other occasions that this made it impossible for people to be libertarianly free. If God already knew what the guerrillas, the missionaries and everyone else involved were going to do tomorrow, there was no point in praying about it today. Tomorrow and all of the future was fixed and certain since God knew it certainly, and the most we could do would be to express our submission to his comprehensive will. Maria rejected Oliver's argument because of her belief in God's timelessness. Whereas Oliver believed that God experiences events in sequence, Maria thought that God experienced everything—past, present and future—"now." God could tell the difference between events that are past and those that are future (to us), but he did not personally experience them that way. For us, tomorrow is future, but for God it is as present as is today, and God knows tomorrow as accurately as he knows yesterday and today.

Andrew (Molinist model) shared Maria's conviction that God knows the future as well as her belief that we are libertarianly free to act in the present and thereby to bring about a different future than would come to be if we acted differently. For Andrew, however, God's comprehensive knowledge of the future and libertarian human freedom were both possible because the future brought about by free creatures is the one that God has chosen from among all the possible futures. God knows today what the guerrillas and the missionaries will do tomorrow because he had chosen this particular history, in which all of these people act in the way that they freely choose to act. As Andrew understood things, God acts in history by intervening to bring about the particular future that is realized. He can do that because he knows (through his "middle knowledge") how every one *would* act in every possible situation. Even though the future is certain, God had been able to plan how he would act in the case of the abducted missionaries because he knew how all of the people involved would respond to particular influences of his own or to factors surrounding them.

In Maria's understanding of God, by contrast with Andrew's, God does not know the counterfactuals (things that *"would* happen *if. . . ."*) he simply knows the future, although for him this is not *fore*knowledge. Through his knowledge of the "future," God is timelessly, eternally aware of what Maria prays now and was therefore able to act in such a way that her request would be answered. Unlike all of those who had prayed before her, Maria believed that God was completely in control in the situation. This gave her great comfort. God had not been taken by surprise, nor did he "foresee" an evil he could not prevent. For reasons that Maria might never understand until she reaches heaven, God had permitted the abduction of Richard and his colleagues. This was not just a general permission, brought about by God's decision to give his creatures libertarian freedom; this was a specific permission with regard to the evil act committed by the guerrillas. God was at work in the world for good, in particular for the salvation of all his creatures, and in his inscrutable wisdom he had decided that this wrong deed should occur for the overall good. As with all of God's action in the world, his work at the moment of the abduction and his work throughout the events yet to unfold would be *concurrent* with the agency of the people involved. God would not work in advance of the human action, thereby determining how the creature acts for that would make him culpable for the wrong done by those creatures. God would enable the people to act as they freely chose, and yet his own concurrent activity would bring about the result that God willed.

Maria had occasionally discussed the matter of God's "will" with her friends at church. As she contemplated Richard's condition, she believed that it *was* and it *was not* according to God's will, in different senses. It was God's antecedent will that people respect one another's persons and property. For the guerrillas to abduct the missionaries from their families was contrary to the antecedent will of God and therefore was sin against the moral will of God. In another sense, however, everything that happened was according to God's will, spoken of as his "consequent" will. God had decided that, in this particular case, he would not prevent the guerrillas from their wicked deed. The abduction succeeded because God sustained the wills of the guerrillas and cooperated with them in their action, though not in a way that would involve him morally. Maria was now confident that, in this sense, the difficult situation had come about by God's will. She did not have a sense of personal helplessness, nor a sense that God had been "defeated" in a struggle with evil.

The primary question for Maria now was: "What does God want me to do to bring about good out of this evil?" She was open to suggestions of ways in which they could get involved in efforts to have the missionaries released. But she knew one thing for sure, God wanted her to intercede in prayer, asking him to bring about good for everyone in the situation. She knew from experience that it would make her feel better when she had acknowledged God's sovereignty and called upon him to act. But, she also believed that good things would happen precisely because she and other believers asked God to bring them about.

With this assurance Maria prayed, "Loving heavenly Father, we approach you as your children, confident that you love us and that you know our every need. We believe that you are active in all that happens and that nothing takes place outside of your control. At the same time, we know that you do not directly will evil acts, and so we do not consider the abduction of Richard and his friends to be something that you have wished to come about although you have permitted it for good reasons that we do not yet understand. I agree with others who have requested that you would bring about the release of these missionaries and that you would advance the cause of the gospel through this event. It is the latter that I seek most; the lives of the three men are valuable, and we believe that it would be a good thing for them to have many more years to serve you. Given our best wisdom at this time, we ask for that. In the meantime, we pray that you would give them grace to remain faithful to you during these trials.

"We know that you desire the salvation of those who have taken the missionaries captive, and we pray that you will work graciously in their lives, drawing them to yourself and making good use of their contact with Richard and the others. Above all, we seek what will be the greatest good in light of your plans for bringing all people (both the missionaries and their captors) to the great blessing of communion with you. We ask, Lord, that even while we pray together, you will strengthen each of us and prepare us to receive joyfully what you wisely bring to pass from this situation. Even now, we praise you for working wisely and lovingly in this and all circumstances of our lives. For Jesus' sake, Amen."

10

The Barthian Model

KARL BARTH IS A GIANT WITHIN THE TRADITION OF REFORMED THEOLOGY, *which has its roots in Calvin. He is best known for his efforts to turn back the tide of theological liberalism, but he did not simply return to Calvinistic orthodoxy, and his theology has therefore been dubbed "neo-orthodox." Barth's Calvinist roots are obvious in his emphasis on divine sovereignty, meticulous providence and comprehensive foreknowledge (which does not include middle knowledge). He affirms the freedom of the creature in a volitional sense but makes it clear that God's will is supreme. What particularly distinguishes Barth's proposal from the classic Calvinist model is his emphasis on the centrality of Christ. Not only salvation but also divine providence must be seen through the perspective offered in the revelation of God in Christ. Only Christ is the revelation of God and hence God's work in the whole range of human history must be viewed within the context of his gracious purpose for creation that was both revealed and accomplished in Christ. Barth's understanding of the role of petitionary prayer is not fundamentally different from Calvin's or Aquinas's, but, again, it is placed within the christological framework. Christ, the representative human being, is the primary intercessor. Our role in petition is to discern God's will as revealed in Christ and to join Christ in praying for what God wills to do in the world. Thus we do not change God's mind when we pray, but our prayers do have a significant part in the realization of God's purposes for the world.*

A second model of providence in the Augustinian tradition that affirms comprehensive divine sovereignty is found in the work of Karl Barth. He worked within the Reformed tradition that is represented in its classical form in the Calvinist model, but he offered a very influential attempt to reformulate that tradition by focusing the whole analysis from a christological perspective. It is difficult to know where to place the Barthian model in our scheme of progressively greater divine control, relative to the Calvinist model. This is because Barth was a dialectical theologian who regularly affirmed both/and when addressing choices. Thus from the openness model, John Sanders finds encouragement in statements made by Barth that seem to acknowledge that God may be conditioned in some way by his creature.[1] This will be considered below, but I see Barth's model as no less strong than Calvin's in its insistence on divine sovereignty, although this is tempered by his conviction that God pronounced both a universal yes and a universal no in Jesus. In particular, Barth's concept of the election of the whole human race in Christ conditions his approach to the general history of humanity. Yet the fact that Barth allowed for the possibility that some people might irrationally reject their election in Christ appears to leave open the possibility that God's eternal purposes are not always realized. For this reason, in spite of Barth's strong affirmations of divine sovereignty, it seems best to place Barth before Calvin. I wondered whether he should even be placed before Aquinas and the Thomist model but decided not because he strikes me as less concerned to emphasize (though not denying) human contingency than Aquinas was.

God's Providential Control Is Comprehensive

Karl Barth made a clear distinction between God's creative act and his fatherly care for that creation. "By 'providence' is meant the superior dealings of the Creator with His creation, the wisdom, omnipotence and goodness with which He maintains and governs in time this distinct reality according to the counsel of His own will."[2] Creation establishes the existence of all things and beings and providence is "the guaranteeing and determination, of the history of creaturely existence by the will and act of God."[3] Providence is more than just foreknowledge, as is evident in Genesis 22:14, where the Hebrew idiom "to see" means "to see about." It is "an active and selective predetermining, preparing and procuring of a lamb to

be offered instead of Isaac. God 'sees to' this burnt offering for Abraham."[4]
For the world, for human beings and for the church, "God sees to that
which in their earthly lot is necessary and good and therefore planned and
designed for them according to His wisdom and resolve. And as He does
so, He cares for them, and therefore sees to the fulfilling of His own purpose for them and to His glory in face of them."[5] Both in creation and in
providence we have to do with the "unconditional lordship of the will and
Word of the divine Creator over the creature—a lordship which in both
cases has its meaning in the divine election and covenant as its final secret
and basis."[6] In Barth's opinion, the Reformed doctrine of providence cor-
rectly carried to the logical conclusion the true relation between God and
the creature, namely, "that it is absolutely the will of God alone which is
executed in all creaturely activity and creaturely occurrence," and that the
concursive operation of God and creaturely agents is irreversible.[7]

God is "always present, active, responsible and omnipotent," and he
always holds the initiative even where he seems to wait or where he permits.[8] God is the "sovereign and living Lord" who precedes, accompanies
and follows the creature, "preserving, co-operating and overruling, in all
that it does and all that happens to it."[9] Through faith in God's particular
revelation in the Word, when we see the history of creation, we see "God
as the One who in concealment but supreme reality is before and over and
in it as the Lord."[10] We recognize that in our confrontation with developments in the world, we have to do with God himself, "with His co-ordinat-
ing and integrating of creaturely occurrence with the history of His
covenant, with the doing of His gracious and saving will, with His providing that all things must work together for good to them that love Him, and
in all these things with God Himself, with the work of His right hand."[11]
Barth confidently affirms Calvinist teaching concerning the sovereign and
predestinating operation of God, provided that it is clear that we are speaking of the God who revealed himself in Jesus Christ.[12]

God upholds and sustains the individual existence of creatures and gives
their existence continuity, and this preservation is for the sake of Jesus. "It
is the outflowing, the presupposition and the consequence of the grace
which God gave to the creature in His Son, and it takes place in order that
in the creaturely world God may be glorified in and through His Son."[13]
This preservation is a free act of God, done according to his own good
pleasure, though he may use creaturely instruments to accomplish it. Yet
even the nourishing power of bread is through the continual influence of

the creative and sustaining Word of God (Mt 4:4).[14] On the basis of the election of grace, God elects the creature to its own specific being and existence, and his faithfulness is therefore the ground of the creature's continued existence.[15]

Both the fact that things happen and the way in which they happen derives from God. "They are decreed and brought to pass by him," and "there are no lacunae in the fulfilment of the decree of salvation and grace without which heaven and earth would not be and in the execution of which they were created; all with the same certainty as that all things and events must serve the one final purpose."[16] Consequently, Barth describes the activity of God and of the creature as a single action: God "is so present in the activity of the creature, and present with such sovereignty and almighty power, that His own action takes place in and with and over the activity of the creature. It is He Himself who does what Moses and David do. . . . It is He who judges when the Assyrians capture Samaria and the Babylonians Jerusalem."[17] Creaturely events take place as God himself acts, not distinct from God's action as though it were above or behind them. "As He Himself enters the creaturely sphere—and He does not cease to do this, but does it in the slightest movement of a leaf in the wind—His will is accomplished directly and His decisions are made and fulfilled in all creaturely occurrence both great and small."[18]

God need not violate the creature in its particularity; he is able to accept and joyfully affirm it, "yet at the same time He can direct all creatures to the one goal, and subordinate all other goals to this one. He has a unified plan which is in the process of execution, and there is no creature which this plan does not embrace, and which does not in its own place and its own way help forward this plan." Nonetheless, this unified plan "has nothing whatever to do with a leveling down and flattening out of individuals and individual groupings"; God takes nothing away from the creature. The one thing that God wills and accomplishes, in and with and by and for all things, is his own glory as Creator within which the creature is also glorified as it realizes its own particular existence as a means of glorifying the Creator.[19]

The older theologians were correct to assert that God concerns himself "with the growth of caterpillars in the grass sprouting in the province of Saxony in any given year" or "with the thread hanging from the beggar's coat" (cf. Ps 139:2; 147:9; Is 34:20; Mt 6:30; 10:29, 30).[20] Both small and great things, those that appear insignificant and those that appear important are the work and possession of God and are ruled by his wisdom and "used in some sense in the fulfilment of His purposes."[21] However, Barth wants to be careful not to give the impression that the small things are means to ful-fill the purpose of a greater whole and therefore of other "better-placed creatures." Each creature has its "own immediacy towards God and there-fore its autonomous validity and worth."[22]

God's Providence Must Be Viewed from the Special History of the Covenant

What distinguishes the Christian view of providence from other views, as Barth sees things, is that the One who is "over us as the Father" is the One who is "for us as the Son."[23] All general world occurrence must be under-stood in relation to the special occurrence that is the history of the cove-nant, grace and salvation.[24] God "coordinates creaturely occurrence under His lordship with the occurrence of the covenant, grace and salvation," and "He subordinates the former to the latter and makes it serve it."[25] Barth urges us to "look at world events in general outwards from the particular events attested in the Bible, from God's activity in the covenant of grace which He instituted and executed in Israel and in the community of Jesus Christ."[26] These particular events are not an end in themselves; they are "an original and pattern of the general events." The history of the covenant is not a private history. "We are dealing with the one act of rule which as such embraces and determines all other events over and above its own ful-filment, which even in its particularity is the centre of a circumference, of all creaturely occurrence both in heaven and on earth."[27] There is no genu-inely secular history because "the general events have their meaning in the particular."[28] General history and the history of the covenant, in Barth's scheme, correspond to general and special providence or ordinary and extraordinary providence in traditional Reformed formulations, but Barth insists that there is only one order in which to approach them. We must move from the salvation history to the general and back again. If proper distinction is not made, then he believes we would be better to abandon the terms altogether.[29] In his summation of "the quintessential features of a Reformed perspective" on divine providence, Benjamin Farley affirms Barth's (and Brunner's) insistence that "ultimately, providence is a function of divine election that in turn constitutes the presupposition on which providence rests."[30]

While approving of the Reformed emphasis on the absoluteness of the will of God in providence, Barth considered it a tragedy that they held this

truth "on the same presupposition of purely formal concepts of God and
His will and work as that of their opponents." Reformed orthodoxy pointed
to the supremacy of God, which is unconditioned by the creature, and they
spoke about God's decree, but they failed to take into account its content.
In this omission, they pointed us "to the dark," and a Stoic or Islamic resignation was unavoidable.[31] "Reformed theology reaped what it had sown as
early as the 16th century with its failure to think out the basis of its doctrine
of providence from a serious Christian standpoint."[32]

When we speak of God, we must understand him to be the "One who
as Father, Son and Holy Ghost is eternal love, and has life in Himself."
When we talk about his will, "we have to understand His fatherly good-
will, his decree of grace in Jesus Christ, the mercy in which from all eternity He undertook to save the creature, and to give it eternal life in the fellowship with Himself." And when we speak of God's work, we must have
in mind his "execution in history of the covenant of grace upon the basis of
the decree of grace, with its fulfilment in the sacrifice of His Son and its
confirmation in the work of the Holy Spirit awakening to faith and obedience."[33] There is nothing capricious about the world rule of the fatherly
goodwill of God and, because it is an activity of grace, "its almightiness
does not in any sense destroy the free activity of the creature."[34]

It is because the decree of grace in Jesus Christ preceded the creation of
all things that the activity of God precedes that of the creature. Before the
creature works, God is there "as the One who has already loved it, who
has already undertaken to save and glorify it," who has already worked
before the creature began to work. "From the very first the purpose of God
was to save and glorify the creature."[35] The God who rules the world
unconditionally and irresistibly in all occurrence is the God who revealed
himself to Abraham and became man in Jesus Christ.[36] The history of salvation is "the centre and key to all events." World history is related to it. "It is
the circumference around that centre, the lock to which that key belongs
and is necessary."[37]

The two spheres of general and salvation history are different only in
that the gracious work of God is revealed in the salvation history and hidden in the general world occurrence, but "even the world-occurrence generally had its beginning by the grace of God the Creator."[38] It was
"decisively altered and conditioned by the love which appeared in Jesus
Christ and was authenticated by His death and resurrection," and "it moves
toward its own perfection and therefore to the end of the age in the still

future revelation of Jesus Christ." Nevertheless, the "lordship and economy" cannot be "directly seen and demonstrated in world-occurrence as such"; we learn this "from the particular history of the covenant and of salvation."[39]

God's Will Sovereignly Precedes Creaturely Being but Does Not Destroy Its Contingency

The freedom of creaturely action within God's control. God alone is "the ruling, determining and conditioning Subject in the history of the covenant of grace," yet he has a partner in human beings.[40] God works through, on and for creation, making it into something with which he is pleased.[41] The creature cannot anticipate its creation or give itself existence and essence, nor can it "anticipate God's providence or its use in God's living hand, as though it already were what it must be in this use, or already had what it must have in it. It can only be ready for God, or more exactly for God's action in the covenant of grace and kingdom of Christ."[42] God gives creatures space and opportunity for their own work, their "own being in action," their own "autonomous activity."[43] But in doing this, God does not leave creatures to their own devices; he accompanies them or cooperates with them. As he works, he allows the creature to work in a freedom that is God's gift. "The free God is always a step in advance of the free creature. The free creature does go of itself, but it can and does only go the same way as the free God. It goes its own way, but in fact it always finds itself in a very definite sense on God's way."[44]

God, who is at work in everything, great and small, does not deal with us as stones but as human beings. He allows creatures to act according to their own nature and limits, but he knows what these are because they are given to creatures by God himself. "The very fact that this God rules as Creator means that in their own way, and at their own time and place, all things are allowed to be, and live, and work, and occupy their own sphere, and exercise their own effect upon their environment, and fulfil the circle of their own destiny." The reality that God is the Master in all things "does not alter the fact that each is allowed to develop in its own activity. On the contrary, the rule and disposition of God consists in the very fact that each may and can do that." Moreover, whenever and wherever the creature acts, "it has to thank the divine rule and disposition for it. It could never do it at all unless from first to last it was allowed to do so by the divine rule and disposition."[45] Since freedom is obedience to God, there is no conflict between being free and being totally ruled by God. Only in God's case does freedom mean self-determination.[46]

In controlling creaturely activity, God does not suspend it and substitute his own activity for it. God "does not do violence to the character and dignity" that the creature has as the reality, which is distinct from God. God pays it high honor by making the activity of the creature the means of his own activity and giving the creature a part in his own operation. Its activity is "free, contingent and autonomous. But God controls the activity in its freedom no less than its necessity."[47] God's will does not destroy the contingence of creaturely being and occurrence, even though it sovereignly precedes it. This happens in the sovereignty of the Creator who is operative in the freedom of His creature without robbing it of freedom. It is true, therefore, without the free will of man having to be understood as unfree in itself." The human will is "free in itself, but in its freedom it is always at the disposal of the ever-active will of God."[48]

There is no contradiction between the sovereignty of God and the freedom of the creature; creaturely freedom includes the fact that it is controlled by God. God limits the creature by law and necessity and yet gives it a sphere in which to exercise its freedom. Accompanying the creature through time, God is "the Lord of the use which it is able to make of its freedom," and the creature uses this freedom. "It is active at every moment. But in every moment it uses this freedom on the basis of the particular divine permission to do so. It works always within the framework and the limits of this permission."[49] As we will see, Calvin was reluctant to speak of divine permission at all, but other Reformed theologians have done so, with reference only to sinful human acts, to differentiate the manner in which they originate in divine causality.[50] Barth, on the other hand, is seen here to attribute both good and evil, all that is in the range of "creaturely freedom," to divine permission.[51] The creature aims at an effect through its action, but "it is God who decides where and how it will actually culminate, what will be its upshot, as the saying goes." This is true both when the culmination and effect are what the creature expected but "also when either by its non-existence or its different form and bearing it is a complete surprise" in relation to the creature's action. In every case the result of the creature's action is something new and something from God, even when the result is what was intended by the creature. Nevertheless, "what happens as the goal of its striving and willing and the result of its working, whether it is non-existent or existent, whether it is what was striven after and willed or something quite different, whether it is good or bad. . . . It is decided, decreed and directed by God. Both in general and particular God Himself fixes for the creature its goals, that is, the goals that it will actually attain. In one way or another it will ultimately realise the divine decree."[52]

The proper use of the language of "causes." Barth suggests that there are a number of possible mistaken perceptions of the relationship between God's work and the work of his creatures, which the older theologies labeled *concursus.* These include (1) a relationship between "an intrinsically unmoved and passive God and a moved order of creation," (2) a relationship "between a living, active and working God and an order of creation which is moved by Him from without, and therefore passively and without any activity on its own account," (3) the concept of a movement that would itself limit the limitation of creaturely action, "which would make creaturely action possible, and then hand over the control to it, leaving it to run its own course," and (4) the concept of "identity between the divine and creaturely action, of the undifferentiated existence of a God-world, which in all its elements and movements might be interpreted equally well as divine or not divine, with a constant amphibole of concepts."[53]

In Barth's reading, the older theologies avoided these misperceptions. Nevertheless, the classical doctrine of God as primary cause, cooperating with second, creaturely causes is viewed by Barth as formally correct but materially incorrect because "it missed completely the relationship between creation and the covenant of grace." It portrayed God as absolute and featureless, and it separated world history from salvation history.[54] Barth does not object to the use of the language of cause, provided certain conditions are maintained. First, it must not be considered as equivalent to a cause that is effective automatically as in modern science or natural philosophy. Barth considers neither Thomas nor the seventeenth-century theologians to have been guilty of this. They left room for contingency, human will and miracle, room for the covenant and the church. Although there is an element of necessity from the divine side, it is not mechanical. Barth grants that "in this respect there are some equivocal statements on the Reformed side, especially in Zwingli and Calvin, and occasionally in the 17th century. But the element of necessity is not to be explained by a foreign concept of mechanical."[55]

A second condition is that "care must be taken lest the idea should creep in that in God and the creature we have to do with two 'things.'" Barth perceives this to have been a danger in Aquinas and in "our own [i.e., Reformed] orthodox fathers." Since theology meditates and speaks *about* God and the creature, "they are always in danger of becoming things. The human thinker and speaker is in constant danger of forgetting the inconceivable mystery of their existence and being, their presence and operation, and of imagining that he can think and speak about them directly, as though both they themselves and also their relationship to each other were somehow below him." Both God and the creature must be *self*-revealed if we are to think and speak about them.[56]

Third, we must not use the term *cause* as "a master-concept to which both God and the creature are subject, nor is it a common denominator to which they may both be reduced." When we apply the term to God and to the creature, "the concept does not describe the activity but the active subjects, and it does not signify subjects which are merely not alike, or not similar, but subjects which in their absolute antithesis cannot even be compared." Of course, there is a comparableness, an analogy, between divine and human causation but not between the two subjects. God is "self-grounded, self-positing, self-conditioning and self-causing," but the creature owes the fact that it is a cause to God who "still posits and conditions it, and then to the other *causae* of its own order, without whose conditioning or partial conditioning it would not exist." This leads Barth to assert that the classic distinction between primary and secondary cause, as it was made in the philosophy of Aristotle or the theology of Aquinas who envisaged an analogy of being between God and creature, did not do justice to the absolute unlikeness of the two causes. The problem could have been avoided, Barth opines, if the older dogmaticians had spoken of divine and creaturely cause rather than primary and secondary, just as they spoke of divine and human nature in Christ. Whether they perceived the proper distinction, in their use of causal terminology, is unclear to Barth.[57]

A fourth condition necessary to proper use of causative language is that we must avoid using it "with the intention or consequence that theology should be turned into philosophy at this point, projecting a kind of total scheme of things."[58] Finally, we must maintain a clear connection between the first article of the creed and the second. We must speak of a concursive action in terms of God having "so loved the world in His election of grace that in fulfilment of the covenant of grace instituted at the creation He willed to become a creature, and did in fact become a creature, in order to

be its Saviour." Even apart from this decision of the covenant and its fulfillment, God accepts the creature. "He takes it to Himself as such and in general in such sort that He co-operates with it, preceding, accompanying and
following all its being and activity, so that all the activity of the creature is
primarily and simultaneously and subsequently His own activity, and therefore a part of the actualisation of His own will revealed and triumphant in
Jesus Christ."[59]

When causation is looked at in this light, Barth believes that we can only
know the primary cause in prayer and the secondary cause in gratitude; we
cannot be above them but only under them.[60] God's operation is almighty,
but his love is primary, and we can only love him in return. God's action is
free in that he does not owe it either to himself or to the creature, yet God
wills to work with the creature, to preserve the creature in its reality, "and
because this reality is change, God accompanies it in this change."[61] By
God's grace "the events of nature and history are authorized and qualified
to co-operate with Him. In itself and as such their activity is their own," but
it cannot go outside the limits of God's grace.

The irreversibility of the concursive action of God and the creature. God
is sovereign, and the concursive action is not reversible. God concurs with
the creature but not vice versa. While the activity of the creature does not
impose conditions on God's activity, God's activity "conditions absolutely
the activity of the creature." It "precedes, accompanies and follows that
activity, and nothing can be done except by the will of God."[62] What keeps
this from producing a submission like that of Stoicism or Islam is "a genuine decision of the Christian obedience of faith." It is not a concept of "sovereign caprice, in the hands of which the creature would appear to act, but
in fact would only be acted upon, and this in pursuance of a purpose
which is utterly obscure." The rule of God must be considered in the light
of his rule in the covenant of grace and of his work and revelation in Jesus
Christ.[63]

Barth is aware that some deny that the divine will is this sovereign in its
operation and assert that the creature also limits the divine activity, that the
concursive work is reversible. Consequently, it is interesting that Ian Barbour, who believes that "God's creation of freedom and law constituted a
voluntary self-limitation" [as in the openness model], wonders if "the same
conclusion might be reached by a more thoroughgoing application of
Barth's own injunction to use the event of Christ as the model of God's
power" since we see in the cross the "power of a love which accepts suf-

fering."[64] Barbour wonders if we might not "describe God's action in the Word as the power of communication, persuasion, inspiration, and evocation rather than as 'unconditioned and irresistible control.'"[65] But although Barth was aware that this way of speaking is attractive to many theologians, he doubted that it really gives us God "when it offers us a supreme being whose will is not sovereignly executed in all the activity of the creature, whose eternal knowledge is not his will and work but only the knowledge of a helpless or disinterested spectator, whose activity is 'concurred' in and conditioned by that of the creature."[66] We cannot "make of the God who is all in all a God who is only much in much."[67]

Barth rejects "the fear-complex which suggests that God is a kind of stranger or alien or even enemy to the creature" and "that it is the better for the freedom and claim and honour and dignity of the creature the more it can call its own a sphere marked off from God and guaranteed against Him, and the worse for it if this sphere is restricted, and worst of all if it is completely taken away." On the contrary, says Barth, because God is the Father of our Lord Jesus Christ it is "better for the creature the more fully it stands under the lordship of God and the worse for it the more that reservations and restrictions are placed upon this lordship."[68]

In Barth's framework we can choose differently from God, but we cannot make a choice that is not delineated by his will, either as something accepted or rejected by him. "We cannot will at all if we are not willing to decide within the sphere fixed by the will of God."[69] God's will can mean that he "loves, affirms and confirms" an action but also that he "hates, disavows, rejects and opposes it." God "still wills it in the sense that He takes it seriously in this way and takes up this position over against it. He wills it in so far as He gives it this space, position and function." On the other hand, he does not will it "as its author, recognising it as His creature, approving and confirming and vindicating it." When he wills it by denying it his authorship and refusing to bless it, "He places it under His prohibition and curse and treats it as that from which He wishes to redeem and liberate His creation."[70] It does not exist without God, and it is under his control and government and subject to his will, otherwise there would be a sphere that was that of another god.

We must not equate with the divine foreordination the determination of our action or "the totality of creaturely activity which accompanies and precedes" our movement; "the sceptre is not in the hands of even the totality of created things in heaven and on earth." The composite of factors that determine the individual "is not an autonomous causal nexus but one which is itself accompanied and dominated and controlled by the divine activity. . . . Its ordering and cohesion are the work of God."[71]

The operation of divine concurrence with human action. How the divine concurrence with human action comes about is a mystery. "It is not merely that God works with a higher or absolute force in beings whose force is less, so that they have no option but to yield and submit to the pressure of His power and accommodate themselves to it."[72] Furthermore, God's work on the creature is not just "an action which stirs up the creature itself to action," nor is it the "first of a series of actions which sets in motion the whole series."[73] God's work is his "moving of all creatures by the force and wisdom and goodness which are His Holy Spirit, the Spirit of His Word. The divine operation is, therefore, a fatherly operation."[74] There seems to be an indissoluble unity between the Word of God and creaturely occurrence; "everything that happens can be traced back to a Word of God. Therefore 'the Lord God will do nothing, but he revealeth his secret unto his servants the prophets' (Amos 3:7). And conversely: 'The word that I shall speak shall come to pass. . . . I will say the word, and will perform it, saith the Lord God' (Ezek 12:25; cf. 37:14)."[75]

Although God is eternal, he acts in time, before, during and after the creature's act is concluded.[76] When we have completed an action or spoken a word, it is irrevocable and unalterable, but God himself "decided concerning my word even before I uttered it. He decides concerning it at the very moment when I utter it. And He will decide concerning it, what it is and what it means, after I have uttered it."[77] Since God decided and ordained what actually happened, we can be confident and hopeful. "For the fact that God does it means that for every effect produced by the creature, whatever it may be, there is in the final and best sense of the word a meaningful and good and right application, that not one of these effects is lost, and that no activity of the creature is in vain."[78]

The nature of miracles. The order of creaturely occurrence that we perceive and describe as ontic laws can be "ruthlessly" ignored by God not because God is disorderly but because he is the God of his own order and is not bound by our concepts of order. When God does this, we see "not a *miraculous* exception but the *rule* of divine activity, the free good-will of God Himself, that is, the law at which we are aiming with our concept of law."[79] Miracles are "ultimately unexpected and inexplicable" because they are "series of creaturely actions and effects directly initiated by God himself," yet "they do not involve any setting aside of such actions and effects." Everything is "absolutely under God, and yet everything attains in freedom to its own validity and honour."[80]

God's Knowledge Is Comprehensive, Eternal and Not Distinguishable from His Will

Rejection of foreknowledge defined as prevision of creaturely acts. The providence of God, Barth insists, is not simply a preceding knowledge, a foreseeing of the work of the creature by virtue of God's eternal knowledge of all things; it is a preceding activity.[81] God does actually know things when they are still future but what is important is that God and his knowledge are "in eternal superiority to all things and eternal independence of all things."[82] God's knowledge is the eternal presupposition of all things. "It is not that God knows everything because it is, but that it is because He knows it."[83] Consequently, God's knowledge is "not actually tied to the distinction between past, present and future being." From all eternity, God knows everything, speaking temporally he knows them "always," and his knowledge of the future is no different than his knowledge of the past and the present.[84]

Barth believes that the Lutherans based God's foreordination upon his foreknowledge route in order to avoid fatalism or the attribution of evil to God's authorship. "But it was done at the price of making God a strangely passive spectator and assistant of the creature, excluding the divine activity at the decisive point where the creaturely activity is itself decision—a truly fateful secularisation of creaturely freedom for which the honour paid to the divine activity in wider spheres was no adequate compensation."[85] God knows what he wills and does what he wills. However, this is not a dangerous proposition as long as we are "clear in our minds that what concerns us is the knowledge and the will and the work of the Father of Jesus Christ."

God's knowledge and his will are always coextensive. "He knows what is real outside Him as that which has been raised to reality by Himself, and as this He also wills it."[86] God knows the possible as that which has its possibility in and by Him, whether as that which He will raise to reality in its own time, or as that which will always be a possibility from Him and by Him, but only a possibility." God wills whether this possibility is to be realized in the future or not. God also knows the impossible, which he has "rejected, excluded and denied; sin as sin; death as death; the devil as the devil. And He also wills it to be this, to be what it is in virtue of His rejection of it, in the way which belongs to it as the impossible."[87]

In Barth's reading, it was to preserve the human agency that Lutheran and Jesuit theologians dissolved predestination into prevision. But he contends that Calvinists did not question the particularity of the activity of creatures, the contingency of natural occurrence or even the freedom of the human will. They did not doubt the spontaneity of human action, although they have been accused of doing so. Calvin may have occasionally described the function of creatures (at least of unconscious ones) as mere instruments used by God,[88] but later divines stated very precisely that we should not believe second causes to be merely instruments of God.[89] "The point at issue between the Lutheran and the Reformed divines was not whether but how to state the autonomy and particularity of creaturely activity in its difference from the relationship with the divine."

Barth recognizes the existence of created wills of angels and humans, and he asserts that these are real wills, that they have freedom of choice and therefore contingency, even though they "have their cause in the divine foreknowledge and are its effect."[90] Both the contingency and the necessity of things is established by God as their originator. God "knows about everything in His creation in its own way. He knows about nature as nature, spirit as spirit, the necessary as necessary, and the contingent as contingent."[91] If people sin, it is not because God knew that they would do so, though he certainly did know from eternity. The object of divine foreknowledge was not fate or fortune "but the man who sinned of his own will."[92]

Barth's rejection of middle knowledge. Barth did not deny that God knew future possibilities or contingencies,[93] but he rejects middle knowledge because of its Molinist association, and he expresses surprise that not all Reformed and Lutheran theologians shared his antipathy.[94] Barth's own rejection of the concept is doubtless explained by his conviction that the purpose of Molinism was "to aid a new semi-Pelagianism to gain its necessary place and right in the new situation in opposition to the Augustinian-Thomist teaching of the Dominicans, whom they accused of being dangerously near to Luther and Calvin."[95] In Barth's view the Molinist model limits God's influence on the free actions of creatures to his giving them a general bias to the good and then seeking to move them in that direction by "moral means, commands, counsels, warnings and threatenings." God knows "(1) what a certain man *can* do with his free will in every conceivable circumstance. He knows (2) what he *would* do in all possible relationships should they become actual." And he knows (3) what the person "*will* do in his freedom when He has given him the necessary external conditions in accordance with His will."[96]

It is Barth's conviction that the middle knowledge concept detracts from the truth and immutability of the divine decrees by attributing certain objects of God's knowledge and will to "free causes" in creation. He cannot understand why A. Walaeus protested against the Jesuits' misuse of the doctrine "as if the doctrine had not been invented for the sake of this 'misuse.'" If we ascribe to the freedom of the creature a decision independent of God's will, it is "too late to profess in the doctrine of grace that it is not a matter of him that wills or runs, but of God who has mercy." In the Molinist model, the outcome is the product both of the decision of the person who wills and runs and of God who has mercy.[97] Quensted, a Lutheran theologian, adopted the concept to preserve election on the basis of foreseen faith, but he changed the language used. Middle knowledge eventually became "a solid constituent of Lutheran doctrine," God's decision in electing individuals to salvation being not absolute but "conditioned by human faith and perseverance." From this perspective human "freedom is not governed by the divine knowledge, nor foreordained in it. It forms a factor over against it which God knows, but cannot, or will not, or at any rate does not control."[98]

Barth asserts that resistance should have been offered to Molinism at the point where the Thomists objected to it. They have "always been more Evangelical in this matter than the wing of our orthodoxy which completely accepted the position of the Jesuits, and obviously much more Evangelical than the popular Protestant Pelagianism which followed."[99] God does not just know human free actions as a spectator, he has "willed and effected their occurrence"; his will and his knowledge are coextensive. Therefore, human free actions are objects of God's knowledge "both as what they are and in the way in which they are." In Barth's opinion, the Thomists were right to object against a limitation of God's omnicausality and omnipotence on the basis of human freedom and to assert that the Molinist position denied God's sovereignty, attacked his deity and made prayer "if not impossible, at least superfluous."[100]

The significance of the doctrine of middle knowledge for prayer was not sufficiently appreciated by Reformed theologians, in Barth's opinion. From Voetius to Turretin, they opposed Molinism too much from the perspective of logic and metaphysics. What prevents the Thomists from effectively countering Molinism is that, when they attempt to do so, their own position reveals that "the door is very slightly open to Protestantism."[101] To effectively reject Molinism, Thomists would have to "become Protestant, and Reformed at that," which is why Barth is convinced that the Roman Catholic magisterium will never decisively reject Molinism. An effective denial of Molinism, in Barth's view, is only possible when one rejects the framework of the analogy of being, within which both God and humans are considered as part of a larger system that includes them both. At that point, "the question of a freedom of the creature which creates conditions for God can no longer arise." To achieve this, theology must be orientated on God's revelation and hence on Christology.[102]

Barth's own opposition to the doctrine of middle knowledge starts from "the simple recognition that the relation between God and the creature is grace, a free act of the divine mercy."[103] There are genuine objects that are distinct from God himself and to that extent independent, and these include "the free creaturely will and all its choice and decision. But it is from God alone that this is what it is." It is by a sovereign decision of grace that God chooses to know the creature, knows it "and competes and cooperates with it." Ours is a "freedom by grace, under grace, and for grace." This leaves no room for the thought "that our will on its side is not completely and omnipotently perceived and therefore foreordained by God in all the possibilities of its choice." There is no possibility that we are given the freedom to assert ourselves in relation to God; yet our wills are not destroyed by this foreordination, and our choices are responsible, and evil choices are not excused. "That it is under divine foreordination does not alter the fact that it is genuine human self-determination."[104]

Prayer Is the Proper Christian Response to God's Providence

Only Christians can confess God's providence because only they know it through their participation in the divine world governance in a "special and inward way."[105] This is not to say that it all makes sense, even to Christians. We "face every day afresh with the riddles of the world-process" and ask "whence, whither, why and wherefore?" Life is an adventure for us as we are "constantly forced to begin afresh, wrestling with the possibilities which open out" to us and the "impossibilities which oppose" us. This is not because we do not know what it is about but because we do. We know "who is its source" and what basically we can expect from it "and what will always actually come from it." But as to the details of the process by which the decision is reached, "and in what form everything will come as it proceeds from this source," we are "as tense and curious as a child, always open and surprised in face of what comes."[106]

We are ready to perceive everything as coming from a positive source and to "co-operate with it instead of adopting an attitude of supercilious and dissatisfied criticism and opposition." In the end we will always be thankful, and in the light of this thankfulness we will "look forward to what has still to come." We will always be the children having dealings with our father.[107] Barth believes that the providence and universal lordship of God are actual to the Christian "in faith, in obedience, and in prayer." If any one of these is missing, it is not a Christian attitude, and there is no antithesis between the contemplative and the active, between "waiting and hasting."[108]

Faith is the source of the Christian attitude and is a receiving of the Word of God.[109] It includes obedience because it lives by the Word, entrusting and surrendering ourselves to the Word's keeping and direction.[110] It includes prayer, particularly thanksgiving and praise as the right of sonship conferred upon us, but also penitence and confession toward the God who gives us this in spite of our own inability and unworthiness. In petition and intercession, faith "ventures to ask about the God who is so near to it and about his benefits which are so near to it, and when it is heard, again receives comfort and blessing, and above all is again given the freedom to be real faith, thus again turning to praise and thanksgiving."[111] In believing, we become Christians, but in doing, we are Christians,[112] and prayer is "the most intimate and effective form of Christian action."[113]

In Petitionary Prayer We Join Christ and His Community as an Act of Obedience to God's Summons and Therefore with Confidence That He Hears

Barth describes prayer as "the true and proper work of the Christian," and he alleges that "the greatest Christian business is only idleness if this true and proper work is not done."[114] In his observation "the most active workers and thinkers and fighters in the divine service in this world have at the same time, and manifestly, been the most active in prayer, and obviously they have not regarded this activity as a waste of time."[115] In prayer we present ourselves to the God whom we can avoid in our activity, but to whom we must present ourselves if we are to have a "genuine and effec-

tive faith and therefore to be capable of a bold and effective obedience."
Prayer is "the act of obedience from which all other acts must spring." In it
we answer the Father who has addressed us, we go to meet the Father
from whose goodness we proceed, and we give direct and natural expression to our great surprise that God is our Father and that we are his children.[116]

By believing, obeying and praying we share in the universal lordship of
God, because God does not preserve, accompany and rule the world without being affected by it. He allows himself to converse with it, and he lis-
tens to what it says. "God is not free and immutable in the sense that He is
the prisoner of His own resolve and will and action, that He must always
be alone as the Lord of all things and of all occurrence. He is not alone in
His trinitarian being, and He is not alone in relation to creatures."[117] In his
freedom God wills to converse with the creature and "to allow Himself to
be determined by it in this relationship." In God's great sovereignty there is
room for us to be "actively present and co-operate in His over-ruling."

Our creaturely freedom cannot limit or compete with the sole sovereignty and efficacy of God, yet God has given us the freedom of his friends
"concerning whom He has determined that without abandoning the helm
for one moment He will still allow Himself to be determined by them." We
do not act autonomously or rebelliously in opposition to the eternal activity
of God's own will and action, "but on the model of His own will and action
there is an individual activity of the creature which is planned and willed
and demanded and made possible and actual by His own eternal activity,
since it is included within it." God does not surrender to the creature, "but
in the very fact that God maintains and asserts himself as King and Lord
there is a divine hearing—on the basis of the incomprehensible grace of
God an incomprehensible hearing—even of the creature which is sinful."[118]

On the basis of this understanding of God's responsiveness to his creatures, Barth has a firm confidence in the importance of petitionary prayer.
It is right for us to wish, to desire and to present our requests to God. God
commands us to call upon him "in the definite expectation that He will
both hear and answer," that our asking "will have an objective as well as a
subjective significance, that is, a significance for his own will and action."
God's will is done "even as the creature calls and presses and prevails
upon it to be done. It is done as the converse with the creature established
by this will is entered into by the creature in the form of this calling and
pressing and prevailing." God's will is done as he "participates in the crea-

ture, and enables it to participate in Himself, and in the purpose and direction of His works."[119]

We come to God in prayer because we seek something from God, we hope to receive what we need from God and do not expect to receive it from anyone else. We cannot petition without worshiping God, giving him praise and thanksgiving and confessing our own wretchedness, but it is in petition that we become praying people. The priority of petition in prayer is evident in the text of the Lord's prayer, "the substance of which is quite clearly and simply a string of petitions, pure petitions, in which the elements of worship and penitence have, of course, their place, which begin and end with worship, but which in themselves and as such are neither adoration nor confession, but simply petition."[120]

What makes our petitionary prayer specifically Christian is that we find ourselves in the relationship of children to God our Father. Since God has drawn near to us, we now turn to him and request from God all that is necessary in our situation as we perceive it. God has showed himself to us as "a Helper and Giver and Deliverer, as the source of all blessing and power and enlightenment and hope," in short of all that we lack, but which the God who has drawn so near to us will allow us to enjoy.[121] Our asking is not impudence. We do not forget the distance between God and ourselves, nor do we seek for things selfishly, but we do what is right and proper in the situation in which we have been placed by the Word of God. We do what God has not only permitted but has commanded us to do, indeed what God has placed us in this situation to do. Consequently, in petition, we are genuinely acting in praise and thanksgiving and in penitence; we magnify God and abase ourselves.[122] It is as members of the body of Christ, and therefore of the community, that we are invited to pray, and we therefore confidently await answers and determine the will of God concerning our personal but not our private needs and petitions.[123]

"Originally and properly the Christian who is at the side of God and has His own voice and responsibility in the divine rule is the one Son of Man, Jesus Christ."[124] It is primarily the asking of Jesus that is answered; this is the work of the creature that includes within it "the fulness of the divine presence and gift, and therefore helps to determine the divine will and action." It is in Christ that God "came to our side and entered into our humility"; and it is in him that "we are lifted up to Him and therefore to the place where decisions are made in the affairs of His government." It is not Christians in and for themselves but Christians in Christ who are at God's side and have "a say and a part in the place where those decisions are made."[125]

What we need most is Jesus Christ. It is in Christ that God controls all occurrence, "upholding it, accompanying it and ruling it." In the Word "the world is already helped, and everything that creation needs, and at the heart of creation man, is already provided." In Christ the church already possesses the grace of God and "looks back and down upon all that is not yet ordered, all that is not yet solved, all that is not yet liberated, all the disturbances and obstructions and confusions and devastations which we still find in the world-process, all the darkness which still tries to obscure and actually does obscure for us the fatherly rule and determination under which this process stands. In Him, it already sees it unobscured."[126] In petition we simply take and receive the "divine gift and answer as it is already present and near to hand in Jesus Christ."[127]

As members of the church we will ask that we may really be Christ's community, that it may not be in vain that the church is founded and maintained and ruled by him; that it may not be in vain that we are separated from the world and sent out into it. We will ask for God's love to unify us, that we may hear and know his Word in a new way, and that our witness might be effective, both by life and speech. It is not our existence as such but our existence in God's service that we will ask for.[128] We need and must desire and request that in every situation we might be "equipped and usable and ready in the service which Jesus Christ has assigned to His people, and in which they can have their salvation and glory."[129]

We will also be intercessors for the world, standing with our Lord before God on behalf of all creation. "Because the community asks, the world in its godlessness is not simply godless, but God finds in the world and has in it a partner, and the history between Himself and the world—which is not merely a history of judgment but also of salvation and grace—moves forward to its ultimate goal."[130]

Barth believed in the effectiveness of petition and intercession, but this was more by virtue of its role within the divine purpose than by a changing of that purpose. "True prayer is prayer which is sure of a hearing," which Barth defines as "the reception and adoption of the human request into God's plan and will, and therefore the divine speech and action which correspond to the human request."[131] In regard to Abraham's intercession for Sodom, for instance (Gen 18:20ff.), Barth says that God "made concessions" to Abraham, step by step, but then Barth denies that it really involves an influencing of God by Abraham. It is rather "confirmation of the fact that according to verse 17 God intended to keep nothing hidden from Abraham of what he proposed to do, and according to verse 19 He had chosen him to command those that came after him to keep the way of the Lord and to do justice and judgment."[132] Clearly, the way of the Lord is "kept" in Abraham's intercession and "manifest in the divine concessions" (cf. Ex 32:9ff.; Num 11; Amos 7:1-6; and especially Jer 18:1-10).

An excursus on the sense in which God makes himself dependent upon our prayer, in Barth's theology. Working within the openness model, John Sanders posits that "God is free to choose to be dependent on the free response of the creatures and to *respond* to them if God so desires."[133] Sanders then cites Karl Barth, giving the impression that Barth shares his perspective in regard to God's choice to be dependent on us and on our response to him. Specifically, he cites Barth's statement: "If ever there was a miserable anthropomorphism, it is the hallucination of a divine immutability which rules out the possibility that God can let himself be conditioned in this or that way by his creature."[134] Admittedly, those words certainly seem representative of the sort of contingency that the openness model attributes to humans within God's self-limited control. I admit to being hesitant when making dogmatic statements about what Barth did or did not believe because of his dialectical approach. Nevertheless, I can say that this statement of Barth's does not connote to me what it does to Sanders, as I read it in its context, which is the section "Prayer" under the general treatment "Freedom before God."

Barth describes prayer, the addressing of our requests to God, as something that we are free to do because God has invited, indeed commanded, us to pray. "God wills to see [the one at prayer] and have him before Him as this praying man and therefore as a free man."[135] Barth faces the objection to prayer from God's goodness and knowledge, namely, "if it rests with God to give us all that we truly lack and desire, and if we may seriously assume that He really can and will do this, and actually does it, then we must obviously suppose that He knows our legitimate needs better than we do, and even before we ourselves discover or state them."[136] But "He is the God who lets man come to Him with his requests, and hears and answers them. He is God in the fact that He lets man apply to him in this way, and wills that this should be the case."[137]

We pray because we know that "God is the Lord of the covenant, that His undoubtedly majestic counsel and will are fashioned as the will and counsel of His grace, that our poor human asking is thus taken up into them from all eternity, that He therefore reckons with it even in time, and that there is thus a necessity of asking."[138] We pray gladly, freely and boldly but in the recognition that "there will never be a human request which does not need to be effectively and definitively rectified on this side by the pure hands with which God receives it."[139] What Barth sees God establishing and revealing to us in the Lord's prayer is a reciprocal relationship but one in which God and his will are clearly dominant. In the first three requests we are invited and summoned "to take up the cause of God and actively to participate in it with our asking."[140] God does not will to work alone but to include us in his work. He wills "that His cause, which as such is prosecuted by Him and is completely in His free and mighty hand, should not only be His but also ours. He does not will to be God without us, or to exist as such. . . . He summons us to make His purposes and aims the object of our own desires."[141]

But God does not need us, and he does not demand our cooperation. However, the last three petitions, in which we focus on our own needs, are offered in the context of the first three. They are the "inversion and consequence of the first three."[142] Nevertheless, when we do bring our requests to God, we have the assurance that God not only receives our petition, it "infallibly passes over into His plan and will and cannot lack the corresponding divine speaking and doing."[143] Our asking and receiving are repeatedly placed in a necessary relationship, within Scripture (Ps 91:14-16; 145:19; Mt 7:7-8; 1 Jn 5:14-15).[144] The reason that we can pray with such confidence is because we pray "in Christ" and in fellowship with the Holy Spirit. Thus God is already on our side, and we are on his. "As Jesus Christ asks, and we with Him, God has already made Himself the Guarantor that our requests will be heard."[145] It is in this context of our prayer in Christ that Barth makes the statement about the possibility that "God can let Himself be conditioned in this or that way by His creature." By contrast with an immovable idol, "His majesty, the glory of His omnipotence and sovereignty, consists in the fact that He can give to the requests of this creature a place in His will." But God does this at the point in creation where He is "concerned with Himself, with His beloved Son and those who are His."[146] God can be no greater than he is in Jesus Christ or "when He lets those who are Christ's participate in His kingly office, and therefore when He not only hears but answers their requests."[147]

In short, Barth's language of divine dependency and of God's willingness to be conditioned by his creatures comes within the framework of his omnipotence, of his sovereignty and of the accomplishment of his own will and purpose for creation. But it also takes us back to Barth's insistence that providence and prayer and everything else that we know and can say about God must be couched in terms of God's revelation of himself in Christ. And it is in this regard that Barth's dialectic comes so much to the fore, since in Christ God says both his "yes" and his "no" to sinful humanity, he both justifies and condemns. Nevertheless, given my previous exposition of Barth's doctrine of providence and prayer and the approval with which Barth quotes Calvin and the Heidelberg Catechism within this section, to elucidate and illustrate his own position, I conclude that Barth should be located primarily within proximity to the Calvinist tradition rather than somewhere further to the "left," within the range of models of "risk providence" and the kind of voluntary divine dependence on the creature that those models include.

The Case Study

Helmut Spiegel had come to faith late in life but had quickly become an avid student of Scripture and a reader of many kinds of theological works. However, his favorite was Karl Barth because he found in Barth's theology not only a strong affirmation of the traditional faith of the Christian church, particularly as it had been formulated within the Reformed tradition, but an approach to all aspects of truth and life that started from the gracious purposes of God in Christ. It was from that perspective that Helmut offered his own petition.

Helmut shared with Maria Sanchez (Thomist model) a strong confidence that God was comprehensively in control of everything in the world. Furthermore, God knows what is future to us in all its details because he knows his own will, not because he foresees our own decisions and actions. Helmut also agreed with Maria and her Thomist teachers that when God makes his decisions concerning the world he brings about he does not utilize a knowledge of what people *would* do in particular circumstances. Helmut saw this Molinist proposal as an inversion of the proper order between God and his creatures. They work together but only in the sense that God works with the creature. Their relationship is not one of mutual dependence. Helmut was concerned that an affirmation of middle knowledge would be a way of making God dependent to some extent upon the creatures and their own self-determination. Although Helmut was generally appreciative of Reformed theology, on this particular question he believed that the Thomists had understood the dangers in Molinism much more clearly than many of the Reformed theologians had done. Where Helmut disagreed with Maria was in regard to the freedom of creatures within God's sovereignty, but Maria was not always clear where the difference between them lay. Helmut was less anxious to insist on the freedom of the creature than Maria was, but he certainly did not deny that creatures act voluntarily within God's overall sovereignty and that they do so by virtue of God's gracious gift.

So Helmut believed that the abduction of the missionaries was neither a surprise to God nor was it something that he had been unable to prevent. In this regard, Helmut and Maria sounded much alike. But Helmut emphasized more strongly than anyone else in his prayer group the centrality of Christ in all of God's action in the world of his creation. Christ is the quintessential human being, but he is also the one in whom we know God. We must not only think about salvation in terms of Christ but also of all of God's working in the world in the broader areas of the general history of the world and its peoples. Since Christ is the one in whom God has spoken both his word of condemnation and of salvation, our contemplation of all things in Christ is a focus on the grace of God at work in his creation. In fact, we know God only in Christ, not first in nature (as Maria proposed) and not in the Bible, as so many others in the church assumed. We come to know God and his work in the world through the testimony of Scripture, but this is because the Bible testifies to Christ, not because it has an intrinsic divine authority. Nevertheless, because the Bible is unique in its testimony to Christ, Helmut studied and quoted it in ways that often made him undistinguishable from the others who believed the Bible itself to be God's Word.

As Helmut contemplated the situation that Fred Henderson had reported, he tried to envision what was going on in terms of the purposes of God in the world as he knew them through the revelation of God in Christ. First and foremost, Helmut was convinced of God's purpose of grace. He considered not only the missionaries but also the guerrillas as elect in Christ, as people whose condemnation had been borne by Christ and whom God was graciously drawing to himself. On the other hand, Helmut did not therefore minimize the wrongness of the rebels' actions nor the fact that they were not living in an acknowledgment of Christ's Lordship. But, in considering God's purpose and action in the situation, Helmut was confident that God was working for the good of everyone in the situation.

Helmut believed that he could have a significant part in the accomplishment of God's purpose through prayer. This was not on the assumption that his prayer would affect God's own decision and change the direction of God's action, but it was because God had purposed to work in the world through those who acknowledged his Lordship and to do much of his work of grace in response to their prayers. Helmut experienced comfort from his conviction that Christ was himself interceding in regard to this situation. Helmut's goal was, therefore, not to change God's mind but to discern his will and to join Christ in prayer that would be offered through Christ himself, the Mediator.

Helmut prayed, "Gracious God, we come to you in the joy of knowing that your purposes for the world are gracious in Jesus Christ. You have chosen humankind in the Word, and you are now working toward the summing up of all things in him. It is from this perspective that we approach the abduction of Richard and his fellow missionaries. We see evil at work in this situation, but we know that it is not evil that is outside of your control. You have invited us to participate with you in your gracious rule of the world through our requests, and so we ask you now that your grace might triumph in this difficult situation. We pray that Richard and his friends might be conscious of your love and care and may seek to be faithful ambassadors for you in their time of trouble. We pray that your own gracious work toward their captors will be evident to them in the behavior of the missionaries, and we ask that their lives may be positively affected through this encounter. Father, what all of those people need, captives and captors alike, is the personal knowledge of your Son, and we pray that this incident may further that purpose. There is no one else to whom we can turn, and so we now turn to you, humbly but expectantly, in the desire that your will may be done there, at this time, as it is always done in heaven. In Jesus' name, Amen."

11

The Calvinist Model

T HE CALVINIST MODEL IS THE MAJOR PROTESTANT FORM OF THE THEOLOGY *that proponents of the process and openness models refer to as "classical theism." Like Thomism, it believes in the omnicausality of God. Everything that happens in the world comes about because God has freely, wisely and in moral goodness, chosen that it should be as it is. This is a "no-risk" model of providence. Like Thomism, the Calvinist model has classically affirmed God's timelessness or time-freeness. Both of them are forms of compatibilism; that is, they believe that everything is determined by God but that creatures are free. The two models differ, however, in their understanding of creaturely freedom. Whereas Thomism asserts libertarian freedom, the Calvinist model believes that God's comprehensive determination can only be coordinated with a creaturely freedom that is volitional or voluntary. Creatures do what they want to do but what they do is always within God's overall determination. Granted that everything that occurs is by God's determination, a distinction is generally made between what God wills to bring about through his personal involvement and what he wills to allow through his not acting preventively. Thus, Calvinists believe, they are able to assert God's sovereign determining of all events while not making God morally responsible for those events in which he has purposed to allow creatures to disobey his commands while not condoning that disobedience.*

This model believes that God's omniscience includes everything in the history of the created world, past, present and future. God's knowledge of the future is not simply foresight, it is a knowledge of his own will, a knowledge of what he has determined the future should be. Classically, Calvinist theologians have agreed with Thomists that God is absolutely time-free so that his foreknowledge is not technically before the time of the event since he himself experiences no before and after, although he is well able to distinguish between what is past and future in the experience of his creatures. Some Calvinist theologians have conceded the possible helpfulness of a divine middle knowledge (knowledge of counterfactuals), but this has not played a significant role in the classical Calvinist portrayal of the formation of God's providential plan.

The Calvinist model of providence has asserted the efficacy of human petition, to the bewilderment of theologians who posit a "risk" view of providence. Although God has determined in his timeless eternity all that would happen in created history, he has planned not only the outcomes but the means by which those outcomes are achieved. God has thus given petitionary prayer an effective role in the outworking of his purposes. There are many things that God does providentially, whether or not anyone asks him to do them. But there are also things that God has purposed to do precisely as answers to prayer. By this means God involves his followers in the work of establishing God's rule in the world, he fosters their sense of dependence on him, and he generates a thankful spirit when things happen as believers have prayed that they should. The ministry of intercession for one another within the community of God's people also fosters the fellowship that God wills for them. So prayer does affect the outcome of things in the world, although it does not do so by changing God's mind about what he will do in the situation.

Among the Protestant Reformers who perpetuated an appreciation for the general approach to God's providence that had been established in the work of Augustine, perhaps none has been more influential than John Calvin. His name has become identified with Protestant theologies that have a strong conviction that God is absolutely sovereign. As was true of Aquinas, many theologians have developed variations of Calvin's theology. We will let Calvin's own doctrine of providence and prayer have a large place in this chapter but will also look at the ways in which a few modern theologians have developed positions within the general framework that

Calvin established. Prominent among these will be G. C. Berkouwer, John Feinberg, Roger Hazelton, Paul Helm, William Pollard and Vernon White.

God's Sovereign Rule in the World Includes
All Occurrences Within It

The all inclusiveness of God's sovereign providence. John Feinberg speaks of God's sovereignty in terms of his having "chosen at once the whole interconnected sequence of events and actions that have and will occur in our world."[1] This was a free choice on God's part and includes both non-constraining means and ends. Nothing external to God, such as the foreseen actions or merits of his creatures, determines his choices, although he accomplishes most of what he does through other agents.[2] Ephesians 1:11 is deemed the clearest statement of this absolute divine sovereignty (cf. Ps 115:3; Prov 16:9, 33; Dan 4:34-35; Acts 2:23; 4:27-28; Phil 2:12-13; Heb 13:21).[3]

Calvin objects against those who contend that the universe, human affairs and humans themselves are "governed by God's might but not by His determination." On the contrary, he insists, nothing is excluded from God's providence: "It is certain that not one drop of rain falls without God's sure command."[4] Having once created the universe, God "governs it, always working to maintain all things in their state and to arrange them by his hand as he sees fit."[5] Calvin denied that God's providence is "an unconcerned sitting of God in heaven, from which He merely observes the things that are done in the world."[6] Rather it is God's governing of the world that he has made. He not only preserves the order of nature that he originally purposed in himself, but he "holds and continues a peculiar care of every single creature that He has created." His providence goes beyond the universal order of nature to the details of people's lives. "Some mothers have full and abundant breasts, but others' are almost dry, as God wills to feed one more liberally, but another more meagerly."[7] In addition to his universal providence, by which "the planets are kept in operation and the seasons recur," he "covers under the wings of His care each single one of His creatures" (cf. Mt 10:29).[8] Human beings are the noblest work of God, and everything contained in the heavens and the earth was created for our good. When Scripture speaks of providence, it is the "care and government of the human race" that is primarily being described.[9]

Like Aquinas (Thomist model), Calvin spoke of God as first cause. He summed up his position with the statement that "the *will of God* is the one principal and all-high *cause* of all things in heaven and on earth!"[10] Calvin warned Christians who have experienced success not to give praise to humans but only to God, in the assurance "that God was the first cause and author of all this good," through whatever secondary medium it came.[11] When someone helps us, we ought to regard the deliverance rendered by a human hand as a divine deliverance. "The sun rises day by day; but it is God that enlightens the earth by his rays. The earth brings forth her fruits; but it is God that giveth bread, and it is God that giveth strength by the nourishment of that bread. In a word, as all inferior and secondary causes, viewed in themselves, veil like so many curtains the glorious God from our sight (which they too frequently do), the eye of faith must be cast up far higher, that it may behold the hand of God working by all these His instruments."[12] God can also work without medium or instrument, giving "strength *without* bread, which He is nevertheless mercifully pleased to supply *by means of* bread."[13]

Inanimate objects have "by nature been endowed" with their own property, but one of them "does not exercise its own power except in so far as it is directed by God's ever-present hand," says Calvin. These are, thus, "nothing but instruments to which God continually imparts as much effectiveness as he wills, and according to his own purpose bends and turns them to either one action or another."[14] By means of a few miracles (Josh 10:13; 2 Kings 20:11; Is 38:8) God has witnessed that "the sun does not daily rise and set by a blind instinct of nature but that he himself, to renew our remembrance of his fatherly favor toward us, governs its course."[15] Consequently, what we designate "natural" occurrences are actually regulated by God's providence, including the south wind that brought birds to Israel in the wilderness (Ex 16:13; Num 11:31), the storm for Jonah (Jon 1:4; cf. Ps 104:3-4; 107:25, 29; Amos 4:9), barrenness and fertility (Gen 30:2ff.; Ps 113:9; 127:3) and the provision of daily bread (Ps 136:25; Is 3:1; Mt 6:11).[16] Paul Helm posits that, in the continuous dependence of all things upon God, even something like a word processor is dependent upon God. The materials were made by God and are upheld by God, and the designers and engineers were or are being upheld by God (cf. Jn 1:3; Acts 17:28; Col 1:17; Heb 1:2).[17] From this perspective, a miracle is "the way in which God has chosen to uphold the universe at that moment."[18]

In every action of a human agent, God is also at work, even to the minutest detail of our lives. Thus Calvin states, "Although men, like brute beasts confined by no chains, rush at random here and there, yet God by

His secret bridle so holds and governs them, that they cannot move even one of their fingers without accomplishing the work of God much more than their own!" However, the faithful who willingly serve God are "in a peculiar manner, *the hands* of God."[19] God uses the wicked to punish human sin but also as instruments of goodness. The Assyrian king, for example, was the rod of God's anger when he made war on Judah (Is 10:5), and God later rebuked him for not acknowledging that he was "an axe and a saw forged by God's hand" (Is 10:15).[20] Joseph's brothers are a classic instance of human wrongdoing that God used for good (Gen 45:5, 8). When Solomon said that "the king's heart is a stream of water in the hand of the LORD; he turns it wherever he will," (Prov 21:1), his intention was to show, "generally, that not only the wills of kings, but all their external actions are overruled by the will and disposal of God."[21]

God even worked through Satan, having him be a lying spirit in the mouths of the prophets, in punishment of Ahab, and later buffeting Paul with a thorn in the flesh. "That is, God, by holding Satan fast bound in obedience to His Providence, turns him whithersoever He will, and thus applies the great enemy's devices and attempts to the accomplishment of His own eternal purposes!"[22] As Vernon White reads the New Testament, it indicates that "the 'works of the devil' may also bring glory to God and provide opportunities of grace and growth [e.g., Jn 9]; the prince of this world has no ultimate power [Jn 14:30], but all will be subject to God who is all in all [1 Cor 15:28]."[23] Even the destruction of the old creation, when viewed from the larger perspective of its recreation, is not "the failure of God followed by a new beginning" but "the pre-ordained means by which the final perfection is to be brought about."

In asserting God's omnicausality, which is to stress the vertical aspect, Paul Helm warns against compromising the horizontal causal relations. Too great a stress on the *immediacy* of creation's reliance on God leads to a continuous creation, as in the position put forward by Jonathan Edwards.[24] In this approach, no room is left for horizontal causes since nothing that exists at a moment can cause any effect at a later moment because the first moment ceases to exist, and the later one is a product of immediate divine power. Helm wishes to avoid any sense of competition between primary and secondary causes. The primary cause is not an event in time but is "an eternal cause which has the whole of the creation as its effect," yet secondary causes are truly causal, even though they have no power independent of God. Helm identifies his position on this matter as consistent with that of both Aquinas and Calvin.[25]

Distinctions between providence, fate, chance and accident. The doctrine of all-inclusive providence Calvin taught was accused of fatalism, but
that was a charge he explicitly rejected,[26] arguing that he was not contriving
"a necessity out of the perpetual connection and intimately related series of
causes, which is contained in nature." On the contrary, he attributed the
government of all things to God's eternal decree, which was made "in
accordance with his wisdom." Furthermore, since every success is God's
blessing, and calamity and adversity are God's curse, there is no place left
"in human affairs for fortune or chance."[27] On the other hand, Calvin
granted that many events appear fortuitous, even though they take place
by God's will, because the "order, reason, end and necessity of those things
which happen for the most part lie hidden in God's purposes, and are not
apprehended by human opinion."[28]

Paul Helm maintains that God's omnicausality would be fatalistic "only if
God decreed ends without decreeing any or all of the means to those ends,
or if God's will was itself fated."[29] But God ordains means as well as ends
and employs our causal powers so that their voluntariness and spontaneity
as well as our responsibility are not overridden. God has ordained that my
choices are exactly the way in which he will accomplish his will. It is critical that we do not know ahead of time what we are going to do, even
though God does.[30] As to chance, we use the term to indicate the "absence
of any imputable cause" or to speak of things that we could not predict,
though they are, in fact, caused and hence predictable. For example, the
numbers in a lottery machine are said to make a winner by "chance."[31]

William Pollard has given particular attention to the place of chance and
accident within divine providence and his account falls within the general
outline of the model of providence under consideration in this chapter. It is
his thesis that "the key to the Biblical idea of providence . . . is to be found
in the appearance of chance and accident in history." What is deemed by
believers to be "an act of divine mercy showing forth our God's restorative
power is for the pagan merely a piece of extraordinarily good luck."[32] Pollard defines chance as "the existence, as a typical feature of natural processes, of alternative responses to a given set of causative influences for
which the laws of nature specify only the relative probabilities. Insofar as
alternatives are typical of all natural processes, chance becomes a universal
ingredient of history."[33] By the term *accident,* he designates "situations in
which two or more chains of events which have no causal connection with

each other coincide in such a way as to decide the course of events." The two chains could each be rigorously determined within themselves yet "their accidental convergence would decisively modify the course of history." For example, one might think of the arrival of a storm at just the right moment to produce a positive military situation.[34]

Tension arises between science and the doctrine of providence because of their different perspectives on events. "Science deals with repeatable events for which the laws of nature determine probabilities of occurrence. Providence in the Biblical sense deals with isolated singular events apprehended in a given historical context as responsive to God's will."[35] Because of this difference in perspective, "one and the same event can equally well be regarded as under the full sway of all laws of nature and natural causality and at the same time under the full sway of the divine will." The laws of nature only prescribe "the chance or probability of the event under the given set of circumstances in which it occurred." Having knowledge of this probability in no way affects the providential character of the event, "which depends only on the circumstance that this particular possibility was the one which actually did occur in the historical sequence of which it was a part." In one context, this can be labeled chance but, in the other context, it "can without contradiction manifest the will of God acting in judgment or in redemption."[36]

The intentional permission of God. Calvin objected to any use of the language of divine permission as a way of evading the action of God in all events. No distinction should be made between what God does and what God permits. "It would be ridiculous for the Judge only to permit what he wills to be done, and not also to decree it and to command its execution by his ministers."[37] Of the hardening of Pharaoh's heart by the Lord, Calvin said: "It is in vain here to flee to the common refuge of God's permission, as if God could be said not to have done that which He only permitted to be done!" Pharaoh exercised his "inhuman cruelty" because "it pleased the Lord; partly, that He might thereby prove the patience of His people; and partly, that He might shew forth His own almighty power."[38] On the other hand, Calvin does not deny that Pharaoh hardened his own heart (Ex 8:32). Pharaoh was not "impelled by any outward influence to do violently," nor did God cause his hardening, but he acted "spontaneously out of his own malice." What Calvin maintained is that when people "act perversely, they do so (according to the testimony of the Scripture) by the ordaining purpose of God."[39] Other instances of this are the men of Gibeon who hardened their hearts against Israel (Josh 11:20); David, whose numbering of the people to satisfy his own pride was spoken of as moved both by God (2 Sam 24:1) and by Satan (1 Chron 21:1); and Saul, who acted from his own wickedness but was urged on by an evil spirit sent from the Lord (1 Sam 16:23-24).[40]

The internal affections of people are no less ruled by God's hand "than their external actions are preceded by His eternal decree" for "God performs not by the hands of men the things which He has decreed, without first working in their hearts the very will which precedes the acts they are to perform." On this point, Calvin cites Augustine with favor: "That is not done without His will which is even done contrary to His will, because it could not have been done had He not permitted it to be done; and yet, He did not permit it without His will, but according to His will."[41] It is wrong to say that "these things happen merely by the permission of God when they are by His will and authority."[42] It was by the secret counsel and decree of God that Adam fell, and "not only by the permission of God."[43]

Calvin's insistence on including the things that God permits within his decree as intended by him drew the charge from his adversary that, in Calvin's theology, "the sins which are committed, are committed not only by the permission, but even by the will of God. For it is frivolous to make any difference between the permission of God and the will of God, as far as sin is concerned."[44] In response to this accusation Calvin argues that God wills in one sense what is contrary to his will in another and that he does so without self-contradiction. For example, God "declares that no false prophets arise, but those whom he ordains to be such, either to prove the faith of His own people, or to blind the unbelieving. 'If there arise among you a false prophet (saith Moses), your God proveth you by that prophet' (Deut 13:1, 3)."[45] If we were to distinguish between willing and permitting as Calvin's opponents wished to do, then riches would not be regarded as "blessings actually bestowed of God" but as having fallen "into our hands by the random permission of God." This is completely unacceptable. The critical point is that God does not permit unwillingly. "If, therefore, God permits willingly, to represent Him as sitting on His throne as a mere unconcerned and unengaged spectator, is utterly profane. Wherefore it follows that God determines and rules by His counsel whatsoever He wills to be done."[46]

G. C. Berkouwer points out that in spite of Calvin's dislike of the term *permission* to speak of God's relationship to human action, the term has

not been totally rejected by Reformed theology because of its "strong distaste—on biblical grounds—for determinism" and on account of "a desire
to express the thought that good and evil do not originate in the same way,
as 'effects' of one general Divine causality."[47] Berkouwer himself suggests
that "when permission is really used to indicate the manner of Divine ruling, by which He grants room *within* His ruling for human freedom and
responsibility, then the line of Biblical thinking has not been wholly abandoned. For this freedom, this creaturely freedom, receives a place in God's
rule of the world."[48]

Roger Hazelton suggests that when we say "God willing" we mean "God
permitting," but we do not regard this permissive power of God as coercive. "It is not the cause to which our wills are but effects. It does not make
us do things, but only gives them leave to happen, gives them room and
scope for becoming real."[49] This implies that unless God allows the outcome, it would not occur since God might refuse his permission. He either
"holds back something of his power, or perhaps confers that power upon
human free will acting as his agent in the world. But in either case," Hazelton posits that "the determining initiative rests with God." This is "not a
device for verbally limiting God or keeping him from getting too much in
man's own way. Rather, it is a way of marking off the limits of *our* compe-
tence to decide and act." To speak in this manner is to concede "the very
positive belief that the entire condition, context, and consequence of
human effort depends finally upon God alone. The stress is throughout on
the primary and prior right of God's will over and above the wills of men
and women in his world."[50] Hazelton states what is commonly the case in
the language of Calvinist theologians, that permission is connected mainly
with human sin and concurrence is connected with human goodness. "It
gives theological statement to the truth of faith that while man by himself
does evil, only God can be the author and finisher of whatever good man
may accomplish."[51]

Paul Helm takes notice of the common objection that this distinction
between the things God wills to permit and those he wills to effect gives
God a split personality. However, he asserts that even in a risk model,
where God does not will or even know events until they happen, God is in
some measure permitting them when they do occur, even though he may
be ignorant in permitting them. Even in those models, therefore, there are
two wills, the will of permission and that of command. Furthermore, a third
sense of *wish* must be added, to designate the will of God that can be frus-

trated. On the other hand, Helm grants that the problem seems more acute in a no-risk model because of the conflict that ensues between God's omnipotence and his goodness.[52]

God Cares for His People in a Special Way, and This May Include Miracles

Among humans, says Calvin, God "keeps a more especial watch over the faithful" (Gen 15; Ps 33:21; 55:22; 91:1,12; 97:10; Is 49:25; Zech 2:8ff.; Mt 10:29-31; 1 Pet 5:7), for "the Church is the great workroom of God, wherein, in a more especial manner, He displays His wonderful works; and it is the more immediate theatre of His glorious Providence."[53] Adoption is "an act of special grace" that brings it about that not all people are "equally the children of God."[54] Perhaps the most quoted text of all in this regard is Romans 8:28, which asserts that, in God's detailed providence, he brings "diverse strands together for the benefit of each Christian and as part of his or her ultimate blessedness."[55]

In spite of this evident distinction between God's general care of all his creatures and his care for those who acknowledge his Lordship, Paul Helm suggests that it is best not to draw too strong a contrast between providence and predestination or general and special providence. This is because God's support and control of his creation as a whole are no less strict and complete than his gracious support and control of the church, and because God controls all persons and events equally, though it is primarily withholding in one case and giving in the other. "All predestination is providential, and all exercises of providence are predestinarian."[56] God's special care for different aspects of the created order is all part of the one providential purpose and program; the ship that carried Paul to Italy was upheld by the same providential care that upholds all other ships going to Italy, yet God's purpose for this particular ship was inextricably tied to the life and health of the church, that is, with the redemptive purposes. God upholds all assembly-line workers, but his intention is different with regard to the Christian. This special providence may work for a time without public evidence, as was the case in Paul's early life, education and Pharisaism, which were preparing him for his ministry as apostle to the Gentiles.[57]

It is within this special redemptive purpose of God for his people that miracles have their particular role. Biblical writers did not work with a rigid distinction between the natural and the supernatural, but they recognized some events as signs and wonders, powerful expressions of God's power and grace. These do not have a "scientific or magical significance of their own" but are integral to the history of God's dealings with his people. "They are intended to make those who believe that God orders the affairs of nature for their good gasp—not only at the power of God in the miracle, but at power of a deeper magnitude in the revelation of saving grace which the miracles signal." This is why they occur at special times of awakening and revelation.[58]

Accordingly, Pollard contends that "in its broadest terms a miracle is an event which is apprehended by a worshipping community as a clear instance of the divine activity in the shaping of history. The question as to whether the event so apprehended does or does not violate known scientific laws is secondary."[59] In the case of the exodus, the storm that opened the way through the sea "is clearly an instance of one of history's great, crucial, and destiny-filled accidents. . . . At this occurrence and from then on throughout their history it was spontaneously and unanimously recognized as a great and mighty act of God on their behalf."[60] Pollard therefore asserts that a miracle "is not a special kind of event possessing a quality which common happenings do not share. It is rather an occasion in which the essentially providential character of all events is made manifest in an especially clear and striking manner." For Israel the exodus became "a clear and decisive guarantee of the providential presence of God in every situation." Consequently, Pollard argues that "the more a given event has the power to reveal some timeless universal property of the world, the less it is capable of making manifest the hand of God in the shaping of events. And conversely, the more an event or sequence of events makes manifest the providential character of history, the more chaotic and fortuitous they will appear to those who seek only to discover universal law and order in history."[61] Most of the miracles in the Bible are seen to be like the exodus, "the result of an extraordinary and extremely improbable combination of chance and accident" (as these terms have been defined above).[62] On the other hand, singular events like creation, the incarnation and the resurrection cannot be spoken of in terms of chance or accident because those terms only apply to events that can happen repeatedly in alternative ways. But a singular event is not repeatable, and there are no alternatives to it, other than its not happening at all. "Such events neither conform to nor violate natural law because their singularity precludes their repetition in accordance with any kind of pattern."[63]

Berkouwer is concerned about attempts to give greater credence to miracles through appeal to quantum theory and Heisenberg's theory of indeterminacy. "He who rediscovers room for the activity of God in a crisis of natural science, however, has already implicitly relativized and limited this activity and has posited it over against a natural order seen as a self-existing reality."[64] This is an abandonment of the biblical manner of speaking about the activity of God in the world. It places faith at the mercy of theories of natural science. On the other hand, Scripture emphasizes the reality of miracles, not their possibility. Its focus is "not so much on the 'point of intersection' of the supernatural with the natural, as on the content and purpose of God's activity in the world."[65] It is not the miraculousness of God's acts that constitutes their significance, it is "their redeeming and informing and instructing content."[66] God's miraculous activity is not against nature but against sin. "A miracle is not an abnormal or unnatural occurrence presupposing the normality of nature, but a redeeming reinstatement of the normality of world and life through the new dominion of God, which stands antithetically against the kingdom of this world."[67] Miracles cause surprise because people have "become accustomed to the abnormality of sin and its curse of death and terror."[68]

Human Agents Are Genuinely Free Within God's Absolute Sovereignty

The definition of freedom. A major difference between Augustinian and non-Augustinian models of providence lies in their definitions of freedom. Both groups of theologians contend that humans are free, but they define freedom in different ways. As we have seen in earlier chapters of the book, non-Augustinians consistently define freedom in an indeterministic manner, what is sometimes spoken of as the "liberty of indifference." By contrast Augustinians, who assert just as strongly that human beings are free agents, consider this freedom to be compatible with detailed divine sovereignty and therefore, in some sense, to be deterministic. This is therefore dubbed the "liberty of spontaneity."[69] In the ensuing discussion it will be helpful also to keep in mind that *determinism* is another term that has different senses, ranging from the soft determinism that a compatibilist affirms to the mechanistic determinism of a fatalist (see the fatalist model in chapter twelve).

Among compatibilists, who argue that God is absolutely sovereign in all the details of the world but that morally responsible creatures (both human and spiritual) are free, there is a difference of opinion concerning our ability to explain or demonstrate this compatibility. Paul Helm cites J. I. Packer as one who affirms a "no-risk" view of divine providence but who considers us unable to explain its reconciliation with human responsibility. This is not on account of an intrinsic incompatibility but because of our ignorance. Helm considers the strengths of such an approach to be that it allows all the biblical data to be given full scope and abandons none of them through rationalism. Its disadvantages are that it offers no criterion for demonstrating that this is an actual antinomy, not just a difficult to reconcile situation, and no criterion for distinguishing an apparent inconsistency from a real one. To conclude that this is an antinomous situation, a large number of attempts at reconciliation would have had to fail. Whereas Packer might argue that since both divine sovereignty and human responsibility are clearly taught in Scripture, they must be consistent, Helm is concerned that in the history of the church much nonsense has been affirmed to be taught by Scripture, and it is, therefore, wise for us to do our best to show the consistency of these two affirmations.[70]

Calvin's insistence on morally responsible human freedom. Because of Calvin's strong emphasis on absolute divine sovereignty and his vigorous opposition to the notion of "free will" that was current in the sixteenth century, he is often described as a determinist. This is a commonplace that Allen Verhey thinks we must challenge and repudiate, because Calvin himself explicitly denied Stoic determinism.[71] Against the Libertines Calvin argued that determinism has "three abominable consequences:" it removes the distinction between God and the devil, it destroys moral conscience, and it leaves us unable to pass moral judgment upon anything.[72] Calvin therefore rejects determinism, but he also refuses to accept indeterminism.

The Libertines spoke as though Calvin were teaching that humans have no more will than a stone,[73] but Calvin wished to preserve for humans a freedom that would constitute them morally responsible for their deeds. The error of the Libertines lay in their failing to observe two essential distinctions. (1) They missed the fact "that Satan and the wicked are not instruments of God in such a way that they do not act for themselves as well."[74] God does not work through iniquitous people in the same way as he does "through a stone or a tree trunk." He uses them "as rational creatures according to the quality of the nature he has given them." Thus Scripture speaks of God whistling to call the impious to arms but "does not fail to recount their own plan and their own will and to attribute to them the work that may indeed have been by the ordinance of God." (2) They failed to note that there is a large difference between the motive or end of God's work and that of the wicked. Creatures act "within their kind," and their deeds are "to be esteemed good or evil according to whether they are obedient to God or offensive to him."[75] God then directs all things to good ends.

Human beings have choice and will, but these are depraved, and so, in his people, God "reforms and changes them from evil to good." As a natural gift we have "capacities to discern, to will and to do this or that." When we choose, desire or do evil, it comes from the corruption of sin, but "when we will to do good and have the power to execute it, this is the supernatural grace of the Spirit."[76] G. C. Berkouwer is thus correct in his assertion that Calvin's approach to the issue of human freedom is from the conflict between sin and grace and that this leaves him "innocent of determinism."[77] Berkouwer himself insists that "determinism and freedom of the will are mutually exclusive" but that the "Divine determining is utterly different from what is generally understood by determinism." God's majestic character is able to "embrace human freedom within itself without being thereby assaulted or even limited," and we must be careful not to depersonalize the God-concept by identifying the doctrine of providence with determinism.[78]

Soft determinism. John Frame indicates that soft determinism is "the position of the Westminster Confession of Faith 9.1 and of Calvinists generally."[79] It is this view that is presented by John Feinberg in preference to others we have already examined, in a collection of essays from which the positions of the other three representatives have already been identified.[80] Feinberg cites a classic definition of determinism as the "general philosophical thesis which states that for everything that ever happens there are conditions such that, given them, nothing else could happen."[81] However, Feinberg warns that determinism in the human sciences should not be confused with determinism in the physical sciences because, in the former, "there do not appear to be general laws covering actions so that one could say 'in instances of type A an agent will always choose action x.'" He also takes a soft determinist (or compatibilist) position, which differs from hard determinist positions, some of which might be fatalistic, that is, they would argue that even God had no choice but to do what he did.

In distinction from the "absolute necessity" of the fatalist model, Feinberg posits "consequent necessity," which holds that "once certain choices are made (by God or whomever) certain things follow as a consequence. But before these choices are made, no inherent necessity dictates what must be chosen."[82] An action is defined as "free," even if it is causally deter-mined, so long as the causes are *nonconstraining*.[83] On this reading, God's decree includes "whatever circumstances and factors are necessary to con-vince an individual (without constraint) that the act God has decreed is the act she or he wants to do. And, given the sufficient conditions, the person will do the act."[84]

Of Norman Geisler's "self-determinism" (Thomist model) Feinberg con-tends that it does not address the fundamental question. He asserts that no one would reject Geisler's point that the actor does the act, but Geisler has not addressed the question of what causes the agent to act. In Feinberg's view, Geisler has left unanswered whether God brings it about that we "do determinedly but unconstrainedly what God has foreordained," whether we do it under constraint, or whether God refuses to exert power in this regard.[85] Feinberg finds specific instances of God's compatibilist working with human agents in the inspiration of Scripture without dictation (2 Pet 1:21) and in the eternal security of the elect, which can only be guaranteed within a deterministic notion of human freedom (cf. Jn 6:37-39; 10:28-30; Rom 8:28-30; 1 Cor 1:8-9; Phil 1:6; 1 Pet 1:5, 9).[86]

It is the claim of indeterminists that determinism removes freedom because it denies that an agent *could* have done otherwise. However, Fein-berg proposes that "could" may have at least seven meanings, only the first of which is not open to the soft determinist.[87] (1) It might assert that, given all the factors in the situation, the individual could have chosen differently than she did; that is to say, there were no "causes" that made the act pre-dictable. This "contracausal" sense is denied by the determinist. But (2) "could" might mean "conditionally," that is, that the agent "would have done otherwise if she had so chosen." (3) "Could" might also mean that the agent had the *ability* to do something or (4) had the *opportunity,* which would include the ability. (5) There may be a "rule consistent" sense, that is, the person can park where rules allow it, if she chooses. There might also be a negative sense (6) in which "cannot" refers to the negative conse-quences that would follow if the agent acted in a certain way. This is a sense that would be used even by a proponent of contracausal freedom. And finally, (7) "could" may mean that the act is deemed "reasonable" by the agent. In short, we must carefully define our terms before asserting that a determinist believes that a person "could" not choose or do differently than they did.

Feinberg has two main philosophical objections to indeterminism. (1) It claims that "although there is no causally sufficient reason for an agent's choices, the agent still chooses," but Feinberg wonders: "if causal influences are not sufficient to move the will to choose, *then what is?*" He asserts with Jonathan Edwards that people act for certain reasons; they do what they consider to be the greatest good.[88] Feinberg agrees with Bruce Reichenbach that God's action is persuasive rather than coercive, in order to leave humans free, but the action one chooses is determined somehow and indeterminists offer no explanation of how the choice is finally made, except that the person just chooses.[89] (2) Indeterminism creates problems for moral responsibility because an act must be intentional to be responsible, and surely there was a set of reasons that were causally sufficient to move the act. If actions are random, they are not free in the sense required for accountability.[90] To the counterargument that a causally determined action is not a morally responsible one, Feinberg responds that people are responsible because they act freely, that is, because the causal determination lies with the agent, not outside of the agent.[91] On the same note, Pollard argues that we cannot find freedom in the "arbitrariness of self-will." The moment that we ask the fatal question, "What made me want this rather than that?" or "What made me do what I did rather than what I could so well have done otherwise?" then the illusion of arbitrariness or indeterminacy is dispelled. "The *I*, too, is seen to be controlled by things and instincts, the product of its given heredity and environment."[92]

Against the appeal to Heisenberg's principle of indeterminacy at the subatomic level, to support *essential* indeterminacy, Paul Helm argues that the principle may indicate a limit of our knowledge. "Even if there are no assignable physical preconditions for a given class of events, it does not follow that these events are *uncaused by God.*" God is not just one physical cause among others; he may have "freely willed into being a succession of events, some of the latter of which are unspecified and unspecifiable in terms of the earlier."[93] Similarly, Donald MacKay posits that "in a world continually dependent upon its Creator as ours is declared to be in Scripture, there is no need whatever to invoke *physical indeterminacy* (Heisenberg or otherwise) in order to make room for the operation of providence. 'Chance' is merely our label for those created events whose rationale escapes us. It does not distinguish such events as either more or less under the control of their Creator than those we term 'lawful.'"[94]

Feinberg fails to see how God can achieve his ultimate purposes if contracausal human freedom is insisted upon. Someone would always be able to overturn God's plans. On the other hand, Feinberg finds no biblical demonstration that God has self-limited his government of events in the world in order to give humans freedom, except the definition of freedom itself, which begs the question.[95] It is this question-begging assumption, that only contracausal freedom is legitimately freedom, which leads Clark Pinnock (openness model) into the error (in Feinberg's opinion) of concluding from the evidences of human rebellion against God that "our actions are not determined but significantly free."[96]

God Is Time-Free

I presented the argument for God's timelessness under our consideration of the Thomist model, and it need not be repeated here, but it is an assumption shared by proponents of this model. However, a few further comments by a Calvinist scholar will add to points made in the previous chapter. Although Paul Helm finds biblical passages that seem to indicate divine timelessness (Ps 90:2; Mal 3:6; Jn 8:58; Jas 1:17), he concludes that the biblical writers neither rejected nor accepted the idea of timeless eternity, but that it is consistent with what they did accept.[97] Helm suggests that it is "better to think of timelessness not as a separate attribute but as a mode of possessing attributes. It is not that God is both omniscient and timeless but that he is timelessly omniscient."[98] It is the distinction between the Creator and the creature that fundamentally grounds the conviction of God's timelessness, as Calvin observes in his commentary on Psalm 90:2.[99] Helm proposes that "timelessness can be regarded as that property or mode of possessing properties which is such that it will ensure that property of immutability that is necessary for explicating the creator-creature distinction as this is understood in Christian theology."[100] Where the concept comes from (the Greek philosophers or elsewhere) is therefore irrelevant provided that it is adequate. It is Helm's conviction that "only timeless eternity prevents the degeneracy of divine omniscience and divine immutability into the idea of a God who changes with the changing world and who is surprised by what he discovers, and that divine timeless eternity does not commit one to logical determinism or fatalism."[101]

Helm suggests that *time-freeness* is a preferable term to *timelessness* because the notions of duration and instantaneousness are banished by it. God relates to his creation, he just does not relate temporally. His knowledge is time-free and hence is not foreknowledge, or memory, or contemporaneous knowledge. It makes no sense to ask how long God has known this or when he came to know it. Thus creation is not "temporally present" to God, but it is not distant either; God simply knows.[102] In Helm's opinion the avoidance of the language of time regarding God's creation is a way to avoid deistic concepts such as were presented in the semi-deist model. God's being "before creation" is ontological or hierarchical rather than temporal, in the sense that the Queen is before the Prime Minister. Helm believes that temporalists are more likely to fall into deism than are non-temporalists.[103]

Helm considers the concept of eternity as endless time to be incoherent "for such a prospect requires that an infinite number of events must have elapsed before the present moment could arrive. And since it is impossible for an infinite number of events to have elapsed, and yet the present moment has arrived, the series of events cannot be infinite. Therefore, either there was a time when God began to exist, which is impossible, or God exists timelessly. Therefore, God exists timelessly."[104] Of William Craig's proposal that time before the creation is undifferentiated, Helm agrees with Richard Swinburne that such a God would be "a very lifeless thing."

In the openness model we encountered the objection that proponents of timelessness equate time and space, which was deemed to be incorrect. Helm does not assume that time and space are analogous in all respects, but he does argue that there is a similarity that makes the temporality of God dubious. "Just as Christian thought portrays God as knowing *when* things take place so he is portrayed as knowing *where* they take place." But an infinite God must be spaceless, therefore there is no good reason for withholding the analogous conclusion that God is outside time.[105] As to the objection that a timeless being could not act, intend or remember as a personal being can, Helm agrees with the Thomist assertion that God knows what he knows "innately, and not as the result of a process of learning." He remembers "in the sense that he can forget nothing he knows."[106] A time-free being can have purposes that are brought about in time without that being having a position in time.[107] It is not by a separate exercise of agency that God has produced every event that the universe contains. Time itself is included in the material universe that God has timelessly produced, and it therefore makes no sense to ask what God was doing "before" creation.[108] However, since "what God timelessly decrees is a complete causal matrix of events and actions, . . . timeless creation entails determinism," but "the fact of the ordination of the causal sequence carries no more adverse consequences for human responsibility" than determinism does on any other account.[109]

God Acts Omnipotently and Always Righteously

Calvin insisted that there is an "inseparable connection and harmony between the power of God and His justice."[110] Everything he does is "moderate, legitimate, and according to the strictest rule of right." His power is always "righteously tempered with equity and justice." Though God's eternal will depends on nothing but himself and has no prior cause to influence it, it "is nevertheless founded in the highest reason and in the highest equity."[111] Calvin's adversaries objected that his position made God the author of evil, but Calvin rejected the charge by appealing to a distinction between the proximate (or mediate) and the remote cause. God is free from blame in those acts that he condemns in Satan and in the reprobate. For instance, when robbers carry off Job's cattle, the deed is cruel and disgraceful; it was intended by Satan in order to do Job evil, but Job discerned God's hand in it.[112] When a person does an injustice out of ambition, avarice or lust, God cannot be charged with sin, even though "by His just but secret judgment" he performs his works by means of such a person. The desires that made the act sinful in its human perpetrator do not exist in God.[113] As Paul Helm puts it, God uses instruments who fulfill his plans, while fulfilling theirs "without either detracting from the evil of their intentions nor contaminating himself by such use."[114]

Similarly, Vernon White speaks of the situation as one in which a primary agent acts "specifically through the event of a secondary agent's own (free) action. The meaning and purpose of the primary agent's action is to be found in the secondary agent's action, but with no guarantee that they are meaning and intending the same thing."[115] White draws on the analogy of an artist at work, to conceptualize this situation. God arranges and orders reality in such a way that whatever intention the creature has and whatever she enacts in her particular context carries God's intention, in a wider context of meaning. To use Kaufman's terminology, it is a situation in which the creature's real act is a subact within God's master act, but they are "playing a different drama." For example, in the case of Judas, God's intention is different from that of Judas, but "Judas's act will be a sub-act in God's overall purpose."[116] Here, "whatever the agent freely does is encompassed without risk in the primary agent's action."

An evil deed must be "estimated according to its end and object," and it is on this account that God is absolved of evil when the evil acts of human beings are included in his providential will.[117] The critical importance of motivation to the moral quality of an act is evident in regard to God's ordaining of the crucifixion of his Son. Once more, Calvin cites from Augustine:

When the Father gave up the Son, when the Lord gave up his own body, when Judas delivered up the Lord, how was it that, in this one same "delivering up," God was righteous and man guilty? The reason was that, in this one same thing which God and man did, the *motive* was not the same from which God and man *acted*. Hence it is that Peter without hesitation declares that Pontius Pilate and Judas, and the other wicked people of the Jews, had done "what God's hand and His counsel had afore determined to be done" (Acts 4:28), as Peter had just before said, "Him being delivered by the determinate counsel and foreknowledge of God" (chap. 2:23). Now if you turn your back on the term "foreknowledge," the definitiveness of the terms, *"determinate counsel,"* will floor you at once. Nor indeed does the former passage leave the least degree of ambiguity behind it, namely, that Pontius Pilate and the Jews, and the wicked people, did "whatsoever God's hand and His counsel had before determined to be done."[118]

A distinction must be made, Calvin insists, between what God commands in his law and what is "hidden in his secret counsel." It is not that God has a double or twofold will or is inconsistent with himself. The will of God is "simple and uniform and one," although a difference between his secret counsel and his general doctrine may be apparent to the ignorant and inexperienced.[119] God always "wills one and the same thing, but frequently in different forms," thus maintaining perfect harmony between these two aspects of his will. There are "different reasons, motives and manners" in God's willing. If God equally and effectually willed that every one should be chaste, he would make them so. "Wherefore, since chastity is a singular gift of God, the prompt and evident conclusion is, that He wills that which He commands in His Word differently from that which He effectually works and fulfils by His regenerating Spirit."[120] Thus God commands children to be obedient to their parents yet he willed that the sons of Eli should not be obedient to their father. God abominates adulterous and incestuous intercourse, yet Absalom's defiling of his father's concubines was not done "in every sense, contrary to the will of God." Through Nathan, God had predicted that Absalom would do this (2 Sam 12:11, 12), and he willed it in punishment of David.[121]

The justice of God's actions, which he has decreed "with most righteous reason," may be indiscernible by us at the present time, but it will be "revealed to us at the last day in all its infinite righteousness and Divine perfection."[122] Nowhere is this more puzzling than in regard to God's not willing to draw all people to salvation by the secret influence of the Spirit. Clearly there is a sense in which God does not will everyone to be saved, and so Calvin interprets 1 Timothy 2:4 (God "desires everyone to be saved") as a reference not to individuals but to groups or orders of people "in their various civil and national vocations."[123] God has "a secret reason why he shuts so many out of salvation."[124]

In addition to the points made by Calvin in defense of God's nonculpability for the sin and evil that are within his decree, we may add Feinberg's argument that God cannot contextualize a contradiction; he cannot be held accountable for failing to do what he could not do. There are two valuable things that God could do, but he cannot do them both because they contradict one another. The option that God chose "is of the greatest value and thus is justified even though it makes it impossible for God to remove evil." God could either create the sort of beings he created (that is, with compatibilistic freedom) or he could maintain a perfect world; he chose to create our world.[125] Feinberg does not believe that there is such a thing as the "best possible world," only good and evil ones. "As long as one can demonstrate that God has created a good possible world, then he has resolved the problem of evil."[126]

God Knows All Occurrences Because He Has Decreed Them Immutably

In the Thomist view of Norman Geisler, God's foreordination and his foreknowledge were neither temporally nor logically prior to one another because God is simple. From Feinberg's perspective this is a "mistake of the first order," to treat God's thoughts as part of his essence.[127] Rather God has always known and foreordained all things at once, not because of his simplicity but because of his omniscience and sovereign will. However, God knows, in his eternal timelessness, the logical and chronological relationship between events.

Paul Helm suggests that we distinguish between two kinds of foreknowledge, O and A. O-foreknowledge is to know ahead of time without bringing the event about. A-foreknowledge is to know the future event as a result of "ordaining or effectively willing or otherwise ensuring that p is true." (O-foreknowledge, also described as "simple foreknowledge," was affirmed by Cottrell in the redemptive intervention model, and it is commonly asserted by Arminian theologians, including Wesleyans.) A-foreknowledge was affirmed by Augustine,[128] Anselm,[129] Aquinas[130] and Calvin.[131] However, Helm considers unclear the extent to which A-knowledge is causative, since even Augustine distinguishes between foreknowledge and predestination, and conceptualizes states that God knows without learning but that he does not cause.[132] Helm proposes that so long as God's A-foreknowledge of the actual world is not necessitated by the laws of logic alone, logical determinism or fatalism is not entailed by it.[133] However, it would not be compatible with indeterministic human freedom.

Helm's judgment here appears to call into question the coherence of the Thomistic model as we described it earlier. Aquinas was endeavoring to hold together divine determination and libertarian human freedom through appeal to divine timelessness and concurrence. The Molinist model tried to help the Thomists out with the proposal that middle knowledge offered a means for God to determine the outcome through his choice of the actual world, while still leaving human actors libertarianly free within the particular world that God chose. But Helm doubts that a compatibilism that defines human freedom as libertarian is viable, thus excluding both the Thomist and the Molinist models.

Calvin believed in God's detailed knowledge of the future, but he did not make a distinction between events that God foreknew and those he decreed. In fact, Calvin complains about many who "babble too ignorantly of bare foreknowledge."[134] God, who holds "the helm of all things which are done in the world, never permits a separation of His prescience from His power!"[135] Calvin agreed with Augustine that "if God foresaw that which He did not will to be done, God holds not the supreme rule over all things." The error of Calvin's calumniator was that he ascribed a prescience to God that portrayed him as "sitting in heaven as an idle, inactive, unconcerned spectator of all things in the life of men."[136] Because future events are uncertain to us, "we hold them in suspense, as if they might incline to one side or the other" but, in fact, nothing takes place that the Lord has not "previously foreseen" and also determined by his decree.[137] Feinberg concurs that if God knows the future, it is, in some sense, set, but this is not because God's knowledge causes the future, it is simply because "what God knows must occur."[138]

Regarding the Fall, Calvin asserted that "God most certainly knew what would take place, both in men and in apostate angels, and He also decreed at the same time what He himself would do." Calvin asks his opponent why God permitted the fall of angels and humans since it was possible for him to preserve them if he had not decreed their destruction. For Adam not to have fallen he would have needed the gift of "fortitude and constancy with which the elect of God are gifted whom God wills to 'keep' sound and safe 'from falling' (Jude 24)." Why God did not do so is among the secret things that belong to the Lord, not one of those he has revealed to his children (Deut 29:29).[139] We must simply confess with Solomon that "the Lord has made everything for its purpose, even the wicked for the day of trouble" (Prov 16:4).[140]

God's decrees are fixed and immutable. Neither his "plan nor his will is reversed, nor his volition altered; but what he had foreseen, approved, and decreed, he pursues in uninterrupted tenor."[141] This is true even when sudden variation may appear to be taking place. The Scriptures that speak of God's repentance (Gen 6:6; 1 Sam 15:11; Jer 18:8) are using the language of accommodation. God represents "himself to us not as he is in himself, but as he seems to us," by this manner of reference to changes in his action that are not changes in his plan. In the cases of Nineveh and Hezekiah, God did not want them to perish, but "it pleased the Lord by such threats to arouse to repentance those whom he was terrifying, that they might escape that judgment they deserved for their sins." There was a "tacit condition in the simple intimation," and the situation was likewise in the case of Abimelech (Gen 20:3, 7).[142]

Feinberg grants that the knowability of the future is problematic philosophically but argues that it must be affirmed, nevertheless, because of the clear biblical testimony that God knows the future and can predict it to and through human prophets.[143] Assessing the explanations of predictive prophecy offered in the openness model, Feinberg finds them thoroughly implausible. He considers it "hard to believe that when God predicted through the prophets the first advent of Christ, for example, he was only expressing what he hoped would happen. If God tells us what he intends to do, he tells us what will happen, and if he intends to do it, he knows it will happen."[144] Of the suggestion that God can predict some things because he knows how the future will grow out of past and present conditions, Feinberg observes that the proposal entails a strong form of determinism and hence is counterproductive to the purposes of those who argue against God's knowledge of the future on libertarian grounds.[145]

Feinberg affirms the understanding of divine timelessness that was presented by the Thomists, as well as the reasoning that God knows "what time it is in *human history*" and what is future *from our perspective,* even though it is all present to God.[146] On the other hand, although Feinberg attributes middle knowledge to God, he does not think that it solves the indeterminist's problem because God could not "*know,* even counterfactually, what *would* follow from anything else unless some form of determinism is correct."[147]

Boethius and Aquinas had appealed to divine timelessness as a way of reconciling divine foreknowledge and human freedom, but Paul Helm does not believe that the strategy works. The problem is that God would not be free if he "knew yesterday that Jones will perform a particular action at some time in the future" because then his knowledge would be past, hence unchangeable and therefore necessary.[148] Helm accepts the premise of objectors to divine foreknowledge that "divine foreknowledge *is* logically incompatible with human (indeterministic) freedom."[149] The concept of foreknowledge applies only to a temporal agent who recognizes timeless knowledge under certain temporal conditions, but for the timeless knower there is no before or after. God timelessly knows all true propositions and believes none that are false.[150] The critical problem in adopting the thesis that the future is indefinite, particularly because of indeterminate human freedom, is that it creates "insoluble problems for the traditional Christian view of God's determinate control over his creation."[151]

The Proper Response to Divine Providence Is to
Recognize God's Activity in Every Detail of Our Lives

When things turn out well, we should experience gratitude to God, recognizing that he is the principal author of benefits received. We may honor humans who were God's ministers in the event, but we must reserve reverence and praise for God since it is by his will that we are "beholden to those through whose hand God willed to be beneficent."[152]

As John Leith points out, Calvin had a hard life. His body was ravaged by disease, and he faced fierce theological and political opposition. The source of his doctrine of providence was therefore not primarily either logic or speculation but "the religious conviction of a believer who takes God very seriously" and who believed that God is infinite in both power and love. "Come what may, either in logic or in history, the Geneva Reformer steadfastly refused to surrender one iota of this conviction." He maintained that God tenderly cared for him although "there were certainly many occasions when Calvin could not square his faith in God's providential care for the world with logic, but on these occasions this man of logic willed to trust the love and justice of God."[153]

Calvin taught that when we face adversities we should take consolation in knowing that "all took place according to the good pleasure of God" and should beware of manifesting "impious obstinacy" against our Maker by complaining about it.[154] We "suffer nothing except by God's ordinance and command," for we are "under his hand."[155] We need to recall that "the Lord has willed it, therefore it must be borne, not only because one may not contend against it, but also because he wills nothing but what is just and expedient."[156] Where we have endured punishments, we should remember the sins that caused them. On the one hand, we should be prepared to accept whatever happens as "decreed by 'the good pleasure' of God"; on the other hand, we must beware of personal indolence, rashness or thoughtlessness that may be "the immediate cause of any adversity under which we are suffering."[157] When we incur a loss through our own negligence, we must therefore impute it to ourselves.[158] For examples of this proper attitude to adversity Helm points us to David, who accepted the death of Bathsheba's child (2 Sam 3:18), to Eli's acceptance of God's judgment on his sons (1 Sam 3:18) and to Paul's response to his thorn in the flesh.[159]

Having God's omnipotence in view, we can face the future with faith that we shall be enabled to surmount "the countless perils of the world." Although we cannot remove contingency from the world, nothing occurs by fortune or chance, as though it were outside of God's purpose. "Anyone who has been taught by Christ's lips that all the hairs of his head are numbered (Mt 10:30) will look farther afield for a cause, and will consider that all events are governed by God's secret plan."[160] If a branch falls from a tree or an axe slips out of a person's hand and kills another, "God did this according to His divine purpose" (Ex 21:13; Deut 19:5).[161] The outcome of the lot (Prov 16:33) and the position of a person economically or socially (Ps 75:6-7) are all part of God's providence, not a matter of luck.[162] Thus when God works through secondary causes, his power is not to be separated from them. A person who wants to eat by God's provision, without working, "would separate and rend asunder those things which God has joined together by an inseparable connection." Our faith in God's providence should therefore make us diligent in performing our duty, hoping for God's blessing in success but "freely prepared to reconcile every contingency with the sure and certain Providence of God."[163]

We can rest safely "in the protection of him to whose will are subject all the harmful things which, whatever their source, we may fear."[164] God's authority curbs Satan and whatever opposes our welfare depends upon God's "nod." Consequently, we ought not to be fearful, as though the things that threaten us "had some intrinsic power to harm us, or might wound us inadvertently and accidentally, or there were not enough help in God against their harmful acts." We should remember "that there is no erratic power, or action, or motion in creatures, but that they are governed by God's secret plan in such a way that nothing happens except what is knowingly and willingly decreed by him."[165] Paul Helm points out that Paul's comprehensive statement concerning God's working of all things together for good (Rom 8:28) is "not *exclusively* of any attitude that the believer might take up, but inclusive of his other obedience"; the promise is to those who love God.[166]

Responding properly to providence, which is an important factor in determining our prayer response to events, is not a simple matter. At one level, the totality of events should be recognized as the pattern of God's providence since everything that happens is divinely providential. On the other hand, Christians are naturally more concerned to discern the particular aspects of God's providence designed for their benefit. In the illustration of Paul Helm, when Mr. Robinson gets a large order from an old school friend who happens to stand next to him after he has missed his train, he discerns God's providence in the incident. He recognizes "an unforeseen and unintended disproportion between what led to the outcome and the outcome itself; and that the outcome was beneficial to him."[167] What complicates this assessment and appropriate gratitude of God is that it is more difficult to discern the manner in which conformity to Christ is achieved through the pattern of events. Thus events deemed beneficial for other reasons may not be discernible as beneficial in this regard, and negative experiences may be seen to contribute more. Consequently, our assessments should be tentative and open to revision in the light of subsequent experience. Since Christians have no guarantee of a happy, long, prosperous or healthy life, the occurrence of such things does not suffice to indicate the pattern of God's providence in our lives.[168] It is from the end of our lives that we are best able to discern the meaning of them and recognize the pattern of God's providence within them. In the meantime, we may have to affirm God's providential government by faith, when we lack the data to demonstrate this.[169]

Vernon White is concerned to point out that a proper response to God's providence calls for a recognition of the activity of God in all of the details of our experience and not only in the big picture that these form. "There is a significant difference between making an unfortunate event serve some further end as a contingency plan, and having no accidents in the first place in the sense that there is always some end related internally to every event."[170] White is particularly concerned that the approach taken by Peter Baelz (openness model) and by process theologians underestimates the extent to which God's initiative and sovereignty include negative factors in the "whole web of events." It is not enough to believe that "God can make tragedies into means to further good ends (the business of redemption)," if there is no sense in which God has "exercised intentional control in relation to the tragedy itself."[171] White is concerned about Gordon Kaufman's approach (the semi-deist model) because "it is a conception where some particular events are *only* understood through reference to further, general purposes."[172] White prefers an approach that insists "that the end is always *internally* related to all those involved in any event in such a way that every event is in some sense 'end' and never purely 'means.'"[173] A fallen tree bringing harm or a car accident can be considered "in some sense an intended action of God in relation to those involved, bearing some intended end for them" and not simply a means to ends for others.[174] However, this is not to deny that the meaning and value of an event are also derived from their interrelation with other events in the wider context. "It is the difference between saying of the crucified Christ that here is constituted something valuable of faith and courage and saying that here is nothing but pain and cruelty."[175] God achieves different ends in the crucifixion and the resurrection, in the death of a child and in its birth, but one is not simply related to the other as means to end.

We May Pray Fervently in the Confidence That Prayer According to God's Will Is Effective Because God Has Determined to Accomplish Some Things in Answer to Our Petitions

Prayer and the fostering of personal relationship. Under the openness model we took note of Vincent Brümmer's contention[176] that both parties must be indeterministically free for a relationship to be personal. Paul Helm doubts that this is true, because no personal relationships are influence-free, although they can be jeopardized by *some* kinds of manipulation or coercion by one of the parties, for example, by brainwashing or intimidation. On the other hand, a relationship can thrive on an appreciable amount of coercion or manipulation if it is benevolently intended. Indeed some relationships are scarcely intelligible without some constraint, but they are still decidedly "personal" relationships, for example, parent-child, husband-wife, teacher-student, manufacturer-customer relationships. Brümmer's argument appears to Helm to assume that prayer is a personal relationship between equals, based on a mutual contract between them. However, this is not Helm's reading of the biblical picture of God's relationship to humans, and many other personal relationships are not based on mutual contract (e.g., family, church and state relationships). Our inherited obligations are God's "providential gift to each of us of a self," and it is "from this self, in its concrete relationships with other selves" that "our volitions and desires engage with those of others."[177]

As Helm understands the situation, the alternatives are not a nonmanipulative personal relationship or a manipulative one. Even on the human level, a relationship without constraints is hardly recognizable as human, and not every instance of a request from one person to another excludes any degree of pressure. The closer a relationship is, the easier it is for the people involved to predict one another's responses. That makes for a stable relationship and indicates that "risk" is not a relevant consideration in assessing the personal quality of relationships. Helm proposes that we consider a relationship to be personal when (1) it is exercised through the structure of belief and desire of each person, and (2) that exercise does not rely upon physical coercion or psychological compulsion. Within this perspective, predictability is an irrelevant factor, and the question of whether providence is risky or risk-free is irrelevant.[178] Assuming these factors, it is possible for prayer to function as a means of fostering closer relationships between God and ourselves even though God is Lord and Father, and we are his obedient servants and his dependent children.

The stimulation to prayer that is produced by confidence in God's providence. Calvin felt no conflict between a firm trust in God's sovereign providence over the details of life and an earnest practice of petitionary prayer. These two go naturally together in the life of believers. The one who "knows and feels that men and their counsels, and the issues of all things, are ruled and overruled by the Providence of God" will commit herself "wholly unto God, and depend entirely upon Him." Where there is this state of mind, "prayers will ever follow, that God will begin and perfect every work which we undertake, while we thus rest on Him in all quietness, and on Him alone."[179] Those who are aware of God's "all-ruling hand" will never hesitate to "cast all their cares upon him," and they "will all the while rest assured that the devil and all wicked men, whatever tumults they may cause, are not only held of God by their feet in chains, but are compelled to do His pleasure, under which assurance they will pass their lives in security and peace."[180] It is precisely because we know that "the dispensation of all those things which he [God] has made is in his own hand and power and that we are indeed his children, whom he has received into his faithful protection to nourish and educate," that we are "to petition him for whatever we desire; and we are to recognize as a blessing from him, and thankfully to acknowledge, every benefit that falls to our share."[181]

Donald MacKay argues that there is "logical indeterminacy in the situation that confronts us moment by moment. This implies that we have a genuine share in determining what the future shall be, and that if our Creator is willing to meet us as God-in-time, then our dialogue with him in prayer may also affect the future in ways beyond the causal reach of our physical powers."[182] Calvin asserts that just as God has ordained labor as a means by which to provide our physical needs, so he has established prayer as a means by which to obtain from God those things we need him to provide.[183] Consequently, God's providence does not relieve us from responsibility, as was argued by Calvin's objectors who said that prayer is superfluous since everything is fixed in the decree.[184] On the contrary, since we know that God is "the master and bestower of all things, who invites us to request them of him," were we not to do so we would be like people who neglect a treasure buried in the earth, after it has been pointed out to them.[185] Prayer is the means by which "we reach those riches which are laid up for us with the Heavenly Father," for there is nothing that is "promised to be expected from the Lord, which we are not also bidden to ask of him in prayers."[186] Moreover, the knowledge that God wishes to give us something is not a disincentive to prayer. Elijah was "sure of God's purpose, after he has deliberately promised rain to King Ahab," yet he "still anxiously prays with his head between his knees, and sends his servant seven times to look (1 Kings 18:42), not because he would discredit prophecy, but because he knew it was his duty, lest his faith be sleepy or sluggish, to lay his desires before God."[187]

Under the fourth petition of the Lord's Prayer, we are instructed to ask God for everything that our bodies need, "not only for food and clothing but also for everything God perceives to be beneficial to us, that we may eat our daily bread in peace." This sort of petition fosters in us an expectation that everything comes from God, "even to a crumb of bread and a drop of water." But we should ask for "only as much as is sufficient for our need from day to day, with this assurance: that as our Heavenly Father nourishes us today, he will not fail us tomorrow." Even when we obtain what we need from use of our skill and our own diligence, we should recognize that "it is by his blessing alone that our labors truly prosper."[188]

Even when we are confident of God's meticulous providence, prayer must not be separated from "the total matrix of events and actions of which it forms a part." Paul Helm illustrates this from the case of a student who studies hard for an exam, prays for success and then passes. On such an occasion it should not be assumed that the success was caused by hard work alone, as though prayer served only to strengthen that will because, if that were true, prayer would be merely talking to oneself.[189] Because of this, we cannot ask what would have happened if a person had not prayed. To do so would be to remove the prayer from the matrix and thereby to change the total matrix. In some cases, the efficacy of a prayer is established by prior promise regarding the item of request, as in the promise "if you seek me you will find me." There may indeed be cases where God indicates that certain events will take place *only if* people pray.[190]

Donald MacKay describes things in a slightly different manner, but the substance of his understanding is similar to Helm's. He claims that "it becomes luminously evident that in general 'had we not prayed,' things *could* have turned out otherwise; for from this standpoint 'had we not . . .' means 'had the Creator conceived the drama differently'—and once we say this, we can use no firm inferences to prescribe or proscribe the outcome, for our only firm ground of inference is our drama as the Creator *has* conceived it, together with his promise to be faithful to that conception (e.g., to Noah in Gen 8:22)."[191] Even where the answer to the request can later be seen to have been dispatched long before the request, MacKay asserts that we cannot say that the prayer was unnecessary. "'Counterfactual hypotheticals' are notoriously treacherous. They require always the preface 'other things being equal.'" The problem, of course, is that "if we postulate a counterfactual situation in which the Creator himself is involved, then other things generally are *not* equal."[192]

Prayer is "not one physical factor—like a chemical or mechanical force—among many other such forces in a set of physical equations."[193] In the unrepeatable history of the universe, the particular matrix of divine and human actions that is focused on for consideration is unique and unrepeatable. It is consequently not subject to scientific investigation, and it is impossible to say what would have happened if the unique matrix had been different, through the addition or omission of a petitioner's prayer. Given that God ordained both ends and the means to them, there are some cases in which people's prayer is part of the total matrix, and God acts because people asked him to do so. If they had not asked, the conditions in the whole matrix would have been insufficient for production of what is asked for. This was Augustine's point when he averred that "prayers are useful in obtaining those favours which He [God] foresaw He would bestow on those who should pray for them."[194] However, Helm suggests that Christians are also invited to pray for things that are unconditional, an example of which would be the coming of the kingdom of God. In these instances, the prayer is not so much a petition as an expression of desire, "an affirmation of solidarity with the unfolding will of God."[195]

Within this model of providence, the reason for answered prayer is not God's benevolence or all prayers would be answered, nor is it the strength of the intercessor. Helm argues that the answer is "not natural but conventional"; the reason "why some prayers are answered and some are not must lie in terms of the structure of will and warrant established by God himself."[196] Within this framework, God carries the burden for answering or not answering prayer, since it is one of the means by which "the already settled mind of God effects what he has decreed."[197] By contrast, Helm contends, those who hold the model of providence in which outcomes are ultimately determined by human agents (a "risk view") place the burden of responsibility for success or failure of the petition upon the one who intercedes or fails to do so. If an evil will be averted only because an intercessor properly intercedes, the responsibility for the continuing evil falls on the shoulders of the intercessor. On this understanding, once Christians know about an ongoing event like the Holocaust, it continues because they do not pray enough, or fervently enough, or faithfully enough.[198]

Helm's thesis regarding the burden placed upon intercessors would apply most strongly to the church dominion model because of its assumption that prayer according to God's general purpose will always be answered. In other risk models that we have examined, such as the openness model or the redemptive interventionist model, God has placed limits on his intervention out of respect for (libertarian) human freedom. Consequently, evil may continue despite the earnest prayers of Christians simply because God has chosen only to intervene in prevention of the evil deeds of sinful people when it is necessary for the achievement of his broad general purpose. On the other hand, the burden upon Christian intercessors does appear to increase in risk models. Even in the openness model, where God loses specific battles with evil, it would appear that the intercession of Christians in those situations might have tipped the scales in God's favor.

Petitionary prayer and the will of God. Since only prayer according to God's will is answered (1 Jn 5:14), God has given us the Spirit to "tell us what is right and temper our emotions" (Rom 8:26). Calvin doubts that the Spirit actually prays or groans, but he "arouses in us assurance, desires, and signs, to conceive which our natural powers would scarcely suffice."[199] We cannot pray in faith if we seek something that is against God's decree, but we do not know the "hidden and unchangeable will" of God, so we must pray according to the will that God inspires in us. When we have no certain promise, "we must ask of God conditionally." God graciously "so tempers the outcome of events according to his incomprehensible plan that the prayers of the saints, which are a mixture of faith and error, are not nullified."[200]

On the other hand, Hazelton observes, "Prayer itself may bring about not only the satisfaction but the actual correction of its dominant desire. I do not always come away from prayer with the same set of impulses that sent me into it."[201] In choosing the object of our petition, Calvin urges us to "pour out our desires before God, seeking both those things which make for the extension of his glory and the setting forth of his name, and those benefits which conduce to our own advantage" (Ps 50:15).[202] We then give thanks for what we receive.

Donald Carson points out how "those who pray in the Scriptures regularly pray in line with what God has already disclosed he is going to do."[203] Examples are found in the prayers of Jesus (Jn 17:1), Daniel (Dan 9:1-19), Paul (Eph 1:15-19) and Moses (Ex 32:9-10). In the latter case, it may appear on the surface as though the intercession of Moses caused God to change his mind, but, on the contrary, had God not relented, his promises to Abraham, Isaac and Jacob would have been nullified. "It is that very point Moses is banking on as he prays."[204] Carson argues that God expects to be pleaded with and that our intercession is "his own appointed means for bringing about his relenting." If we fail in this respect, God's wrath is poured out.[205] Not that God's appointed ends will fail if we do not pray, leaving God frustrated, but our prayerlessness can be the sad instrument of divinely appointed judgment both of ourselves and of those for whom we failed to intercede.[206] Speaking of the function of prayer within the purpose of God, Harry Blamires likewise posits that "when we pray, even in petition, we do not initiate. God is always the initiator. If we are praying for something which is in accordance with God's will, then we can be sure that he is already operating towards the end we pray for."[207]

When we pray the Lord's Prayer, asking that God's will may be done on earth, our request is not concerning his secret will, "by which he controls all things and directs them to their end.[208] For even though Satan and men violently inveigh against him, he knows that by his incomprehensible plan he not only turns aside their attacks but so orders it that he may do through them what he has decreed." The will concerning which we are praying is that "to which voluntary obedience corresponds," the moral will of God.[209]

James indicates that God brings some things about because people ask him to do so (Jas 1:5), and some passages even speak of God as changing his mind because of prayer (cf. Is 38:1-6). On these grounds Paul Helm asserts that, like any other human action, prayer is "warranted because God commands it under certain conditions and circumstances, permits it in some circumstances, and forbids it in others." Therefore, there is a morality of praying, and a request must be warranted by God, at least by being permitted, to have a prospect of being answered; prayer is never a natural human right.[210] On the other hand, Hazelton suggests that there are no boundaries placed on what we can ask for. Anything we wish or need is an appropriate subject of prayer because we thereby acknowledge that all of our life is within God's rule. He suggests that "it is far better to ask God for whatever we desire than to play God by deciding on our own what we ought to pray for. That would simply be pious magic all over again, wanting to control God by praying only for the right things in a way that is sure to get results."[211] We should let God be the judge, abandoning ourselves to his providence, even in our prayer. "We must ask abundantly, since the measure of our asking shall be that of our receiving."[212] Prayer "begins by calling upon God and ends by resting the case with God. We address ourselves to one who reserves the right to grant or to withhold, one who in short remains God."[213]

John Porteous calls upon us to have a sense of proportion in our prayers and not to allow them to be self-centered. Some might assume, on this basis, that it is not appropriate to pray for good weather for a picnic, but Porteous is not convinced that such is the case. He proposes that "it does not follow at all that my picnic is too small a thing to be within the providential care. Bad weather, meaning discomfort, upset of arrangements, chills, loss of work, and other ills may be serious enough." Therefore, "it is quite right and dutiful to pray about it, with the quiet assurance that God in the multitude of big concerns will not let so small a thing escape His notice, but it is reverent to pray with a due recognition of what we might call the world-wide responsibilities of God, as well as the needs of our fellow-men, and with an entire willingness to accept disappointment, and even suffering, in the interests of the general scheme and larger whole, if it must be so." Nevertheless, even in the matter of a picnic we can be quite sure that God's providence "will be real, effective and adequate."[214] I would assume that Porteous might give this same response to the people I mentioned, in Oxford, if they were to ask him about the appropriateness of asking God to provide a parking spot in London.

The benefits of petition additional to the specific answers obtained. Calvin recognized the seeming superfluity of petition, since God knows what we need, but he believed that God had ordained prayer for our benefit. This occurs in a number of ways. In petitionary prayer we "invoke the presence" of God's providence, "through which he watches over and guards our affairs, and of his power, through which he sustains us, weak as we are and well-nigh overcome." Having disclosed to the Lord the needs that were pressing upon us, "we even rest fully in the thought that none of our ills is hid from him who, we are convinced, has both the will and the power to take the best care of us."[215]

In another passage, Calvin lists six reasons for prayer.[216] (1) We pray to rekindle the "burning desire ever to seek, love and serve him [God], while we become accustomed in every need to flee to him." (2) We express our desires to God to protect ourselves from any thoughts or desires that we would be ashamed of before God. (3) We request things from God to prepare ourselves to receive his benefits with true gratitude. (4) Having obtained what we asked for, "we should be led to meditate upon his kindness more ardently." (5) We "embrace with greater delight" what was obtained through prayer. And finally, (6) we pray so that our experience will confirm God's providence, which invites us to call on him and also "extends his hand to help his own."

From delayed answers we gain the benefit of being roused from idleness or laziness "to seek, ask and entreat him to our greater good."[217] Blamires suggests that what we have a right to expect when we pray is that our experience will be rendered meaningful. A venture for which we have prayed may fail, but "provided that we continue to pray in submission to God's will that our efforts may be blessed, the fruits of this creaturely dependence will undoubtedly emerge. And they will emerge in the form of a new realization of the meaningfulness of the part we are playing."[218] Blamires posits that few of us have achieved a degree of self-surrender that will stand continual success, and "God loves us too much to shower upon us, as a result of our prayers, the very circumstances that will more readily feed our pride, vanity, and self-dependence." In this way God delivers us from temptation and does not lead us into evil and thus actually answers our prayer.[219]

The effectiveness of the petitions of unbelievers. Although faith is a stated condition of answered prayer, even for God's children, Calvin suggested that God may graciously answer the prayers of unbelievers when they cry out in desperate need. He has occasionally punished "the cruelty, robberies, violence, lust, and other crimes of the ungodly, silencing their boldness and rage, also overturning their tyrannical power," when people who are being wrongly oppressed "beat the air with praying to an unknown God." In Psalm 107, in particular, Calvin finds clear teaching "that prayers which do not reach heaven by faith still are not without effect. The psalm lumps together prayers which, out of natural feeling, necessity wrings from unbelievers just as much as from believers," and "from the outcome it proves that God is gracious toward them" (Ps 107:6, 13, 19). This is not an indication that those who pray are acceptable to God. "Nay, it is by this circumstance to emphasize or illumine his mercy whenever the prayers of unbelievers are not denied to them; and again to incite his true worshipers to pray the more, when they see that even ungodly wailings sometimes do some good." Other illustrations of this mercy of God are seen in Ahab's feigned penitence (1 Kings 21:29) and the cries of the Israelites in the days of the judges. "Just as God causes his sun to shine alike upon the good and the evil (Mt 5:45), so he does not despise the weeping of those whose cause is just and whose distresses deserve to be relieved."[220]

The Case Study

Peter Vandervelde had been reared in a Presbyterian home where he had been taught the Scriptures in the way that is most commonly associated

with the name of John Calvin. Early in his life he had developed the conviction that God rules in the world in such a way that nothing occurs
except by God's direct action in and through others, or by his express permission of the actions of his creatures. In his understanding of God's work
in the world Peter had much in common with Maria (Thomist model) and
Helmut (Barthian model). All three of them shared the belief in God's
meticulous providence, his determining of all that occurs in the world. But
how this came about with regard to the free agency of God's creatures was
somewhat differently perceived by Peter than by Maria. She wanted to
assert libertarian freedom as well as God's comprehensive determining of
outcomes, and Peter found that incoherent. They both believed that God is
time-free, experiencing everything that occurs within human history within
his timeless present. But even so Peter doubted that this would allow for
libertarian human freedom. It seemed clear to Peter that if everything that
happens is determined by God, either effectuated or deliberately permitted,
then people and angelic beings can be free only in the sense that they do
what they want to do. God does not force people to do things that they do
not want to do, but he understands them so thoroughly (their motives,
their habits, their desires, their genetic strengths and weaknesses, their
fears and hopes, etc.), and he works so continuously in the physical world,
that God is able to achieve in each moment what he wills. Thus nothing
surprises God, and nothing happens that he did not at least will to permit.
He could have prevented it, had he chosen to.

Oliver (openness model) often told Peter that if God was so completely in
control in every specific event, then he was morally responsible for the evil
that people do. But Peter denied this and frequently referred to the experience of Joseph and to the crucifixion of Jesus as illustrations of the way in
which God's intentions are fulfilled through evil human intentions, but the
humans are morally accountable for their evil intentions, and God is guilt
free because his own intentions are good. God did not inspire Joseph's
brothers to sell him into slavery nor the religious leaders of Jerusalem to put
Jesus to death. They wanted to do that. On the other hand, God could have
prevented both of those situations. On previous occasions when people had
murderous intent toward Jesus, he avoided death. There was a sense in
which God "wanted" Joseph sold into slavery in Egypt and "wanted" Jesus
put to death despite his innocence. God's secret will, the will of his eternal
purpose, was accomplished even though his moral will was disobeyed.

Tom (redemptive intervention model) had a larger place for God's control than Oliver did and believed that this was specifically enabled by God's knowledge of the future. But even so, Tom did not accept Peter's understanding (or that of Maria and Helmut either) of the extent to which God's will was done in every event. Tom argued that the biblical cases of Joseph and Jesus were special. In order to achieve his redemptive purposes in the world, these things needed to happen. In Tom's view, Peter Vandervelde's error was that he generalized from specific biblical incidents in a way that Scripture does not warrant.

Peter Vandervelde knew that his understanding of the missionary abduction set him apart significantly from Oliver and Tom (as well as a number of others in the group) because of his strong conviction that this event was a part of the decree or eternal purpose of God. This was an event no different than the one that occurred to Joseph in patriarchal times. Peter believed that he could say exactly the same thing about Richard Henderson as Moses recorded from the mouth of Joseph. God was intentionally involved in the abduction, but his intention was different from that of the guerrillas. Actually, it occurred to Peter that there may have been significant overlap in the divine and human intentions in this instance. The guerrillas were seeking political justice, which had been persistently denied to their tribe. Given God's deep concern for justice, Peter thought it just possible that God had a very good reason for permitting this abduction. Granted, it was hard on the missionaries and their families, but it could result in significant gains both for the gospel and for the cause of civil justice. Of course, without a divinely revealed interpretation of the missionary crisis, Peter could not know God's intention. Nevertheless, Peter was confident that things were under God's control and that he planned good things, particularly for those who loved him, but not necessarily for them alone. He reminded himself, however, that God's intention for the guerrillas might be judgmental rather than merciful. It could just be that God had let these guerrillas go to this extreme as a way of bringing down upon them the punishment that their rebellion deserved.

Contemplating the situation of the missionaries, Peter was again aware that there were a variety of possible intentions on God's part. Peter did not doubt that God had intentionally permitted the abduction to occur, but he could not know for certain why. Perhaps this was an opportunity for the missionaries to spend otherwise boring days in a guerrilla camp talking about Jesus. Or maybe the missionaries had gotten rather lax in their dependence on God. Missionary work, like other kinds of work, can be done in purely human strength and can become a thoroughly autonomous venture. Peter didn't know Richard Henderson or the other missionaries intimately, but it did occur to him that they might have needed to be put into a situation where they were no longer in control, where they were desperately dependent on God. This was an opportunity to test their faith as God had tested Job's faith and Abraham's faith. Job's experience demonstrated that Satan might have destructive intentions for the missionaries, but God could still allow him to move against the missionaries because God intended to use the experience for their spiritual growth. The complexity of God's work in the world was immense, but at least Peter could trust the good and holy God to do his whole project wisely and well.

There was one good in the situation that Peter saw immediately. It had already occurred. God loves for his children to acknowledge their dependence upon him. He loves to have them pray and then to give them the joy of answered prayer, eliciting praise and thanksgiving. The very fact that this group of believers was now so earnestly engaged in prayer was obviously part of what God wanted. The fact that they had such different conceptions of God's role in the situation was, in the final analysis, not the most important thing. The good thing was that, for slightly different reasons, they were all united in prayer that God's good purposes for the world would be achieved at this time. Even Millie (semi-deist model) wanted that to happen, although she did not expect God to intervene at all. She still found it meaningful to acknowledge God in the situation and to commit herself to be an agent of the good that God wished for his creation. Crises had this positive outcome when people truly believed in God.

Working from within the openness model, Oliver could never quite figure out why Peter thought that his prayer would actually affect the situation. If every little event in the whole of human history had already been determined by God in his eternal purpose, then the outcome of the abduction situation was already settled. What was going to happen to both the guerrillas and the missionaries was already certain within God's plan. So, Oliver sometimes asked, why did Peter bother to ask God to do anything? Why didn't Peter just submit to God's eternal will and acknowledge that nothing he did could make any difference? Sandra (church dominion model) agreed with Oliver and called Peter a fatalist. But Peter would have none of that. A fatalist, he explained, is someone who believes that the outcome or end of everything is absolutely fixed, but who gives no room for the part that actions along the way play in achieving that end. Peter called that "hyper-Calvinism" and insisted that what sets true Calvinism apart from hyper-Calvinist fatalism is the conviction that God ordains means as well as ends. Peter knew that the outcome of this abduction was already settled in God's eternal plan, but he also believed that there are many things that God has ordained to accomplish in response to the prayers of his people. Peter knew that he could not change the future, but he did believe that his prayer now could have a significant part in bringing about the future that God had planned. If he failed to pray when he should, God would hold him responsible for that failure and for the less beneficial outcome that might result if God had decided that he would not do some particular good unless he were asked to do so.

Peter now prayed, "Gracious Father, there are many occasions when we do not understand why you allow evils to come upon your children, and this is one of those times. On the other hand, we are not shaken in our confidence that you are in control and that you have good purposes for what you have permitted to happen to Richard and his colleagues. You could have protected them, or warned them, or delivered them. That you did not do so indicates to us that you have reasons for allowing this difficult set of events to come about. Now that it has happened, however, we are also confident that you want us to be involved in prayer and perhaps in other ways that you may show us as we make ourselves available to you for the accomplishment of your will.

"Lord, we pray for Richard and his friends that you will keep them safe and bring them out of their captivity unharmed. We ask that you will comfort and strengthen them and cause their lives to be a powerful witness of their faith in you. We know that you may have allowed them to come into contact with their abductors because of good that you wish to come to these men, even though their own intentions are evil. We ask that you would be gracious to them and bring good out of this for them as well as for the missionaries. Father, please encourage Fred and the family members of the other missionaries, assuring them that you are in control and that they need not be fearful. It is not that you have given us any guarantee of your children's physical safety, but you have promised us that you will always be with us and that you will work everything together for the good that is our conformity to Jesus Christ. Please help all of those who are at work on the situation, give them wisdom and courage and faith in your care. All this we ask in the name of Jesus, Amen."

12

The Fatalist Model

CALVINISM IS OFTEN CHARGED WITH FATALISM, BUT THE MODELS ARE DIS-
*tinct. Like previous models of the "no-risk" variety, the fatalist model views
God as absolutely in control. Its distinctive is that God not only determines
the outcome of all events, he is, to all intents and purposes, the only actor in
them. Everyone else is simply acting by God's will and their sense of having
significant agency of their own is illusory. God is the only cause in the
world, everything else is effect. Petitionary prayer is ruled out by this uni-
causal model. Prayer is an act of worship in which one acknowledges God's
greatness and expresses one's own willing submissiveness to the all-powerful
will of the all-wise God.*

The models presented in the three preceding chapters (Thomist, Barthian and Calvinist) all asserted that God is absolutely in control of the events
that occur in the cosmos, but they also contended that this control does not
negate the freedom and contingency of creaturely action. Humans are able
to decide and act spontaneously even when their action is within the eternal plan of God. The theologians represented in those three models have
all carefully distinguished their position from fatalism, and this has been
necessary because proponents of the models that define human freedom as
libertarian often equate Augustinian or compatibilist positions with fatalism.

Indeed, the remarks of the women whose view Brother Andrew cited (see church dominion model) as evidence for his legitimate concern about fatalism could possibly have arisen within one of the models we have just been examining, all of which deny that they are fatalistic. On the other hand, it is distinctly possible that those women did, unwittingly, have a fatalistic view of life. Andrew himself is concerned about the teaching that "*nothing* happens outside His [God's] will," and dubs it Christian fatalism, a "false doctrine that has infected the thinking of an alarming number of Christians in our time."[1]

Roger Hazelton notes that "Karl Heim, several decades ago, observed that it was fate which expressed more than any other term the direction in which men were looking for the meaning of life," and Hazelton believes that Heim's "statement holds true."[2] In his opinion, "fate is a powerful contemporary substitute for the providence of God," and he asserts that "there are surely multitudes of people, whether in or outside churches, who have a very fuzzy and hazy working notion of Providence but betray an appallingly plain and practical notion of fate."[3] The notion was expressed in a song popular some decades ago, a line of which said: "*Que sera sera,* whatever will be will be." On the other hand, Dorothy Sayers suggests that no one actually lives in a consistently fatalistic way for "even the most thoroughgoing philosophic determinist will swear at the maid like any good Christian when the toast is burned."[4]

Unlike all of the other models, this one has no Christian theologians who admit to holding it as a biblical doctrine of providence. G. C. Berkouwer notes that there are deterministic tendencies in Martin Luther and Ulrich Zwingli's protests against free will, by which he presumably means "hard determinism." In Luther's case, however, it was not an issue of determinism versus free will but an attempt to "focus the entire problem of freedom on the central, religious relationship of man to God, which relationship is defined, not by the concept of necessity, but by the antithesis between sin and grace."[5] Berkouwer observes that "determinism seeks to solve the anthropological problem by means of the scheme: causes, causing, caused." Both Luther and Zwingli made use of this determinist design, drawing on the heritage of medieval thought, "undoubtedly because of its apparent parallelism to the decreeing, foreordaining, and ruling of God."[6]

When Luther writes concerning the betrayal of Jesus by Judas as an act within God's providence, he "seeks to distinguish between two kinds of necessity: one that implies a blind coercion and another that implies only that something must occur." It is the latter that Luther affirms in order to magnify God's rule, independence and majesty. Judas betrayed Christ freely and without coercion, and when Luther expresses his conviction regarding free will, "he speaks not about a determining first cause which excludes freedom of the will, but about the wrath of God revealed from heaven against man's suppression of the truth in unrighteousness." Luther did not base his argument against Erasmus on the relationship between first and second causes "but on the fettered, fallen will of man and on the wrath of God. The argument against free will was not a logical *deduction* from the all-embracing activity of God."[7]

Given that no Christian theologian intentionally asserts fatalistic determinism, why would I include this among our models? I do so for three reasons. (1) There are positions that are clearly headed in this direction, although their proponents back away from the conclusion. We will look at two of these directions: single causality and the embodiment of God. (2) The accusation is often heard that the positions presented under the Thomist, Barthian and Calvinist models are fatalistic,[8] and (3) it is apparent that people who are taught those models may unwittingly lapse into fatalism. Indeed a number of the models expounded earlier, particularly the openness model, have taken stances such as the denial of divine foreknowledge specifically to avoid the fatalism that they assume such a belief entails. Given the way in which an Augustinian view of providence is viewed by those who oppose it, one is sometimes unsure what it is that such opponents are naming "fatalism."

Terence Fretheim, for instance, argues from the biblical teaching concerning divine repentance that "the future is genuinely open," and God "does not have an unchangeable will with regard to every matter the prophets ever discussed concerning the future." But he posits that "in much prophetic interpretation, it is as if there is nothing God or people could do about the future; it is only a matter of those words making their way across history until they find their 'home.'" For such interpretations, he suggests "one should really use the language of fate" because "the future is all locked up in prophecies spoken in earlier times."[9] On the one hand, none of the theologians who were represented in the exposition of the Thomist, Barthian and Calvinist models would argue that neither God nor people can do anything about the future. On the other hand, they do believe in predictive prophecy through which God reveals the future as it will actually occur. Whether Fretheim refers to these theologians or not is unclear to me, but I suspect that to be his intention simply because it is a position like theirs that Fretheim is countering throughout his article. Consequently, it seems helpful to describe a fatalistic model and, thereby, to distinguish it from the models often described by opponents as fatalistic but which reject that designation.

**Everything Is Absolutely Determined by God, and
There Are No Secondary Causes**

John Fischer defines *fatalism* as "the doctrine that it is a logical or conceptual truth that no person is ever free to do otherwise,"[10] but this definition has a libertarian ring to it, which may explain why some theologians consider the Calvinist model, at least, to be fatalistic. By this definition, if creatures do not have libertarian freedom, they are subject to "fate." Roger Hazelton more helpfully suggests that fate is "a sort of Providence-in-reverse, which is to say a malevolent, teasing parody of God's guiding, guarding, governing power."[11] The word *fate* means what is "decreed or spoken, which cannot be taken back but must be carried out or executed."[12] Fatalism usually begins by distinguishing what humans can control and what they cannot, but "ends up by absorbing the former into the latter—which obviously makes nonsense of the initial distinction."[13] It "denotes that strange and spectral something which controls, determines, hedges about the life of man, overriding our wishes and disregarding our needs."[14] Alternately, it identifies fate with doom and equates it with chance or fortune. In the first case, the stress is on inevitability and necessity; the second emphasizes the accidental and unpredictable. The two come together in that our vulnerability to chance is seen as the effect of doom upon us. In the fatalism Hazelton has encountered, it is assumed that all the events of life have been decided in advance and that they are contrary to our self-fulfillment.[15]

A thoroughgoing theological determinism replaces the impersonal fate with God, a God who wills everything just as it happens and brings it about *without any genuine second causes*. The proper response to this situation is resignation. John Feinberg holds a "soft determinist" position (see the Calvinist model) but insists that determinism is not the same as fatalism except in the case of some "hard deterministic" positions. By his definition "a position is fatalistic if it claims that there is an inherent necessity in the way things are so that they could not be any other way." On those terms, even God had no choice but to do what he did, that is, the necessity was absolute. Over against this stance, Feinberg holds to "consequent necessity" that "once certain choices are made (by God or whomever), certain things follow as a consequence. But before these choices are made, no inherent necessity dictates what must be chosen."[16] The Stoics have been identified as "the first philosophers to maintain, in any systematic way, the law of universal causation."[17] Consequently, Christian theologians distinguishing their own views of providence from fatalism have characteristically identified Stoicism as the position from which their own theology needs to be differentiated. Peter Baelz cites words of Epictetus as epitomizing this Stoic doctrine of providence:

> We ought to approach God as we approach a guide, dealing with him as we deal with our eyes, not beseeching him to show us one sort of thing rather than another, but accepting the impressions of things as they are shown us. But instead of that, we tremble and get hold of the augur and appeal to him as if he were a god, and say "Master, have pity, suffer me to come off safe." Slave! Do you not wish for what is better for you? Is anything better than what seems good to God?[18]

This attitude of resignation to the divine determinism is later encouraged by Epictetus in the following words:

> Have courage to look up to God and say, "Deal with me hereafter as Thou wilt: I am as one with Thee. I am Thine: I flinch from nothing, so long as Thou thinkest it good. Lead me where Thou wilt. Put on me what raiment Thou wilt. Wouldest Thou have me hold office, or eschew it, stay or fly, be poor or rich? For all this I will defend Thee before men. I will show each thing in its true nature, as it is.[19]

On the other hand, Benjamin Farley asserts that the Stoics, though rigorously deterministic, espoused divine providence "by which they clearly meant nature's capacity to bring about good in spite of physical and moral evil."[20] This puts their position in a little different light than the "post-Christian" fatalism that Hazelton observes in people today.

John Sanders has noted that while it is true that "many Stoics spoke of events as the product of an impersonal source," as necessarily caused by the chain of events, "one of the frustrating things about them is that some of them speak of God as personal and as directing all events towards the good of the whole." In such cases "the contrast with Calvinism is not so strong, if a contrast at all."[21] This is an important warning. References to Stoicism within this chapter should be read in respect of the mechanistic and impersonal formulation that is most often associated with the Stoics by their critics.

The Thomist, Barthian and Calvinist models are all later expressions of the earlier proposal of Augustine. Since one of our intentions in this chapter is to show how fatalism is a model different from the Augustinian, it is helpful to note here that Augustine considered the Stoics to be right in believing that "God allows all things before they come to pass" but wrong in failing to understand "that what God allows in the moral order includes the free choices of men. Hence, Augustine is willing to concede that God 'is the Cause of all causes,' but 'not of all choices.'"[22] Augustine used the term *fate,* but he rejected the popular, astrological understanding of it. T. J. Gorringe posits that Augustine kept the term because he erroneously traced the word *fatum* to *fari,* "to speak," in Psalm 61:11, "God has spoken once," that is, immovably. God knows all that is to happen and he "leaves nothing unordered."[23]

Boethius, who significantly influenced Augustine, said that "Providence includes all things at the same time, however diverse or infinite, while Fate controls the motion of different individual things in different places and in different times. So the unfolding of the plan in time when brought together as a unified whole in the foresight of God's mind is Providence; and the same unified whole when dissolved and unfolded in the course of time is Fate."[24] Gorringe understands "fate," as Boethius used it, to refer to "the causal nexus, the rules which constitute an orderly universe (more or less what Tillich in this century called 'destiny')."[25] Aquinas also agreed that "fate" refers to the series of secondary causes, for he says that "the divine power or will can be called fate, as being the cause of fate." Aquinas asserted that "'Fate' refers to the fact that anything God foreknows will happen will certainly do so. What God foreknows must be: the ordained cause of things is immutable."[26] Gorringe is correct to note that these uses of the term were not intended to confuse the Stoic concept of fate with the Christian doctrine of providence.

John Calvin is frequently dubbed a determinist and was thought by a theologian as astute as the Lutheran Philip Melanchthon to be defending a Stoic doctrine.[27] But in Calvin's treatise "Against the Libertines" he spelled out "three abominable consequences" that follow from the determinism that was being espoused by his Libertine opponents: (1) it makes no distinction between God and the devil; (2) it robs people of moral conscience; and (3) it leaves us with no means of passing moral judgment on anything.[28] Calvin rejected determinism while also avoiding radical indeterminism. In his *Institutes* Calvin argued that "the doctrine of providence is no Stoic belief in fate," and he did so precisely because his objectors charged him with fatalism. Calvin protested: "We do not, with the Stoics, contrive a necessity out of the perpetual connection and intimately related series of causes, which is contained in nature; but we make God the ruler and governor of all things, who in accordance with his wisdom has from the farthest limit of eternity decreed what he is going to do, and now by his might carries out what he has decreed."[29] We see here what Calvin understood by Stoic fatalism and why he denied propounding the doctrine himself, his detractors not withstanding.

It is precisely in an effort to avoid the fatalistic risks inherent in a theology of absolute divine sovereignty that Karl Barth insists that the rule of God be considered in the light of his rule in the covenant of grace and in the work of Jesus Christ. Not to do so would leave us with a concept of "sovereign caprice, in the hands of which the creature would appear to act, but in fact would only be acted upon, and this in pursuance of a purpose which is utterly obscure." Barth suggests that in such a theology submission would be like that of Stoicism or Islam but would not be "a genuine decision of the Christian obedience of faith."[30]

Barth posits that the traditional Reformed way of speaking of God's rule led, in practice, to a Stoic or Islamic resignation and incited "the murmuring of the clay against the potter (Rom 9:20ff.), the revolt against a capricious sovereign rule, and the despair or frivolity which is the inevitable consequence of this revolt." He notes that the Lutherans even accused the Calvinists of apostasy to Islam and protested "that they themselves had more fellowship with Rome than with a Geneva which maintained such a doctrine" of the divine concursive operation.[31] Barth's own assessment is that the older theologians avoided both the Stoic doctrine of fate and the Epicurean doctrine of chance that had been revived in the Renaissance, although neither the Lutherans nor the Reformed thought that the other had succeeded.[32]

As indication of the avoidance of fatalism by classic Reformed scholars, Barth cites H. Heidegger, who identified the following five points of distinction between the Christian doctrine of divine world governance and fatalism:[33] (1) divine governance is located in God himself, but fatalism places fate in things, in the series of causes and effects; (2) in the Christian view, God is a free agent, whereas fatalism imprisons God within the order of causes;[34] (3) faith distinguishes between the eternal (divine) and temporal (immanent) necessity of world occurrence, but fatalism confounds the two; (4) although faith has room for both "contingency in general and for a freedom for the human will in particular," fatalism "involves a mechanisation and destruction of the two"; and (5) in a proper theology God's governance extends to sin but not in a way that makes him its author, but in fatalism "sin is one of the necessities posited by God side by side with others."

God as the only cause. G. C. Berkouwer notes that Ulrich Zwingli was more inclined than Luther to argue from God as first cause and prime mover, a cause that excludes freedom of the will in a libertarian sense. "He shifts the problem from the dynamic relationship between grace and freedom to an abstract logical relationship between Providence and freedom."[35] One might think that Zwingli, with his denial of genuine secondary causes could therefore be cited as an example of a fatalistic determinism, but Zwingli himself denied this. In spite of his insistence that God is the author of every human action, Zwingli argued that "only the unbeliever interprets this in a deterministic way, and so regards all human action as vain."[36] In the elect, belief in providence ought not to lead to indolence and a leaving of everything to God because they know that God requires their work, even though it is only produced as the Holy Spirit acts.[37]

In spite of the moves Zwingli makes to avoid fatalistic determinism, he speaks so strongly of God's sole causing of everything that takes place that it is hard to see how he can coherently avoid what he denies. Zwingli argues his case for comprehensive divine providence from God's supreme goodness, which necessitates that he provide for all that he creates.[38] God is the only cause and all creatures are his instruments. "It is the kindly power of the Deity that giveth all things; the earth, the tree, the sun, and the rest are the stalk and branches which hold that bounty and supply it to us." Consequently, "those nearer things which we call causes, are not properly causes, but the agents and instruments with which the eternal mind works, and in which it manifests itself to be enjoyed."[39]

Earlier we noticed how Calvin responded to the charge that God is the author of sin because he is the primary cause of sinful actions. Calvin rejected the charge on the ground of genuine secondary causation, and because God's intention in the acts produced by double-agency was pure and good. Zwingli takes a similar approach but speaks of emotion rather than intention. However, his major argument for absolving God (who is the *only* cause) from unrighteousness in causing sinful deeds is that God is not under the law that humans are obligated to obey and the breaking of which makes them sinners. Consequently, God "sinneth not when He does in man that which is sin to man but not to Himself."[40]

Zwingli illustrates his point by describing a situation in which a human instrument sins but God, the cause, does not. "Even when He slays a man whom He kills by the hand of a robber or of an unjust judge, He sins no more than when He kills a wolf by means of a wolf or an elephant by means of a dragon. For all things are His, and He has no wrong feeling towards anything. Therefore He is not under the law, because he who cannot be influenced by any evil emotions has no need of law." From this perspective "the same deed which is done at the instigation and direction of God, brings honor to Him, while it is a crime and sin to man." This is because the human actors have "sinned against the law, not as principals, but as accessory instruments, which God can use as He will more freely than the father of a family may drink water or pour it out upon the ground." Furthermore, although God "impels men to some deed which is a wickedness unto the instrument that performs it, yet it is not such unto Himself. For His movements are free." God does no wrong in using human instruments in this way "since all things are His more than any artisan's tools are his own, and to these he does no wrong if he turns a file into a hammer or a hammer into a file." Moreover, when God "instigates the robber" even to kill the innocent or those who are unprepared for death, the robber is guilty because he sinned against the law, but God is not because he did not sin against the law and because he transported the righteous to the abode of the blessed or the sinner to just punishment. God influenced both the robber and the judge whose conscience goads him to punish the robber. "In short, God instigated the killing, but He instigates the judge just as much to sacrifice the slayer to justice."[41]

What keeps Zwingli's position (coherently or otherwise) from being thoroughgoing fatalism is his insistence that the human instruments are morally responsible for their evil deeds. Zwingli specifically warns believers against explaining providence "so as to say, 'I will, therefore, indulge my inclinations. If I am elect, I shall attain felicity however I live.' Men who speak thus give evidence either that they are not elect or that they have not yet acquired faith and the knowledge of God." This is evident because "those who have the knowledge of God know that life must be ordered according to God's will, and those who have faith know that they are elect. And the elect, knowing this, cannot help seeing that they must refrain from whatever the law forbids."[42]

The world as God's body. Grace Jantzen notes that the Stoics considered God and the world to be composed of the same stuff and hence conceived of God as corporeal. This was an idea she also discerns in some of the early fathers, like Tertullian, who may have been influenced by the Stoics.[43] Jantzen herself argues that the whole universe is God's body, which thus gives him an unmediated knowledge of it, since it is the parts and processes of his own body that he knows.[44] This is her explanation of God's feeling of our pain: he does not just sympathize with us; he feels the pain, but he can cope with far more than we can.[45] Similarly, God's actions on the world are understood as direct and basic, not like the moving of a pencil, for which we must move our hand, but like the direct movement of our hand.[46] God controls the universe and all its parts directly, because its movements are his basic actions. This removes the question of miracles since it is just one part of God's continuous action, indeed "the whole unfolding of nature, including at least to some degree humankind's part in it, will be the manifestation of divine activity."[47] The inappropriateness of frequent divine "intervention" is affirmed by embodiment theologians as it is by those committed to divine incorporeality, since the regularities that God has established in nature (his body) are overall good, though they sometimes bring pain and suffering. Evil is in God, on this model of divine being, but God is not evil because he does not have an evil will.[48] His omnipresence is particularly easy to conceive, though the model requires that God not be spatially infinite, and his loving awareness and ability to intervene are affirmed (cf. Ps 121:4-7; 139:7-10). God does reveal himself specially, on occasion, in particular actions.[49]

Jantzen proposes that God transcends his own body in the same way that humans are self-transcendent. "If human embodiment does not reduce personal significance to physiology, neither would the postulate that God's body is the universe mean that God is finally describable in exclusively physical terms." Transcendence is therefore compatible with embodiment, without reverting to metaphysical dualism.[50]

On this model, everything that exists is God's self-expression. "It is God's self-formation, and owes its being what it is directly to God's formative will." God is in complete control, and nothing exists apart from his will. This sounds like the pantheism and determinism that the early fathers criticized in Stoicism, but Jantzen rejects that identification. On the one hand, she asserts, "If pantheism is thus understood as an affirmation that all reality is God's reality, that there can be nothing without God or utterly apart from him or independent of him, then pantheism is not an alternative to Christian theology but an ingredient in it." Yet mechanistic determinism need not follow.[51] Though God and the world are a single reality, "this does not mean that God is reducible to mechanism and physical statistics any more than personhood is reducible to physiological data."[52]

Through most of Jantzen's book I expected that her model of God's being and action were going to be a clear case of the absolute, single agent determinism that constitutes this last model.[53] Right at the end of her treatment, however, she avoids that conclusion and places herself within the openness model. The "solution" to the apparent assault on human freedom lies in God's "self-restraint." God has given some parts of his body a measure of autonomy within his gracious self-manifestation. Although Jantzen has removed her own model from the position being examined in this chapter, it is easy to see how a theology of divine embodiment could provide a thoroughly deterministic picture of God's relationship to the world and its events.

Mind, brain and fatalism. One last area of contemporary theological discussion deserves consideration for its implications in regard to human freedom. For centuries, philosophers and theologians have struggled to define the nature of human being and to establish how many distinct parts of us there are. The traditional struggle between dichotomists (two parts: body and soul/spirit) and trichotomists (three parts: body, soul and spirit) has increasingly led theologians to question whether there are any parts at all to human being. The primary factor contributing to this trend of substance monism has been the scientific difficulty of describing how mind (soul) and brain (body) interact if they are two distinct things.[54] The trouble with committing oneself to a thoroughgoing monism of human being is that if there is only one part to us, then ultimate reality must be either idea (mind) or matter (brain and body). It is beyond our scope in this study to pursue this anthropological question, but efforts are being made to construct a substantial monism that avoids the problem of reducing humans to the purely material. The importance of this is evident when one looks at the consequences of a thoroughgoing materialism, which necessarily leads to fatalism. An example of this can be found in John Searle's discussion of the freedom of the will.[55]

John Searle concludes that mind and body are "not two different things, since mental phenomena just are features of the brain."[56] As a materialist, Searle is a determinist who posits that "since nature consists of particles and their relations with each other, and since everything can be accounted for in terms of those particles and their relations, there is simply no room for freedom of the will."[57] Searle finds no support for a doctrine of the freedom of the will even in the physicists' proposal that there is indeterminism at the level of particles. This is because "the statistical indeterminacy at the level of particles does not show any indeterminacy at the level of the objects that matter to us—human bodies, for example."[58] Searle finds "no evidence that there is or could be some mental energy of human freedom that can move molecules in directions that they were not otherwise going to move," and so he concludes that contemporary physics forces us to deny any form of human freedom.[59]

Compatibilists have posited that we can affirm both divine determinism and human freedom. This has frequently (in the Calvinist model especially) been done by arguing that we are free as long as we do what we want. Provided our action is directed by our own desires rather than coerced from outside of ourselves, we can be considered free in our action. It is because we act for "reasons" that God, who knows us thoroughly, can predict and direct our action without robbing us of freedom. But Searle argues that "the problem about the freedom of the will is not about whether or not there are inner psychological reasons that cause us to do things as well as external physical causes and inner compulsions." The critical issues is "whether or not the causes of our behaviour, whatever they are, are sufficient to *determine* the behaviour so that things *have to* happen the way they do happen" and Searle thinks that this is not so.[60]

Those who believe that human freedom is libertarian get no better support from Searle's materialism than do the compatibilists. For libertarianism to be true, Searle argues, "We would have to postulate that inside each of us was a self that was capable of interfering with the causal order of nature . . . some entity that was capable of making molecules swerve from their paths." Since this is not consistent with what we know about the world from physics, Searle rejects the possibility and therefore rejects libertarian freedom.[61] Searle rejects psychological determinism, the idea "that our states of mind are sufficient to determine everything we do," but he is stuck with a more fundamental form of physical determinism. Even if we grant that our minds affect our bodies, in a top-down causation, the problem remains because "the top level is already caused by and realised in the bottom levels."[62]

Searle himself hangs on to a "modified form of compatibilism" in which he holds together physical determinism and psychological libertarianism. As far as psychological factors were concerned, people could have done otherwise, but "as long as we accept the bottom-up conception of physical explanation, and it is a conception on which the past 300 years of science are based, then psychological facts about ourselves, like any other higher level facts, are entirely causally explicable in terms of and entirely realised in systems of elements at the fundamental micro-physical level. Our conception of physical reality simply does not allow for radical freedom."[63] Searle concludes that for reasons he does not understand, evolution has given us a form of experience of voluntary action in which we sense that we have alternative possibilities even though this is illusory.

I have not included Searle's materialistic account because he himself is approaching the critical issue of human freedom from a theological perspective. I mention it because it illustrates the challenge that confronts theologians who are attracted to monistic conceptions of the human constitution. A thoroughgoing materialism will lead to a fatalistic model of the world and our place in the progress of human history. However difficult it is to explain the relationship between the mind and the brain as distinct, immaterial and material entities, the consequences of reducing human being to one or the other of these are far-reaching.

Petitionary Prayer Is Futile in a Fatalistic Structure

In the hard determinism or fatalism that allows no genuine creaturely causation, it is obviously futile to make requests to God, since they can have absolutely no effect. As H. H. Farmer put it, "Petition expresses the confidence that the ultimate reality of man's world is not uncongenial or unresponsive to his life task, whereas the petitionless man is always in danger of falling into a fatalistic despair which sees man, for all his endeavours, the plaything of forces over which in the last resort neither he, nor any power the least concerned with him, has any control."[64] From the church dominion model, this was Brother Andrew's concern when he heard the two women discussing a hostage taking by Middle Eastern terrorists. One of the women said: "I feel sorry for those poor men and their families, but really, this is God's problem not ours. We have to remember that He has already decided how their stories are going to turn out."[65] Andrew considers such an attitude completely crippling as far as petitionary prayer is concerned.

Thomas Aquinas observed that the Stoics "claimed that prayers were of no use, as if they thought that the wills of men and their desires, from which prayers arise, are not included under that universal order."[66] They argued that "whether prayers are offered or not, in any case the same effect in things follows from the universal order of things," thereby isolating "from that universal order the wishes of those who pray." Once again it is helpful to hear the distinction Aquinas makes between his own view and the fatalist or hard determinist one. He does not deny that human prayers are included in the universal order established by God, but he contends that "if these prayers be included under that order, then certain effects will result by divine ordination by means of these prayers, just as they do by means of other causes." Consequently, "prayers retain their power; not that they can change the order of eternal control, but rather as they themselves exist under such an order."[67]

The Case Study

One of the newest additions to Fred Henderson's congregation was Ahmed Kalil, a young man who had very recently come to faith in Christ, having grown up in a Muslim home. He was an earnest believer but one who was still learning to think about things in a distinctively Christian way. By the time of the prayer meeting, Ahmed thought of God as the almighty One whose will was absolutely sovereign in the world. Indeed, so complete was God's control that there were not really any other genuine agents in the world. Ahmed felt most at home talking about God and his work in the world when he was in conversation with Peter Vandervelde (Calvinist model). In Peter he found a reverence for God and a submissiveness to the all-powerful will of God, which was similar to his own religious sense. Ahmed was still trying to figure out why Peter was unsatisfied with Ahmed's own conception of God and with his manner of praying. Others in the church indicated that Peter and Ahmed believed pretty much the same thing, but this upset Peter, who insisted that God's comprehensive control within his creation was not exercised apart from the genuine agency of his creatures. Peter insisted that what we do is meaningful and that it has an effect on the outcome. How this could be was hard for Ahmed to see, but he was eagerly reading both the Bible and books that he borrowed from the church library in order to grow in his Christian understanding.

In conversations about God's providence, as the others called it in religious language that Ahmed was still learning, he was shocked at the conceptions voiced by most of the group. The common view of a God who had given up his own ability to guarantee that his will was done at every moment scarcely seemed like a description of God at all. In a peculiar way, Ahmed felt an affinity with Millie (semi-deist model). She had the least sense of God's involvement in the world of anyone in the group, and that should have made Ahmed most uncomfortable. But when Millie prayed, Ahmed found himself fairly comfortable with the general tenor of her request or, more accurately, the *absence* of any requests. In Millie's understanding, God had acted to create a good world and had built into it the dynamics capable of achieving his purposes for it, but beyond that he was not continually involved. The good thing about this, from Ahmed's perspective, was that when Millie prayed, she didn't act as though her praying was going to bring about changes in the world. In particular, she did not assume, as Oliver did (openness model), that she could actually contribute to God's decision-making process about what he was going to do next and even *change* God's mind about what he was planning to do.

In Ahmed's view of the situation reported by Fred, the abduction of the missionaries had obviously happened within God's will as everything does. It was not their prerogative to understand the will of the Almighty and certainly not to influence or change it. God does in his world what God wants to do, and we simply submit and acknowledge his greatness and his right to do this because he is God. Whatever God would do in Richard Henderson's case was up to God. It was not Ahmed's place to instruct God, to reason with God or to plead with him about the need of Richard, the needs of the guerrillas, the troubles of the related families or anything else. The attitude of prayer is an attitude of humble submission to God and whatever he wills.

Ahmed knelt on the floor and bowed his head low as he prayed, "Almighty God, your power is complete and all things are in your hands so that your will is always done. It is according to your plan that Richard and his friends have been taken captive, and we do not yet understand your will in this matter, but we accept it as good and wise. We submit to it, and we look forward to the time when we will comprehend what you are doing. Accept our praise for your goodness in all things, and make us and all who acknowledge your name to be obedient servants. Amen."

Part 2

One More Model Proposed

13

A Middle Knowledge Calvinist Model of Providence

T*HIS LAST MODEL IS MY OWN. AS THE NAME SUGGESTS, IT AFFIRMS THE MAIN features of the Calvinist model. God is comprehensively in control in the world, accomplishing purposes that he has determined in eternity. Because his will is always accomplished, it is evident that God's creatures (human and angelic) do not have libertarian freedom. This is a compatibilist model that affirms both meticulous providence and human freedom of a spontaneous or voluntary kind. This model is less certain than the traditional Calvinist model that God is absolutely timeless because of a concern that such a concept may not do justice to God's highly relational personal being. In a significant sense, God is not only determining human history, he is responding to his creatures within it. This divine responsiveness is facilitated by God's possessing knowledge of how creatures would act in particular circumstances (so called "middle knowledge"). God not only knows the actual future, he has determined that future. But in order to do this, God needed to know how creatures would respond to situations, including their response to his own persuasions or actions. God can know this because creatures are not libertarianly free and he must know this in order to plan how he will act to bring about his purposes. With simple foreknowledge God would know the future but be unable to do anything about it. With "middle knowledge" God*

is able to plan and then to accomplish his plan without violating the respon-
sible freedom that he has given to his creatures.

I have presented ten models of providence formulated by theologians
attempting to represent the biblical teaching concerning God's care for his
creatures, and I have shown how petitionary prayer works within each of
those models. I hope that the process has helped readers to refine their own
model of providence and prayer through personal assessment of the positions presented. In this last part of the book I will present my own understanding and say what I have appreciated and accepted from the various
models examined in the first part of the book. Having presented the argu-
mentation of the proponents of those models, I do not need to repeat the
premises, but I will refer to lines of exegesis and reasoning that I find convincing as I develop my own model. In this chapter I will present a model
of providence, and the next chapter will deal with the function of petitionary prayer within this model of providence. It will quickly become clear that
my own understanding falls squarely within the Augustinian end of the
spectrum, and of the three representative positions expounded, it is closest
to the Calvinist model. In several ways, however, my understanding is influenced by aspects of other models studied in the first part of the book and
this changes the picture. I am particularly impressed with the significance of
God's knowledge of what *would* have happened in situations that never
actually occur (counterfactuals). The most enthusiastic proponents of this
concept have been found in the Molinist model, which called it "middle
knowledge." I am somewhat reluctant to use the term to describe my own
position because it is usually associated with a commitment to libertarian
human freedom. However, it is a simple handle to refer to the concept of
God's knowledge of counterfactuals of human freedom, and I will use it in
my own model even though I do not believe human freedom to be libertarian. It is my hope that reasons for accepting and rejecting aspects of the various proposals already presented will become clear as I go on.

God Cares for All of His Creation with a Comprehensive,
Detailed and Loving Control

As I read the narrative of Scripture, the picture that comes through very
clearly to me is much like the one that John Calvin saw. I meet a God who
brought things into reality where nothing existed before *(creatio ex nihilo)*
and who then preserves their continuing existence and rules over creation

in a sovereign and all powerful way. He is the Lord God Almighty upon whom all creaturely existence depends and whose will, in the sense of his eternal purpose or plan, is always done. We know, after the fact, that all events have been either brought about by God's active working or by his willing permission. Either God acted to ensure that just these circumstances arose, or he restrained himself and allowed things to develop through the decisions and actions of creatures, without God's specific assistance or prevention. In that sense we can say that everything that happens is "God's will."

Clearly, there is also a sense in which God's will is not done. He is not the only agent, for he created other spiritual beings, angelic and human. God made them like himself as persons, creatures that have a power of self-determinacy and an ability to discriminate between good and evil and to choose from among the options within their power. He made them creatures in relationship with himself and with one another, able to love and to be loved. He made them good but not independently so, and he allowed both the angels and the first human beings to disobey his command (his moral or prescriptive will) for reasons that are beyond our comprehending. It has not been our purpose to analyze those complex reasons, but each model of providence that we have examined has its own way of dealing with evil in creaturely experience.

It is necessary for us to say, therefore, that God's sovereign will or purpose is always done but that his moral will is not. The moral will of God describes how creatures ought to behave to be true to their own nature as creatures who bear a likeness to the God who made them. Only in obedience to this will can we be fully human and therefore truly free, being our true selves and living in harmonious relationship with God who is himself consistently good and whose being is the definition of moral goodness.

There is nothing that happens within the created reality outside of God's good and wise care and control. In creating other beings with self-determination, God has surrendered none of his control. This does not mean that God is effectively the only agent, as the final model would suggest. It means that God can work within his creation so that free self-determining creatures do what they want to do but always within a context over which God maintains his sovereign prerogative and in which he could prevent things from taking place or bring about different outcomes, without taking away the creature's self-determination. We may not want to use the language of primary and secondary cause in the way that Aquinas or even

Calvin did, but the idea is valid. There is a double agency at work in the events of human history, and those agents are not equal in their control and determination of outcomes. Humans have genuine agency, they make decisions and effect outcomes, but always within the total supervision of God, so that everything happens at least because he allows it and sometimes because he contributes to the event in ways that influence the outcome. In either case, what happens is within God's purpose. However, it is often not possible for us to discern the nature of God's involvement. We are usually not able to say when God permitted and when he acted directly or through his means of influence to bring about some state of affairs. Nevertheless, knowing his complete control, we are grateful to God for all the good things we receive, and we trust his wisdom and care even in the midst of painful circumstances.

That God is concerned about the little things in his creature's lives and not only about the general conclusion of things is shown in Jesus' instructions to his disciples regarding worry. Among the items about which Christians need not be anxious are the most basic ones, food and clothing (Mt 6:25), and the reason such anxiety is inappropriate is God's knowledge and provision. God knows what we need (Mt 6:32), and the assurance that he will provide derives from the observation of his care for creatures who are less valuable than we (Mt 6:30; 10:31; Lk 12:7).[1] The detailedness of God's providence is evident in Jesus' picture of God "clothing" grass and lilies (Mt 6:28-30) and feeding the birds of the air (Mt 6:26). Jesus speaks of God's awareness of the fall of every sparrow and of the numbers of the hair on our heads (Lk 12:6-7) to indicate how comprehensively God cares for his creation and how silly it is for believers to worry about the necessities of life. In the same context, however, Jesus establishes priorities for us. Without denying that God cares for the details of the lives of his creatures, Jesus notes that the rule of God in his creation is the larger matter for God and that it should likewise be our primary concern. It is precisely because we are freed from anxiety about the little things of life that we are freed to "strive for the kingdom of God and his righteousness" (Mt 6:33) and to make those permanent realities our greatest treasure (Lk 12:31-34).

The big picture of God's establishment of his rule in all of creation should keep us from presumption about what God will provide. It is obviously wrong to assume that Jesus has given us assurance that none of God's children will ever be hungry or naked. Experience indicates otherwise, and there is no guarantee that Christians in a sinful world will not be among the victims of drought and war, famished and naked. That this would be true of God's people is evident in Jesus' words about the identification between believers and himself. In the judgment day he will commend or condemn people for having fed and clothed him or for not having done so when he was hungry, thirsty and naked (Mt 25:34-45). The only sense I can make of this is that it is God's prerogative to decide when even the basic essentials of life are no longer his will for us. If we starve to death, our faith in God need not be shaken. He could feed us by ravens as he did Elijah, or with manna and quail as he did Israel in the wilderness. Indeed there are instances of his doing similar things in our own day. There is no guarantee that God's people will not suffer hardship, but when they do so they can still rest in the knowledge that God is aware of their suffering and has reasons for not intervening supernaturally to prevent it. Furthermore, human beings who are aware of that suffering and able to alleviate it are culpable if they do not do so.

With regard to God's provision, Paul was confident that God would care for the needs of the Philippians precisely because they had been good stewards of the resources God had given them and had sacrificially given for the support of Paul and his ministry (Phil 4:15-19). It is also clear that James had the same understanding of the comprehensiveness of God's will in our lives, in mundane details and not only in matters of grave eternal significance. He rebuked those who make plans for the future on the assumption that their lives are completely at their own disposal, announcing that "Today or tomorrow we will go to such and such a town and spend a year there, doing business and making money" (Jas 4:13). Instead we ought to make all plans for the future with the awareness that what actually happens is determined by God. Consequently, we ought rather to say, "If the Lord wishes, we will live and do this or that" (Jas 4:15).

From this perspective Fred Henderson need have no fear that things have "gotten out of hand," if it is God's "hand" that he keeps in mind. The men who abducted Richard and his fellow missionaries sinned in so doing. What they are doing in holding those three men captive and demanding ransom is contrary to the moral principles God has defined for human relationships. There is a definite sense in which we can say that God did not "want" the abductors to do what they did. On the other hand, we must grant that there is a sense in which God did "want" it to happen or he would have acted to prevent it. There are numerous ways in which God could have done that, some of which would have been exceptional and would be dubbed miraculous, but some of which would be imperceptible. God could have timed an earthquake like the one that would have set Paul and Silas free in Philippi if they had wished to leave the jail. He could have sent an angel to lead them out of jail as he did Peter. He could have surrounded them with angels, as he did Elijah. He could have warned them directly so that they would flee, as he did Joseph and Mary, or prompted them to do things that would have removed them from the danger. This might have happened in a way that would enable them to look back and conclude that God had providentially protected them, or they might never become aware that they had even been in danger. The point is that they and their loved ones could accept the admittedly bad situation with confidence that God was still in control and that he would bring good out of the evil, both for his children and for others.

It will be apparent that I do not share John Calvin's aversion to the language of permission in regard to God's sovereign care of creation. I share Calvin's conviction that when God permits, he does it willingly and is not simply passive. God's permitting is as much a part of his eternal purpose as is his acting and effectuating. It is not "mere" permission. I understand that to be Calvin's concern, and so I am not disagreeing with him, but I am speaking in a way that he was reluctant to do because of the way the language of permission was being used by his contemporaries who rejected comprehensive divine providence. In fact, I would argue that *only* those who believe in meticulous providence *can* use permission to speak of God's relationship to particular incidents of evil in life. It puzzles me when people who believe that human freedom is libertarian speak of God's "permission" of an event such as an accident or an illness. I suspect that this is frequently the result of widespread Calvinistic influence within evangelicalism, which has contributed a way of speaking that is not truly consistent with the general framework or theological model within which these people understand God and his work in the world.

Like other Augustinians whose treatment of the passage I have described, I find the words of Joseph to his brothers (Gen 50:20) to be an excellent paradigm for our approach to situations where other people transgress God's moral precepts, and we suffer as a result. The distinction between God's intention and the intention of human actors is important; God's intention was (and always is) good. Even more significant for distinguishing our model from those earlier in the book is the assumption that God himself had an intention and was acting to realize that intention in and through the very different intention and evil action of Joseph's brothers.[2] At that point, Joseph was able to discern God's intention and to understand why God had allowed him to be sold into slavery in Egypt. Joseph could see the good that had resulted, but the text "does not picture God as *post eventu* deflecting the evil action of the brothers and transforming it into something good"; both God and the brothers had intentions in the act itself.[3]

When evil befalls us, we often do not have the benefit of this sort of perception. At the point that Fred Henderson was asking prayer for his son, he knew something of the intention of the abductors, but he was completely unaware of the intention of God in the situation. What distinguishes the Augustinian from the non-Augustinian models is the conviction that God is realizing his intention at every point. For various reasons, the first six models assume that there are instances when God will have to act in some way to achieve his general intentions but that in the particular circumstance only the creaturely intention is at work. God will work to bring good out of evil, but the evil itself happens apart from his intention.

More important than Joseph's experience is that of our Lord himself. Here I take Peter's words at Pentecost (Acts 2:23-24) and the prayer of the church after the apostles' release (Acts 4:27-28) to be a paradigm for our understanding of the interaction of God and humans. Nothing could have been more evil than putting to death as a blasphemer the man who had always done the will of the Father (Jn 5:19; 15:10) and who revealed the Father in all his words (Jn 12:50) and actions (Jn 14:9). Yet Peter tells the crowd gathered at Pentecost that Jesus had been handed over to those who crucified and killed him "according to the definite plan and foreknowledge of God" (Acts 2:23). Likewise, as the believers gathered in prayer following the release of Peter and John, they told God that they knew that what had been done by Herod, Pontius Pilate, the Gentiles and the peoples of Israel against God's anointed one was whatever God's hand and plan "had predestined to take place" (Acts 4:28). Given that conviction of God's controlling providence, they asked God to take note of the continuing threats being made against the followers of Jesus and to give them boldness to proclaim him faithfully, while God acted through them in signs and wonders done in the name of Jesus. I take Paul's statement to the Ephesians to be a statement of this detailed and comprehensive providence of God accomplishing in the events of creation and history what he has purposed, counseled and willed (Eph 1:11).

Spiritual Beings Are As Much Within God's Sovereign Control
As Human Beings Are

Just as I do not perceive human beings to be operating independently of God, I do not agree with Gregory Boyd's portrayal within the openness model of the spiritual conflict between God and the evil spiritual powers.[4] Within my model, Satan and the demons are never able to act contrary to God's sovereign purpose. Even in their evil action they accomplish the will of God. I have significant appreciation for Boyd's treatment of the biblical material concerning spiritual conflict, but I disagree in regard to the level of risk that God has undertaken or the level of the threat that the rebellious spirits pose to his rule in the world. Satan himself is very powerful and is indeed the enemy, the Satan, the opponent of God, but God is always completely in control.[5] As Stephen Noll puts it, "God has committed himself to rule through the free, and thus potentially wicked, wills of his creatures."[6] It is for this reason that Satan is sometimes represented as God's servant rather than God's opponent. Noll is correct to reject the suggestion that this is indication that the Satan is "a title designating an officer of the divine council, like a prosecuting attorney in a courtroom"[7] God is able to use Satan in punishing sin because "his malicious intent is overlapped by the Lord's righteous indignation."[8] In 1 Kings 22:19-23 and 1 Chronicles 21:1 "Satan operates in heaven, not because he occupies a post or wants to serve God but because the repaying of evil in this case is 'an act of God,' that is, not the normal working out of natural justice by which the wicked steps into his own trap (Ps 7:14-16)."[9]

God's use of evil spirits as a form of judgment is exemplified in the experience of Abimelech, who murdered sixty-nine of his brothers to consolidate his power. Because of this, "God sent an evil spirit between Abimelech and the lords of Shechem" after he had ruled over Israel for three years (Judg 9:23) and this resulted in much civil strife, war and death. The phrase "evil spirit" that is used here is identical to the term used of the spirit that troubled Saul,[10] and that evil spirit is described as "from the Lord" six out of the seven times that it is mentioned (1 Sam 16:14; cf. 18:10; 19:9).[11] "The contrast between the Spirit of Yahweh and the evil spirit virtually demands that the evil spirit be understood as an external power that existed independently of Saul," not simply as a psychological problem, but it is best not to view this as an Old Testament counterpart to the demonization encountered in the New Testament. It was periodic, was from the Lord, was judgment for sin and was relieved by music.[12]

Similarly, King Ahab was lured to his death by an evil spirit that was serving God (1 Kings 22:19-22), and John writes of demonic torture (like the sting of a scorpion) in the fifth trumpet (Rev 9:1-11). It is particularly noteworthy that these demons were restrained by God so that they were not permitted to harm grass or plants or those who had the seal of God on their foreheads (cf. Rev 13:5-7; 16:1-4). In fact, commenting on the Revelation of John, G. B. Caird writes, "Throughout his book John is constantly trying to show how God's hand may be detected in the affairs of the world; but he is equally insistent that Satan can do nothing except by the permission of God, who uses Satan's grimmest machinations to further his own bright designs.'"[13] Gregory Boyd notes the almost universal recognition of spiritual conflict except where the Enlightenment has removed this awareness. Consequently, it is significant to note that this biblical portrayal of the power of God over the evil spirits is very much unlike the African traditional religious idea where "spirits, witches and sorcerers appear to be very largely autonomous in their activities. As creator, God may be the ultimate cause of all things, but actual, present causation in the spiritual realm is effectively located elsewhere."[14]

As already mentioned, the story of Job is one of the clearest illustrations of God's *permission* relative to Satan. I strongly disagree with Brother Andrew's assessment that Job was guilty of the error of fatalism when he said, "The LORD gave, and the LORD has taken away" (Job 1:21).[15] Granted, it was the Sabeans who killed some of his sons and daughters (Job 1:13-15); it was lightning that killed his sheep and shepherds (Job 1:16); it was Chaldeans who raided and stole his camels (Job 1:17); it was a great wind that knocked down the house that killed more of his children (Job 1:19); but Job rightly understood that forces of nature (wind and lightning) and greedy, violent people (on that occasion, Sabeans and Chaldeans) all do their deeds within God's providence. Job did not then realize that he was also under assault from Satan, who sought to destroy Job's faith in God. What the narrative tells us, however, is that Satan himself, the most powerful of all evil beings, is restrained or released by God to do what he does (1:6-12).[16]

God repeatedly establishes the boundary within which Satan can work. God first gives Job's possessions and then his body into Satan's hand (Job 1:12; 2:6), but Satan "is not granted the right to seize Job's most important possession, his soul (compare Lk 12:16-23)."[17] God authorizes Satan's action and takes responsibility for its effects on Job (Job 2:3; 42:11), but then he blesses him even more richly in his later days than in his earlier life. On the other hand, the apostle John acknowledges the extent to which humankind has submitted to Satan's rule when he speaks of him as the one in whose power the whole world lies (1 Jn 5:19). But John also notes that "the evil one does not touch" those who are born of God (1 Jn 5:18).

Most of What Happens Within Human History Is Determined by the Will of Creatures Without Special Action by God to Bring It About

In insisting that absolutely nothing takes place outside of the purpose of God, either effectuated or permitted by him, I stand squarely within the Augustinian tradition, and my model sounds much like Calvin's. However, I now begin to add features to the model that distinguish my proposal from any of those encountered in part one.

Proponents of comprehensive and detailed divine providence wish to preserve a place for God and his activity in the world when factors I have identified previously have threatened to squeeze God out. The growing modern confidence in the abilities of mechanistic science, coupled with an evolutionary theory of the development of the cosmos, appeared to make God less and less necessary as an explanation for what we experience. On the other hand, it is easy to get the impression from certain statements by Calvinist theologians that God is unceasingly active in every little thing that happens. I am reminded of Calvin's comment that "although men, like brute beasts confined by no chains, rush at random here and there, yet God by His secret bridle so holds and governs them, that they cannot move even one of their fingers without accomplishing the work of God much more than their own!"[18] In fairness to Calvin we must note that he does not say that God does something particular to get each finger moved. What Calvin says is that God's work is accomplished when people's fingers are moved, and I have also asserted this perspective. Even when God has exercised no special influence in order to bring about an event, his decision to permit it is deliberate. Nevertheless, it is my conviction that special acts of God, in ways that might legitimately be called "interventions," are by definition unusual.

The natural order. My thesis is quite widely accepted among Augustinian theologians when it comes to the inanimate part of creation. Most if not all of the non-Augustinian positions that we examined, after treating the semi-deism of the first model, are very willing to allow God to act in nature in special ways that would be called miraculous. God can and does heal directly and immediately, for instance, but this is unusual. As to God acting to redirect hurricanes or to cause or prevent earthquakes, one encounters widespread caution if not skepticism from theologians of widely different persuasions. There is a common perception that, while nature is not a closed continuum into which God cannot or will not venture, most of the time he is content to allow "nature," which is his normal providential work, to take its course. He has instituted an orderly system and he sustains all its components in their existence but allows them to operate according to the order that he established.

To some extent this is a perception more appropriate within a Newtonian view of physics than it is from the perspective of quantum physics. Now many physicists accept a randomness at the subatomic level that only reaches a state of statistical order at a more complex level. Some have found, in this indeterminism, room for God to work within nature without his having to intervene in an otherwise orderly process. I am personally reluctant to give too large a place within a doctrine of providence to a scientific theory whose life span as a credible account is uncertain. Whether nature is fundamentally indeterministic or not is irrelevant from the standpoint of comprehensive providence. How God accomplishes his will in nature is not the issue; that he is free to do so, even if he must act differently than he normally does, is the point being asserted. At the macro-level we observe an orderliness in nature that enables us to predict how things will work and to act accordingly. To what extent that macro-level orderliness is the result of God's direct action at the subatomic level, none of us knows.

The point is that God is not bound by the orderliness of his own usual ways of working in nature. Miracles are not God's work "contrary to" or "against" or even "super" nature. Since even the normal order is there by virtue of God's continual sustaining, he is free to act differently. When he does act in ways that strike us as demonstrative of his loving, redemptive work in a world marred by sin, we say that a miracle has occurred. God has signified to us his gracious concern for us in a way that causes amazement; it is a "sign and wonder." Because God can and does do this, it is not wrong for us to ask God to act in a way that would require him to act unusually or miraculously. We can pray for healing if it seems to us that God would be glorified and his purposes advanced by such healing. On the other hand, we must not question his benevolent intentions when he does not do miracles to alleviate the effects of sin in human experience. Furthermore, a look at the biblical record indicates that God's miraculous working has not been equally prevalent throughout the course of biblical history. There have been periods of particular frequency, but through most of history, miracles have been a rarity.

From the relative infrequency of "supernatural" (in the sense of "beyond the usual") or miraculous activity by God, I draw a number of conclusions. First, this is to be expected from the very definition of terms. Were God to act this way frequently, it would become "natural" or normal and would cease to be *sign*ificant or to cause wonder. Second, it is a part of God's grace, as expressed in the covenant with Noah (seedtime and harvest, summer and winter [Gen 8:22]), that we can plan our activities with an expectation that the inanimate creation will "behave" in predictable ways. Third, and perhaps most important, the comprehensiveness and integratedness of God's eternal purpose is such that God has ordered and "coordinated" things in such a way that the normal course of the natural world serves his purposes, and he does not have to be tinkering with it continually to accomplish what he intends. It is a sign of his greatness and of his complete foresight that he does not need to be stepping in continually to change the way things are going in the natural world. Given the "chaos principle" regarding the interrelatedness of the cosmic order, when we understand the effect that a butterfly in Beijing can have on weather in London, we realize both how easily (and imperceptibly) God can bring about the natural circumstances he wishes and how wonderfully his greatness enables him to bring together the immense multitude of particulars in order to achieve his purposes for each of his creatures in a personal way.

The complexity of human experience. What I have asserted about God's providential action in inanimate nature I believe to be also true in the realm of moral creatures. It is here, perhaps, that my proposal differs a bit from the common Calvinist portrayal of God's providential activity, although G. C. Berkouwer also noted that God's purpose is often reached "without radical intervention."[19]

Jack Cottrell has suggested (in the redemptive intervention model) that special action on God's part, what may be called "intervention" in human affairs, occurs only when things are particularly important for the accomplishment of God's redemptive purposes.[20] That obviously covers the two biblical instances we described above, Joseph and Jesus. What Cottrell questions is the assumption that God is actively involved in the small details of the lives of individuals or even in the large details of national history, when those are not significant for the overall establishment of God's goals for the world. God *can* influence the heart of kings but generally has no reason to do so. This almost certainly rules out the requests for parking spaces which I mentioned in the introduction since it would be virtually impossible to demonstrate that the provision of such parking spaces was of significance in the big redemptive-historical picture.

Concerning the capture of Richard Henderson and his colleagues, from Cottrell's perspective, one might be able to argue that their situation had significance because they were missionaries, and God's purposes for the world are understood as primarily related to salvation. On the other hand, Cottrell's account leaves me doubtful that this one incident in the lives of three missionaries would qualify. When it comes to safety on one's vacation trip or the need of a job or the sickness of a child, in the lives of average people, it is extremely difficult to demonstrate that this is a situation in which any particular action can be expected from God. One gets the impression that most of the time life goes on pretty much as the acts of creatures cause it to and that the most we can expect from God is what is helpful for our sanctification. This is not to be demeaned, for it would include gifts of courage and strength to deal with the vagaries of life in ways that will make us more Christlike. God is at work in us in the midst of our circumstances to conform us to his image, but it is not likely that he is at work in the mind of a prospective employer to enhance our chances of employment. In the church dominion model, which urged earnest prayer by the church, since God has committed himself to act only in response to those prayers, the focus was again completely on items of eternal or salvation-related importance.

I affirm the value system that puts things of eternal consequence ahead of those that are only temporarily important or strictly materialistic. Jesus prescribed this hierarchy for us in passages such as Matthew 6:33 (or Lk 12:31). On the other hand, the approaches offered in the church dominion and redemptive intervention models do not do justice to the New Testament's own picture of God's intimate concern for the daily details of the existence of all his creatures. They also run the risk of encouraging a dualistic approach to our lives. There is a psychosomatic wholeness about human being that makes it difficult to draw too clear a line between body and soul. The health of both is intricately intertwined, and the value of both is attested in the biblical promise of bodily resurrection. Furthermore, the interrelatedness of the lives of individuals within the human race is complex and far-reaching. It is true that the Old Testament focuses on the history of Israel, but there were many other nations who had contact with Israel and whose rise and fall, morality or immorality, had an impact on Israel's situation. Even so, we must grant that Scripture tells us nothing about tribes in North or South America (as we now call it) when God was at work with Israel, working out his covenant promises to Abraham and David. Yet I am unwilling to deny that God was at work among those peoples also. I do not believe that their lack of contact with Israel excluded them from God's salvific purposes for all people,[21] and I do believe that God had a careful concern for them as creatures in his image. Surely it was not only the grass and the lilies or the ravens and the sparrows in Israel that God clothed; he cares for all his creatures everywhere. The same hierarchy of values that pertained between sparrows and human beings in Israel was operative in the Americas. There too God "clothed" and "fed" the nonmoral parts of his creation and sent rain upon the fields and forests of the righteous and the unrighteous alike, making his power and his deity known to all of his sentient creatures everywhere.

There is no question in my mind about the comprehensiveness and the detailedness of God's providential care for all his creatures. I affirm that God's care for all his creatures is appropriate to their God-given nature. God cares for and works with rocks, grass, birds and humans all differently, in ways that are appropriate to their manner of being. God also cares for and acts with human and angelic beings differently, in ways appropriate to their relationship to him. I affirm the Thomist and Calvinist teaching that God exercises a special loving care for his children; it is for those who love him and are "called according to his purpose" that God is working all things together for good (Rom 8:28). In asserting God's providential operation, however, we must not forget the way Paul defines that good, namely our conformity to the image of God's Son (Rom 8:29). With E. D. Bebb I affirm that "providence is a real and gracious fact, but it is concerned with personality rather than prosperity."[22] By this I do not mean that God does not providentially give his children (or even unbelievers) material things. If we believed that to be true, we would lose all sense of gratitude for physical blessings, for our daily bread and for the ability and opportunity to work for it. On the other hand, we gain a perspective in which material things are not an end in themselves, either as prayer requests or as items of thanksgiving.

Since all the good things that we experience are gifts of God, we may both ask and thank God for things that are good for us in our physical being, but we must view them in their place within the larger purpose of God for our lives. On occasion we discover that a failure to maintain this proper perspective renders God's kind gifts a hindrance to our spiritual growth in dependence upon God. The Chronicler illustrates this from the life of Uzziah who was "marvelously helped" by God until he became strong, "but when he had become strong he grew proud, to his destruction" (2 Chron 26:15-16). By contrast we find ourselves growing in spiritual maturity as we experience hardship, even though we may find it difficult to maintain a spirit of thankfulness in the midst of those difficulties. All of our practical reflection on God's meticulous providence must bear in mind the goal to which God is leading his creation. A. B. Bruce captures this point nicely in his classic treatment of providence: "In the providential order, events are relative to moral ends, and are to be interpreted in their bearing on these. The interpretation is a delicate problem in which not merely the outside world but even the subjects of the experiences to be interpreted may easily err."[23]

This is not to say that God is not also at work in beneficent ways in the lives of unbelievers. He sends rain on the fields of the unrighteous, and he feeds and clothes them too, graciously giving them what their rebellion and unbelief make particularly undeserved. It is their ingratitude for this goodness toward them that stirs the just wrath of God against them (Rom 1:18-21). What they lack is the comfort that comes from the knowledge of God's providence in their lives. Even disobedient believers receive better than they deserve, and obedient believers who experience God's blessing have no cause for pride in it because their very status as God's children is a gift of God's grace (Eph 2:8-9). So I do not question the comprehensive providence of God, but I am suggesting that God's providential care for the details of the lives of all his creatures does not require ceaseless "interventions" on his part.

The gracious influence of God's Spirit is continually at work in human lives, and the heart of kings is in his hand (Prov 21:1), but we need not assume that God is continually making suggestions to them or influencing them in one direction or another. On this point, Jack Cottrell's message deserves to be heard. This is not, however, because only decisions made by kings involved in the line of redemptive history are of concern to God. It is because God's foresight and planning in human affairs, as in the natural order, is such that he need not be continuously working in people's minds to assure that they make the "right decisions."

There is a fine balance to be sought here, and I tread lightly in seeking it. It should be clear that I want to affirm the comprehensiveness of God's providence. In doing so, however, I do not want to leave the impression that God is more continuously effecting things than the biblical account warrants. What is true of the natural order is also true, I believe, of the human order. Much of what takes place in any given day, in the lives of most of us, is on the order of divine permission, but it is a deliberate permission, and it is in the context of God's immense control of all that has gone before. I have a sense that, in reaction to the embarrassment concerning the doctrine of providence that arose in response to modern enthusiasm for the capabilities of science and the assumptions that the world is a closed system, some theologians of Augustinian bent may have overreacted. I sympathize with Harry Blamires when he objects to people speaking about God *intervening* because his "hand is daily and hourly upon the affairs" of people. He asks: "Must we speak as though God only occasionally wakened up to the cries of human distress, to make a quick saving sally into the world of men—like a guerilla warrior operating in enemy territory—thence to retire immediately to his long sleep of neglect?" Then Blamires answers his rhetorical question with the affirmation that "God is ceaselessly active among men and within man."[24] I would hate for readers to think that I am denying God's ceaseless activity, for I am not doing so. On the other hand, I do believe that God, who is constantly watching over his creatures, is not always acting in the same way and that his own action leaves much room for the action of creatures without making them independent of God.

The trickiness of finding the biblical balance in our perspective may be illustrated further by comment on the thesis of John Boykin that most of the time things happen by human decision. I affirm this, and I agree with Boykin that God's normal work is by the Holy Spirit changing us inside, making us better believers. I agree with Boykin's suggestion that God plants ideas in our heads but that it is up to us to act on or ignore them and that, once planted, God's inspirations must compete for our "attention and cooperation on precisely the same basis as all the other ideas" in our heads, but *we* choose. God changes our inner essence, and these changes express themselves as changes in what we want and what is important to us.[25] In commenting on an earlier draft of this book, John Sanders wondered whether my compatibilism creates a conflict between those last two sentences. In the first sentence it sounds to Sanders "as though we can reject God's inspiration, while the next sounds as though we cannot reject it—after all, if God changes our inner essences which changes our wants, then, given compatibilism, our wants will be those God desired us to have."

Sanders has raised a helpful question that may come to the minds of other readers as well. It calls for a reminder that in the Calvinist doctrine of the Spirit's work of regeneration and sanctification we are not perfected in this life. God has changed, and is continuing to change, our inner essence so that we are more and more conformed to the image of his Son. Where once we were unable to please God by acting from faith (Rom 14:23), now we can do so. But even the regenerate are not *always* obedient; they can also displease God. True believers do not always respond positively to God's inspirations because there are still sinful desires at work in our minds and hearts. With these wrong desires God's promptings must compete, and the sin too often triumphs. Our wants are not always the ones that God wishes us to have. Indeed we need to vigorously use the means of grace (Scripture, prayer, the fellowship of the church) in order to further the process of inner transformation and the conforming of our desires to God's. It is precisely here that my point about God's limited "intervention" comes to bear. God gives sufficient grace so that we need not sin, but he does not always intervene with an "efficient" grace to *ensure* that we do not disobey him. With Calvinists in general I believe that God graciously limits the extent to which his children can wander in pursuit of sinful desires and preserves them from apostasy. Short of that point, however, there are many occasions on which the Spirit is prompting us in a direction or away from an action, and we resist; we quench the Spirit rather than being filled by him. God *could* do a work of grace to ensure that a Christian never sins again, but he will not put us in this position until the final transforming work that we speak of as "glorification."

I now get back to my interaction with John Boykin. At the conclusion of his book he expresses the "fervent hope" that "this perspective will make us think twice before saying such nonsense as, 'God was so gracious in arranging for me to get this job,' or 'I guess this tragedy was just God's will.'"[26] Here my model drastically parts company from Boykin's. My point in asserting God's comprehensive providence is that we can and should be grateful to God when things turn out well for us and that we can and should view tragedies with a similar trust in God's loving control of *all*

things. The cause of our divergent conclusions rests on at least these differences in our convictions: (1) I insist on the deliberateness of God's permitting what he allows to happen, whether that be the beneficial decisions of
prospective employers or the evil intentions of wicked people; (2) in my
model of God's comprehensive and omniprescient providence, God is able
to see many of his purposes accomplished without his special action
("intervention"); and (3) it appears that I have a greater confidence in the
ability of God to effect his will through the noncoercive persuasion of
spontaneously free agents.

G. C. Berkouwer describes Calvin's objection to the term *permission* as a
concern that "when the word is used in order to bring the relation between
Divine and human (sinful) activity into a logical synthesis the Divine activity is limited, since it is then placed on the same level with human activity."
The word "permission" seems to suggest "that God allows the sinner to
decide in freedom against God's command."[27] This is certainly not my
intention, and I use the term for the reason that Berkouwer surmises other
Reformed theologians have not totally repudiated it, from a distaste for
mechanistic determinism and "a desire to express the thought that good
and evil do not originate in the same way, as 'effects' of one general Divine
causality."[28] Berkouwer himself suggests that "when permission is really
used to indicate the manner of Divine ruling, by which He grants room
within His ruling for human freedom and responsibility, then the line of
Biblical thinking has not been wholly abandoned. For this freedom, this
creaturely freedom, receives a place in God's rule of the world."[29] It is precisely in that sense that I use the term.

Going back to the instance ridiculed by G. K. Chesterton, therefore, I am
prepared to be thankful to God that I slipped on a banana peel and missed
a bus that had an accident. On the other hand, I do not thereby assume
that God worked in some special way to have the banana peel dropped,
directed the length of my stride and drew my attention away from the
ground at the critical moment, so that I stepped on the peel and fell down.
He could do so, but it is neither likely nor necessary that he would. All of
the details are part of a huge picture that is within God's control, yet he
does not need to be continuously doing special acts, precisely because of
the comprehensiveness of his control. It seems to me quite possible, as
William Pollard indicated, that "chance" is operative here. God may well
have foreseen that I would step on the banana peel and have chosen to
permit it, neither having effectuated it nor doing anything to prevent it. His

deliberate permission of this event would lie in his awareness that the outcome of my missing the bus would be the avoidance of harm for me in its crash. On the other hand, God would also have known that the woman just ahead of me would see the peel and step over it, catch the bus and then be hurt or killed. He could have acted to bring about her stepping on the peel but chose not to. In such a situation, I might legitimately say, after the serious bus accident that I had escaped, that "by chance" I had slipped on a banana peel and missed the bus. This would not be a denial of God's comprehensive providence, it would simply be a recognition that he had not *done* anything by way of special providence to bring about my deliverance.

On the other hand, because I am unable to discern when God does act in special providence, I would want to give God thanks that I was spared from death or injury. By contrast, someone who postulates a less detailed involvement of God in the routine affairs of human life might be likely to consider this less an occasion for a prayer of gratitude and more a matter of "good luck." Maurice Wiles (semi-deist model) is correct that any model of providence that prompts me to be thankful to God that I stepped on the peel and was saved, must also be prepared to factor God into the situation of the woman who stepped over the peel and was hurt. In order to do this, however, we need not assume that our stepping or not stepping on a banana peel that may or may not have been dropped on the platform is something completely outside of God's purpose and providence. He sees each banana peel that drops as surely as he sees each sparrow that falls. He may not prevent it, but in some sense, he is prepared to take responsibility for what happens as a result.

General providence, special providence and miracle. In light of the perspective I have developed here, I have some sympathy for those who are cautious about distinguishing between general and special providence. In making such a differentiation we would not wish to make too large a distinction between God's active involvement in the two kinds of care. In the natural order that God has instituted, and in the complex of human actions and interactions, even when God does nothing particular, direct or special to bring about an outcome different from the one that would come about through the action of creaturely forces, God is at work. He is at work in each day's sunrise and every rainfall, even though these come about because of a pattern that he has established. When the rain falls on the farmer's field, he is right to thank God for it and to appreciate it as a sign of

God's care, without assuming that God intervened in the normal process of nature to ensure that his field received rain. In short, a distinction between general and special providence must not blind us to the fact of God's action in all things.

Nevertheless, there is benefit in making a distinction between general and special action by God. On the one hand, by the term "general providence" we identify God's permissive order, his normal action in natural processes and human actions according to the principles of operation that he has established. God sustains all these creatures in existence and gives them the ability to do what they do, but he does not act in a particular way to bring about effects that would not come about if the creatures were left to their own decision and action. On the other hand, there are times when God acts to bring about a situation that would not come about if he did not do something specific. This we may rightly call "special providence." To cite the prime example in Israel's experience, their crossing the Red Sea on dry land was an act of special care on God's part. It may have been brought about by natural means. God did not need to "blow" on the waters to part them. Yet the timing of the natural occurrence was unmistakably beneficial and intended for their deliverance. Likewise, the dying down of the wind that caused the waters to drown Pharaoh's soldiers was within God's action on Israel's behalf. When circumstances quite unexceptional in themselves come together to produce a situation beneficial to us, we rightly attribute this to the kindness of God and assert that we have experienced special providence. In fact, the line between these is difficult for us to perceive because God's action in the world is usually hidden. Nevertheless, it is appropriate for us to be thankful for good things and to accept bad things without resentment against God, because of our recognition of his control of all things, even when we are prepared to grant that he acts specially on some occasions. Some writers object to the use of "intervention" to speak of God's special action. I have not shrunk from using the term and the sense in which I do so has hopefully been made clear

A further distinction between special providence and miracle is legitimate. Not all events that appear to us to give evidence of God's special action for our good (or punishment as the case may be), should be called miracles. In special providence, we discern God's action through the concurrence of actions or events that are, in themselves, unexceptional. Chance meetings, beneficial changes in weather, the opening of opportunities for work or evangelism or education, delays that turn out to be helpful, sudden "inspirations" that prompt us to do something that turns out to be very wise and productive of good, these are all normal in themselves, and one is hard put to demonstrate to an unbeliever in God's providence that it was anything more than luck. So we ought not to say that it was miraculous that a particular employer became aware of our availability at just the right time, or that a government official making a decision about our visa "happened" to know a mutual friend and was favorably disposed to our case. On the other hand, when things happen that are inexplicable by anyone in the context, where things operate in ways that are completely unusual, unrepeatable and unpredictable, we say that a miracle has occurred. When more than five thousand people are satisfied by the repeated division of five loaves and two fishes, when a large tumor suddenly disappears, when a blind person instantly receives perfect sight, we say that a miracle has been done. Miracles are a form of special providence done with particular intent of revelation and of victory over effects of sin, but not all special providences are miracles.

People Act Freely Within God's Overall Determination

The nature of human freedom has been a frequent point of contention between the models presented in the first part of this book. I accept the plausibility of arguments made under the Calvinist model concerning the genuine freedom of people who do what they want to do without external constraint. It does not appear that consensus is ever going to be achieved either among theologians or philosophers on this point. My own position derives from the necessity of holding together two truths very clear to me in the biblical record; namely, (1) God is absolutely sovereign in the comprehensive manner described above, and (2) humans are morally responsible.[30] As G. C. Berkouwer notes, the providence of God and human responsibility "do not exist together in the Scriptures as something problematic. They both reveal the greatness of the Divine activity, in that it does not exclude human activity and responsibility but embraces them and in them manifests God on the way to the accomplishment of His purposes."[31] Berkouwer neatly sums it up in the statement that "the Divine activity is all inclusive, but not all exclusive."[32]

> Anyone who does not take both this Divine ruling and human responsibility seriously can never rightly understand history. He will always assume one or the other of two basically erroneous perspectives: either he will make man the lord of history, creator of events, holding history in his hand or propel-

ling it through the power of his personality—with the 'leaders of men' blazing the trail; or he will make history a Divine game in which human beings are pushed about like chessmen, void of responsibility.[33]

To be morally responsible, humans must be significantly free since everyone agrees that a person is not responsible for action that was coerced or forced. This significant freedom entails that they do what they choose to do; they are, in that sense, self-determining. It does not require that there be no reasons for the decision a person makes. Consequently, someone who knows all the factors in a situation and all the facets of a person making a decision (e.g., genetic inheritance, hormonal makeup, mood, temperament, values, tastes, habits, relationships, inclinations, moral standards, reasoning pattern, fears, hopes, desires and motives) can know what that person would choose to do in a particular situation. This does not mean that the person who makes the decision does not actually make the choice, as though it were made for her by the complex of factors that make up her person. The self who decides is not like a computer choosing numbers randomly. Were that the case, it would not be a personal decision, and it would not be a moral one. Each decision obviously contributes to the forming of the self that makes the next one. This is the reality underlying the truth of the old chorus, "Yield not to temptation, for yielding is sin, each victory will help you some other to win." A decision not to do something deemed wrong by the person's conscience strengthens the moral fiber of that person so that it is a slightly different self that confronts the next temptation of the same kind.

Donald MacKay has helped the case for the liberty of spontaneity by demonstrating that in a deterministic world people's future is not "inevitable" for them. His proposal is summed up as follows:

> There exists no complete description of A's future which would have an unconditional claim to A's assent, in the sense that A would be correct to believe and mistaken to disbelieve it, if only A knew it. In this sense A's future is *logically indeterminate* and from A's viewpoint that future is open and "up-to-A" to determine. For MacKay, this is the essence of freedom. He asserts "it is not brains but persons who choose."[34] There is an indeterminacy on the level of our conscious experience irrespective of any indeterminacy at the level of the brain [emphasis added].[35]

MacKay thinks it unlikely that the world is totally physically deterministic, but he shows that even in this "worst-case" scenario freedom can be imagined, and such freedom is therefore compatible with theological determinism.

No one ever acts without influences coming to bear on the decision to commit the action. To be personal is to be a being in relationship, and all of those relationships and the value that we give to harmony within them play a part in our decisions. People who know us well are able to influence us most effectively because they can appeal to the desires, values and motives that are strongest in our selves. Advertising is effective to the degree that those who create the ads have successfully discerned these factors in the decision-making activity of their target population. Those who know us best are most able to manipulate us if they choose to do so. When we use the term manipulation to describe the influence one person exerts on another, we imply a misuse of that power for self-serving goals. To manipulate people is to get them to do what we want for reasons that are important to us but that may not be in the best interests of the persons being influenced. On the other hand, benevolent influencers such as loving parents are able to lead their children to do what is in the children's best interest by understanding the desires and values of their children. They learn what motivates one child does not motivate another. This information could be misused, but it is not intrinsically bad. If the parent is wise and loving, it is good for the child to have a parent who has this understanding of the child's personality.

The fear I sense in people who deny that God is all-determining in his providence is that even if this does not exactly rob human beings of their freedom, it depicts God as the master manipulator. The fact is that God would be immensely dangerous if he were not good. Knowing us and our circumstances completely, God is able to bring influences to bear in our lives so that we do what he wants us to do. Thankfully, in God's goodness he never uses his immense ability to influence us in ways that are bad for us. Berkouwer rightly distinguishes the biblical description of God's determining "from what is generally understood by determinism," a structure that is both rigid and violent. "The essential error of identifying the Providence doctrine with determinism is the de-personalization of the God-concept. God is looked on as the beginning of a sequence out of which all things emerge."[36] The choice for Christian theologians is not between determinism and indeterminism "but a Divine activity over and in the creaturely activity of man," the exact nature of which is admittedly beyond our complete understanding or explanation.[37] What matters is that "the nature of the personal living God absolutely defines the nature of the determining."[38]

The great attractiveness of universalism is that it assumes that given enough time God can and will influence every one of his creatures to choose what is truly good for them and to love God. Christian theologians have generally resisted this attractive hypothesis because of Scriptures that indicate that some will never be reconciled to God. It is difficult to believe, however, that eternal condemnation is best for any individual, and this fact confirms my earlier assertion that God has decided to do a great deal of his control through the permissive operation of his will in the world. It would appear that, in order to achieve what is genuinely best for each person, there are instances in which God's influence would have to be so strong that it would be coercive and God will not coerce his creatures in ways that would finally rob them of self-determination in every significant sense.

The way in which I am speaking may seem to echo the point that is being made by the openness model, but it differs in a number of important ways, including particularly (1) the extent to which human freedom provides a constraint upon God's ability to achieve the best for each individual without robbing those persons of their very personhood; and (2) the extent to which the decision concerning people's destinies rests in God's sovereign and gracious purpose. In the openness model as in the process model, God appears to be doing his best to lead all individuals to what is best for them, but the outcome rests finally in the response of the creature. Finding myself within the Augustinian understanding of Scripture, I must assert a larger role for God in determining the grace individuals experience both for their general well-being in the details of their lives in this world and for their eternal situation. In models of providence as in models of salvation, there is a great divide between those who find the explanation for differences in the human decision and those who believe that God is the one determining this. I am in the latter group, in the form that is most often identified with the Reformed tradition.

It appears to me that my model differs from the openness model particularly in its insistence that people do not decide in an ultimately random or indeterministic way. Indeed it is my conviction that radical indeterminism is as destructive of moral responsibility as coercion would be. If there are no reasons for a person's choices, then those choices are as random as the number-selecting computer in a lottery and just as amoral. To be responsible, an act must be intentional. Thoroughly indeterministic or libertarian freedom is therefore not only unnecessary to "significant freedom," it would destroy the intentional selfhood of that very freedom that indeterminists are so anxious to preserve. As Jonathan Edwards stressed, people act for certain reasons, based upon their assessment of what is the greatest good.[39] In that vein, John Feinberg asks the critical question, "If causal influences are not sufficient to move the will to choose, *then what is?*"[40] What preserves the freedom of the person who acts freely though predictably is that the causal determination lies within the person and not outside and that no other agent is forcefully coercing the individual who makes the decision to act *against her will*. Like Norman Geisler and other Thomists, I want to assert that people are *self*-determining, but I also recognize that the *self* which decides and acts has a character out of which she acts.

John Sanders has questioned that I have accurately represented the libertarian perspective in these comments because "Libertarians reject that our decisions are 'random.'" He notes that libertarians do not consider reasons to be causes and that "choices are made with reasons." This is an important point, and I can understand why libertarians might take mild offense at my description of their libertarianly free decisions as "random." Nevertheless, my contention still seems valid to me. I am not arguing that every decision a libertarianly free person makes is done thoughtlessly or carelessly or irrationally. I have no doubt that a person with libertarian freedom could assess a situation carefully and identify a list of reasons for doing various things in the context. I presume that she would even be prepared to explain afterward *why* she made that particular decision. But as libertarian freedom is characteristically defined, she had to be in a position where she could just as easily have made a different decision or her choice was not libertarianly free. Therein lies the problem from the perception of a compatibilist. If a person's actual decision can validly be explained *afterward* by a set of "reasons," including a whole range of factors, both internal and external to the person deciding, then knowledge of those reasons *beforehand* would have made the decision predictable. On the other hand, if the complete set of factors leaves the person with a final choice that is influenced by nothing in or outside of himself, then it escapes me how the decision between two equally viable and possible courses of action can be anything but arbitrary. Granted, there are many contributing factors or "reasons" but, since the sum total of them is insufficient to explain this choice rather than that one, the decision appears to be "random." I see no way to escape that conclusion given all the premises.

I grant that the person making a decision, even if libertarianly free, may think he knows why that particular decision was made, much of the time. Obviously there are trivial decisions in life that we would have no hesitation making by the drawing of straws. But when the really important decisions are carefully thought through and concluded upon, it is understandable that people would resist the judgment that they had decided arbitrarily. Nevertheless, I still see only two possibilities. *Either* there was, in fact, some "reason" why this particular decision was made and that "reason" could have been predicted beforehand by someone as knowledgeable as God, *or* the person's sense of having had a "reason" for this particular choice rather than another is illusory, and the decision was actually arbitrary or random.

The biblical writers were able to speak confidently of God's ability to accomplish his purposes through the decisions and actions of free human agents because they knew how completely he understands all of us and how active his Spirit can be within the mental worlds of rational beings. God is able to ensure that his purposes are accomplished regardless of the power of creatures who are committed to preventing the realization of those purposes. However, the authors of Scripture also believed that people are responsible for the actions they take within God's all-determining providence because God always deals with people as people and not as stones, to use Calvin's terminology. He never acts so overwhelmingly that people lose their own self-determining capacity. However alien from my own model the panentheism of process theology may be, I affirm its assertion that God always acts in loving persuasion and never coercively. It is this self-restraint that preserves the moral freedom of the creature, but it does not limit God's control as much as is assumed by those who are convinced that freedom must be contracausal in order to be significant.[41]

I see some validity in the proposal of the libertarians that in giving people freedom God has placed a restraint on the means of his own unilateral action. It does seem likely that it would be impossible for God, or anyone else, to get an individual to do absolutely anything, in a particular situation, without resorting to force or coercion. The biblical record leaves us in no doubt that people often resist God's persuasive work and grieve him in so doing (cf. Mt 23:37; Lk 13:34). However, given God's presence everywhere and always with his creation, and given the benefit of his comprehensive knowledge of all things actual and possible, this is not a major hindrance to God. What God purposes to accomplish, he is able to achieve in and through and with his creatures, but he can do so without taking away their genuine creaturely agency. The fact that God cannot get everyone to do absolutely anything at any moment is not a significant limitation on God's sovereign work in the world because he is able to ensure that situations do not develop in which there is no way for him to fulfill his purpose without robbing creatures of responsible agency. God is therefore always able to accomplish the will of his eternal purpose in the world, even though there are things that he *could* not do in a given situation. This means that God's creatures, and particularly morally responsible creatures, have a significant role in determining outcomes, especially in determining their own role in those outcomes, but that they never do so independently or beyond the general control of God.

In spite of my strong sense of God's sovereign rule in the world, I am reluctant to speak of God's "omnicausality." It gives the impression that God is the *only* cause, when in fact history is brought about by the complex interaction of many self-determining agents, even though none of them are ever completely independent of God and his agency in the world. Berkouwer suggests that the language of first and second cause was used with good intent but that "this distinction has not brought the Church essentially further in her reflection; in fact, it has more often obscured her insight into Divine Providence." The main problem is that it implies that God is "only the most important cause among equal causes *(causa prima inter pares)*," which runs the risk that God will be viewed as "enclosed within a system of causality."[42]

God's Providential Care of His Creation Is Greatly Facilitated by His Knowledge of All Things Both Actual and Possible, Past, Present, and Future

God's knowledge of the actual future. In the writing of some theologians who affirm libertarian human freedom, we have met the conviction that God does not know the future because, if he did, humans would not be significantly free. Without restating the argument, I believe that the demonstration of the compatibility of foreknowledge and human freedom, even libertarian freedom, which was offered by William Lane Craig (Molinist model) is completely adequate. Foreknowledge is not causative, nor would it be an instance of backward causation.[43] What God knows ahead of time (from our perspective) is the future that comes about through the decisions of free human agents (and would be so, even if they were libertarianly free, which I do not believe is the case, though Craig does). If people decided differently, God's knowledge would have been different. This does not entail that the future must be undecided; it affirms rather that the future that actually comes to be is determined by responsible agents at that time, that those actual decisions have truth value, and that God knows their truth value. Thus God's knowledge a week ago that Richard Henderson was going to be kidnapped did not rob his kidnappers of their self-determination today. It is correct to say that a week ago it was true that they would decide to abduct Richard today, but the truth of that fact was established by their action today, not by knowledge of it a week ago.

Without repeating the biblical evidence that God does know the actual future and that he has often revealed that future to his prophets, I affirm the biblical position presented under models that included a conviction that God does know the future, that he knows and declares the end from the beginning (Is 46:10).[44] Furthermore, I see no philosophical difficulty in affirming that God knows the actual future. The future differs from the past, not in its certainty, but in the opportunity for people acting now to affect it. We cannot change the past, and we cannot *change* the future, but we can, in significant measure, determine the future, whereas the past is outside of our ability to affect it. All of this is true whether people are libertarianly free or only voluntarily free. However, when it comes to consideration of the *possible* future, the situation changes.

God's knowledge of purely hypothetical future events (counterfactuals). David Basinger observes that "an increasing number of philosophers are coming to believe that the traditional theistic perspectives on most important issues—for instance, the traditional perspectives on the creation of the world, divine guidance, prophecy and salvation—presuppose Middle Knowledge." He notes that it is particularly favored by indeterminists who desire to preserve God's control.[45] I too have become increasingly convinced that God's knowledge of what *would* happen in hypothetical situations is an essential element in his wise planning and predestining of the future of the world's history. Basinger concludes that "generally speaking, the providential capacities of a God with Middle Knowledge have been greatly overstated,"[46] but this assessment is made only with reference to the model of providence that attributes middle knowledge to God in a world where people are libertarianly free. His criticisms of that model are justified, but they do not apply to my own compatibilist model, which puts together divine knowledge of the outcome of hypothetical situations and human freedom of a voluntary type.

On the matter of God's knowledge of counterfactuals, I agree with critics of the Molinist appeal to middle knowledge who argue that it is impossible to know a libertarianly free decision before it is made. Actual libertarianly free future events can be known because they have truth value. The same is not true of libertarianly free counterfactuals, events that would have happened if important factors had been different than they were. By definition of the terms it is impossible to know what a person would decide to do in a given situation if the person's decision is conceived to be indeterministically free. Surely, as Craig says, there are many future counterfactuals that do have truth value. This seems correct, particularly of negative statements concerning the future. One who has God's comprehensive knowledge of the past and present can identify with certainty many things that will not happen in the future. Unfortunately, this is not enough to satisfy the requirements of Molinist middle knowledge. For the proposal to work, God must know what a person would do in every possible situation, and one cannot know that if the person's decision is ultimately indeterminate, awaiting the apparently arbitrary choice of the free agent when the moment of decision arrives.[47]

In other words, I believe that a knowledge of future, contingent, purely hypothetical events is only available to God in a situation such as I have described above, where free selves determine their actions in ways that implement all the facets of their selfhood. If one knows all those facets of the person and all the factors of the situation in which the person will make a decision, one can predict what that decision would be. Therefore, I agree that Molinist middle knowledge of future contingent possibilities that are never actualized is incoherent. However, I do not agree with Augustinians like Karl Barth that we must reject the concept of middle knowledge because of the use for which the theory was formulated by Molina, namely the harmonizing of absolute divine sovereignty with libertarian human freedom. In fact, I am convinced that the critique of simple foreknowledge by middle knowledge theologians as well as open God theologians is correct. If God only has simple foreknowledge, that is, knowledge of the actual future, his knowledge is useless to his providential care. By the time that God knows what is actually going to happen, it is "too late" for him to do anything about it, and this is true whether or not creatures have libertarian free will.[48]

There may be some validity in Anna Case-Winters's critique of Calvin's approach to God's foreknowledge. She observes that "for Calvin, divine foreknowledge is not a matter of foreknowing the actions of free beings; it is a matter of foreknowing how *God* will dispose such."[49] Her concern about Calvin's perspective is that the noncontingency of the future seems to limit even God's freedom. She approaches the issue of God's action in the future from a different angle but supports our concern that, if God eternally foreknows his own action in time by way of a simple foreknowledge, there seems to be no room for divine purposing or planning. In particular, there is no place for divine *response* to human actions.

Basinger identifies three commonly propounded options regarding God's knowledge, present knowledge, simple foreknowledge and middle knowledge. His own position favors present knowledge, the approach described under the openness model. In a recent article his primary objective is to demonstrate that simple foreknowledge does not have significant advantages over present knowledge, particularly as an aid in God's control over earthly affairs. He does grant, however, that "a God with MK [middle knowledge]—a God who knows before he acts exactly what will occur as a result—is in a better position to ensure his desired ends than is a God without MK."[50] The same is not the case if God has simple foreknowledge. Basinger illustrates with the case of a lottery player who knows the winning numbers ahead of time.

> Our lottery player can beneficially utilize her foreknowledge of the winning numbers *only if* she has access to this information *before* she decides what numbers she will play. However, if our player has always possessed complete foreknowledge, then there has never been a time at which she foreknew what the winning numbers would be but did not already know at this same time what numbers she would choose to play. Thus if our player has complete foreknowledge, her knowledge of next week's winning numbers cannot influence what numbers she chooses to play and thus is of no practical benefit.[51]

The application of this illustration to the planning of God's eternal purpose or decree is obvious.

It may appear to some that the concept of God's eternity as timeless solves the problem. Since God does not know things at any time but knows them timelessly, the concept of that knowledge being "too late" is inappropriate. This does not really solve the problem. In his description of middle knowledge, William Craig explicitly stated that the three moments of God's knowledge (natural, middle and free) are not chronologically sequential moments; they are logical moments. When I say that God's foreknowledge is "too late," my words can be understood in those terms of logical relationship and need not imply temporality or succession in God's decision-making. The problem still pertains: if God only has simple fore-knowledge (i.e., completely knows the *actual* future), then he cannot decide how he will act on the basis of a knowledge of how other creatures would respond. He knows, eternally, his own action and the creature's at the same logical moment.

The situation is not improved by positing that God's knowledge of the future is not simple foreknowledge but is the knowledge of his own will, that is, the knowledge of the future that will be what it is because he has decided that it should be so. Without middle knowledge I cannot concep-tualize God's decision as either wise or cognizant of the freedom of his creatures. If God simply decided the future in one logical moment without regard to the possible responses of creatures to his own initiatives and the wisest responses that he could make to those creaturely decisions, then any appearance of significance in those human decisions is thoroughly illusory.

For these reasons I am convinced that God has middle knowledge, understood as his knowledge of all future counterfactuals. He is able to know this because his moral creatures are voluntarily but not indeterminis-tically free. Therefore, at the logical moment in eternity when God deter-mined all that would come to be in created time, thereby establishing his eternal purpose or decree, he did so by a process in which he discerned what each of his creatures would do in a particular situation and then decided what influences he would bring to bear to change the situation so that the outcome, as decided freely by the creatures involved, would move things along in the direction of his purpose. I have posited that in many instances God chose not to insert his influence in a forceful way and that he chose never to do so in a coercive way. He was still able to bring all of those creaturely decisions and their effects together in a history that culmi-nates with his triumph over evil, and that demonstrates to all the greatness of his wisdom and his grace. Every incident along the way has meaning in the light of the whole, and he is never out of control, even when he wills to allow creatures to be disobedient, sustaining their lives even as they reject his right to their worship and love and obedience.

I agree with William Craig that there are no biblical passages that con-clusively demonstrate God's knowledge of possible future events. The two passages that have been used to bolster the case are adequately explained on the basis of God's comprehensive knowledge of the past and the future. My belief in God's knowledge of all that could possibly have happened in the future is like Craig's; it rests on the immense usefulness of this concept to understanding God's wise planning and the implementation of his plan in and through a world in which some of his creatures have their own free agency. I believe that everything that occurs in world history is part of the eternal purpose of God, but I believe that, in forming his plan, God knew what all of his creatures would do in what circumstances, and he decided which circumstances would come about through the joint agency of God and his creatures, so that everything that happens is as God planned it, but God is not the only agent who works to bring it about.

Cottrell has complained that it is a "farcical use of the term *freedom*" to claim that the will is free if it acts voluntarily, since God determines the desires, motives or circumstances that lie behind the volition.[52] He contends that if human actions are free, then God must respond to them. If God cannot respond, then he must cause, and this is deemed to be the problem of the unconditional decree.[53] This criticism evidences a misunderstanding of the nature of the unconditionality of God's decree as understood by Calvinists. The point is that God's decree is determinative, whether by permission or by effectuating action. God's decree is not conditional upon another's decision, which he has no power to prevent or permit. Everything that happens is within his purpose, and that purpose is not determined for him by someone else. For this to work, however—for there to be authentic human decision and divine response, given that God's purpose was established before his act of initial creation—it is essential that God's purpose have been determined with knowledge of the possible actions that might have been taken by his creatures in given circumstances. With that knowledge God was able to purpose his own action and to discern the responses this would trigger from his creatures. This is a scenario of divine knowledge and purpose that allows for both authentic human freedom and divine responsiveness, while preserving God's sovereign control of his creation and its history. Cottrell proposes that contrary to the concerns of determinists, "the fact that God's knowledge of free acts is derived from those acts themselves via foreknowledge does *not* make God 'dependent upon the world.'"[54] This is true but only if we also posit that the actual events of history are such as they are because God has purposed them to be so and had determined either to allow or to effectuate them. We need not use the language of divine "omnicausality" if it leaves the impression (as it seems to do) that God is the *only* cause. It is precisely God's foreknowledge of counterfactuals that allows him to accomplish his own purposes without denying humans or angels their own free agency.

God's relationship to time. In our discussion of God's knowledge of the future, I have inevitably used temporal language. Among the models we have examined, there is a marked difference between those asserting that God is temporal and those positing that God is timelessly eternal, without duration or succession; between those who view eternity as everlasting and those who view it as timeless. Like Augustine, I think that I know what time is until I am asked to explain it. I will not attempt to do that here because I do not think that it is essential to my model of providence. Nevertheless, I believe that there are some assertions we can make about God and time that are important to an understanding of his providence. For starters, our time is God's gift to us, and we do better to think of our time as being within God's "time" than of him as being within ours. God transcends the time that limits us just as he transcends the space that limits our existence. *Eternity* is the term we use to indicate this time-transcendence of God's being, which means at the very least that he is without beginning or end. All created things had a beginning; for all of them there was a time when they were not. They would all come to an end if God did not sustain their existence. But God is not dependent on any other in this way. There was nothing "before" him, and his continued being depends on nothing else.

This God who lives eternally is, nevertheless, a God who acts in time. All that he created exists in time relationship to all else that is created, it has an existence that can be measured and that is experienced as a succession of moments. We call "now" the moment we are presently experiencing, but we recollect moments in our past experience, and we anticipate that there will be moments that we have not yet experienced. Whether or not God has any personal experience of this succession of moments I do not know, but I know that our experience of such succession is "real" to him as the one who created us in this mode of being. Yesterday may not be the "past" to God in the way it is to us, but he knows that what we are experiencing (and what he is experiencing with us) today comes after what we experienced yesterday and before what we will experience tomorrow.[55] For this reason I doubt that an assertion of timelessness is helpful in our effort to understand how God knows a future that is yet to be effected by our free agency. Even if God does not experience the difference between today and tomorrow in the same way that we do, it is still true (if God has foreknowledge, as we assert) that God knows today what will happen tomorrow. Since his knowledge is "before" the event, even though the time relationship may be only *from our perspective,* the perceived problem of the actuality of the future is not avoided by asserting that it is not "before" in God's experience. At best, this may be our way of asserting that God's experience of time is not the same as ours, although our experience of it is real and known to him.[56] But as I indicated above, I do not think it is a problem for God to know the truth value of propositions about the future even though that truth value is yet to be effected by the actors who will make the propositions true as statements about the present.[57] At the time that I call "yesterday," God knew that I would write these words today, even though it was not an actuality until today when I chose to do this rather than something else.

The Thomist model has affirmed God's absolute control and his comprehensive knowledge of what is future to us, but it has also asserted that human freedom is libertarian. The timelessness of God has been critical for Thomists in establishing the conjunction of these factors. We are deemed to be libertarianly free in the acts we do "today," even though God knew perfectly that we would do so, and knew this at a time that was "yesterday" for us. This is thought to be possible because all of our times—past, present and future—are "present" for God. Given the great appeal of a libertarian concept of freedom and yet the widespread desire to preserve God's control of his creation and its history, this proposal may appear attractive as a means to avoid the conflict between these notions. Alvin Plantinga believes in libertarian freedom, but he expresses well my own doubts that divine timelessness is the answer to concerns about determinism.

I think that Aquinas, in company with much of the theistic tradition, is mistaken in taking God to be timeless. God's life is of endless (and beginningless) duration; he has always existed and always will. His knowledge, furthermore, is not temporally limited; he knows the future in the same minute detail as he knows the present and the past. But to add that he is somehow timeless, somehow not in time at all, is to court a host of needless perplexities. There is nothing in Scripture or the essentials of the Christian message to support this utterly opaque addition, and much that seems *prima facie* to militate against it. God spoke to Abraham and did so, naturally enough, during the latter's life time. God created Adam and Eve and did so well before he created, say, Bertrand Russell. God led the children out of Egypt; he did so after he created Abraham and before he spoke to Samuel. On the face of it, then, God acts in time, acts at various times, and has done some things before he did others. It is at best Quixotic to deny this *prima facie* truth on the tenuous sort of grounds alleged by those who do deny it.[58]

It was "when the fullness of time had come" that God sent his Son (Gal 4:4), and it was "at the right time" that Christ died for the ungodly (Rom 5:6); it was not until his "hour" came that Jesus went to Jerusalem (Jn 13:1), and it will be "when his time comes" that the lawless one will be destroyed by Christ (2 Thess 2:6). Jesus did not know when that time would be, when questioned about it by his disciples, although the Father did know (Mt 24:36). In short, whatever God's own experience of time may be, he is not excluded from acting in our own time or from knowing the time-relatedness of all the events of created history. Indeed he determines the very time at which those events occur, while not negating the agency of creatures that bring events to reality at a time. I find most helpful Alan Padgett's proposal (as presented under the Thomist model) that God's action is *zero time related* to the created effect and that God himself is "relatively timeless" in the sense that his eternity does not have "measured time" as our temporal lives do.[59]

More recently another idea has been put forward by Millard Erickson that also appears to be helpful.[60] Following a presentation of the arguments for God's existence as atemporal and of the case for his temporality, Erickson observes that "we seem, in some ways, to have come to an impasse."[61] He finds it not surprising that philosophers like Thomas Morris and Ronald Nash have been unable to choose between the two views.[62] Erickson proposes that the key may lie in a proper understanding of the transcendence and immanence of God in relationship to time, similar to that which is traditionally affirmed regarding his relationship to space. We have no difficulty considering God as both transcendent and immanent within space. God is aspatial or ontologically outside of space, and yet he is able to act within space and in the realm of physical objects. Although God does not have spatial location, he can act within space.

Erickson cites the argument of Einstein that space and time are inseparable and the proposal that time is a fourth dimension. These lead to the Einsteinian concept that "simultaneity is in part a matter of space as well as time. A being that is everywhere is also 'everywhen.'"[63] In theory, every event in the physical universe is still current at some place in the universe and, though time travel is technically impossible for us, the problem does not exist for God. "Thus, the events that occurred at a particular place five minutes ago are present to him, as are those that happened ten minutes ago."[64] Erickson therefore suggests that God is "atemporal/aspatial in his fundamental nature, or is ontologically atemporal/aspatial but actively or influentially present within the space-time universe."[65] With regard to his immanence, we might therefore speak of God as "omnitemporal" while calling him "supratemporal" in his transcendence.[66] Given this framework, Erickson suggests that God was both absolutely timeless and spaceless prior to creation but that he became related to the universe once he created it and hence immanent within it. Although still without location or extension, he is present and active everywhere within the universe.[67] Erickson is agnostic about whether God experiences succession and sequence within himself because, if we assume that he does, we work from the assumption that his existence and experience are of just the same nature as ours, and this takes us beyond our knowledge of God through his self revelation.

My one hesitation regarding Erickson's proposal is the suggestion that God was absolutely timeless before creation. Even granting Erickson's warning about drawing analogies from our experience to God's, I have a difficult time conceiving of a tripersonal God who existed eternally in loving relationship as completely timeless. The concept seems too static and lifeless to me. In this regard, it seems to me that space and time are slightly different, but my lack of training in Einsteinian science could be a difficulty. I assume that space does not exist until there are objects that can have a spatial relationship to one another and that this did not occur until God created the first material things. On the other hand, I view time as the possibility of events occurring in sequence. Without it nothing happens, relationships would be frozen in an instant where no interaction of a give and take or responsive nature would be possible.

Under the Molinist model, theologians were careful to note that God's three forms of knowledge were in a logical but not chronological order. This is a language with which we are also familiar from Calvinist discussions of the "order of the decrees." But all of those discussions were carried out in the assumption of an absolutely timeless eternity. I struggle to see the adequacy of such a concept to a God as relational and dynamic as the one who is eternally Father, Son and Holy Spirit. I favor Padgett's proposal concerning the "relative timelessness" of God's inner experience. Within that framework, I am inclined to believe that God's experience within himself and his deliberative process in planning the course of creation and of its history under his providential guidance was not absolutely timeless. In God's infinite wisdom and transcendence, his plan for the unfolding of creation history was made with the benefit of the knowledge of how his creatures would act in various circumstances. From our own standpoint, that deliberation and decision could have been made with a speed that would make it virtually unmeasurable by any instrument of time that we possess. This becomes increasingly easy for us to comprehend, however, as the speed of computer processing grows. I am, however, not presently comfortable with the proposal of either Molinists or Calvinists that the deliberations of God leading up to his final plan were completely timeless. A certain reverent agnosticism is in order here, and this leaves me unable either to conclusively confirm or deny a chronological rather than purely logical relationship between the orders of God's knowledge as utilized in the establishment of his eternal purpose. However we understand the very difficult matter of God's relationship to time, our conceptualization must include the possibility of God's acting in our time, and this has not been denied by any Christian theologian, regardless of the definition given to God's eternity.

The suffering and responsiveness of God. The understanding of providence that I am offering has been described as a "no-risk" view because God has determined before creating anything that his purpose will be accomplished in and through the creation. There is never any risk that his purpose will not be achieved. Unfortunately, this has created the impression in the minds of some that God is not involved with his creatures in a way that he is affected by them or is responsive to them. Indeed God's impassibility has been cogently defended by Paul Helm who proposes that the biblical portrayal of God as one who is angry, repents, laughs, has people in derision and takes delight in them is anthropopathism. As such, they must be controlled by the biblical statements of God's infinity, eternity, immutability, omniscience and omnipotence. God's character is essential to him and is not dispositional, therefore we are wrong to "think of him as having passions." Helm does not believe that God is inactive or uninterested, but his will is determined from within rather than moved from without, and he cannot be changed by emotion. He is never portrayed as acting under the sway of emotion. However, God presented himself as a person from whom response is possible, "as one who acts in time," because he wanted people to respond to him. But there could not be timelessly eternal affects in God because a God who has emotional changes (whether time-lessly eternal or not) "also has changes in belief or knowledge, and either was not or is not omniscient."[68]

I described this view as "unfortunate" because, despite my significant agreement with Helm's understanding of God and providence, I do not consider this stance on divine passibility necessary or valid. While never questioning God's control in his world, I do not assert that the history of his relationship with creation is without pain for him. Of course, given the model I am proposing, this is not a pain that takes God by surprise. It is a pain he foresaw and he purposed to bear. For this reason, God's pain does not constitute a change in his belief or knowledge, which is what Helm rightly wishes to avoid. On numerous occasions the biblical writers give us glimpses of God's pain at the rejection of his rebellious creatures, particu-larly those to whom he has been most kind. Their ingratitude for his good-ness to them, their decision to worship creatures rather than the Creator, their failure to keep his commands when those precepts are given them for their own good—all of this is a source of pain to God who, in the days of Noah, reached the point of being "sorry that he had made humankind on the earth, and it grieved him to his heart" (Gen 6:6). Given God's compre-hensive knowledge, it cannot be that he did not know that Noah's genera-tion would sin so persistently for their doing so was, in part, the result of his decision not to graciously turn them from their sin. God "foreknew" both what these sinners would do and the grief that it would cause him.

I see no reason why we should assume God's grief of which Genesis speaks to be anthropopathism, although the "heart" in which God experi-enced that grief is clearly an anthropomorphism. This raises the question of criteria for our discernment of when descriptions, even self-descriptions, of God are anthropomorphic or anthropopathic. On the one hand, it is always dangerous to assume that God is like us simply because he uses analogical language to communicate truth about himself to us. On the other hand, we are persons created in God's image, and I think that it is reasonable to assume that biblical language about God means the same thing about him as it would mean about us unless there are compelling reasons, such as his purely spiritual nature, to indicate otherwise. I do not deny the possibility of anthropopathic speech in God's revelation to us of his reaction to human actions. I do, however, find implausible any construct that rules out any possibility of reaction or response on God's part. When we are displeased by the actions of our children whom we love, if they deliberately spurn our love and disobey us, we experience grief and perhaps anger, and we have physical experiences concomitant with these emotions. God does not have a body and so any experience that he describes as an emotion does not include the physical experiences that we have. But I see no reason why our own embodied experience of emotion should be made an exclusive or normative one. God is love, and we are called upon to be loving, after his image and his example. When we love, we experience the emotion of love in an embodied way that is clearly creaturely. However, we must be careful not to assume that love or the joy and pain that come from it are not experiences of God in some genuinely analogous way. They are responsive experiences that are always appropriate.

God is only angry when it is right to be so and he only rejoices over what is good. For God to change from approval to anger because of what we do is not a change in his nature, it is brought about by the consistency of his nature. Were God not to respond to deliberate disobedience with righteous anger, he would not be the holy God that he is. I assert that God is responsive, but I deny that this makes him dependent upon his creatures. His experience of changing emotions appropriate to the actions of his creatures is an emotional experience that he determined to allow himself when he determined to allow the creaturely action. We have the power to give God joy or to give him pain, but it is his prevenient grace that enables us to give him joy, and it is his decision to permit our disobedience that enables us to give him pain.

Obviously, the issue of God's relationship to time is closely related to this matter of his experiencing emotion. Erickson's proposal concerning the immanence of God relative to time may bear fruit here. If we affirm that, in his immanence, in his relatedness to the creature, God is active in time, we can see how that immanence also makes it possible for him to feel and to act in response to the actions of his creatures. I agree with Millard Erickson that "if it is the case that God has planned from eternity all that occurs, and that this includes the various events in the lives of all persons, then although God may experience certain emotions, make certain choices, and take certain actions in connection with those events, they really are not the cause of these events in God's life. Those actions and feelings are actually the result of his choices and plan, which is now being worked out within history."[69] Here lies a significant difference between risk and no-risk doctrines of providence. In risk views, God's experience of emotion in response to his creatures is a greater self-chosen dependence upon them than in non-risk models. In non-risk models, I believe that it is possible to affirm both divine responsiveness and divine passibility without positing any significant divine self-limitation or contingency.

In addition to the pain of rejection by his creatures, God graciously willed to bear immeasurably greater pain in order to deliver a large multitude of people from the terrible consequences of their willful rebellion. Although God had no obligation to deliver sinners from their just punishment, he chose to bear the punishment of his people himself, in the person of the incarnate Word, thus being just but justifying sinners (Rom 3:25-26). The God who is in control is not an impassible God, nor is he a God helpless in the face of that which gives him pain. Patiently he endures the rebellion of his creatures and continues to work graciously among them until his purpose is accomplished and "the kingdom of the world has become the kingdom of our Lord," until he is "all in all" (1 Cor 15:28).

I think that Hendrikus Berkhof has overstated the case when he says that "the first impression one gets from the biblical account of revelation is that of God's impotence, of how man has taken the initiative away from him, of what we shall call here his 'defenselessness.'"[70] From my statements thus far it is clear that I hear a strong testimony to God's omnipotence throughout the biblical witness. On the other hand, I am sympathetic to Berkhof's assessment that "God's history with Israel is to a large degree the history of a God who sees his plans fail and who repeatedly must react to a hostile or at least disobedient initiative of his partner, without apparently having (or wanting to have) the power to force that partner to his will."[71] I disagree with Berkhof because I do not conceptualize God's providence in terms of ad hoc responses to events that happen differently than he planned, that is, responses made on the spur of the moment rather than premeditatedly. I see a situation in which God anticipated the rebellion of his people, indeed he predicted it and warned them of how he would *respond* when it happened. In his eternal purpose, God knew what they were going to do, and he knew what he was going to do when they did it. In some cases God actually prevented the coming of judgment by a conditional prophecy that he would punish people for their sin, without making it explicit that he would withhold that judgment if they repented. Nineveh is the classic case of this principle, but I understand God to be effectively using the same approach in the warning passages of Hebrews 6 and 10.

God uses the warning that apostasy would be irrevocable to keep his children from it. For our present purposes, however, it is important to note that God's foreknowledge of his people's rebellion and of the judgment that he would have to exercise did not save him from the pain of rejection either at the "eternal moment" when he willed to permit that disobedience or at the time that it occurred. Then, as now, the Spirit of God is grieved when his loving overtures are spurned, and Scripture appropriately enjoins us not to "grieve the Holy Spirit of God" (Eph 4:30).

The Son cried out in agony as he experienced the Father's forsaking, and he did it for us. I assume that this must have been matched by the Father's pain at the Son's suffering, although neither of them flinched from that pain because of the great saving good that they lovingly accomplished through it. It might be suggested that Jesus could experience pain because of his humanity and his embodiment, but the purely spiritual and impassible Father could not. For the reasons I have already noted, the incarnation gave Jesus the ability to experience emotions in an embodied way, more closely analogous to our own experience of them. But there was no incoherence between the divine and the human natures. I see no reason to assume that passibility was an experience made possible for the incarnate Word only because of that embodiment. We divide the divine and human natures too strongly, if we assert that God felt the pain of the Father's abandonment only in his humanity. It was precisely as the divine Word who had known the Father's good pleasure from all eternity that the Son then suffered the terrible sense of the loss of that approval as he was made sin for us.

It was "for the sake of the joy that was set before him" that our Lord endured the cross and disregarded its shame (Heb 12:2), but it would be folly to blunt the reality of the suffering God experienced. It was all part of God's "definite plan and foreknowledge" (Acts 2:23; cf. 4:28) but that made it no less painful. Nowhere do we find a greater demonstration of God's responsive love than in the cross (Jn 3:16; Rom 5:8). Berkhof writes:

> The cross is the climax of our resistance and hostility toward God and therefore the nadir of God-forsakenness. Here free and guilty man seems to have the final and only say. Yet this God-forsakenness is enclosed by an unfathomable presence of God whereby the God-forsakenness becomes the way leading to a new and reconciled communion between him and man. Since this has happened we know that even the greatest horrors do not happen apart from God. He does not want them, but they cannot thwart his purpose and must ultimately serve it.[72]

This is movingly said, but we must qualify the sense in which God "does not want them." Here I simply refer to the discussion under the Calvinist model concerning the senses in which Scripture speaks of God's will. There is a sense in which he does not want it but also one in which he wills it. Between these two there is no inner conflict within God, but we dare not deny God's sovereign providence to avoid the difficulty in our expression of the relationship between these two aspects of God's "willing."

In a model of comprehensive providence that includes both deliberate divine action and deliberate divine permission, there is ample room for God to be responsive to his creatures so long as middle knowledge is included in the divine planning. In that logical moment when God foreknew all that could happen and decided what he would permit, he was also involved in determining how he would respond. God knew that under certain circumstances evils would occur, and he determined not to permit them to do so by introducing influences of his own or other factors that brought about a better situation for his creatures and glorified himself. One of the great incomprehensibles for theists is why God deliberately permitted so many evils if he was able to prevent them. A number of the models we surveyed have proposed that God could not prevent those evils without robbing his creatures of their freedom. That does not adequately represent the control of God within his creation as I (along with Thomists and other Calvinists) understand Scripture. We are left to assert that in God's goodness and wisdom he has decided to permit some of these evils because of a good that is served by them, even for the creatures who suffer those evils. Although not able to develop the case in this book, I have found the approach to evil that is offered by representatives of the Calvinist model to be adequate, without removing the element of mystery that remains in our finite knowledge of God's ways.

Summing Up

Before I begin to unpack the model of petitionary prayer that derives from this model of providence, it may be helpful to sum up in a few brief theses my understanding of providence.

1. God's providential care of his creation includes every detail, and it is an outworking of his detailed eternal purpose (decree), not the pursuit of a general purpose on an ad hoc basis. Furthermore, God exercises a particular care for those who are specially related to him in Christ. However,

God's special providences for his children, though apparent to his grateful children, are difficult to demonstrate conclusively to others, particularly to unbelievers. Furthermore, in special providence, as in miracle, special divine action (intervention) is by definition not God's usual practice. God's "foresight" and comprehensive control enable him to arrange circumstances for the furtherance of his purposes, without continual intervention. Nonetheless, though God's special acts to effectuate events are unusual, nothing transpires without his express permission.

2. God has established a usual way of upholding his nonsentient creation. He is not bound by it, but he works differently only on relatively rare occasions so that we can order our own lives with a predictable expectation of the way in which "nature" will act. When God acts unusually in order to draw our attention to himself in sign and wonder, we call his action a "miracle."

3. God's eternal purpose is the ground of his comprehensive knowledge of created reality, and it encompasses all of that reality, including things that are past, present and future from our standpoint.

4. In establishing his eternal purpose God "had" middle knowledge (that is, knowledge of future contingent possibilities or counterfactuals) but, contrary to the assumptions of Molinist forms of middle knowledge, precognition of libertarianly free actions is not possible even for God.

5. God's comprehensive providential care is exercised in such a way that creatures act spontaneously, normally choosing what they do without external constraint. Consequently they are morally responsible for their acts, even though God has included those acts within his eternal purpose. The good things we do as a result of God's gracious influences upon us bring glory to God, and the evil we do by his permission is strictly our own culpability.

6. God's "foreknowledge" of our spontaneous actions does not make the freedom of our decisions illusory. We have a significant role in deciding the actual future. Were we to decide differently than we do, God's eternal knowledge of the future would be different than it is.

7. God's relationship to time and, hence, the nature of eternity is mysterious. However, we can affirm that God transcends our time (as he does our space), in the sense that he is not limited by it as we are. He is present in all time (and space) but is not restricted by it. We can also affirm that God is nevertheless able to act in time, as he does in space, and to establish and discern the time relationship of different events.

8. Given our creation as morally responsible creatures, God's direction

of our lives is through commands and through persuasion (both external and internal). God's perfect knowledge of us and of all the circumstances of our lives (including his middle knowledge) enables him to accomplish his purposes without coercion and with a minimum of "intervention."

9. Although God is completely in control at all times so that the accomplishment of his purposes is never at risk, voluntarily free creatures often act contrary to God's moral precepts. This causes grief and pain for God, but he has willed to bear that pain and has graciously chosen to increase his own suffering by absorbing the consequences of the disobedience of those who are in Christ, in order that they might not have to do so. There is a sense in which God is a fellow sufferer with his creatures living in a sinful world, but his is never a suffering that is forced upon him by an inability to remove its cause even if that would entail the destruction of the creature. In his comprehensive providence God shows himself gracious and patient as well as wise and powerful.

The Case Study

Having grown up in a Presbyterian home, Gail Wellwood learned her catechism faithfully as a young girl. During her early adult years she struggled particularly with the existence of evil in the world as it had been explained to her by her parents and teachers. "If everything that happens is part of God's decree or eternal purpose, then didn't that make God responsible for sin?" she wondered aloud. Millie Dennis (semi-deist model) assured her that it does indeed, and both Mark Peterson (process model) and Oliver Dueck (openness model) agreed with Millie. During that time of theological unsettledness, Gail discussed the matter frequently with them. But as time went on, the alternatives to the position that she had been taught became more clear but also less plausible. She never did think that Millie's position was a possibility; it viewed God as too uninvolved to fit with the story of God's working in the world that she found in the Bible. Mark's position was fascinating, but in the end it also looked too far from the biblical material to work for Carol. She did not initially object to the strong use of Whitehead's philosophy that the model used. She realized that everyone's theological construction uses philosophy, and so we must make a judgment about which understanding of the basic nature of reality (metaphysics) and of truth (epistemology) best enables us to make sense of the biblical narrative. Whitehead certainly had a fascinating proposal, but when God was included in the framework, Gail felt very uncomfortable with the outcome. It was impossible for her to view God as so intricately involved in the world that he himself was affected in his own personal development.

It was Oliver's way of explaining the situation that seemed to Gail to be the most likely alternative to the position she had accepted up to that point. By asserting that God had willingly limited himself by giving his creatures libertarian freedom, Oliver greatly reduced the likelihood that people would hold God responsible when evil occurs. Not everything that happens is part of God's eternal purpose, either effectively brought about or permitted by him. In a very general sense, God permitted evil in the world by giving creatures libertarian freedom, but he did not permit specific evils. These things happened because creatures (human and angelic) opposed God and did what he did not want, in spite of all his gracious efforts to prevent them from doing something destructive, not only to others but also to themselves.

So Gail could see an advantage in moving toward Oliver's position, but would the biblical account allow her to do this? As time went by and Gail tried Oliver's model on for size, she concluded that even Oliver's position did not give God the kind of control that she believed the Scripture gave to him. It might be helpful in getting God off the hook for the Holocaust, but there were too many occasions in the Old Testament where God had clearly drawn the line regarding what happened to Israel. He said when the oppression in Egypt was enough, he delivered Jerusalem from Sennacherib's army, even though it meant drastic intervention through an act of the Angel of the Lord that killed 185,000 soldiers in one night. Yet when the Babylonians eventually came back, God informed Jeremiah that he was not going to deliver them this time. He told Habakkuk that he was "rousing the Chaldeans" (Hab 1:6) against Judah as an instrument of his judgment. But God clearly did not condone the Chaldean's violence, and he later brought judgment upon them too. Having seen the way God placed boundaries on the development of nations and used them for his purposes, without condoning their willful sin, Gail did not see how she could leave God out of the tragedy that was perpetrated by the Holocaust.

It was at that point that Tom Stransky's contribution (redemptive intervention model) had to be considered. Tom argued that the spectacular interventions of God to which Gail was referring were related to his special purpose of redemption and that Gail should not extrapolate from those events that God is always involved in the same intentional way in all historical incidents. Gail liked to cite Joseph's words about God's intention, which was different from that of Joseph's brothers, and she believed that it provided a paradigm for interpreting all human happenings. Where evil occurs, it comes about through the wicked desires and intentions of disobedient creatures. God permits them to fulfill their desires on many occasions, but he does so with good intentions frequently hidden from us. But Tom insisted we cannot make a general principle from specific biblical incidents like Joseph's life, which were so obviously important to God's plan for the establishment of his covenant people as a nation.

Tom's view initially seemed a bit more palatable to Gail than Oliver's, particularly since Tom believed that God knows the future completely. Gail remembers being a bit shocked when Oliver first made the statement that God did not know exactly what she or anyone else was going to do tomorrow. But when he explained that this was a natural consequence of the libertarian freedom that God had given to these people, it was a bit less startling. Oliver argued that until Gail had decided what she was going to do tomorrow, her own future was open. Obviously her choices were fairly limited, but they were not completely fixed. Until she chose and acted, there was nothing there to be known, and so it was no aspersion on God's omniscience to recognize that he did not know what could not be known. That point brought Andrew Martin (Molinist model) into the conversation. Like the others who were in conversation with Gail until then, Andrew believed that people are libertarianly free, but he also believed that God knew what they would do even though they had not yet made their free decision about it. When they did decide and act, their action would give truth value to a statement about their action. Since God knows all truth, he knows the truth value of all statements, and so he knows what Gail will do tomorrow as a true proposition. Furthermore, Andrew said, God not only knows what Gail will do tomorrow, he knows what she *would* do in an infinite variety of circumstances. He had that knowledge (what Andrew called "middle knowledge") before he created the world, and so he chose to create this particular world, knowing full well what every creature in it would do of their own libertarianly free choice. The Holocaust came about through the free choices of evil people, but God had chosen the world in which he knew those choices would be made, and he was at work to bring good out of it all.

Gail was definitely interested in maintaining her belief in God's comprehensive foreknowledge, and so she had pretty much given up on Oliver's proposal. Maria Sanchez (Thomist model) seemed to be holding together the features that Gail considered nonnegotiable: God's foreknowledge (although she said it was not technically beforehand, for God), God's complete control and a strong view of human freedom. However, it was both Oliver and Andrew who convinced Gail that Maria's position wouldn't work. For one thing, the concept of God as absolutely timeless sounded a bit unlikely, but, more significantly, Oliver pointed out that simply knowing the future ahead of time would do God no good. By the time God knew what Gail was going to do tomorrow, it was already a truth, and there was nothing that God could do about it. That was going to be a problem with Tom's (redemptive intervention) model as well. So Andrew's idea of middle knowledge was beginning to sound really good. It was a way in which God could use his knowledge of future possibilities before they became actual truths, in order to decide how he would act in particular situations and bring about the outcomes he wanted. But Oliver pricked that balloon too. Even if Andrew was correct about God's knowledge of the actual future as a knowledge of all true propositions, his proposal about God's knowledge of counterfactuals of libertarian human freedom was not going to work. Unlike the statements about actual future events, the counterfactuals do not have truth value. Their truth value is established only when the free creatures make the decision. If Gail is libertarianly free, as Andrew believes, then even God cannot know what she *would* do tomorrow in circumstances that never actually exist.

Oliver's objection to middle knowledge, in the way that Andrew used it, made good sense to Gail, and it was seriously narrowing her options. It looked as though Oliver's openness model was the only one that would work if she wanted to assert that humans are libertarianly free. But for reasons that she had stated to Oliver previously, there was too much in Oliver's construction that did not square with her reading of the Bible. God does know the actual future, and he predicts it through his prophets, on occasion. God is completely in control, and he has planned how he will act in history to bring about the outcome that he wills. This meant that her parents had been right all along about the nature of human freedom. People are not libertarianly free, but they are genuinely free in the sense that they act according to their own desires. God knows how they will act because he has determined what he will permit in his eternal purpose and has also determined how he will act to bring things about, on occasion, that would not occur if creatures were left to themselves. It looked as though Gail and Peter (Calvinist model) were going to come out on pretty much the same page. But Gail could see that Peter's position suffered from the same problem that Oliver and Andrew had pointed out in connection with Maria's view: simple foreknowledge was not going to enable God to plan how he would respond to possible situations that he foresaw. Middle knowledge was going to be necessary. She agreed with Oliver that Andrew's way of incorporating middle knowledge into the mix was not going to work because libertarian freedom made it impossible. Since she had backed away from libertarian freedom, that problem no longer existed for her.

Gail was now at peace and convinced that she had the best of all possible constructions. God was completely in control, but his morally responsible creatures are genuinely free. God knows not only the actual future but also all possible futures, and it is precisely his knowledge of what people *would* do in given circumstances that enables him to plan how to respond and to act in ways that move history toward the achievement of his own goals for his creation. There were still moments at which the awful tragedies of life gave Gail pause, but she was convinced now that, although God had allowed these events to happen, he was not personally evil in doing so. Only from the end, looking back on human history from glory and with God's explanation, would the workings of God in and through it all make complete sense. But, as Helmut Spiegel (Barthian model) often insisted, it is in Jesus Christ that we have to contemplate God and his ways. Nowhere was the power of double intention more clear to Gail than in the crucifixion of Jesus. Surely no greater human evil could have been committed, and it was clearly a work in which the devil was very active, and yet through it God had accomplished the defeat of Satan and the liberation of a great host of those whom Satan held captive.

By the time Gail heard Fred Henderson's prayer request, she had settled on her theological model, and it gave her a framework within which to understand what was going on. She could see that the act of the guerrillas was evil, in and of itself, but she was confident that God had permitted it with a deliberate and good intention. He had not only foreknown that the abduction would take place, he had included it in his eternal purpose as something that he would permit. Furthermore, he had been aware of other possibilities that could have been brought about through changes in the circumstances. Having considered the full range of possible outcomes, God had decided that he would permit this particular one, but he was not passive in doing so. He was continually at work in the situation, moving toward purposes of his own.

14

A Middle Knowledge Calvinist Model of Prayer

P RAYER IS ONE OF THE MEANS THAT GOD HAS DETERMINED TO USE IN THE *accomplishment of his will. In his eternal purpose God has included all of the events of human history, but he does not act alone, as though he were the only agent in the world. He has given his children the privilege of participation in his program for establishing his kingdom on earth. One of the most significant means of our involvement is through petitionary prayer, because it is here that we attempt to discern God's will in particular situations, we align our own desires with his, and then we ask God to do what we believe he wants to do. Although God could work without us, he delights to answer the prayers of his children and to be glorified by their thanksgiving when he does so. It is particularly because God has middle knowledge that he is able to accomplish his purposes while at the same time being responsive to the desires and petitions of his children. In prayer we do not seek to change God's mind. We seek to discern his will and to pray accordingly, believing that there are some things that God has determined to do in answer to prayer so that our prayers are a necessary—though not a sufficient—"cause" of the ultimate outcome. Our prayers do affect the outcome as one of the essential factors in the whole complex of events as they transpire through God's superintendence.*

Throughout this book our focus has been on the providence of God, his action in the world that he created. We have particularly been observing how one's model of providence affects the practice of petitionary prayer. Having described my own model of providence in the previous chapter, I will now describe my understanding of prayer as an effective means to influence the way things go in the world as we work together with God. I will lay out some general principles about the role of prayer in effecting things in the world and then focus on three arenas of prayer, namely, the physical world, the developing history of the human world and our own lives as God's children.

Response to Prayer Is One of the Means by Which God Has Chosen to Accomplish His Purposes in the World

I have presented a picture of God's sovereign action in the world that portrays God as intimately involved in all that takes place. In fact, the whole history of creation has been determined by God in his eternal purpose. As we have seen, this appears to many theologians to leave no place for genuine human agency. However, I share with many others the view that within God's overall control, human beings are free agents who act responsibly in the world and that our actions influence the outcome of events within history. Granted, freedom has to be understood as the ability to act according to one's own wishes, without coercion, rather than in terms of the power of contrary choice (libertarian free will), which is favored by most of the models we have studied.

Prayer as an effective contributor to final outcomes. If God has eternally purposed everything that will happen, then it seems to some theologians that it is futile for us to ask God to act now. What he will do has already been determined, and nothing we do or say can change that. It is my proposal that, in God's knowledge of the possible future, he has foreseen our prayers and has determined to act in response to them. Consequently, some of what happens comes about because we prayed and because God answered those prayers. There is a sense, therefore, in which it is legitimate for us to say that if we had not petitioned God to do something, he would not have done it. God acts according to his own wise and perfect will, and yet our prayers are instrumental in the final outcome because of the occasions upon which he acts with the intention of giving us what we desire. In this sense we can say that *prayer changes things.*[1] On the other hand, it is impossible for us to say for certain that our prayer was an essential ingredient of the total situation, without which God would not have acted in any particular instance. When we ask God to act in a certain way and he does so, we can legitimately be thankful that our prayer was answered. But we must not assume that we *determined* the outcome by virtue of our request.

There are obviously many things that God does for us without anyone asking him to do them. As Jesus said, God sends rain upon the fields of both those who are in fellowship with him and those who are in rebellion (Mt 5:45), and in both cases God often does this whether or not he is asked to do it. But those who have asked God for rain are much more likely to be thankful when it comes and are right to believe that their prayers were answered. They now have two things for which to give thanks to God, the rain and the answer to their prayer. I am convinced that one of God's reasons for choosing to involve us in the determination of outcomes, by inviting us to entreat him to act in the world, is that he is glorified in our gratitude for his responsive action on our behalf. It is among the most basic complaints of God against unbelievers, that they do not acknowledge his role in the world or give him thanks (Rom 1:21).

Prayer according to God's will. First John 5:14-15 is a fundamental passage in my understanding of the role of prayer within the accomplishment of God's purposes. In that encouragement, John tells us that "if we ask anything according to [God's] will, he hears us. And if we know that he hears us in whatever we ask, we know that we have obtained the requests made of him." I hear the apostle John affirming what I have earlier developed, that God's will is done in the world. In prayer, we do not cajole God into doing something that he did not purpose to do; we ask him to do what he wants to do. Our first task in petitionary prayer is therefore to discern God's will for the situation. The better we know God through our knowledge of his Word and through our fellowship with him, the more likely we are to accurately discern his will. As Harry Blamires observes, "If we are praying for something which is in accordance with God's will, then we can be sure that he is already operating towards the end we pray for."[2]

Obviously Scripture does not tell us specifically what God wants to do in most of the situations that we face. But he has given us a picture of his general desires. He gives us wisdom by his Spirit so that we can examine situations and make judgments concerning what development in the situation would move things along toward the goals that we understand to be God's goals for the world. Nevertheless, on many occasions we find ourselves unsure of the specific action that God would wish to do in the situation that confronts us, and so we present our requests, but we qualify them with the condition "if it is your will." This is not a lack of faith; it is a lack of knowledge. We believe that God will do what is best, but we are uncertain what that is and so we ask according to our best wisdom.[3] If God does not act as we have asked him to, we accept that our prayer was not answered, and we seek his will in the new circumstances that surround us. Often the object of our request remains a possibility, and we have been given no indication by God that he does not intend ever to answer this particular request, and so we persist until we either get the answer we seek or believe that God has told us no.

In this process, if our motives are right, we need not be afraid of praying "against God's will." Along this line Harry Blamires suggests that "unless one is consciously perverse, it is not at all easy to pray against God's will." Indeed Blamires is "not sure that it is even possible."[4] For example, although a friend may be sick by God's intention to discipline him, "prayer for a friend's well-being inevitably has the character of an act of obedience to the divine will, even though ignorance may frame the request in a form which God rejects."[5] Indeed, we learn from the cases of Nineveh and Hezekiah that God may make predictions about the future specifically to elicit prayer. In these instances a failure to pray would bring the foretold judgment, but appropriate prayer forestalls it (cf. Is 38:1-6). Moses' intercession for Israel functioned similarly (Ex 32:9-14), saving the lives of the people with whom God had made a covenant. The principle at work here is stated by God in Ezekiel 33:13-16.

We must distinguish between the prayer of *submission to God's will* and the prayer *according to God's will*. The first is the sort of petition about which we have been speaking, when we are unsure of God's will in a situation because it has not been revealed to us, and so we pray conditionally, "If it be your will." The second type is what I also call the prayer of "appropriation," and Jesus spoke of it in Mark 11:24: "So I tell you, whatever you ask for in prayer, believe that you have received it, and it will be yours." To have that sort of faith when we make a request, we must know not only that God is *able* but also that he is *willing* to grant it. It is a serious mistake to assume that this text provides us with a blank check with which we can get anything we want from God if only we have enough faith.

Jesus made another broad promise, which is recorded in John 14:13-14: "I will do whatever you ask in my name, so that the Father may be glorified in the Son. If in my name you ask me for anything, I will do it." Here the condition for answered prayer is identified as the warrant of Jesus' name rather than the faith of the petitioner. But again the context of the promise is critical. M. M. B. Turner rightly notes that the "greater works" Jesus predicted would be done by his followers (Jn 14:12) is in the context of Jesus' doing the works of the Father. Until Jesus has been glorified in the cross and resurrection, and the Spirit has been given, his works cannot achieve their true end. "It is in this salvation-historically defined sense that the works will be greater than Jesus' own."[6] The "anything" that we ask is also related to that context and its content is thus "limited to 'works' that will reveal the unity of the Father and the Son in new creation (which might include anything from healing, to giving grace to bear suffering for Jesus; or from providing the disciples' material needs to granting their prayers for powerful witness, or wisdom in the church)." This is why our requests must be made in Jesus' name, that is, "bound up with his purposes and intended to reveal and glorify him."[7]

It is sometimes said that prayer is always answered: God says "yes" or "no" or "wait." I do not consider this a helpful way to speak. If we mean to say that God always hears us and that he is not unresponsive to our appeals, then it is correct. But I think that we do best to consider positive responses to our requests to be "answers" and to grant that when those do not occur, our prayers have not been answered. There are various reasons for unanswered prayer that are well treated in books on prayer. We will not address them here since our purpose is to demonstrate how a particular model of providence affects our practice of prayer, not to offer a treatise on all aspects of petitionary prayer.[8] It is worth noting, however, that God's will includes a timing factor, and so we cannot assume that an unanswered request was necessarily contrary to God's will. This is the truth in the suggestion that one of God's answers is "wait." If we have reason to believe that a particular request conforms to the general purposes of God revealed in Scripture, and if God does not make it clear to us that our request is contrary to his will, we are warranted in persisting in prayer concerning that need. Keith Ward, although he works within a different model of providence, aptly encourages us that "prayer will always make a difference to the world. It will sometimes make precisely the difference we desire. For it is part of the way in which God decrees that his creative and redemptive action in the world should be given a particular shape and form."[9]

I propose that petitionary prayer is effective in accomplishing things in the world because God has chosen to involve us in the establishment of his purposes. It is not that we simply do what God forces us to do as though we were not willing agents in the world. God is genuinely responsive to our desires precisely because our good desires are the fruit of his liberating grace in our lives. It is also not the case, however, that God is unsure of what he will do and is waiting for us to decide what we want so that he can act accordingly. We do not seek to *change* God's mind, we seek to change the situation in the world through an understanding of how God wishes things to be and through fervent petitions that he will do what is necessary for that state of perfect shalom to be realized. It is true that prayer is good *for us*. It fosters our sense of dependence on God, it develops closer fellowship with God, and it opens us up to God's strengthening work within us.[10] But I reject all models of providence in which prayer has no effect on the way the world goes. Prayer changes us, but God also changes our circumstances in response to prayer. It is God, however, and not prayer that *changes things,* even though his doing so is an answer to prayer.[11]

Prayer as an effective "cause" of God's response. Into the providence model I have factored God's knowledge of future possibilities (counterfactuals), sometimes designated middle knowledge. I believe that this is an important ingredient in defending this model of prayer from the charges that are often brought against deterministic models. Vincent Brümmer, for instance, contends that impetratory prayer would be meaningless in a deterministic universe where God infallibly foreknew every event and human action. This is because "no event could take place differently from the way it in fact does, and no human agent could act differently from the way it in fact does, for that would falsify God's infallible foreknowledge, which would be logically impossible."[12] Some have attempted to avoid the difficulty by asserting that God is timeless.[13] Brümmer does not think that approach successful, and I do not consider it to be very helpful for reasons I indicated in the previous chapter. However, if we assume that the establishment of God's eternal purpose included a rational assessment of options, including the possible prayers that could or would be offered, then I believe the difficulty is resolved.

While it is true that God infallibly knows what is going to happen, he knows it because he has willed that it should be, and he has willed that his own action in the situation should be a response to foreseen prayer. This does not make God's purpose *conditional* upon the foreseen human prayer, as though God's will is dependent on his foreknowledge, as Barth fears. But it does permit God to act *responsively,* while maintaining his sovereign independence. The certainty of the future is established by God's eternal will, but that future comes about through the genuine agency of God's creatures, including their petitionary prayer. God determines his own action, and he determines the ultimate outcome, but some of what he has determined to do, he has chosen to do in response to prayer. He both knows what he will do and that he will do it because his people asked him to (cf. Ezek 36:37).

Brümmer argues that within the scheme proposed by Aquinas "petitionary prayers are not impetratory at all. They are the (eternally decreed) direct causes of the events prayed for and not requests to bring these events about. To say that God brings about events *by means of* our prayers is not the same as to say that he brings about events *because of* our prayers."[14] I contend, however, that this disjunction is overcome by the positing of the knowledge of future possibilities. Since God has chosen to respond to our prayers, we can speak of his acting *because of* them, but since he has chosen to include those very prayers within his eternal purpose, we can also say that he accomplishes his will *by means* of them.[15] The fact that our petition has itself thus become a part of God's decree does not detract either from its genuine agency or from the personal relationship that exists between God and us.[16] As Paul Helm puts it, there are cases in which people's prayer is part of the total matrix, and God acts *because* people asked him to. Had they not done so, the conditions in the whole matrix would have been insufficient for production of what is asked for.[17] Thus, also, Augustine's statement that "prayers are useful in obtaining those favours which He foresaw He would bestow on those who should pray for them."[18]

In a similar vein to Brümmer's, Clark Pinnock has posited that prayer is a demonstration that the future is open,[19] but this is only true if he is correct in his rejection of divine foreknowledge. Rightly assuming that God does know the future, Norman Geisler notes that "God knew who would freely pray when he predetermined to use prayer to achieve his ends. So it is open to us to change the world by prayer, but it will not catch God by surprise when we do."[20]

Recently John Sanders raised this question once more. He concluded that in "no-risk" models of providence we cannot validly speak of God as *responding* to prayer because he is "'responding' in terms of his own decrees. The 'God who hears' prayers is the God who hears himself speaking through second causes."[21] Sanders argues that in no-risk models, "God is not dependent on our prayers; rather, our prayers are dependent on God's decreeing them. Thus God may be said to do X 'because' we prayed only in the sense that God has always decreed that God was going to do X after we prayed the prayer he also decreed."[22] As evidence of his case, Sanders cites Jonathan Edwards who wrote: "Speaking after the manner of men, God is sometimes represented *as if* he were moved and persuaded by the prayers of his people; yet it is not to be thought that God is properly moved or made willing by our prayers. . . . He is self-moved. . . . God has been pleased to constitute prayer to be antecedent to the bestowment of mercy; and he is pleased to bestow mercy in consequence of prayer, *as though* he were prevailed upon by prayer."[23]

Most seriously, Sanders argues that no-risk models consequently have difficulty making sense of the apostle James's statement that "you do not have, because you do not ask" (Jas 4:2). This follows because "if God's will is never thwarted in any detail, then we can never fail to receive something from God *because* we failed to ask for it." There is therefore "no place for impetratory prayer in this model," in the opinion of Sanders.[24] If Sanders were right, it would not trouble me to agree with him that my model (and other no-risk models, such as the Thomist, Barthian and Calvinist models we have presented) do not have a place for impetratory prayer, in the strong sense of the term, which is the sense in which Sanders and Brümmer always use it. We could simply grant that, given the greater weight these models give to God's control over human control of outcomes, impetratory prayer is excluded from the model. But it *would* disturb me if I offered a model that excluded specific biblical teaching. However, I do not think that this is the case.

James draws an explicit connection between our asking and our receiving. This is common in Scripture, as was noted by Barth in material I cited from him under that model. Barth himself did not hesitate to use the language of contingency and dependence as a consequence of this biblical manner of speaking. Clearly, in the no-risk model presented by Calvin and represented in the earlier citation from Edwards, God does not do things *because* we request them, in the sense that he had intended to do something else but changed his mind on account of our prayer. That is precisely the position taken within the openness model, and it is not surprising that they wish to preserve the language of causal dependence for the sense that it carries within their model. But, I would argue, it is legitimate to use this language in a sense that coheres with the no-risk model and to interpret James in a manner equally consistent with it. James can be heard to teach us that there are occasions upon which the whole complex of factors contributing to the outcome includes prayer as one of its *necessary* ingredients. It really makes no difference whether this is by God's predetermination or not. For example, God could have predetermined that he would act to deliver Richard Henderson and his colleagues from harm and that he would do so even though no one prayed about it or even knew that Richard had been captured. On the other hand, God could have determined that this particular act of deliverance would be one that would rightly be discerned by his people as a response to their prayers and that would elicit appropriate praise of God for his greatness and kindness.

What troubles theologians of the openness model as they contemplate no-risk models is that the prayers themselves are as much part of God's eternal purpose as are the answers. It gives them the impression that God is actually the only one who is at work, and the people who pray are simply manipulated by him to produce the whole "puppet show." It is at this point that I find the inclusion of middle knowledge within the model to be helpful. In fact, I would argue that the Calvinist model implicitly assumes it and will not work without it. Furthermore, only such a no-risk model *could* include it, for reasons presented previously. By introducing the logical (or even, in some sense, chronological) moment of middle knowledge, we allow for God's eternal purpose to be established with the creaturely desires "in mind." God knows what Fred Henderson and his fellow believers would do freely or spontaneously, being the people they have become through an amazingly complex array of factors physical, psychological, relational and divinely gracious. Certainly God has played a part in bringing them to that point in their human and spiritual maturity, but he has not done so coercively. He has graciously worked by his Spirit, along with the "natural" and circumstantial factors of their lives, to bring them to this point in the conformity to the image of Christ, which is his goal for them. So in one sense it is true that they are what God has "made" them. But in another very significant sense, the people they have become through a multitude of choices made during their lives are the people that God has considered in forming his eternal purpose. No one determines who will be the objects of God's special grace; that is God's free prerogative, or it would be earned, a proposal that Christian theology has regularly rejected though not always with equal consistency. At the moment that these people pray, however, it is they, not God, who do so. And it is to them and not himself that God responds to when he acts in the way that they have requested. They then have *because* they asked, just as, in some situations, they would *not* have had *because* they did *not* ask. I cannot deny that the human action is *less* determinative of the outcome in my model than it is in the openness model. But I do insist that within God's overall control he has given us genuinely effective agency so that our actions, including our prayer, are real (though secondary) "causes" of the way things turn out and hence may legitimately be spoken of in the language of "because."

In his review of my earlier manuscript John Sanders made the statement that proponents of a no-risk model of providence and prayer "should use the same careful word selection they use when discussing the doctrine of election so as not to mislead people into believing that God is actually affected by our prayers." This is an important analogy, and it does form a significant warning to those of us who believe and teach no-risk models. Since the Arminian controversy within Calvinism, Reformed theologians have clearly asserted that God's electing grace is unconditional. God does not elect people because of anything about them, including their faith, which he merely foresees; he chooses them in free and sovereign grace, and the faith he foresees is the faith he has chosen to give, from before the creation of the world. Calvinist or Reformed theologians affirm the instrumentality of faith in salvation but insist that we are saved *by* faith but only *because* of the work of Christ. We are not saved *because* of faith, and God's choice of us was not *because* of our faith, our faith is *because* of his choice.

By analogy, using the terms in the same way, a Calvinist would have to say that prayer is instrumental but not causal. God acts upon or subsequent to our petition, which was part of the complex of factors included in his plan to act as he does, but his *choice* to act in this way was not *caused* by our prayers. In other words, God's *act* of delivering Richard Henderson may have been caused by the believers' petition, but his *decision* to deliver Richard was not. On the other hand, the openness model can assert that even God's decision to deliver the missionaries was caused by the petitioners. So there is a difference, and that difference needs to be clearly explained to those with whom we converse, but it is not a difference between one legitimate use of the language of cause and another illegitimate use.

If someone asks a Calvinist why God justified her, she may legitimately answer: "Because I believed in Jesus." But if asked further: "Why did you believe in Jesus?" she might answer: "Because my pastor preached the gospel and the Spirit of God drew me to Christ, opened my heart and gave me faith." If God had not chosen her to salvation, the gospel preaching of her pastor would have been ineffective. On the other hand, since gospel proclamation was the instrument God chose to bring her to faith, it would not be incorrect for her to say to her pastor: "Thank you for explaining the good news of salvation so clearly. I was saved because you preached the gospel."

In the same way, if Richard is freed and someone asks Fred Henderson, "Why did God deliver Richard from the rebels?" he might properly answer, "Because we prayed." In saying so, however, Fred ought not to think that God's *decision* within his eternal purpose was caused by their prayer. God freely and graciously decided that he would deliver Richard, just as he decided that he would deliver the apostle Peter but not deacon Stephen. He decided, however, that he would do this in response to the prayers of Fred and his friends. Yet the salvation that put Fred into a relationship with God, which gave him the right to pray in the name of Jesus, and the sanctifying grace that kept him growing as a faithful intercessor were the work of God's grace. Thus there is a sense in which the very prayers of Fred are God's work, and Fred can give God praise not only for delivering Richard but for so graciously bringing him into a relationship in which his own prayer could be a causal factor in that deliverance. In such an understanding, all the glory must unmistakably go to God!

Speaking of the efficacy of prayer, Donald M. MacKay aptly suggests that there is no guarantee "that if God had created a drama in which you had not prayed, he would still have made it one in which help was sent off in time to rescue you."[25] We have God's promise that he hears prayer and that he cooperates for our good, and so we pray, "confident that if the Creator sees that good would be served by a positive response, he will have ordered accordingly events that may otherwise have no 'causal connection' (in the scientific sense) with the action of praying."[26] Consequently, "there is no inconsistency between recognizing an event as an answer to prayer and recognizing that it was predictable by others—even if the prediction could have been validly made by them (though not by you) before the prayer was offered."[27]

Prayer as seeking the kingdom in fellowship with God our Father. In teaching his disciples about prayer, Jesus stressed their relationship to God as their Father in heaven. In prayer we seek to find the proper balance between our awe before the God who is absolutely sovereign Lord of his creation and our intimate fellowship with our loving heavenly Father. These two aspects are wonderfully brought together in the comfort of knowing that the Father who cares for us is the sovereign Lord who controls all things and leads them toward the consummation of his purposes in the world. Prayer is a means that God has provided for us to be involved in establishing his rule in the world. It is also a way through which we grow in our personal knowledge of God and our love for him. As we learn to desire above all else the coming of God's kingdom and the doing of his will in the world, our prayer for daily needs and for forgiveness is subsumed under the overall quest for God's glory. Prayer becomes a natural activity in our lives, an ongoing conversation with God, through which we acknowledge our dependence upon him for everything that we need and, yet, also participate in the establishment of God's will through our petitions. It is in prayer that we become "willing agents of God's purpose" rather than the "unwitting instruments" that we would be if we did not consciously seek to obey and serve God.[28]

The framework that Jesus provided to us in his model prayer establishes an important criterion for our requests. We are encouraged to ask God for the little but necessary details of our lives but to do so in such a way that these things are not ends in themselves but are part of what is needed for us to work for God's kingdom and will. Thus Roger Hazelton encourages us: "Let there be no limit to what we take to God in prayer, so that there may be no limit to God's reign and rule in all of life. It is far better to ask God for whatever we desire than to play God by deciding on our own what we ought to pray for. That would simply be pious magic all over again, wanting to control God by praying only for the right things in a way that is sure to get results. God himself will be the judge; ours is the task of putting everything up to him."[29]

In an earlier time John Porteous addressed the question whether we should pray for good weather for a picnic and wisely advised his readers to

> have some sense of proportion even in our prayers. . . . Yet it does not follow
> at all that my picnic is too small a thing to be within the providential care. Bad
> weather, meaning discomfort, upset of arrangements, chills, loss of work, and
> other ills, may be serious enough. It is quite right and dutiful to pray about it,
> with the quiet assurance that God in the multitude of big concerns will not let

so small a thing escape His notice, but it is reverent to pray with a due recognition of what we might call the world-wide responsibilities of God, as well as the needs of our fellow-men, and with an entire willingness to accept disappointment, and even suffering, in the interests of the general scheme and larger whole, if it must be so. We are quite sure all the same, that God's providence, even in the matters of the picnic, will be real, effective and adequate.[30]

The function of prayer within the personal relationship that we have with God is nicely described by H. H. Farmer, who suggests that petition is the heart of prayer as "the expression of a genuinely personal relationship with God."[31] Here the duality between an I and a Thou is preserved. Farmer notes a common objection that prayer is superfluous since God already purposes good, but he replies that "the divine purpose may be such that petitionary prayer is indispensable to its realisation."[32] Against the further objection that petitionary prayer is presumptuous, Farmer argues that, on the contrary, because the end God is seeking is personal, such personal responses must be included. After all, the "essence of a personal relationship is precisely . . . that one will acts differently from what it would otherwise act because it meets another will."[33] I believe that my model of providence, which includes a responsiveness in God's planning of his own action, gives room for precisely this reciprocal relationship. It is right for us to seek "the good things of life," provided that our petition "expresses the conviction that the will of God is directed to [our] succour in and through the circumstances of this present world."[34]

The benefit of corporate prayer. Within my model of providence, where God's sovereign control is absolute and predetermined, even if we satisfactorily explain the role of personal petition, it may seem peculiar that corporate prayer has additional value. If we are not changing God's mind by our praying, there is certainly nothing to be gained through a concentrated lobbying effort by a group of Christians who are agreed together about their requests. Yet Jesus does suggest that such agreement is valuable (Mt 18:19-20). My basic assumption is that this has to do with the efficacy of prayer according to God's will. When we have a consensus concerning the appropriate petition in a given situation, it may indicate that we are accurately discerning the promptings of the Spirit of God. Farmer offers another helpful suggestion, however, that has to do with this matter of our corporate seeking of the kingdom of God in growing fellowship with him.

Farmer proposes that the value and, possibly, an additional effectiveness of corporate prayer is "because such prayers are prayers of fellowship, prayers of the Church. They rest on, and carry the power of, at least a partial realisation of that to which all true prayer is directed, namely that membership one of another in the love of God, which is the kingdom."[35] Thus it is not simply an "addition sum," for "more people at prayer means more effectiveness in prayer only if it represents an extension and a deepening of fellowship, a passing of more personalities out of the lower and sinful status of isolation into the higher and redeemed status of loving co-operation in God for the high ends of His kingdom" (Mt 28:19).[36]

God's Providential Operation in the Physical World Makes Requests for Him to Work in Nature Legitimate Under Certain Conditions

In the church where my wife and I were married, and which she had attended for most of her life, Wednesday night was prayer meeting night. I can remember what used to happen when the Sunday school picnic was coming up on Saturday. Inevitably someone would suggest that we pray for good weather, and we would do so. The appropriateness of that prayer depends on the model of providence within which we operate. In the model that I have proposed, the prayer may be legitimate if certain conditions are fulfilled.

The validity of this prayer is based on a number of assumptions, although it is doubtful that these had been thought through by those who offered the petition. For starters, we have to recognize that our weather is part of a very complex system governed by high and low pressure situations, ocean currents and many other factors and that the weather we are now experiencing began to develop about eleven days beforehand. That raises the question of whether there is any point in praying about the weather on Saturday when that is just four days away or whether we should only pray for rain or sunshine if we can give God twelve days advance warning so that he can start to do something about it. The fact is that many urgent prayers are offered for safety well after a weather system has developed and the news is announcing an impending hurricane or tornado.[37]

Theological assumptions underlying our prayer for God's activity in "nature." These prayers are legitimated in my model by the following assumptions:

☐ What we call the "course of nature" is the usual providence of God, and it does not run on its own. In the poetic words of the psalmist, it is God "who makes the clouds rise at the end of the earth; he makes lightnings for the rain and brings out the wind from his storehouses" (Ps 135:7). Job's friend Elihu was mistaken in the application of his doctrine of providence to Job's situation, but he was right in asserting God's intimate involvement in natural events. "For to the snow he says, 'Fall on the earth'; and the shower of rain, his heavy shower of rain, serves as a sign on everyone's hand, so that all whom he has made may know it" (Job 37:6-7). The weather system does not operate independently of God, it serves him. He established its order, and it operates within his providential control, which is so all-encompassing that he does not need to be doing constant interventions to accomplish his purposes or to answer prayer.

S. G. Hall has commented that it is widely taught that the "only point of praying to God for things is that it does something to the one who is praying. If you pray for the poor, it is not so that God will provide for their needs and relieve their poverty; that would be too much to expect." It is supposed that God does not "change the course of events because some people asked him." Hall opines that this is the reason that "we have stopped praying against bad weather, drought, flood, storm, and pestilence," since "those are all things we can do nothing about."[38] But Hall wisely dubs this perspective "illogical and seriously atheistic."

It is illogical because prayer of the kind that is asking God to change us so that we can change things in the world "does not in fact get rid of the difficulty that it perceives." If we ask God to still a storm or stop a drought, we are asking him to "interfere" with natural processes. "But that is no less true if you ask him to make you more generous. Your generosity, like every virtue you possess and every thought of holiness, is fixed in microcircuits in your brain cells. To ask God, to expect him, to alter your brain is just as much an interference with the natural order as stilling a storm." The attitude is atheistic because it "assumes that we are ourselves free to change our attitudes, our behaviour, and hence to act differently in the world and change it in ways large and small. It allows God no such freedom. He can only act by our leave, at our consent."[39] In praying for God to act in nature, therefore, we are granting him the sovereign freedom within his creation that is truly his as Creator and Lord.

☐ God's foreknowledge makes it possible for God to answer the prayers of his people even when those prayers have been offered too late for an answer to be effected without miraculous intervention. God knows the future, and he knew ahead of time, for instance, that we would pray for rain tomorrow or for sunshine on Saturday. He started to answer that prayer even before we prayed it.[40] Perhaps this is what God is talking about when he says through Isaiah (Is 65:24): "Before they call I will answer, while they are yet speaking I will hear."[41]

When we hear reports of Christians gathered after a time of drought and earnestly praying for rain, which comes even while they pray, we can accept that as a response from God and give thanks both for the rain and for the answered prayer. We need not decide whether the answer was a "miracle" or whether it was something that God had prepared beforehand to happen only after their prayer. Whether by normal or unusual providence, God has met our need in answer to our petitions, and we give him thanks. This would still be true even if a meteorologist later postulated that the rain was on its way and that it would have rained at that time whether or not anyone had prayed. Given God's role in nature, such a statement is beyond the meteorologist's expertise within the scope of his observation. He can say what "would have happened," and he may be able to discern quite accurately the "natural" causes involved, but the hand of God's providence in the matter is invisible to his technology, and hence so is the role of Christians at prayer.

Prayer for miracles. Particularly important in regard to our prayer concerning things in the natural world is the position we described concerning miracles in God's special providence. Because we believe that God is in control of his creation and that he is able to act differently than he usually does (i.e., "supernaturally"), we are able to ask God to do the miraculous when we believe that it may conform to what we understand of his purposes in the world and that it would bring him glory. When opportunities are given for prayer requests in an evangelical gathering, I am always struck by the large percentage of requests that have to do with physical healing. From one standpoint this is not surprising because we have biblical instruction to pray for the sick, and we have examples both in Scripture and in our experience of people who were healed dramatically and in ways that mystify medical science. From another perspective, it is a significant indication of firm Christian faith in the biblical teaching concerning God's providential ability, since our experience of miraculous organic healing is extremely rare, even in churches that make the most radical statements about God's healing power.

This is another instance in which we do well not to draw too sharp a line between God's normal and his unusual providence. In praying for the sick, we are acknowledging that our bodies are "fearfully and wonderfully made" by God and that even when we treat our bodies wisely and remain healthy, we ought to be thankful to God for that health. We know of the amazing health-maintaining and restorative "powers" that God supports in sustaining our lives. We grant, therefore, that it is not a large thing to God whether he overcomes illness in our physical systems through "natural" processes such as the steady but gradual healing of a wound or whether he does something "supernatural" such as the dramatic removal of a tumor.

Efforts have been made to demonstrate the healing power of prayer, and a recent article reports that "there is a growing body of evidence that suggests prayer can be an effective tool for combating illness and disease."[42] However, none of it has provided us with evidence supporting Christian faith in the triune God as the true and living One. Siang-Yang Tan points out that the landmark study done by Randolph Byrd "showed a benefit gained through prayer," but it "did not establish the superiority of prayer to the God of the Bible since no control groups were used in which the help of other deities were sought."[43] Albert Ellis, president of the Institute for Rational Emotive Therapy, is typical of the critics of the healing powers of prayer. He believes that patients get better after praying or having been prayed for "because faith bolsters their immune system, not because a personal God actually intervenes."[44]

I would argue that we should not put much trust in the apologetic value of these experiments in prayer for the sick precisely because of the model of divine providence I have offered. The studies indicate that any form of prayer is beneficial to health and that prayer by a supportive community is even more so. However, our confidence when we pray for the sick is not in the power of prayer, it is in the power of God. When we pray, God remains sovereign, and we rarely know that healing is God's will in a particular instance so that we must almost always pray that God will heal if he wills to do so. Neither the faith of the sick person nor the faith of the intercessors provides a guarantee that God will heal. Consequently, it is impossible to demonstrate in experimental fashion that Christian prayer has "healing power."[45] At most such a study can show that some people are healed by God when Christians have prayed for them, but we must also grant that people have been healed when shamans or Muslims have prayed for them. Strange as it seems, within God's providential control, the demonic powers also appear to have been given the ability to effect physical healing on occasion. On the other hand, there is no reason to doubt that, in some instances where prayer has been offered ignorantly to someone other than the God who revealed himself in Jesus, God still answers those prayers. He may do this as part of his gracious drawing of people to himself or simply out of the same benevolence that sends rain on the fields of the wicked.

Given God's Providential Rule in the History of the World, We May Ask Him to Act Even When Other Beings Are Genuine Agents in the Situation

With the unprecedented access to information that we have these days, we are very aware of the many troubled areas of the world. We know that it is not God's will that populations should be oppressed by corrupt governments or that citizens should kill one another in orgies of tribal and ethnic hatred. We are particularly disturbed when these situations bring suffering to Christ's church and when its members are specifically the target of discrimination and persecution. Given our knowledge of the world situation, we know of more kings and leaders upon whose authority the peace depends than Paul could have imagined when he instructed Timothy that prayer should be offered for such individuals (1 Tim 2:2). The general harmony and universal well-being (shalom) that we look forward to and long for, in God's kingdom, is the cry of our hearts. But here we face difficulties that we do not encounter when we pray for blessings in the physical world. What God does in that area is amazing, but in some ways it is comparatively simple because clouds and tumors do not have wills of their own. God can remove a brain tumor without getting any cooperation from the tumor, but the same is not the case when we ask him to bring peace to Yugoslavia or other trouble spots where the war goes on because people make it happen, because there is ethnic pride and suspicion and hatred, and because there is greed and hunger for power.

James described the situation very clearly: "Those conflicts and disputes among you, where did they come from? Do they not come from your cravings that are at war within you? You want something and do not have it; so you commit murder. And you covet something and cannot obtain it; so you engage in disputes and conflicts" (Jas 4:1-2). This is what is going on in many areas of the world, but what do we expect God to do about it? Indeed what *can* God do about it, given that decisions in the situation are being made by human beings? It is here that the issue of the nature of human free agency and the options open to God, given his creation of human wills, becomes critical.

I have stated my own conviction that God is in control of what happens in human history. In the big picture, things turn out in history according to

God's plan and purpose (cf. Ps 33:8-11; Is 14:24-27; 46:8-11; Dan 4:25-26, 35; Acts 17:26), but God accomplishes his purposes in history without forcing human wills. He persuades, but he does not coerce. In their sinful rebellion against God, the rulers of nations are greedy, oppressive of their own people, proud and aggressive toward other nations. God does not stir these rulers up to go to war against others; he does not have to because that is their inclination unless the Spirit of God transforms their hearts. Yet as Calvin has so well argued, God is not powerless in the face of this sin in human hearts.

On the one hand, the Spirit of God is always and everywhere at work. God works directly, immediately and mysteriously in the minds of people. He can prompt them with good thoughts; he can stimulate within them a fear of doing things that would incur his wrath. He convinces people of their sin, of his righteousness, of the sureness of his judgment. So people act freely, but they act within the boundaries of God's overall control. This was clearly the framework of the early church's doctrine of providence as they reflected upon the crucifixion of Jesus. Praying after the release of the apostles from prison, they acknowledged to God that "both Herod and Pontius Pilate, with the Gentiles and the peoples of Israel, gathered together against your holy servant Jesus, whom you anointed, to do whatever your hand and your plan had predestined to take place" (Acts 4:27-28).

As we pray for the holders of power in the world, we should therefore pray confidently, hopefully rather than despairingly, remembering that the situation is not out of control. God still rules in the kingdoms of the world. He establishes their boundaries. He sets up rulers and puts them down. He determines the length of their lives and of their rule. Consequently, we can pray about these difficult situations with the confidence that God is in control and that he is able to work good in them and through them.

In this area, as in many others, it is difficult for us to pray precisely "according to God's will" because we only know what God reveals to us about what he is doing in the world when he tells us, and he has not done this very often. It is difficult for us to know what exactly God is planning and accomplishing in a given situation. On the other hand, God has revealed to us the basic outline of what he wants for his world in his law and in the instructions of the prophets, in the teaching of Jesus and of the apostles. We know that he desires justice between people in a society, between employers and employees, between the rulers and the governed and between nations. God wants peace, for people to live in harmony with one another and with the rest of creation. He wants a society in which the poor are cared for, where mercy is shown to the defenseless and the needy. He desires a society in which people are free to worship God and to grow into what he wants them to be in the world. We can assume that God wants these things in every society. Ultimately, when God overcomes all his enemies and establishes his kingdom, it will be that kind of kingdom. So we can ask God to bring that situation about in the troubled parts of the world today.

Given the model of God's working that I have proposed, we can pray for the victory of God's gracious persuasion in the minds of those who rule. We can pray for the spread of the gospel in societies and that God will work directly on the hearts and minds of rulers, giving them impulses to do good, a desire for justice and mercy toward those whom they govern. God can send them good advisors and encourage them to take that good advice. He can restrain them externally in various ways. He can limit their health or even their lives. He can "use" Satan to send them bad advisors, with lying spirits, as he did Ahab, causing them to make bad, self-destructive decisions (1 Kings 22:19-23). Or he can restrain Satan who is also at work influencing rulers to do evil (Dan 10:13).

We may also pray for God's providential work in the circumstances of other nations, economies and so forth, which can affect the situation where the trouble is going on. In our shrinking world, nations are more interrelated than ever, and God is able to do things in one nation through the actions of another. We do not always know how best to bring about a desirable situation, through strategies of economic embargo, mediation, armed peacemaking and so on, but God can give wisdom to other rulers too, and he can providentially assist them in their efforts.

We live in God's world, and he has not abdicated his government of it. Things are not out of control, and God will not indefinitely allow evil to flourish. In the meantime God is calling out a people for his name from all over the world, in and through some of the most difficult situations. He invites us to join in the work, through prayer for kings and all in authority so that God's people "may lead a quiet and peaceable life in all godliness and dignity" (1 Tim 2:2).

God Has a Special Providential Interest in the Lives of His Children

As I listen to students in theology classes, it intrigues me that there is so often a discrepancy between their convictions regarding providence and concerning salvation. I have taught in environments where most of my students were not of Augustinian or Calvinist convictions in regard to salvation. In that regard, I encounter a widespread commitment to libertarian free will; if election is viewed as referring to individuals, it is characteristically assumed to be conditioned upon God's foreknowledge of human faith. Peculiarly, the situation changes when it comes to God's providence in the details of their daily lives. They do not want to live in a world where God's ability to protect and care for them is significantly limited by his having given creatures libertarian freedom. When they walk down a dark street at night, they want to believe that God is protecting them and that evil people who could do them harm are not operating outside of God's control. Likewise, when reflecting on situations in which they or other Christians have been the victims of evil, they often acknowledge that this happened within God's providential control or his "permission." Things did not get out of his hands. This general trust in God's providential government of the world is also reflected in their prayers for safety and provision of their needs. (In fact, when it comes to prayer, there is frequently a similar inconsistency between their theology of salvation and their petitions for the unsaved, but that is a matter for a different book.)

It is in the area of our daily lives as God's people that the model of providence proposed in the previous chapter offers the greatest encouragement and comfort and also where it is likely to inform Christian prayer most specifically. My model posits that the God who rules in creation and history has a special interest in the needs of his children. This is one of the blessings that comes to us through our relationship with God as his own treasured people. It is what theologians often describe as God's "special providence," and the passage most often quoted in this regard is Romans 8:28-29.

As I read that text, I hear Paul assure us that God is always at work in every situation of the lives of those who love God. He has our good constantly in mind, and the greatest good of all is the work that God is doing in our lives to make us like Jesus. In Matthew 6:25-34 Jesus urges us not to worry because worry does no good but, more importantly, because God knows what we need, and we are more important to him than the birds and flowers he takes care of. Yet bad things happen to God's children. We have no guarantees of health and wealth in this fallen world because God does not protect his children from all of the effects of other peoples' sinfulness or even of the brokenness of the world that brings sickness and natural disasters. God can and does protect us from evil circumstances on many occasions, probably more than we are even aware of. But on other occasions God allows bad things to happen to us because he plans to bring about good through them. We have cited Joseph as a prime exhibit of this truth. It is painful to consider, but sometimes God allows bad things to happen to us as part of our education. He may not protect us from the consequences of actions we take that are foolish or wrong because we need to learn by our mistakes. That too is a good that God allows to occur. Or these difficulties may be disciplinary, part of our learning of obedience through the things that we suffer (Heb 5:8) or bringing us back to God when we have wandered away (Heb 12:5-11). Given my proposal that there is an economy of God's special interventions, I believe that sometimes bad things happen because it is a sinful world and God does not intervene but chooses rather to work with this evil to bring about good further along the way. There is a limit to how often or how dramatically God can act in the form of special interventions without making the world so unpredictable that normal human planning would be impossible.

A doctrine of providence that thanks God for protection must also factor God into the situation when protection does *not* occur. In this regard, Maurice Wiles is correct (in the semi-deist model) that we must either include both the good and the evil in our reckoning concerning God's providence or that we should include neither.

Taking all these things into account, I believe that we should pray for *all* the things we need, considering them part of the "daily bread" for which Jesus instructed us to petition. It is true that God knows what we need, but he loves to hear us acknowledge our dependence upon him and to give us things that we ask him for. As we have noted earlier, God can give us good things even when we do not ask. But when we ask, he has the additional joy of answering, and we are led to be more consciously thankful. Furthermore, believing that prayer is one of the means God has ordained to be effective in the world, we can assume that some goods will not be experienced without prayer, even though we are unable to identify when prayer or its absence has been the critical factor in the obtaining of or lack of some good thing. James warns us that one reason we do not have what we want is that we do not ask God for it (Jas 4:2)

It is precisely because of God's loving control of all the events of our lives that Paul urges us to be thankful in all circumstances (1 Thess 5:18).

This does not mean that we never feel the pain of the harm that befalls us in a sinful world, but we trust God in the midst of it, and we entrust ourselves to him to accomplish his good purposes in our lives and in the life of the world.

The Case Study

Gail Wellwood was the last to pray that evening when the major focus of the group's prayer at Fred Henderson's church had been the abduction of Richard and the other missionaries. As Gail prepared her thoughts, she recalled that, in planning the history of the world, God foreknew the circumstances that would have developed on the day that the missionaries were abducted if all factors prior to that point had been as they were. In that plan God had options. He could have influenced situations prior to that day to bring about a different set of circumstances. That approach would have required the least "intervention" at the moment of the crisis. Or God could have let the situation develop but then acted to keep the missionaries safe. This could have been done in many ways. God could have warned the missionaries of the danger so that they could escape (as he did Joseph and Mary when the life of Jesus was in danger from Herod). He could have prevented the guerrillas from accomplishing their intended abduction by causing things in the natural world that would foil their plans, or he could suggest to their minds ideas that would deter them from their plan. In short, God's control was not curtailed significantly, even though his creatures were morally responsible agents with wills of their own.

Given all these factors in the situation of God's providence, Gail was confident that the abduction had taken place within God's purpose, although she could not know what it was, specifically, that God was intending to do. Because Gail had no revelation to the contrary, she assumed that God willed the physical safety and the spiritual growth of the missionaries and that he desired the salvation of the abductors, that he wanted the church to grow and desired peace and justice to prevail in the society. Gail realized that God might not be graciously inclined toward the guerrillas at this time. He might just be allowing their own wickedness to bring upon them the consequences of their wrong decisions. God might even have some disciplinary purpose in mind for the missionaries. But while these were possibilities, Gail did not know this to be the case, and so she assumed that God's intention was gracious.

Gail was also confident that God was able to do what would most result in his own glorification and that what he actually did would be good and wise. She could pray with the firm conviction that her prayers mattered and that they would be effective instruments in the spiritual struggle that is going on in the world and in the ultimate achievement of God's wise purposes for the history of the world. She wanted to be sensitive to the leading of the Spirit as she prayed, but she was careful not to speak as though she understood what God was about when this had not been made plain to them.

When Gail had talked about God's providence with the others in her church, they had sometimes suggested that there was really no point in Gail making requests of God. If everything had already been planned by God and the future was already fixed in God's foreknowledge, then what was the point of asking God to do something now, except that the exercise made her feel better. Sandra Buxton (church dominion model), in particular, had made this point to Gail. Sandra believed that God had committed himself not to do many things that he could do unless he was asked to do them by his church, so that the church could develop in its exercise of the dominion that God had given to humankind when he created them in his image. Gail respected Sandra and appreciated her fervency in intercession, but she rejected the proposal that her own model of providence made petitionary prayer meaningless.

Gail was aware that, if they had been able to talk about the situation for which they were praying, Oliver (openness model) would tell her that her prayer could not change things for Richard Henderson. Oliver knew that Gail believed that all of the details of history were already fixed in God's eternal plan. So it looked to Oliver as though nothing Gail prayed or did not pray could make any difference to the situation of the abducted missionaries. God didn't only know what was going to happen, as Tom (redemptive intervention model) believed, he had actually decided what would happen. If God's mind was made up and the outcome was already fixed, there did not seem to Oliver to be any point in asking God to do things now. But Gail contended that this complaint about the lack of a significant place for prayer made sense in regard to Ahmed Kalil's understanding of providence (fatalistic model) but not to her own. She argued that God had not only decided what would happen but *how* it would come about. Included among the factors contributing to the occurrence of events in the world was petitionary prayer and God's action in response to it.

It was here that Gail believed her model to be more helpful than Peter Vandervelde's (Calvinist model) because God's middle knowledge gave

God the opportunity to foresee what prayer would arise from the complexity of people's personal being, in particular situations, and then to decide how he would respond to those prayers. In this way God could genuinely *respond* to prayer. If God only had simple foreknowledge, response would be impossible, but with middle knowledge God could know what prayers would be offered by people and could determine how he would respond to them. Of course, his control of the situation was secured by the fact that it was God who determined which of all those possible situations would come about through the actions and interactions of both physical entities and spontaneously free moral creatures.

So Gail approached her prayer for the missionaries in need with a confidence that her prayer would make a difference in the situation. It would not change God's mind or prompt him to do something that he would not otherwise have done, but it was a potentially significant part of the whole complex event that also included God's action. Gail believed that God had already decided what he was going to do but that he had factored into that decision her own prayer. Consequently, she had a sense of being heard by God, and she anticipated the time when they would be able to look back on the event and thank God for what he had done, including his answer to their prayers. Gail knew that God could do what he wanted without their prayer, but he had chosen not to. He had chosen to involve them in his ministry in this way and determined that there were some things he would not do without their prayer. Gail realized that she would never be able to say that something would not have happened if she had not prayed (as Sandra believes), but she did have a keen sense that whether or not she prayed had significance to the final outcome.

Gail was the last to pray that evening: "Dear Father, each of us has brought to you our concern for Richard and his two colleagues and for all the people who are affected by this terrible thing that has happened to them. We thank you for inviting us to pray and promising to hear and answer the cries of your children. We don't all agree about what you are able to do in this situation or how our prayer will affect the outcome, but you know the desires of our hearts and you work through us, even with our limited understanding. I thank you, Lord, for being the almighty God whose will is done in all the earth. But this does not mean that everything you permit is good, although you have the power to bring good out of it, particularly for those who love you and whom you have called according to your gracious purpose.

"From our perspective, what has happened is both wrong and dangerous, but at least it has not taken you by surprise. You knew what the guerrillas were planning, and you knew what it would take to change their plans or to prevent them from realizing their intentions. So we accept your wisdom in having allowed this particular situation to develop. We pray for the guerrillas, that you will restrain their evil intentions and use this time with the missionaries as a means of softening their abductors' hearts toward you. We do want to see justice done for the tribal people, and although we do not approve of their methods, we ask that you will work in the situation for good in this regard. Father, please strengthen and encourage Richard and his friends. Give them a sense of your nearness and a confidence in your control of the situation. Give them wisdom in dealing with their captors. Lord, please comfort their families and give them peace. Help those who are involved in negotiation with the guerrillas. Please give them wisdom and open the hearts of the guerrilla leaders to a peaceful solution. Their hearts are in your hand, as are the hearts of all human authorities, so please do your persuasive work in their minds. You know how they would respond to particular initiatives, and so we ask you to direct the thoughts and efforts of those who are seeking resolution.

"Father, we know that the adversary is constantly at work, trying to hinder the spread of the gospel and to frustrate your rule in the world. Please foil his evil efforts in this situation. Your ways are frequently hidden from us, Lord, but we want to be sensitive to your Spirit and discerning of your will. If there are things that we should be doing, please prompt us to do them. Thank you for promising that you would hear and answer our prayers when we ask according to your will. We are not entirely sure what you want in this situation, but I am assuming that the things for which I have prayed are in accordance with your gracious purposes. Thank you for the peace that comes when we commit ourselves and this situation into your care and submit to your perfect will. May your name be magnified through this event and may it contribute to the advancement of your kingdom on earth. In Jesus' name we ask. Amen."

Epilogue

The Lord God omnipotent reigns. We live in that confidence and in the awesome awareness that he has chosen to give us significant agency within his creation. Prayer is one of the means that God has given us to be workers together with him in bringing about God's perfect rule. To him alone be glory.

Appendix

A Comparative Chart of the Eleven Models

	Semi-Deist	Process	Openness	Church Dominion	Redemptive Intervention	Molinist
God's experience of time	?	temporal	temporal	timeless (?)	could be either	timeless
God knows the actual future totally	No	No	No	?	Yes	Yes
God knows counterfactuals	No	No	No	No	No	Yes
God takes a risk in creation	Yes	Yes	Yes	Yes	Yes	Yes
God specifically permits all evils	No	No	No	No	No, only generally	Yes, in choosing this world
Human freedom is	libertarian	libertarian	libertarian	libertarian	libertarian	libertarian
Prayer affects the outcome	No	Yes	Yes	Yes	Yes	Yes
Prayer changes God's mind	No	Yes	Yes	Yes	influenced the plan but does not change it now	No

	Thomist	Barthian	Middle Knowledge Calvinist	Calvinist	Fatalist
God's experience of time	timeless	timeless	probably temporal	timeless	temporal (?)
God knows the actual future totally	Yes	Yes	Yes	Yes	Yes
God knows counterfactuals	No	No	Yes	No	there are none
God takes a risk in creation	No	No	No	No	No
God specifically permits all evils	Yes	Yes	Yes	Yes	No, but brings them about
Human freedom is	libertarian	volitional	volitional	volitional	illusory
Prayer affects the outcome	Yes	Yes	Yes	Yes	No
Prayer changes God's mind	No	No	No	No	No

Glossary

compatibilism: Compatibilism contends that a person can act freely even though that action is determined by God. To the compatibilist, actions are free if the actors do them voluntarily, spontaneously or willingly, without coercion by anything outside of themselves, even though their action may be predictable as an expression of their own desires.

conditional election: Conditional election is the thesis that God has chosen individuals to salvation based upon their action (i.e., faith), which he has foreseen. Thus God has chosen to salvation those whom he foreknew would believe.

contingent causes: Contingent causes are those factors upon which an effect depends for its coming to be but particularly those that are not certain or are not directly determined by God.

contracausal: An event is contracausal if its occurrence was not necessitated by any of its precedents. "Contracausal freedom" is the sort of freedom people have if they are free to act differently than they act even though all the causative factors influencing them remain exactly the same.

corporate election: Corporate election posits that God has established and revealed the conditions by which individuals can be saved and has chosen the communities made up of the individuals who meet these conditions, namely, Israel and the church. God does not decide which individuals are part of the group that is saved, but he has elected the group to salvation. Thus the true church is elect, but those who are part of the church have not been individually chosen to salvation by God.

counterfactuals: Events that do not in fact occur but that *would* occur if the circumstances were different are counterfactuals. They are hypothetical but true, as hypotheses about what would pertain in a given situation if it were realized, although this particular situation never actually occurs.

decretive will of God: The decretive will of God is the decision by God that an event should happen. The actual production of those events may be by the exclusive action of God (as in initial creation) or it may include the actions of others (as in most of human history). The models disagree about how comprehensive God's decree is. The term is used particularly within the Calvinist model, to identify events that will surely occur because God has purposed that they should (cf. "moral will" and "permissive will").

deism: In the seventeenth and eighteenth centuries, deism presented a picture of God as detached from the world that he created. The term is commonly used to denote a theology in which God functions like "an absentee landlord" or like a "watchmaker" who does not need to be active to keep the watch running once he has made the whole mechanism.

determinism: In the *scientific* sense, determinism is the theory that each event is necessarily as it is because of the factors or events that precede it. *Theological* determinism believes that events are as they are because God has determined they should be so. There is an ongoing controversy between compatibilists and incompatibilists whether a human act can be both free on the part of the human actor and determined by God. (See also "hard determinism" and "soft determinism.")

efficient cause: The efficient cause is the immediate agent in the production of an effect.

final cause: The end or purpose of a process is called the final cause in Aristotelian philosophy and theologies that use it, such as Thomism.

general providence: General providence is the way that God normally works within and usually through his creation. It is often described as the natural order because of its visible regularity that makes scientific study possible.

hard determinism: Hard determinism, as contrasted with "soft determinism," is mechanistic in its assumption that an event is completely the product of the preceding state so that the idea that the event was brought about by someone's will is completely illusory.

impetratory prayer: To impetrate is to ask for or to entreat, but it is particularly used to speak of *obtaining* by request or entreaty. The term "impetratory prayer" is generally used in the stronger sense, to describe prayer that is successful in getting what is asked for, where the receiving of what was requested is considered a response to the request. It may, therefore, be contrasted with the term "petitionary prayer," which indicates that a request has been made but does not indicate that the request was granted.

incompatibilism: Incompatibilism insists that people do not act freely if their action is determined by God even if they act willingly. It posits that genuine freedom must be libertarian and indeterminate.

indeterminism: In the theological sense, indeterminism is the belief that most, if not all, events are determined neither by God nor by the preceding factors. All other things being equal, the event could have been different than it actually was if the intelligent agents involved had chosen to act differently.

individual election: Individual election (by contrast with "corporate election") posits that God has chosen which individuals will be saved, whether conditionally or unconditionally.

libertarian freedom: Libertarian freedom is the state of freedom in which there is a real possibility that one could make at least two different choices in exactly the same circumstances, both external and internal. It is frequently referred to as the "power of contrary choice" and is the type of freedom affirmed by "incompatibilists."

middle knowledge: The term "middle knowledge" is most often associated with Luis de Molina, who asserted that God has three kinds of knowledge. I use the term in this book to speak more generally of knowledge concerning what *would* happen if the circumstances were different than they actually are.

moral will of God: The moral will of God is all that he commands his creatures to do. They may disobey him so that God's will, in this sense, is not always done.

necessary cause: If a particular effect could not occur without a particular cause, then that cause is described as a necessary cause.

panentheism: Panentheism is the belief that God is intimately *in* everything in a much stronger sense than is generally affirmed by the classical Christian doctrine of divine immanence. It is not, however, to be confused with "pantheism," which is the belief that everything *is* God.

permissive will of God: The permissive will of God is the decision of God to permit things to occur but not to be the one who actually brings them about.

petitionary prayer: Petitionary prayer is prayer that makes requests to God.

power of contrary choice: The power of contrary choice is the ability to have done something other than one actually did in exactly the same circumstances. Everything else being equal, one has the ability to choose at least two courses of action.

second cause: Assuming God to be the first or primary agent at work in bringing about a particular effect, a second cause is an agent other than God that also has a role in bringing about that effect.

soft determinism: Essentially the same thing as compatibilism, soft determinism affirms that everything is determined by God, but it denies that this can be understood in regard to moral creatures in a mechanistic fashion analogous to the form of determinism that may occur in the physical world.

special providence: Special providence is God's action in creation that departs from his usual way of sustaining the natural order. It is usually redemptive, and it may be spoken of as divine intervention because of its relative infrequency by comparison with the way God usually works (i.e., his general providence). Miracles are a particular form of special providence.

simple foreknowledge: Simple foreknowledge is prescience or precognition, that is, knowing for certain what will occur before it happens. Simple foreknowledge includes a knowledge of the one future that will actually happen but not knowledge of the other possibilities that might have occurred if circumstances were different.

sufficient cause: A sufficient cause is one that is adequate to account for the effect that came about. Whatever other causes may actually have been involved, the event would have occurred even if this had been the only cause at work in the situation. On the other hand, it is not a "necessary cause" because the same effect could have been brought about by other causes.

theodicy: Theodicy is the attempt to justify God in the face of evil.

unconditional election: Unconditional election posits that God has chosen particular individuals to salvation as an act of his own free will rather than on the basis of some foreseen act (e.g., faith or perseverance) by those individuals. Having chosen them, he graciously gives them the necessary means of salvation.

Notes

Chapter 1: Introduction

[1]Langdon B. Gilkey, "The Concept of Providence in Contemporary Theology," *JR* 43, no. 3 (July 1963): 171.

[2]Ibid.

[3]While appreciating Gilkey's astute analysis of the state of the doctrine of providence in this century, Charles Cashdollar demonstrates that "the debates and attacks on the doctrine reach back into the nineteenth century with more vigor and substance than might be inferred from his article." "The Social Implications of the Doctrine of Divine Providence: A Nineteenth-Century Debate in American Theology," *HTR* 71, no. 3-4 (July-October 1978): 265-84.

[4]Cashdollar, "Social Implications," p. 282.

[5]Gilkey, "Concept of Providence," p. 172.

[6]Ibid., pp. 173-74.

[7]Ibid., p. 174.

[8]Jonathan Tucker Boyd, "If We Ever Needed the Lord Before," *Books and Culture* (May-June 1999): 41.

[9]Langdon B. Gilkey, *Reaping the Whirlwind: A Christian Interpretation of History* (New York: Seabury, 1976).

[10]John Polkinghorne, *Science and Providence: God's Interaction with the World* (London: SPCK, 1989), p. 5.

[11]Ibid.

[12]Frederick Ferré, "Mapping the Logic of Models in Science and Theology" in *New Essays on Religious Language*, ed. Dallas M. High (New York: Oxford University Press, 1969), p. 75.

[13]Sallie McFague, *Models of God: Theology for an Ecological, Nuclear Age* (London: SCM Press, 1987), p. 34.

[14]Ferré, "Mapping the Logic," p. 88.

[15]Ibid.

[16]Ibid., p. 91.

[17]Ibid., p. 88.

[18]Paul Helm, *The Providence of God*, Contours of Christian Theology (Downers Grove, Ill.: InterVarsity Press, 1993), pp. 32-34.

[19]Ian G. Barbour, *Issues in Science and Religion* (New York: Prentice-Hall, 1966; reprint, New York: Harper & Row, 1971), p. iii.

[20]This particular story is fictional, but most readers will know of real-life situations just like it.

Chapter 2: The Semi-Deist Model

[1]Maurice Wiles, *God's Action in the World: The Bampton Lectures for 1986* (London: SCM Press, 1986), pp. 1-2.

[2]Ibid., p. 1.

[3]Nancey Murphy, "Of Miracles," *CTNSB* 10, no. 2 (spring 1990): 16.

[4]Maurice Wiles, "Divine Action: Some Moral Considerations," in *The God Who Acts: Philosophical and Theological Explorations,* ed. Thomas F. Tracy (University Park: Pennsylvania State University Press, 1994), p. 21.

[5]Stanislaus Grabowski, however, thinks that this was probably the attitude of many church fathers before Augustine and that Augustine may himself be deistic on occasion. (*The All-Present God* [St Louis: St. Louis University Press, 1954], p. 152; cited by Stephen Bilynskyj, "What in the World Is God Doing?" in *The Logic of Rational Theism: Exploratory Essays,* ed. William Lane Craig and Mark S. McLeod Lewiston [New York: Edwin Mellen Press, 1990], p. 158.)

[6]Bilynskyj, "What in the World," p. 158.

[7]Ian G. Barbour, *Issues in Science and Religion* (New York: Prentice-Hall, 1966; reprint, New York: Harper & Row, 1971), p. 61.

[8]Georges De Schrijver, "Religion and Cosmology at the End of the 20th Century," *CTNSB* 14, no. 1 (winter 1994): 10.

[9]Bilynskyj, "What in the World," pp. 155-68.

[10]Ibid., p. 167.

[11]Ibid., p. 168.

[12]Gordon D. Kaufman, "On the Meaning of 'Act of God,'" *HTR* 61, no. 2 (April 1968): 175.

[13]Ibid.

[14]Ibid., p. 177.

[15]Ibid., pp. 177-78.

[16]Ibid., p. 178.

[17]Ibid., p. 180.

[18]Ibid., p. 187.

[19]Ibid., p. 183.

[20]Ibid., p. 184.

[21]Ibid., p. 187.

[22]Ibid., p. 188.

[23]Ibid., p. 190.

[24]Ibid., p. 191.

[25]Ibid.

[26]Ibid., p. 192.

[27]Ibid.

[28]Ibid., p. 196.

[29]Ibid., p. 198.

[30]Benjamin Wirt Farley, *The Providence of God* (Grand Rapids, Mich.: Baker, 1988), p. 210.

[31]Ibid.

[32]Ibid.

[33]Kaufman, "On the Meaning," p. 200.

[34]Ibid.

[35]Wiles, *God's Action,* pp. 28, 96.

[36]Ibid., p. 25.

[37]Ibid., p. 28.

[38]Ibid., pp. 96-97.

[39]Ibid., p. 51.

[40]Ibid., p. 52.

[41]Ibid., p. 60.

[42]Ibid., p. 62.

[43]Ibid.

[44]Ibid., p. 64.

[45]Ibid.

[46]Ibid.

[47]Ibid., pp. 66-67.

[48]Ibid., p. 66.

[49]Ibid., p. 69.

[50]Wiles, "Divine Action," p. 26.

[51]Wiles, *God's Action,* p. 76.

[52]Ibid., p. 81.

[53]Ibid., p. 83.

[54]Ibid., p. 85.

[55]David Brown, *The Divine Trinity* (London: Duckworth, 1985), p. x. Cited in Wiles, *God's Action,* p. 85.

[56]Wiles, *God's Action,* p. 89.

[57]Ibid., p. 90.

[58]Ibid., p. 91.

[59]Ibid., p. 92. Cf. also Wiles, "Divine Action," p. 28.

[60]Ibid., p. 93.

[61]Ibid., p. 97.

[62]Ibid.

[63]Ibid., p. 98.

[64]Ibid.

[65]T. J. Gorringe, *God's Theatre: A Theology of Providence* (London: SCM Press, 1991), p. 15.

[66]Wiles, *God's Action,* p. 99.

[67]Ibid.

[68]*On Prayer,* pp. 3, 5; cited in Wiles, *God's Action,* p. 100.

[69]S. G. Hall, "The Prayer of the Church: What We Ask and How We Ask It," *ExpTim* 96, no. 3 (December 1984): 76.

[70]Cited in Wiles, *God's Action,* p. 100.

[71]Ibid., p. 101.

[72]Ibid.

[73]Ibid., p. 102.

[74]Ibid., p. 103.

[75]Ibid., p. 104.

[76]Ibid.

[77]Ibid., p. 105.

[78]Ibid.

[79]Ibid., pp. 107-8.

[80]John Polkinghorne, *Science and Providence: God's Interaction with the World* (London: SPCK, 1989), p. 6.

[81]Richard Sturch, *The New Deism: Divine Intervention and the Human Condition* (Bristol, U.K.: Bristol, 1990), p. 3.

[82]Ibid.

[83]Wiles, *God's Action,* p. 2.

[84]Tom Harpur, *The Uncommon Touch: An Investigation of Spiritual Healing* (Toronto: McClelland and Stewart, 1994).

[85]Ibid., p. 187.

[86]Ibid.

[87]Ibid., pp. 187-88.

[88]Ibid., p. 188.

[89]Ibid., pp. 188-89.

[90]Larry Dossey, *Recovering the Soul: A Scientific and Spiritual Search* (New York: Bantam, 1989), p. 44, cited in Harpur, *Uncommon Touch,* p. 189.

[91]Harpur, *Uncommon Touch,* pp. 189-90.

[92]Paul N. Duckro and Philip R. Magaletta, "The Effect of Prayer on Physical Health: Experimental Evidence," *JRHealth* 33, no. 3 (fall 1994): 216.

[93]Ibid., p. 218.

Chapter 3: The Process Model

[1]John B. Cobb and David Ray Griffin, *Process Theology: An Introductory Exposition* (Philadelphia: Westminster Press, 1976), p. 50.

[2]Ibid., p. 49.

[3]Ibid., p. 50.

[4]Norman Pittenger, *God's Way with Men: A Study of the Relationship Between God and Man in Providence, "Miracle," and Prayer,* The Library of Practical Theology (London: Hodder & Stoughton, 1969), 23.

[5]Ibid.

[6]Ibid., citing Barth's *Church Dogmatics* (hereafter *CD*) III, *The Doctrine of Creation,* part 3, trans. G. W. Bromiley and R. Ehrlich, ed. G. W. Bromiley and T. F. Torrance (Edinburgh: T & T Clark, 1960), pp. 31, 118, 146-47.

[7]Barth, *CD* III/3, pp. 99-100.

[8]Cobb and Griffin, *Process Theology,* p. 51.

[9]Citing *Jesus Christ and Mythology* (New York: Charles Scribner's Sons, 1958), p. 65.

[10]Citing *Kerygma and Myth,* ed. Hans Werner Bartsch, trans. Reginald Fuller (London: SPCK, 1953), p. 197.

[11]Ibid.

[12]Cobb and Griffin, *Process Theology,* p. 51.

[13]Ibid., p. 52.

[14]Ibid.

[15]Charles Hartshorne, *The Divine Relativity: A Social Conception of God* (New Haven, Conn.: Yale University Press, 1948), p. 41. Cited in Anna Case-Winters, *God's Power: Traditional Understandings and Contemporary Challenges* (Louisville: Westminster John Knox, 1990), p. 132.

[16]Cobb and Griffin, *Process Theology,* p. 47.

[17]Ibid.

[18]Ibid., p. 48.

[19]Pittenger, *God's Way with Men,* p. 39.

[20]Norman Pittenger, *Process-Thought and Christian Faith* (Digswell Place, U.K.: James Nisbet & Co., 1968), pp. 12-13.

[21]Speaking of the "lure of the future," one is reminded of the important work of Wolfhart Pannenberg, though he will not emerge significantly as a representative of any of the models that are developed in this study. I have some sympathy with the suggestion that "the crucial ideas in Pannenberg's work are more at home in the setting of process theology than anywhere else" (David McKenzie, "Pannenberg on God and Freedom," *JR* 60, no. 3 [July 1980]: 326 n. 51), and Lewis Ford has made a similar suggestion in "A Whiteheadian Basis for Pan-

nenberg's Theology," *Encounter* 38 (1977): 307-17. It would be misleading, however, to reference Pannenberg's work in the exposition of this model because his own proposal of the working of God from the future is quite different from that of theologians who consciously identify themselves with Process thought.

[22]Pittenger, *Process-Thought* , p. 13.

[23]Ibid., pp. 14-15.

[24]Ibid., p. 15.

[25]Ibid.

[26]Ibid., p. 16.

[27]Ibid., p. 44.

[28]Ibid.

[29]Ibid., pp. 44-45.

[30]Ibid., pp. 20-21.

[31]A. N. Whitehead, *Process and Reality* (Cambridge: Cambridge University Press, 1927-1928), p. 521. Cited by Pittenger, *Process-Thought,* p. 26.

[32]Pittenger, *Process-Thought,* p. 27.

[33]Ibid.

[34]Ibid., pp. 21-22.

[35]Ibid., p. 28.

[36]Ibid., p. 29.

[37]Ibid., p. 40.

[38]Lewis S. Ford, "Divine Persuasion and the Triumph of the Good," in *Process Philosophy and Christian Thought,* ed. Delwin Brown, Ralph James, and Gene Reeves (New York: Bobbs-Merrill Co., 1971), excerpted in Peter C. Hodgson, and Robert H. King, eds., *Readings in Christian Theology* (London: SPCK, 1985), p. 137.

[39]Ibid., p. 138.

[40]Cobb and Griffin, *Process Theology,* p. 28.

[41]Pittenger, *God's Way with Men,* pp. 32-33.

[42]Cobb and Griffin, *Process Theology,* p. 28.

[43]Pittenger, *Process-Thought,* p. 46.

[44]Ford, "Divine Persuasion," pp. 138-39.

[45]Ibid., pp. 140-41.

[46]Pittenger, *Process-Thought,* p. 33.

[47]Ibid., p. 49.

[48]Ibid., p. 34.

[49]Hartshorne, *Divine Relativity,* p. x.

[50]Pittenger, *God's Way with Men,* p. 50.

[51]Ibid., pp. 50-53.

[52]Ibid., p. 73.

[53]Ibid., pp. 68-69.

[54]Pittenger, *Process-Thought,* pp. 29-30.

[55]Cobb and Griffin, *Process Theology,* p. 20.

[56]Ibid., p. 16.

[57]Case-Winters, *God's Power,* p. 139.

[58]Pittenger, *Process-Thought,* p. 41.

[59]Cobb and Griffin, *Process Theology,* p. 26.

[60]Pittenger, *God's Way with Men,* p. 117.

[61]Ibid., p. 120.

[62]Ibid.

[63]Cited from *Reality as Social Process* (Glencoe, Ill.: Free Press, 1953), p. 107, in Ian G. Barbour, *Issues in Science and Religion* (New York: Prentice-Hall, 1966; reprint, New York: Harper & Row, 1971), p. 445.

[64]Barbour, *Issues in Science*, p. 445.

[65]Ibid.

[66]Pittenger, *Process-Thought*, p. 42.

[67]Pittenger, *God's Way with Men*, p. 130.

[68]Ibid., p. 129.

[69]Cited from "To Pray or Not to Pray: A Confession" (Nashville: Upper Room, 1974), p. 18, in Phillip Allen Cooley, "Selected Models of the God-World Relationship in Twentieth Century Theology: Implications for a Contemporary Doctrine of Providence" (Ph.D. dissertation, Southern Baptist Theological Seminary, December 1981), p. 143.

[70]Cooley, "Selected Models," p. 143.

[71]David Basinger, *Divine Power in Process Theism: A Philosophical Critique,* SUNY Series in Philosophy (Albany: State University of New York Press, 1988), p. 85.

[72]Basinger, *Divine Power,* p. 90, drawing on Marjorie Suchocki, "A Process Theology of Prayer," *AJTP* 2 (May 1981): 39.

[73]Basinger, *Divine Power,* p. 91.

[74]Pittenger, *God's Way with Men,* p. 23.

[75]Ibid., p. 146.

[76]Ibid., p. 147.

[77]Hartshorne, *Divine Relativity,* p. 51.

[78]Case-Winters, *God's Power,* pp. 144-45.

[79]Pittenger, *God's Way with Men,* p. 150.

[80]Ibid., p. 152.

[81]Ibid.

[82]Ibid., pp. 153-54.

[83]Ibid., p. 154.

[84]Ibid.

[85]Ibid., pp. 156-57.

[86]Ibid., p. 158.

[87]Ibid., p. 159.

[88]Ibid., p. 160.

Chapter 4: The Openness Model (1)

[1]John Polkinghorne, *Science and Providence: God's Interaction with the World* (London: SPCK, 1989), p. 6. This is a book that was stimulated by Maurice Wiles's Bampton Lectures, which were cited as representative of the semi-deist model.

[2]For example, according to William Hasker's definition of libertarian or incompatibilist freedom, "an agent is free with respect to a given action at a given time if at that time it is within the agent's power to perform the action and also in the agent's power to refrain from the action." By contrast, the compatibilist believes that "an agent is free with respect to a given action at a given time if at that time it is true that the agent can perform the action if she decides to perform it and she can refrain from the action if she decides not to perform it" (in Clark Pinnock, Richard Rice, John Sanders, William Hasker and David Basinger, *The Openness of God: A Biblical Challenge to the Traditional Understanding of God* [Downers Grove, Ill.: InterVarsity Press, 1994], pp. 136-37).

[3]Clark Pinnock, Richard Rice, John Sanders, William Hasker and David Basinger, *The Openness of God: A Biblical Challenge to the Traditional Understanding of God* (Downers Grove, Ill.: InterVarsity Press, 1994).

[4]William Hasker, "The Openness of God," *CSR* 28, no. 1 (fall 1998): 111.

[5]For example, by Millard J. Erickson, in a chapter entitled "Free Will Theism," under the general heading "Challenges to the Traditional Understanding of God," *God the Father Almighty: A Contemporary Exploration of the Divine Attributes* (Grand Rapids, Mich.: Baker, 1998), chap. 4.

[6]Norman Geisler, *Creating God in the Image of Man? The New "Open" View of God: Neotheism's Dangerous Drift* (Minneapolis: Bethany House, 1997).

[7]David Basinger, *The Case for Freewill Theism: A Philosophical Assessment* (Downers Grove, Ill.: InterVarsity Press, 1996), p. 55.

[8]John Sanders's work *The God Who Risks: A Theology of Providence* (Downers Grove, Ill.: InterVarsity Press, 1998) was published after my manuscript was substantially written. He has drawn heavily on many of the people whom I have cited in this chapter, but his own name is referenced less often than would probably have been the case if his book had appeared before I wrote this section. He has presented us with the most complete case for the openness model of providence from a thoroughly evangelical perspective.

[9]Marcel Sarot, "Omnipotence and Self-Limitation," in *Christian Faith and Philosophical Theology: Essays in Honour of Vincent Brümmer Presented on The Occasion of The Twenty-fifth Anniversary of His Professorship in The Philosophy of Religion in The University of Utrecht*, ed. Gijsbert van den Brink, Luco J. van den Brom and Marcel Sarot (Kampen, The Netherlands: Kok Pharos, 1992), pp. 176-77.

[10]Ibid., p. 174.

[11]In "The Concept of God After Auschwitz: A Jewish Voice," *JR* 69 (1987): 109-10, cited in Sarot, "Omnipotence and Self-Limitation," p. 175.

[12]Sarot, "Omnipotence and Self-Limitation," pp. 178-82.

[13]Keith Ward, *Rational Theology and the Creativity of God* (Oxford: Basil Blackwell, 1982), p. 123.

[14]Peter Baelz, *Does God Answer Prayer?* (London: Darton, Longman & Todd, 1982), p. 26.

[15]Ibid.

[16]Ibid., p. 28.

[17]Polkinghorne, *Science and Providence*, p. 52.

[18]Vincent Brümmer, *What Are We Doing When We Pray? A Philosophical Enquiry* (London: SCM Press, 1984), p. 67.

[19]Ibid., pp. 67-68.

[20]Peter R. Baelz, *Prayer and Providence: A Background Study. The Hulsean Lectures for 1966* (London: SCM Press, 1968), p. 68.

[21]Polkinghorne, *Science and Providence*, p. 66.

[22]Ibid., p. 67.

[23]Baelz, *Prayer and Providence*, p. 69.

[24]Polkinghorne, *Science and Providence*, p. 32.

[25]Ward, *Rational Theology*, p. 208.

[26]Ibid.

[27]Ibid., p. 209.

[28]Brümmer, *When We Pray*, p. 68.

[29]Ibid.

[30]Baelz, *Prayer and Providence*, p. 66.

[31]T. J. Gorringe, *God's Theatre: A Theology of Providence* (London: SCM Press, 1991), p. 106.

[32]Polkinghorne, *Science and Providence,* p. 84.

[33]Richard Rice, *God's Foreknowledge and Man's Free Will,* rev. ed. (Minneapolis: Bethany House, 1985), p. 73.

[34]In John Feinberg, Norman Geisler, Bruce Reichenbach and Clark Pinnock, *Predestination and Free Will: Four Views of Divine Sovereignty and Human Freedom,* ed. David Basinger and Randall Basinger (Downers Grove, Ill.: InterVarsity Press, 1986), p. 146.

[35]Hendrikus Berkhof, *Christian Faith: An Introduction to the Study of the Faith,* trans. Sierd Woudstra, rev. ed. (Nijkerk, The Netherlands: Uitgeverij G. F. Callenbach B. V., 1985; trans., Grand Rapids, Mich.: Eerdmans, 1986), p. 141.

[36]Ibid., p. 223.

[37]David Bartholomew, *God of Chance* (London: SCM Press, 1984), pp. 14-15.

[38]Ibid., p. 67.

[39]Ibid., p. 68-75.

[40]Ibid., p. 95.

[41]Ibid., p. 102.

[42]Ibid., p. 107.

[43]Ibid., p. 141.

[44]Richard Rice, in Pinnock et al., *Openness of God,* p. 17.

[45]Ibid., p. 26.

[46]Ward, *Rational Theology,* p. 151.

[47]Ibid.

[48]Ibid., p. 161.

[49]Brümmer, *When We Pray,* p. 35, citing Origen *Treatise on Prayer* V.6.

[50]Ibid., p. 40.

[51]Rice, *God's Foreknowledge,* p. 63.

[52]Ibid., pp. 64-68.

[53]Ibid., p. 70.

[54]Ibid., p. 73.

[55]Terence E. Fretheim, "The Repentance of God: A Key to Evaluating Old Testament God-Talk," *HBT* 10, no. 1 (June 1988): 59.

[56]Rice, in Pinnock et al., *Openness of God,* p. 27.

[57]Ibid., p. 28.

[58]Polkinghorne, *Science and Providence,* p. 79.

[59]Rice, in Pinnock et al., *Openness of God,* p. 28.

[60]Fretheim, "Repentance of God," p. 61.

[61]Aristotle *Physics* 4.2.220a25.

[62]Cited by Ward, *Rational Theology,* p. 150.

[63]Ward, *Rational Theology,* p. 163.

[64]Ibid., p. 164.

[65]Ibid., p. 166.

[66]Ibid., p. 169.

[67]Ibid.

[68]Ibid., p. 42.

[69]Ibid.

[70]Richard Swinburne, *The Christian God* (Oxford: Clarendon Press, 1994), p. 140.

[71]Brümmer, *When We Pray,* p. 41. In regard to knowledge concerning true propositions, Richard Swinburne states this point succinctly: "If humans are sometimes free in the sense that

sometimes their choice at a time as to how they will act is not determined by any prior cause (nor does reason make it inevitable how they will act), then they are sometimes in a position to make false any belief that some person has about how they will act. Whatever proposition I believe in advance about what you will do, if you act freely in this sense, you have it in your power to make my belief false. Hence no one can be guaranteed to have true beliefs in advance about the actions of free agents" (*The Christian God* [Oxford: Clarendon Press, 1994], p. 131).

[72]Ibid., p. 42.

[73]J. R. Lucas, *The Future: An Essay on God, Temporality and Truth* (Oxford: Basil Blackwell, 1989), p. 227.

[74]Swinburne, *Christian God,* p. 132.

[75]Ibid., p. 134.

[76]Ibid.

[77]Bartholomew, *God of Chance,* p. 148.

[78]As Swinburne puts it, God's omniscience must be defined "not as knowledge at each period of time, of all true propositions, but as knowledge of all propositions that it is logically possible that he entertain then and that, if entertained by God then, are true, and that it is logically possible for God to know them without the possibility of error" (*Christian God,* p. 133).

[79]Rice, *God's Foreknowledge,* p. 56; citing 1 Sam 16:7; Ps 94:11; 139:2-4; Mt 10:30; Heb 4:2.

[80]Brümmer, *When We Pray,* pp. 43-44.

[81]Polkinghorne, *Science and Providence,* p. 78.

[82]Ibid., p. 79.

[83]Ward, *Rational Theology,* p. 131.

[84]Brümmer, *When We Pray,* p. 44.

[85]Rice, *God's Foreknowledge,* p. 59.

[86]Ward, *Rational Theology,* p. 163.

[87]Rice, in Pinnock et al., *Openness of God,* p. 53.

[88]Hence Norman Geisler's criticism of Clark Pinnock's position: "If God cannot know the future for sure, then even traditional Arminianism is impossible, for Arminians believe predestination is based on infallible foreknowledge of our free choice. So, in the historic sense, if Pinnock's view of God is right, then he cannot even be an Arminian!" (in John Feinberg et al., *Predestination and Free Will,* p. 170).

[89]Rice, *God's Foreknowledge,* p. 85.

[90]Rice, in Pinnock et al., *Openness of God,* p. 44.

[91]Rice, *God's Foreknowledge,* pp. 85-87.

[92]Ibid., p. 87.

[93]Ibid., p. 91.

[94]Ibid., p. 93.

[95]Rice, in Pinnock et al., *Openness of God,* p. 55.

[96]Ibid., p. 55.

[97]Ward, *Rational Theology,* p. 131.

[98]Ibid.

[99]Polkinghorne, *Science and Providence,* p. 79.

[100]Rice, *God's Foreknowledge,* p. 77.

[101]Rice, in Pinnock et al., *Openness of God,* p. 51.

[102]Sanders, *God Who Risks,* p. 137.

[103]Rice, *God's Foreknowledge,* pp. 77-81.

[104]Hasker, "Openness of God," p. 121.

[105]Ibid.

[106]Sanders, *God Who Risks,* p. 195.

[107]Ibid.

[108]Fretheim, "Repentance of God," pp. 65-66.

[109]Lucas, *Future,* p. 224.

[110]Rice, *God's Foreknowledge,* p. 95.

[111]Ibid., p. 96.

[112]Michael J. Langford, *Providence* (London: SCM Press, 1981), pp. 100-101.

[113]Rice, in Pinnock et al., *Openness of God,* p. 52.

Chapter 5: The Openness Model (2)

[1]John Polkinghorne, *Science and Providence: God's Interaction with the World* (London: SPCK, 1989), p. 6.

[2]Vincent Brümmer, *What Are We Doing When We Pray? A Philosophical Enquiry* (London: SCM Press, 1984), p. 65.

[3]Ibid., p. 66.

[4]Ibid.

[5]Ibid.

[6]Ibid., p. 91.

[7]Ibid.

[8]Peter R. Baelz, *Does God Answer Prayer?* (London: Darton, Longman & Todd, 1982), p. 34.

[9]Ibid., p. 35.

[10]Ibid.

[11]Ibid.

[12]Ibid., p. 36.

[13]Polkinghorne, *Science and Providence,* p. 33.

[14]Ibid., p. 34.

[15]John Polkinghorne, "Can a Scientist Pray?" *Col* 26, no. 1 (1994): 4.

[16]Ibid.

[17]Polkinghorne references J. Gleick, *Chaos* (London: Heinemann, 1988), p. 8, for this notion. John Polkinghorne, "A Note on Chaotic Dynamics," *SCB* 1, no. 2 (1989): 125.

[18]Polkinghorne, "Can a Scientist Pray?" p. 7.

[19]William G. Pollard, *Chance and Providence: God's Action in a World Governed by Scientific Law* (London: Faber & Faber, 1959).

[20]David J. Bartholomew, *God of Chance* (London: SCM Press, 1984), p. 139.

[21]Ibid., p. 140.

[22]Keith Ward, *Divine Action* (London: Collins, 1990), p. 140.

[23]Ibid., p. 143.

[24]Ibid., p. 145.

[25]Ibid., pp. 145-46.

[26]Ibid., p. 153.

[27]Ibid.

[28]Baelz, *Does God Answer?* p. 36.

[29]Brümmer, *When We Pray,* p. 61. Cf. also Ward, *Divine Action,* p. 171: "such exceptions must be rare. From the point of view of the structure, they will be anomalies which can be safely ignored in setting up the 'laws' which govern the working of the system."

[30]Brümmer, *When We Pray,* p. 61.

[31]Ward, *Divine Action,* p. 172.

[32]Ibid., p. 178.

[33]Ibid., p. 180.

[34]Polkinghorne, *Science and Providence,* p. 51; referring particularly to Mt 11:2-6. On another occasion, he defined a miracle as "an unexpected providence in an unprecedented circumstance" ("God's Action in the World: 1990 J. K. Russell Fellowship Lecture," *CTNSB* 10, no. 2 [spring 1990]: 7).

[35]Brümmer, *When We Pray,* p. 63.

[36]Ibid., p. 64.

[37]Ibid.

[38]Ward, *Divine Action,* p. 75.

[39]Ibid., p. 77.

[40]Ibid., p. 93.

[41]Ibid., p. 114.

[42]Ibid.

[43]Ibid., p. 115.

[44]Brümmer, *When We Pray,* p. 69.

[45]Polkinghorne, *Science and Providence,* p. 48.

[46]Ibid., p. 50.

[47]Ward, *Divine Action,* p. 183.

[48]Ibid., pp. 185-86.

[49]Polkinghorne, *Science and Providence,* p. 41; citing Vernon White, *The Fall of a Sparrow: The Concept of Special Divine Action* (Exeter, U.K.: Paternoster Press, 1985), p. 19.

[50]Polkinghorne, *Science and Providence,* p. 42.

[51]Ibid., p. 43.

[52]Nancey Murphy, "Of Miracles," *CTNSB* 10, no. 2 (spring 1990): 16.

[53]Gregory A. Boyd, *God at War: The Bible and Spiritual Conflict* (Downers Grove, Ill.: InterVarsity Press, 1997).

[54]Ibid., p. 13.

[55]Ibid., p. 14.

[56]Ibid., p. 19.

[57]Ibid., p. 20.

[58]Ibid.

[59]Ibid., p. 22.

[60]Ibid., p. 49.

[61]Ibid., p. 50.

[62]Ward, *Divine Action,* p. 160; citing Aquinas *Summa Theologica* 2a.2ae.83.2.

[63]Ward, *Divine Action,* p. 160. Polkinghorne suggests that the rationale offered by Aquinas makes prayer "a kind of spiritual exercise in providential pattern recognition" (*Science and Providence,* p. 70).

[64]Ward, *Divine Action,* pp. 160-61.

[65]Ibid., p. 164.

[66]Ibid., p. 169.

[67]Clark Pinnock, in John Feinberg, Norman Geisler, Bruce Reichenbach and Clark Pinnock, *Predestination and Free Will: Four Views of Divine Sovereignty and Human Freedom,* ed. David Basinger and Randall Basinger (Downers Grove, Ill.: InterVarsity Press, 1986), p. 152.

[68]Brümmer, *When We Pray,* p. 29.

[69]Ibid., p. 30.

[70]Ibid., p. 33.

[71]Ibid., p. 34.

[72]Hendrikus Berkhof, *Christian Faith: An Introduction to the Study of the Faith,* ed. and trans. Sierd Woudstra, rev. ed. (Nijkerk: The Netherlands: Uitgeverij G. F. Callenbach B. V., 1985; reprint, Grand Rapids, Mich.: Eerdmans, 1986), p. 499.

[73]John Lucas, *Freedom and Grace* (London: SPCK, 1976), p. 41.

[74]John Boykin, *The Gospel of Coincidence: Is God in Control?* (Grand Rapids, Mich.: Zondervan, 1986), p. 101.

[75]Ibid., p. 203.

[76]Ibid., p. 102.

[77]Ibid., p. 103.

[78]Ibid., p. 192.

[79]Peter R. Baelz, *Prayer and Providence: A Background Study. The Hulsean Lectures for 1966* (London: SCM Press, 1968).

[80]Ibid., p. 110.

[81]Baelz, *Does God Answer?* p. 43.

[82]Berkhof, *Christian Faith,* p. 497.

[83]Ibid.

[84]Richard Rice, in Clark Pinnock, Richard Rice, John Sanders, William Hasker and David Basinger, *The Openness of God: A Biblical Challenge to the Traditional Understanding of God* (Downers Grove, Ill.: InterVarsity Press, 1994), p. 163.

[85]Ibid., pp. 164-65.

[86]Ibid., p. 168.

[87]Ibid., p. 166.

[88]H. D. McDonald, *The God Who Responds: How the Creator Relates to His Creation* (Cambridge: James Clarke & Co. Ltd., 1986), p. 116.

[89]Ward, *Divine Action,* p. 169.

[90]Brümmer, *When We Pray,* p. 40.

[91]Ibid., p. 45.

[92]Ibid., p. 47.

[93]Ward, *Divine Action,* p. 162.

[94]Ibid.

[95]Berkhof, *Christian Faith,* pp. 450-51.

[96]Ibid., p. 494.

[97]Brümmer, *When We Pray,* p. 57.

[98]Ibid.

[99]Ibid., p. 69.

[100]Ibid., p. 58.

[101]Ibid., p. 69.

[102]Ibid., p. 70.

[103]Baelz, *Prayer and Providence,* p. 116.

[104]Ibid.

[105]Brümmer, *When We Pray,* p. 72.

[106]In A. Alhonsaari, *Prayer: An Analysis of Theological Terminology* (Helsinki: Kirjapaino Tamo, 1973), pp. 47-48; cited by Brümmer, *When We Pray,* p. 72.

[107]Brümmer, *When We Pray,* p. 72.

[108]Lucas asserts: "Our wanting something does give it some value in the eyes of God," *Freedom and Grace,* p. 41.

[109]Polkinghorne, "Can a Scientist Pray?" p. 9.

[110]Lucas, *Freedom and Grace,* p. 38.

[111]Ibid., p. 34.

[112]Ibid., p. 230.

[113]John Sanders, *The God Who Risks: A Theology of Providence* (Downers Grove, Ill.: InterVarsity Press, 1998), pp. 268-69.

[114]Ibid., p. 270.

[115]Ibid., p. 271.

[116]Ibid.

[117]Ibid., p. 272.

[118]Ibid., p. 273.

[119]McDonald, *God Who Responds,* p. 115.

[120]T. J. Gorringe, *God's Theatre: A Theology of Providence* (London: SCM Press, 1991), p. 78.

[121]Ibid., p. 80.

[122]Ibid., p. 91.

[123]Baelz, *Prayer and Providence,* p. 112.

[124]Ibid., p. 118.

[125]Baelz, *Does God Answer?* pp. 36-37.

[126]Polkinghorne, *Science and Providence,* p. 32.

[127]Ibid.

[128]Baelz, *Does God Answer?* p. 37.

[129]Ibid.

[130]Ibid.

[131]Baelz, *Does God Answer?* p. 51.

[132]Ibid.

[133]Polkinghorne, "Can a Scientist Pray?" p. 9.

[134]Ibid.

[135]John Polkinghorne, "Setting the Problem," *CTNSB* 10, no. 2 (spring 1990): 8. Ian Barbour believes that "Polkinghorne is much closer to process thought than he realizes, and that some of his criticisms of Whitehead and Hartshorne are based on dubious interpretations by other authors" ("Time and Eternity" *CTNSB* 10, no. 2 [spring 1990]: 26). Were Barbour correct, it might appear that Polkinghorne belongs in the previous chapter rather than this one. Barbour himself, however, notes that one very important difference exists between Polkinghorne's dipolar theism and Hartshorne's. For Polkinghorne, God's power is voluntarily self-limited, whereas the limitation is necessary rather than contingent in process thought. That significant difference is what places Polkinghorne legitimately in this chapter.

[136]Bartholomew, *God of Chance,* pp. 159-62.

[137]Ward, *Divine Action,* p. 165.

[138]Ibid., p. 166.

[139]Ibid.

Chapter 6: The Church Dominion Model

[1]Brother Andrew and Susan DeVore Williams, *And God Changed His Mind Because His People Prayed* (1990; reprint, London: Marshall Pickering, 1991), p. 11.

[2]Ibid., p. 12.

[3]Ibid., p. 20.

[4]Ibid., p. 14.

[5]Ibid., p. 22.

[6]Ibid., pp. 24-25.

[7]Ibid., p. 13.

[8]Ibid., p. 15.

[9]Nee To-Sheng (Watchman Nee), *What Shall This Man Do?* (London: Victory Press, 1961), p. 146.

[10]Ibid., p. 147.

[11]Ibid.

[12]Paul Billheimer, *Destined to Overcome* (Minneapolis: Bethany House, 1982; reprint, East-bourne, U.K.: Kingsway, 1982), p. 41.

[13]Ibid., p. 15.

[14]Ibid., p. 16. Cf. also Andrew and Williams, *God Changed His Mind,* p. 118.

[15]Ibid., p. 17.

[16]Ibid., p. 20.

[17]Ibid., pp. 21-22.

[18]Ibid., p. 23.

[19]Andrew, *And God Changed His Mind,* p. 169.

[20]Ibid., p. 170.

[21]Paul Billheimer, *Destined for the Throne* (London: Christian Literature Crusade, 1975), p. 26.

[22]Ibid., 41.

[23]Ibid., 47.

[24]Andrew and Williams, *And God Changed His Mind,* p. 13.

[25]Ibid.

[26]Ibid., p. 17.

[27]Nee To-Sheng (Watchman Nee), *Sit, Walk, Stand,* 4th ed. (Bombay: Gospel Literature Ser-vice, 1957; reprint, London: Victory Press, 1962), pp. 48-49.

[28]Ibid., p. 51.

[29]Ibid., p. 53.

[30]Nee, *What Shall This Man Do?* p. 148.

[31]Billheimer, *Destined to Overcome,* p. 25.

[32]Ibid., p. 26.

[33]Ibid., p. 27.

[34]Ibid., p. 42.

[35]Ibid., p. 44.

[36]Ibid., pp. 45-46.

[37]Ibid., p. 28.

[38]Ibid., p. 47.

[39]Billheimer, *Destined for the Throne,* p. 48.

[40]Ibid., p. 50.

[41]Ibid., p. 65.

[42]Ibid.

[43]Ibid.

[44]Andrew and Williams, *And God Changed His Mind,* p. 14, and Nee, *What Shall This Man Do?* p. 148.

[45]Nee, *What Shall This Man Do?* p. 148.

[46]Ibid.

[47]Ibid., p. 48.

[48]Nee, *Sit, Walk, Stand,* p. 57.

[49]Nee, *What Shall This Man Do?* p. 146.

[50]Ibid., p. 148.

[51]Ibid., p. 149.

[52]Ibid.

[53]Ibid., p. 49.

[54]Ibid., p. 50.

[55]Ibid., p. 55.

[56]Andrew and Williams, *God Changed His Mind,* p. 94.

[57]Ibid., pp. 100-101.

[58]Ibid., p. 29.

[59]Ibid., p. 35.

[60]Ibid., p. 40.

[61]Ibid., p. 42.

[62]Ibid.

[63]Ibid., pp. 54-56.

[64]Ibid., pp. 75-77.

[65]Ibid., p 77.

[66]Ibid., p. 90.

[67]Ibid., p. 105.

Chapter 7: The Redemptive Intervention Model

[1]John Feinberg, Norman Geisler, Bruce Reichenbach and Clark Pinnock, *Predestination and Free Will: Four Views of Divine Sovereignty and Human Freedom,* ed. David Basinger and Randall Basinger (Downers Grove, Ill.: InterVarsity Press, 1986), pp. 102-3.

[2]Ibid., p. 103-4.

[3]Ibid., p. 105-6.

[4]Ibid., p. 108-9.

[5]Ibid., p. 113.

[6]Ibid., p. 114.

[7]Ibid., p. 113.

[8]Ibid., p. 111.

[9]Ibid., p. 133.

[10]Ibid., p. 53.

[11]Ibid., p. 176.

[12]Ibid., p. 111.

[13]Ibid.

[14]Ibid., p. 50.

[15]Ibid., pp. 115-16.

[16]Ibid., p. 117.

[17]Ibid., p. 118.

[18]Ibid., p. 52.

[19]Jack Cottrell, *What the Bible Says About God the Ruler* (Joplin, Mo.: College Press, 1984), p. 194.

[20]Ibid.

[21]Ibid., pp. 223-24.

[22]Ibid., p. 29.

[23]Ibid., pp. 67, 84.

[24]Ibid., p. 77.

[25]Ibid., p. 83.

[26]Ibid., pp. 188-89.

[27]Ibid., p. 189.

[28]Ibid., pp. 215, 217.

[29]Ibid., p. 276.

[30]Citing Karl Barth, *CD* III, *The Doctrine of Creation,* part 3, trans. G. W. Bromiley and R. Ehrlich, ed. G. W. Bromiley and T. F. Torrance (Edinburgh: T & T Clark, 1960), p. 166.

[31]Cottrell, *What the Bible Says,* pp. 218-20.

[32]Ibid., p. 221.

[33]Ibid., p. 222.

[34]Ibid., p. 224.

[35]Ibid., p. 118.

[36]Ibid., p. 119.

[37]Ibid., p. 120.

[38]Ibid., p. 121.

[39]Ibid., p. 213.

[40]Ibid., p. 139.

[41]Ibid., p. 140.

[42]Ibid., p. 141.

[43]Ibid., p. 208.

[44]Ibid., p. 281.

[45]Ibid., p. 278.

[46]Ibid., pp. 214-15.

[47]Ibid., p. 225, citing L. S. Chafer, *Systematic Theology* (Dallas: Dallas Seminary Press, 1948), 1:230.

[48]Ibid., p. 226.

[49]Ibid., p. 283.

[50]Ibid., p. 96.

[51]Ibid., p. 99.

[52]Ibid., p. 106.

[53]Ibid., p. 277.

[54]Ibid., p. 107.

[55]Ibid., p. 109.

[56]Ibid., p. 112.

[57]Ibid., p. 114.

[58]Ibid., pp. 114, 195.

[59]Ibid., p. 158.

[60]Ibid., p. 142.

[61]Ibid., p. 143.

[62]Ibid., p. 144.

[63]Ibid., pp. 147-48.

[64]Ibid., p. 149.

[65]Ibid., p. 156.

[66]Ibid., p. 130.

[67]Ibid., pp. 134-35.

[68]Ibid., pp. 305-6.

[69]Ibid., pp. 312-13.

[70]Ibid., p. 195.

[71]Ibid., p. 196.

[72]Ibid., p. 139.

[73]Ibid., p. 278.

[74]Ibid., p. 276.

[75]Ibid., p. 197.

[76]Ibid., p. 200.

[77]Ibid., p. 202.

[78]Ibid., p. 203.

[79]Ibid.

[80]Ibid., p. 204.

[81]Ibid., pp. 206-7.

[82]Ibid., p. 208.

[83]Ibid., pp. 166-67.

[84]Ibid., pp. 237-43.

[85]Ibid., pp. 260-61.

[86]Ibid., pp. 253-54.

[87]Ibid., p. 261.

[88]Ibid., pp. 262-63.

[89]Ibid., p. 133.

[90]Ibid., p. 149.

[91]Ibid., p. 367.

[92]Ibid., p. 368.

[93]Ibid., p. 370. Here Cottrell cites a passage that makes this point, from Arthur Pink, *The Sovereignty of God,* rev. ed. (London: Banner of Truth Trust, 1961), p. 116.

[94]Ibid., p. 371.

[95]A. H. Strong, *Systematic Theology* (Valley Forge, Penn.: Judson Press, 1907), p. 434; cited by Cottrell, p. 374.

[96]Cottrell, *What the Bible Says,* p. 375.

[97]Ibid., p. 376.

Chapter 8: The Molinist Model

[1]William Hasker deems middle knowledge to be "almost certainly the strongest view of providence that is possible short of complete theological determinism" (William Hasker, *God, Time, and Knowledge* [Ithaca, N.Y.: Cornell University Press, 1989], p. 19).

[2]Barry E. Bryant, "Molina, Arminius, Plaifere, Goad, and Wesley on Human Free-Will, Divine Omniscience, and Middle Knowledge," *WesleyTJ* 27, no. 1-2 (spring-fall 1992): 93.

[3]Thomas P. Flint, "Two Accounts of Providence," in *Divine and Human Action: Essays in the Metaphysics of Theism,* ed. Thomas V. Morris (Ithaca, N.Y.: Cornell University Press, 1988), p. 148.

[4]William Lane Craig, *The Problem of Divine Foreknowledge and Future Contingents from Aristotle to Suarez,* Brill's Studies in Intellectual History 7 (New York: E. J. Brill, 1988), 219.

[5]Ibid. Maurice Wiles (whose views we examined under the semi-deist model) cites a similar idea from Gregory of Nyssa who said that God "does nothing without a reason." Consequently, when an infant dies, it is because God out of his love for the individual is withdrawing the material for evil; it is a matter of one, whose character is well-known to God through his foreknowledge, being allowed no time to display his true nature by the actual commission of wicked deeds when his propensity to evil would have had the opportunity to show itself" (*On the Deaths of New-Born Infants,* PG 46, 185c), cited in *God's Action in the World: The Bampton Lectures for 1986* (London: SCM Press, 1986), p. 72. The testimony to a

belief in middle knowledge is significant. Also of interest, however, is the comment of Wiles that "It is difficult to know whether the purported love to the individual or the eternal fore-knowledge of future vice is the more open to objection" (ibid., pp. 72-73).

[6]Indeed Karl Barth surmises that the purpose of Molinism was "to aid a new semi-Pelagian-ism to gain its necessary place and right in the new situation in opposition to the Augustin-ian-Thomist teaching of the Dominicans, which they accused of being dangerously near to Luther and Calvin" (Karl Barth, *CD* II, *The Doctrine of God,* part 1, trans. T. H. L. Parker, W. B. Johnson, Harold Knight and J. L. M. Haire, ed. G. W. Bromiley and T. F. Torrance [Edinburgh: T & T Clark, 1957], p. 569).

[7]C. D. Broad, "The Philosophical Implications of Foreknowledge," in *Knowledge and Fore-knowledge* (London: Harrison & Sons, 1937), p. 207; cited by William Lane Craig, *Divine Foreknowledge and Human Freedom: The Coherence of Theism: Omniscience* (Brill's Studies in Intellectual History, ed. A. J.Vanderjagt, no. 19. Leiden: E. J. Brill, 1991), p. 136.

[8]Craig, *Divine Foreknowledge,* p. 158.

[9]Ibid., p. 161.

[10]Ibid., p. 171.

[11]Ibid., p. 274.

[12]D. A. Carson, *Divine Sovereignty and Human Responsibility: Biblical Perspectives in Tension,* Marshalls Theological Library 7 (London: Marshall, Morgan and Scott, 1981), pp. 24-35.

[13]William Lane Craig, *The Only Wise God: The Compatibility of Divine Foreknowledge and Human Freedom* (Grand Rapids, Mich.: Baker, 1987), p. 45.

[14]Carson, *Divine Sovereignty,* pp. 18-22; Craig, *Only Wise God,* p. 45.

[15]Craig, *Only Wise God,* p. 45.

[16]Craig, *Divine Foreknowledge,* p. 237.

[17]Craig, *Only Wise God,* p. 129.

[18]Ibid.

[19]Morris, "Two Accounts," p. 157.

[20]Craig, *Only Wise God,* pp. 130-31.

[21]Ibid., pp. 22-23.

[22]Ibid., p. 24.

[23]Ibid.

[24]Ibid., p. 119.

[25]Ibid., pp. 56-59.

[26]Nelson Pike, "Divine Omniscience and Voluntary Action," *PhRev* 74 (1965): 27-46; also reproduced in *God, Foreknowledge, and Freedom,* ed. John Martin Fischer (Stanford, Calif.: Stanford University Press, 1989), pp. 57-73.

[27]Cited in Craig, *Divine Foreknowledge,* p. 25.

[28]Craig, *The Only Wise God,* p. 70.

[29]Ibid., pp. 73-74.

[30]Ibid., p. 128.

[31]Craig, *Divine Foreknowledge,* p. 42.

[32]Craig, *Only Wise God,* pp. 81-82.

[33]Craig, *Divine Foreknowledge,* pp. 90-91.

[34]Ibid., p. 93.

[35]Craig, *Only Wise God,* p. 121. This was also the understanding followed by Francisco Suarez (Craig, *Divine Foreknowledge,* p. 268).

[36]Craig, *Divine Foreknowledge,* p. 268.

[37]Ibid., p. 26.

[38]Cf. Francis J. Beckwith, "Limited Omniscience and the Test for a Prophet: A Brief Philosophical Analysis," *JETS* 36, no. 3 (September 1993): 357-62.

[39]Craig, *Only Wise God,* p. 28.

[40]Ibid., pp. 27-28.

[41]Ibid., p. 28

[42]Ibid., pp. 35-36.

[43]Ibid., p. 36.

[44]Ibid., p. 28

[45]Ibid., p. 32.

[46]Ibid., p. 33.

[47]Ibid.

[48]Ibid., p. 30.

[49]Ibid., p. 40.

[50]Ibid., pp. 40-41.

[51]Ibid., pp. 41-42.

[52]Ibid., pp. 42-43.

[53]Craig, *Only Wise God,* p. 131.

[54]Craig, *Divine Foreknowledge,* p. 242.

[55]Robert R. Cook, "God, Middle Knowledge and Alternative Worlds," *EvQ* 62 (1990): 299.

[56]Craig, *Only Wise God,* p. 137; cf. Craig, *Divine Foreknowledge,* p. 245.

[57]Bryant, "Molina, Arminius, Plaifere," pp. 96-101; Richard A. Muller, *God, Creation and Providence in the Thought of Jacob Arminius: Sources and Directions of Scholastic Protestantism in the Era of Early Orthodoxy* (Grand Rapids, Mich.: Baker, 1991), pp. 235-85.

[58]Cook, "God, Middle Knowledge," p. 299.

[59]Cited from D. Zohar, *Through the Time Barrier* (London: Paladin, 1983), pp. 34-35.

[60]Cook, "God, Middle Knowledge," p. 299.

[61]Lindsay Dewar, *Does God Care?* (London: Hodder & Stoughton, 1936), p. 61. Particular note is made of part 134 of vol. XLII of the *Proceedings* of the Society.

[62]Ibid., pp. 63-65.

[63]Craig, *The Only Wise God,* p. 140.

[64]Ibid., p. 141.

[65]Ibid., p. 147.

[66]Ibid., p. 148.

[67]S. T. Davis., ed. *Encountering Evil: Live Options in Theodicy* (Edinburgh: T & T Clark, 1982), pp. 80-81; cited by Cook, "God, Middle Knowledge," p. 303.

[68]Craig, *Only Wise God,* pp. 149-50.

[69]Ibid., pp. 150-51.

[70]Alvin C. Plantinga, *God, Freedom, and Evil* (1974; reprint, Grand Rapids, Mich.: Eerdmans, 1980), p. 30.

[71]Although not personally arguing for middle knowledge, William Hasker supports this criticism of simple foreknowledge. By the time God foreknows, it is "too late" for him to do anything about it. This would be true whether or not creatures have libertarian free will (*God, Time, and Knowledge*), pp. 53-62.

[72]Craig, *Divine Foreknowledge,* p. 244.

[73]*Concordia* 6.1.1; cited in Craig, *Divine Foreknowledge,* p. 200.

[74]Craig, *Only Wise God,* p. 134.

[75]Ibid., pp. 134-35.

[76]Ibid., p. 136.

[77]Ibid., p. 135.

[78]Craig, *Divine Foreknowledge,* p. 241.

[79]*Concordia* 4.53.3.17; cited in Craig, *Problem of Divine Foreknowledge,* pp. 200-201.

[80]*Concordia* 4.53.2.

[81]Ibid., 4.53.3.2.

[82]Craig, *Divine Foreknowledge,* p. 201; cf. *Concordia* 4.53.3.7.

[83]Craig, *Divine Foreknowledge,* p. 202.

[84]Craig, *Only Wise God,* p. 137.

[85]Craig, *Divine Foreknowledge,* p. 242.

[86]Craig, *Divine Foreknowledge,* p. 203.

[87]Craig, *Only Wise God,* pp. 136-37.

[88]Craig, *Divine Foreknowledge,* p. 204.

[89]"How Can I Turn the Tables in Witnessing?" Campus Crusade for Christ, Great Britain, booklet, p. 5; cited by Craig, *Only Wise God,* p. 138.

[90]Eleonore Stump, "Petitionary Prayer," *APQ* 16, no. 2 (April 1979): pp. 87-90.

[91]Michael J. Murray and Kurt Meyers, "Ask and It Will Be Given to You," *RelS* 30 (1994): 324.

[92]Ibid.

[93]Ibid., p. 330.

[94]Craig, *Only Wise God,* p. 137.

[95]Ibid., p. 87.

[96]Craig, *Divine Foreknowledge,* p. 96.

[97]Craig, *Only Wise God,* p. 88.

Chapter 9: The Thomist Model

[1]Clark Pinnock, Richard Rice, John Sanders, William Hasker and David Basinger, *The Openness of God: A Biblical Challenge to the Traditional Understanding of God* (Downers Grove, Ill.: InterVarsity Press, 1994), pp. 11-12.

[2]Norman Pittenger, *Process-Thought and Christian Faith* (Digswell Place, U.K.: James Nisbet & Co., 1968), p. 41.

[3]I have deliberately referred to Thomism rather than to the work of Thomas Aquinas, accepting the validity of an observation made by Thomas Flint. He was confident in presenting the position of Molina, but, of his exposition of Thomism, he would only say that it "can be confidently ascribed only to a large segment of Aquinas's intellectual heirs, not necessarily to their eponymous philosophical progenitor" (Thomas P. Flint, "Two Accounts of Providence," in *Divine and Human Action: Essays in the Metaphysics of Theism,* ed. Thomas V. Morris [Ithaca, N.Y.: Cornell University Press, 1988], p. 149). Given the massive literature on Aquinas and the disputes about what he really taught, this seems to be a wise course.

[4]Thomas Joseph Loughran, "Theological Compatibilism" (Ph.D. diss., University of Notre Dame, University Microfilms International, 1986), 1. Cf. Thomas Aquinas, *The Summa Theologica,* trans. The English Dominican Fathers (London: Burnes Oates & Washbourne, 1911-25), Ia, q.14, a.5; Ia, q.22, a.2. (Hereafter cited as *ST.*)

[5]Benjamin Wirt Farley, *The Providence of God* (Grand Rapids, Mich.: Baker, 1988), p. 124, citing Aristotle's *Nichomachean Ethics,* bk. 1, chap. 3.

[6]Ibid.

[7]Ibid., p. 127.

[8]Ibid., p. 128.

[9]Stephen Bilynskyj, "What in the World Is God Doing?" in *The Logic of Rational Theism: Exploratory Essays,* ed. William Lane Craig and Mark S. McLeod (Lewiston, N.Y.: Edwin

Mellen Press, 1990), p. 161, citing Aquinas, *On the Power of God* (Westminster, Md.: Newman, 1952), q.3, a.7, with emphasis supplied; cf. Aquinas: "The causality of God extends to all beings, not only as to the constituent principles of species, but also as to the individualizing principles," *ST,* Ia, q.22, a.2.

[10]Bilynskyj, "What in the World," p. 161.

[11]Ibid., p. 163.

[12]Farley, *Providence of God,* p. 128.

[13]Ian G. Barbour, *Issues in Science and Religion* (New York: Prentice-Hall, 1966; reprint, New York: Harper & Row, 1971), p. 426. Barbour's own account of neo-Thomism draws particularly on the work of Etienne Gilson and Reginald Garrigou-Lagrange.

[14]Farley, *Providence of God,* p. 129.

[15]Aquinas, *ST* Ia, q.22. a.4, cited by Barbour, *Issues in Science and Religion,* p. 426. See also q.19, a.4; and q.105, a.5.

[16]Reginald Garrigou-Lagrange, *Providence* [La Providence et la confiance en Dieu], trans. Bede Rose (London: B. Herder, 1937), pp. 162-66. As indication of its universality, he cites Wisdom 6:8; 8:1; 11:21; 12:13; 14:1-5; and Judith 9:3-17. Evidence of its infallibility is seen in Esther 13:9-17; 14:12-19; Prov 21:1; Is 14:24; and Ecclus 33:13. The end of providence is described in Ps 22:1-5; 24:4-7, 10; 30:1, 16, 17, 20; 32:4-5.

[17]Ibid., p. 168.

[18]Ibid., p. 200.

[19]Aquinas, *ST,* Ia, q.20, a.3, cited by Garrigou-Lagrange, *Providence,* p. 201.

[20]Garrigou-Lagrange, *Providence,* p. 201.

[21]Alan G. Padgett, *God, Eternity and the Nature of Time* (New York: St. Martin's Press, 1992), p. 19.

[22]Aquinas, *ST,* Ia, q.104, a.1.

[23]Padgett, *God, Eternity and the Nature,* p. 20.

[24]Aquinas, *ST,* Ia, q.104, a.3, ad 3, cited in ibid.

[25]Padgett, *God, Eternity and the Nature,* p. 20.

[26]Ibid., p. 21.

[27]Aquinas, *ST,* Ia, q.25, a.5.

[28]Ibid.

[29]Aquinas, *ST,* Ia, q.103, a.4, cited in Eleonore Stump, "Providence and the Problem of Evil," in *Christian Philosophy,* ed. Thomas P. Flint (Notre Dame, Ind.: University of Notre Dame Press, 1990), p. 58.

[30]Aquinas, *ST,* Ia, q.19, a.6.

[31]Stump, "Providence and the Problem of Evil," p. 58.

[32]Ibid., p. 59.

[33]Ibid., p. 60, referring to Aquinas, I *Sententiae* 46.1.1.

[34]Ibid. Emphasis supplied.

[35]Ibid., pp. 60-61, citing Aquinas, *De veritate,* q.23, a.2.

[36]Garrigou-Lagrange, *Providence,* p. 152, citing Aquinas, *ST,* Ia, q.19, a.11-12.

[37]Ibid., citing *ST,* Ia, q.19, a.11.

[38]Ibid., p. 153.

[39]Flint, "Two Accounts of Providence," p. 162.

[40]Ibid., p. 168.

[41]Ibid., p. 149. God's complete and perfect foreknowledge was also asserted by Vatican I (Heinrich Denzinger and Adolf Schonmetzer, eds., *Enchiridion symbolorum,* 23d ed. [Freiburg: Herder, 1963], nos. 3001, 3003), cited by Flint.

[42]Garrigou-Lagrange, *Providence,* p. 138.

[43]Ibid., p. 139.

[44]In this description, I am relying largely on Vincent Guagliardo's exposition of Aquinas's thought in *De Potentia,* q.6, a. 1 & 2, and *ST,* Ia, q.105, a.5-8, q.110, a.4, and q.114 ("Nature and Miracle," *CTNSB* 10, no. 2 [spring 1990]: 17-20).

[45]Guagliardo, "Nature and Miracle," p. 17.

[46]*De Potentia,* q.6, a.1, ad 1.

[47]Augustine, *On Free Will,* cited by Farley, *The Providence of God,* p. 101.

[48]Augustine, *City of God,* V, 9. Cf. Bartholomew R. De La Torre, *Thomas Buckingham and the Contingency of Futures: The Possibility of Human Freedom,* Publications in Medieval Studies, ed. Ralph Mcinerny, no. 25 (Notre Dame, Ind.: University of Notre Dame Press, 1987), p. 51.

[49]Farley, *The Providence of God,* p. 104, citing Augustine, *The City of God,* V, 8.

[50]Ibid., citing *City of God,* V, 9.

[51]Ibid., p. 105. For this, Farley commends Augustine.

[52]Loughran, "Theological Compatibilism," p. 2.

[53]Aquinas, *ST,* IIa, IIae, 83, 2, as cited by Vincent Brümmer, *What Are We Doing When We Pray? A Philosophical Enquiry* (London: SCM Press, 1984), p. 50.

[54]Loughran, "Theological Compatibilism," p. 2, referring to Aquinas, *ST,* Ia, IIae, q.9, a.6; q.10, a.2; q.17, a.1.

[55]Ibid., pp. 10-11, drawing upon Reginald Garrigou-Lagrange's interpretation of Thomism in *God: His Existence and His Nature,* trans. Dom Bede Rose (St. Louis: Herder, 1936), p. 297.

[56]Loughran, "Theological Compatibilism," p. 11.

[57]Ibid., p. 54, referring to Aquinas, *ST,* Ia, q.105, a.4; Ia, IIae, q.9, a.4, ad 1.

[58]Ibid., p. 54, referring to Aquinas, *De Potentia,* q.3, a.7.

[59]Garrigou-Lagrange, *Providence,* p. 161. Cf. Aquinas, *ST,* Ia, q.22, a.3.

[60]Flint, "Two Accounts of Providence, p. 174, citing a "classic statement" by Thomas Reid, *Essays on the Active Powers of the Human Mind* (Cambridge, Mass.: MIT Press, 1969), p. 259.

[61]Flint, "Two Accounts of Providence," p. 174.

[62]Ibid, p. 175.

[63]Aquinas, *ST,* Ia, q.105, a.5, ad 3.

[64]Loughran, "Theological Compatibilism," p. 219, cf. Aquinas, *ST,* Ia, IIae, q.6, a.1, ad 1.

[65]John Feinberg, Norman Geisler, Bruce Reichenbach and Clark Pinnock, *Predestination and Free Will: Four Views of Divine Sovereignty and Human Freedom,* ed. David Basinger and Randall Basinger (Downers Grove, Ill.: InterVarsity Press, 1986), p. 74.

[66]Ibid., pp. 74-75.

[67]Ibid., p. 132.

[68]This is Geisler's basic criticism of the contribution made by John Feinberg to the collection in which Geisler's essay is found. Feinberg's position appears under our treatment of the Calvinist model.

[69]Ibid., p. 46.

[70]Ibid.

[71]Ibid., p. 48. This is what Geisler believes Romans 7 to be teaching.

[72]Ibid., p. 76.

[73]Ibid., p. 78.

[74]Ibid., pp. 78-79.

[75]Ibid., p. 48.

[76]Ibid.

[77]Ibid., pp. 132-33.

[78]Barbour, *Issues in Science and Religion,* p. 427.

[79]Thomas Aquinas, *The Summa Contra Gentiles,* trans. The English Dominican Fathers (London: Burns Oates & Washbourne, 1923-29), III, 94 (referred to as *SCG,* in future citations).

[80]Richard Downey, *Divine Providence,* Treasury of the Faith Series 7 (London: Burns Oates & Washbourne Ltd., 1928), p. 29.

[81]Garrigou-Lagrange, *Providence,* p. 160. Cf. also Aquinas, *ST,* Ia, q.103, a.5-8; q.105, a.4,5; q.106, a.2.

[82]Ibid.

[83]Stump, "Providence and the Problem of Evil," pp. 62-63.

[84]Ibid., p. 65.

[85]Ibid., citing Aquinas *ST,* Ia, q.19, a.8.

[86]Ibid., citing Aquinas, *ST,* Ia, q.19, a.9; q.22, a.4; q.103, a.7; Ia, IIae, q.10, a.4.

[87]Ibid., p. 76.

[88]Padgett, *God, Eternity and the Nature,* p. 42.

[89]E.g., Garrigou-Lagrange, *Providence,* p. 115.

[90]Paul Helm, *Eternal God: A Study of God Without Time* (Oxford: Clarendon Press, 1988), p. 95.

[91]Cited by Padgett, *God, Eternity and the Nature,* p. 42.

[92]Ibid., p. 43.

[93]Augustine *Confessions* 11.13; cited ibid., p. 44.

[94]*On the Consolation of Philosophy,* 5.6; here cited from John Polkinghorne, *Science and Providence: God's Interaction with the World* (London: SPCK, 1989), p. 77.

[95]Padgett, *God, Eternity and the Nature,* p. 45.

[96]Aquinas, *ST,* Ia, q.3, 1.4.

[97]Padgett, *God, Eternity and the Nature,* p. 47.

[98]Aquinas, *ST,* Ia, q.9, a.1.

[99]Ibid., Ia, q.10, a.1.

[100]Ibid., Ia, q.10, a.2.

[101]Ibid., Ia, q.10, a.2, ad.4.

[102]Padgett, *God, Eternity and the Nature,* p. 50; citing Aquinas, *SCG,* II, 35.

[103]Aquinas, *ST,* Ia, q.14, a.5,7.

[104]Padgett, *God, Eternity and the Nature,* p. 50, referring to *SCG,* I, 66.

[105]Padgett, *God, Eternity and the Nature,* p. 64.

[106]Feinberg, *Predestination and Free Will,* p. 133.

[107]Norman Geisler, *Creating God in the Image of Man? The New "Open" View of God: Neotheism's Dangerous Drift* (Minneapolis: Bethany, 1997), p. 97.

[108]Ibid., p. 98.

[109]Aquinas, *ST,* Ia, q.14, a.6.

[110]Gerard J. Hughes, *The Nature of God,* Problems of Philosophy, ed. Tim Crane and Jonathan Wolff (London: Routledge, 1995), p. 69.

[111]Ibid.

[112]Ibid., p. 70.

[113]Ibid., pp. 72-74.

[114]Aquinas, *ST,* Ia, q.14, a.13. Cf. De La Torre, *Thomas Buckingham,* p. 63, and Barbour, *Issues in Science and Religion,* p. 427.

[115]Hughes, *The Nature of God,* p. 75. Cf. Aquinas, *SCG,* III, 66.

[116]De La Torre, *Thomas Buckingham,* p. 65. Cf. Aquinas, *ST* Ia, q.14, a.15; Ia, q.19, a.3; Ia, q.19, a. 7 ad 4; Ia, q.23, a.6 ad 3.

[117]Feinberg et al., *Predestination and Free Will*, pp. 67, 170.

[118]Ibid., pp. 70, 74.

[119]Padgett, *God, Eternity and the Nature*, p. 19.

[120]Ibid., p. 22.

[121]Ibid., p. 123.

[122]Ibid., p. 126.

[123]Ibid., p. 129.

[124]Ibid., p. 137.

[125]Garrigou-Lagrange, *Providence*, pp. 216-17.

[126]Ibid., pp. 218-22.

[127]Ibid., p. 227, citing Aquinas, *ST*, IIa, IIae, q.72, a.3; q.73, a.3ff.

[128]Garrigou-Lagrange, *Providence*, p. 227.

[129]Ibid., p. 229.

[130]Ibid., p. 262.

[131]David J. Bartholomew, *God of Chance* (London: SCM Press, 1984), p. 109, citing Aquinas, *SCG*, II, 39.

[132]Citing Aquinas, *SCG* III, 74.

[133]Aquinas, *SCG*, III, 74.

[134]Ibid.

[135]Garrigou-Lagrange, *Providence*, p. 263.

[136]Ibid.

[137]Brümmer, *When We Pray*, p. 23.

[138]Appendix 3 to vol. 39 of the Blackfriars edition of Aquinas, *Summa Theologica* (London, 1964), cited by Brümmer, *When We Pray*, p. 10.

[139]Chapter seventeen of *Letters*, in Nicene and Post-Nicene Fathers, Vol. 1, cited by Brümmer, p. 23.

[140]Augustine, Sermon 56, 4, cited by Hugh Pope, O. P., *The Teaching of St. Augustine on Prayer and the Contemplative Life: A Translation of Various Passages from the Saint's Sermons and Other Writings* (London: Burnes Oates and Washbourne Ltd., 1935), p. 37.

[141]Aquinas, *ST*, IIa, IIae, q.83, a.2.

[142]Ibid., IIa, IIae, 83, 9, as cited by Brümmer, *When We Pray*, p. 24.

[143]Garrigou-Lagrange, *Providence*, p. 207.

[144]Downey, *Divine Providence*, p. 30.

[145]Ibid., pp. 30-31.

[146]Garrigou-Lagrange, *Providence*, p. 136.

[147]Ibid., pp. 136-37.

[148]Aquinas, *ST*, IIa, IIae, q.83, a.2.

[149]Ibid., IIa, IIae, q.83, a.2.

[150]Cited in Pope, *Teaching of St. Augustine*, p. 75.

[151]Augustine, *Enarratione* 1, 14 on Ps 62, cited by Pope, p. 76.

[152]Ibid., p. 37, citing Augustine, Sermon 56, 4.

[153]Feinberg et al., *Predestination and Free Will*, p. 171.

[154]Aquinas, *ST*, IIa, IIae, 83, 2.

[155]Ibid.

[156]Garrigou-Lagrange, *Providence*, p. 195.

[157]Ibid., p. 204.

[158]Ibid.

[159]Ibid., p. 205, cf. Aquinas, *ST*, IIa, IIae, q.83, a.2.

[160]Ibid.

[161]Aquinas, *ST,* Ia, q.23, a.8.

[162]Ibid.

[163]Aquinas, *SCG,* III, 96, 8.

[164]Ibid.

[165]Ibid., III, 96, 14.

[166]Ibid.

[167]Garrigou-Lagrange, *Providence,* p. 208.

[168]Ibid., p. 209.

[169]Ibid., p. 210.

[170]Geisler, *Creating God?,* p. 142.

[171]Augustine, *Enarratione 1,19 on Ps 144,* cited in Pope, *Augustine on Prayer,* p. 38.

[172]Pope, *Augustine on Prayer,* p. 76, citing Augustine, Sermon 21, 9.

[173]Augustine, *Enarratione 1,* 8 on Ps 85, cited in Pope, *Augustine on Prayer,* pp. 79-80.

[174]Augustine, *Enarratione 1,* 7 on Ps 59, cited in Pope, *Augustine on Prayer,* p. 81.

Chapter 10: The Barthian Model

[1]John Sanders, *The God Who Risks: A Theology of Providence* (Downers Grove, Ill.: InterVarsity Press, 1998), p. 185, citing Karl Barth, *CD* III, *The Doctrine of Creation,* part 4, trans. A. T. Mackay, T. H. L. Parker, H. Knight, H. A. Kennedy and J. Marks, ed. G. W. Bromiley and T. F. Torrance (Edinburgh: T & T Clark, 1961), pp. 108-9.

[2]Karl Barth, *CD* III, *The Doctrine of Creation,* part 3, trans. G. W. Bromiley and R. J. Ehrlich, ed. G. W. Bromiley and T. F. Torrance (Edinburgh: T & T Clark, 1960), p. 3.

[3]Ibid., p. 8.

[4]Ibid., p. 3.

[5]Ibid., p. 4.

[6]Ibid., pp. 8-9.

[7]Ibid., p. 115. Barth references Calvin's *Institutes* I.16-18, Zwingli's *De providentia* and the work of the orthodox Reformed of the sixteenth and seventeenth century, as seen in Questions 26-28 of the Heidelberg Catechism.

[8]Ibid., p. 13.

[9]Ibid.

[10]Ibid., p. 44.

[11]Ibid.

[12]Ibid., p. 131.

[13]Ibid., p. 58. Biblical evidence of this divine preservation is found in 1 Chron 29:11ff.; Neh 9:6ff.; Ps 104:27ff.; 36:6ff.; 73:23; Is 40:26; Rom 11:36; 1 Cor 8:6; Heb 1:3.

[14]Ibid., pp. 63-67.

[15]Ibid., pp. 70-71.

[16]Ibid., p. 132.

[17]Ibid.

[18]Ibid., p. 133, citing agreement by Aquinas, *ST,* Ia, q.105, a.5.

[19]Barth, *CD* III/3, p. 168.

[20]Ibid., p. 174.

[21]Ibid.

[22]Ibid., p. 176.

[23]Ibid., p. 29.

[24]Ibid., p. 37.

[25]Ibid., p. 41.

[26]Ibid., p. 183.

[27]Ibid.

[28]Ibid., p. 184.

[29]Ibid., p. 185.

[30]Benjamin Wirt Farley, *The Providence of God* (Grand Rapids, Mich.: Baker, 1988), p. 229.

[31]Barth, *CD* III/3, p. 115.

[32]Ibid., p. 117.

[33]Ibid.

[34]Ibid., p. 118.

[35]Ibid., p. 119.

[36]Ibid., p. 148.

[37]Ibid., p. 186.

[38]Ibid., p. 196.

[39]Ibid.

[40]Ibid., p. 45.

[41]Ibid., p. 47.

[42]Ibid., p. 52.

[43]Ibid., p. 91.

[44]Ibid., pp. 93-94.

[45]Ibid., p. 148.

[46]Karl Barth, *CD* II, *The Doctrine of God,* part 1, trans. T. H. L. Parker, W. B. Johnston, Harold Knight and J. L. M. Haire, ed. G. W. Bromiley and T. F. Torrance (Edinburgh: T & T Clark, 1957), p. 580. Cf. comments by Anna Case-Winters, *God's Power: Traditional Understandings and Contemporary Challenges* (Louisville: Westminster John Knox, 1990), p. 115.

[47]Barth, *CD* III/3, p. 165.

[48]Barth, *CD* II/1, p. 596.

[49]Barth, *CD* III/3, p. 166.

[50]Cf. G. C. Berkouwer, *The Providence of God,* trans. Lewis B. Smedes (Grand Rapids, Mich.: Eerdmans, 1952), p. 138.

[51]For this Barth is commended by Jack Cottrell, who finds it problematic to attribute only evil to divine permission because then good acts must be caused and that is too deterministic a conception for him (*What the Bible Says About God the Ruler* [Joplin, Mo.: College Press Publishing Co., 1984], 220). See chapter seven in this volume.

[52]Barth, *CD* III/3, p. 167.

[53]Ibid., pp. 95-96.

[54]Ibid., pp. 98-100.

[55]Ibid., p. 101.

[56]Ibid., pp. 101-2.

[57]Ibid., pp. 102-4.

[58]Ibid., p. 104.

[59]Ibid., p. 105.

[60]Ibid., p. 106.

[61]Ibid., pp. 107-9.

[62]Ibid., pp. 112-13.

[63]Ibid., p. 113.

[64]Ian G. Barbour, *Issues in Science and Religion* (New York: Prentice-Hall, 1966; reprint, New York: Harper & Row, 1971), pp. 424-25.

[65]Ibid., p. 424.

[66]Barth, *CD* III/3, pp. 114-15.

[67]Ibid., p. 119.

[68]Ibid., pp. 147-48.

[69]Barth, *CD* II/1, p. 556.

[70]Ibid.

[71]Barth, *CD* III/3, pp. 121-22.

[72]Ibid., p. 135.

[73]Ibid., p. 136.

[74]Ibid., p. 142.

[75]Ibid., p. 143. Barth also cross-references 2 Sam 16:10; Job 37:6; Ps 50:1-6; 90:3; 105:31; 147:18; Is 40:7; 40:26; 41:4; 44:26ff.; 44:38; 46:11; 48:15; Jer 1:15; 18:7ff.; 25:29; Ezek 17:24; 36:29; Hos 11:1; Jon 2:11.

[76]Alan Padgett discerns in Barth's detailed discussion of the issue of God's own time and eternity "an attempt to blend the timeless with the temporal," which has obvious similarities to the work of Hegel. Alan G. Padgett, *God, Eternity and the Nature of Time* (New York: St. Martin's Press, 1992), p. 54, remarking on Barth's treatment in *CD* I, *The Doctrine of the Word of God,* part 2, trans. G. T. Thomson and H. Knight, ed. G. W. Bromiley and T. F. Torrance (Edinburgh: T & T Clark, 1956), pp. 45-70; and *CD* II, *The Doctrine of God,* part 1, trans. T. H. L. Parker, W. B. Johnson, H. Knight and J. L. M. Haire, ed. G. W. Bromiley and T. F. Torrance (Edinburgh: T & T Clark, 1957), pp. 608-78.

[77]Barth, *CD* III/3, pp. 152-53.

[78]Ibid., p. 154.

[79]Ibid., pp. 129-30.

[80]Ibid., p. 186.

[81]Ibid., p. 120.

[82]Barth, *CD* II/1, p. 559.

[83]Ibid.

[84]Ibid.

[85]Barth, *CD* III/3, p. 120.

[86]Barth, *CD* II/1, p. 551.

[87]Ibid., p. 552.

[88]Cf. Calvin, *Institutes,* I.16.2.

[89]Barth, *CD* III/3, p. 145.

[90]Barth, *CD* II/1, p. 560.

[91]Ibid.

[92]Ibid., p. 568.

[93]Cf. ibid., p. 552.

[94]Ibid., p. 575. Among Reformed scholars who affirmed Molinism, Barth cites F. Gomarus and A. Walaeus, and he cites J. Gerhard and J. Quensted as Lutherans who adopted the view.

[95]Ibid., p. 569.

[96]Ibid., p. 570.

[97]Ibid., p. 575.

[98]Ibid., p. 577.

[99]Ibid., p. 578.

[100]Ibid.

[101]Ibid., p. 582.

[102]Ibid., p. 583.

[103]Ibid., p. 585.

[104]Ibid., pp. 585-86.

[105]Barth, *CD* III/3, p. 239.

[106]Ibid., pp. 242-43.

[107]Ibid., p. 243.

[108]Ibid., p. 245.

[109]Ibid., p. 246.

[110]Ibid., p. 252.

[111]Ibid., pp. 252-53.

[112]Ibid., p. 254.

[113]Ibid., p. 264.

[114]Ibid., p. 265.

[115]Ibid.

[116]Ibid.

[117]Ibid., p. 285.

[118]Ibid.

[119]Ibid., p. 286.

[120]Ibid., p. 268.

[121]Ibid., p. 169.

[122]Ibid., p. 270.

[123]Ibid., p. 287.

[124]Ibid.

[125]Ibid.

[126]Ibid., p. 272.

[127]Ibid., p. 274.

[128]Ibid., pp. 277-78.

[129]Ibid., p. 281.

[130]Ibid., pp. 279-80.

[131]Barth, *CD* III, *The Doctrine of Creation,* part 4, trans. A. T. Mackay, T. H. L. Parker, H. Knight, H. A. Kennedy and J. Marks, ed. G. W. Bromiley and T. F. Torrance (Edinburgh: T & T Clark, 1961), p. 106.

[132]Barth, *CD* II/1, p. 497.

[133]Sanders, *God Who Risks,* p. 185.

[134]Ibid., p. 185, citing Barth, *CD* III/4, pp. 108-9.

[135]Barth, *CD* III/4, p. 89.

[136]Ibid., p. 91.

[137]Ibid., p. 93.

[138]Ibid., p. 96.

[139]Ibid., p. 101.

[140]Ibid., p. 103.

[141]Ibid., p. 104.

[142]Ibid., p. 105.

[143]Ibid., p. 106.

[144]Ibid.

[145]Ibid., p. 108.

[146]Ibid., p. 109.

[147]Ibid.

Chapter 11: The Calvinist Model

[1]John Feinberg, Norman Geisler, Bruce Reichenbach and Clark Pinnock, *Predestination and Free Will: Four Views of Divine Sovereignty and Human Freedom*, ed. David Basinger and Randall Basinger (Downers Grove, Ill.: InterVarsity Press, 1986), p. 29.

[2]Ibid., p. 30.

[3]Ibid., pp. 29, 31.

[4]John Calvin, *Institutes of the Christian Religion*, The Library of Christian Classics 20, 21 (London: SCM Press, 1960), I.16.4-5.

[5]John Calvin, "Calvin's Treatise 'Against the Libertines,'" with an introduction by Allen Verhey, trans. Robert G. Wilkie and Allen Verhey, *CTJ* 15 (November 1980): 208.

[6]John Calvin, *A Defence of the Secret Providence of God, by Which He Executes His Eternal Decrees: Being a Reply to the "Slanderous Reports" (Rom. iii.8) of a Certain Worthless Calumniator Directed Against the Secret Providence of God [Calvin's Calvinism II]*, trans. Henry Cole (Geneva: 1558; trans. London: Sovereign Grace Union, 1927), p. 224.

[7]Calvin, *Institutes*, I.16.3.

[8]Calvin, *Secret Providence*, pp. 224-25.

[9]Ibid., p. 225.

[10]Ibid., p. 246.

[11]Ibid., pp. 230-31. In this affirmation of the reality of secondary causes Calvin differed from Zwingli, who denied their reality because of his method of presenting "the idea of providence as a deduction from the idea of divine supremacy and truth," Paul Helm, "Calvin (and Zwingli) on Divine Providence," *CTJ* 29 (November 1994): 403, citing Zwingli's "Sermon on Providence," in *On Providence and Other Essays*, ed. Samuel Macauley Jackson, trans. William John Hinke (1922; reprint, Durham, N.C.: Labyrinth, 1983), pp. 132-36, 151-55.

[12]Ibid., p. 231.

[13]Ibid., p. 232.

[14]Calvin, *Institutes*, I.16.2.

[15]Ibid.

[16]Ibid., I.16.7.

[17]Paul Helm, *The Providence of God*, Contours of Christian Theology (Downers Grove, Ill.: InterVarsity Press, 1993), pp. 81-82.

[18]Ibid., pp. 82-83.

[19]Calvin, *Secret Providence*, p. 238.

[20]Ibid., p. 239.

[21]Ibid., p. 241.

[22]Ibid., p. 240.

[23]Vernon White, *The Fall of a Sparrow: The Concept of Special Divine Action* (Exeter: Paternoster Press, 1985), p. 47.

[24]*The Great Christian Doctrine of Original Sin Defended* (1758), IV.3, cited by Helm, *Providence of God*, p. 86.

[25]Helm, *Providence of God*, pp. 84-87.

[26]As does John Feinberg, regarding his own "soft determinism" (Feinberg et al., *Predestination and Free Will*, p. 23).

[27]Calvin, *Institutes*, I.16.8.

[28]Ibid., I.16.9.

[29]Helm, *Providence of God*, p. 139.

[30]Ibid., p. 140.

[31]Ibid., p. 142.

[32]William G. Pollard, *Chance and Providence: God's Action in a World Governed by Scientific Law* (London: Faber & Faber, 1959), p. 66.

[33]Ibid., p. 73.

[34]Ibid., p. 74.

[35]Ibid., p. 94.

[36]Ibid.

[37]Calvin, *Institutes,* I.18.1.

[38]Calvin, *Secret Providence,* p. 241.

[39]Ibid., p. 242.

[40]Ibid.

[41]Ibid., pp. 243-44, 253.

[42]Ibid., p. 244.

[43]Ibid., p. 267.

[44]Ibid., p. 284.

[45]Ibid., p. 287.

[46]Ibid., p. 295.

[47]G. C. Berkouwer, *The Providence of God,* trans. Lewis B. Smedes (Grand Rapids, Mich.: Eerdmans, 1952), p. 138.

[48]Ibid., p. 140.

[49]Roger Hazelton, *Providence: A Theme with Variations* (Nashville: Abingdon, 1956; reprint, London: SCM Press, 1958), p. 68.

[50]Ibid., pp. 68-69.

[51]Ibid., p. 77.

[52]Helm, *Providence of God,* pp. 132-33.

[53]Ibid., pp. 226-27, and Calvin, *Institutes,* I.17.6.

[54]Ibid., p. 271.

[55]Ibid., p. 19.

[56]Ibid., p. 20.

[57]Ibid., pp. 95-96.

[58]Ibid., pp. 106-7.

[59]Pollard, *Chance and Providence,* p. 106.

[60]Ibid., p. 109.

[61]Ibid., pp. 112-13.

[62]Ibid., p. 115.

[63]Ibid., p. 117.

[64]Berkouwer, *Providence of God,* pp. 202-3.

[65]Ibid., p. 204.

[66]Ibid., p. 206.

[67]Ibid., p. 211.

[68]Ibid., p. 212.

[69]Cf. Helm, *Providence of God,* p. 67.

[70]Helm, *Providence of God,* pp. 63-66. See also David M. Ciocchi, "Reconciling Divine Sovereignty and Human Freedom," *JETS* 37, no. 3 (September 1994): 395-412.

[71]"Calvin's Treatise 'Against the Libertines': Introduction by Allen Verhey, trans. Robert G. Wilkie and Allen Verhey," *CTJ* 15 (November 1980): 198.

[72]Ibid., p. 207.

[73]Ibid., p. 205.

[74]Ibid., p. 210.

[75]Ibid., p. 211.

[76]Ibid., p. 212.

[77]Berkouwer, *Providence of God,* p. 10.

[78]Ibid., pp. 151-52.

[79]John M. Frame, "Review of *The Providence of God,*" by Benjamin Wirt Farley, in *WTJ* 51 (fall 1989): 400.

[80]Feinberg et al., *Predestination and Free Will.* In my book, Pinnock is identified in chapters four and five, Reichenbach in chapter seven and Geisler in chapter nine.

[81]Richard Taylor, "Determinism," in *The Encyclopedia of Philosophy,* ed. Paul Edwards (New York: Macmillan, 1967), 2:359, cited by Feinberg, p. 21.

[82]Feinberg, *Predestination and Free Will,* p. 23.

[83]Ibid., p. 24.

[84]Ibid., p. 26.

[85]Ibid., pp. 87-88.

[86]Ibid., pp. 34-35.

[87]Ibid., pp. 26-28.

[88]Ibid., p. 35.

[89]Ibid., p. 126.

[90]Ibid., p. 36.

[91]Ibid., p. 37.

[92]Pollard, *Chance and Providence,* p. 161.

[93]Helm, *Providence of God,* p. 144.

[94]Donald M. MacKay, *The Open Mind and Other Essays* (Leicester, U.K.: Inter-Varsity Press, 1988), pp. 195-96.

[95]Feinberg et al., *Predestination and Free Will,* pp. 125, 166.

[96]Ibid., p. 149, with critique by Feinberg, p. 164.

[97]Paul Helm, *Eternal God: A Study of God Without Time* (Oxford: Clarendon Press, 1988), pp. 3-4.

[98]Ibid., p. 17.

[99]Cited in ibid., p. 18.

[100]Ibid., p. 20.

[101]Ibid., p. 150.

[102]Ibid., pp. 36-37.

[103]Helm, *Providence of God,* p. 80.

[104]Helm, *Eternal God,* p. 38.

[105]Ibid., pp. 42-55.

[106]Ibid., p. 59.

[107]Ibid., p. 62.

[108]Ibid., p. 69.

[109]Ibid., p. 170.

[110]Calvin, *Secret Providence,* p. 248.

[111]Ibid., p. 283.

[112]Ibid., p. 247.

[113]Ibid., p. 251.

[114]Helm, *Providence of God,* p. 109.

[115]White, *Fall of a Sparrow,* p. 111.

[116]Ibid., p. 116.

[117]Calvin, *Secret Providence,* pp. 303-4.

[118]Ibid., pp. 299-300.

[119]Ibid., p. 307.

[120]Ibid., p. 310.

[121]Ibid., pp. 254-55.

[122]Ibid., p. 267.

[123]Ibid., p. 275.

[124]Ibid., p. 277.

[125]Feinberg et al., *Predestination and Free Will,* p. 39.

[126]Ibid., n. 57.

[127]Ibid., p. 86.

[128]*On the Trinity* XV,13.

[129]*On Foreknowledge, Predestination and the Grace of God,* in *Trinity, Incarnation and Redemption,* ed. and trans. Jasper Hopkins and Herbert W. Richardson, p. 166.

[130]Aquinas, *ST,* Ia, q.14, a.8.

[131]*Institutes,* III.23.6.

[132]*On the Predestination of the Saints,* XIX, cited by Helm, *Eternal God,* p. 131.

[133]Helm, *Eternal God,* p. 149.

[134]Calvin, *Institutes,* I.16.4.

[135]Calvin, *Secret Providence,* pp. 280-81.

[136]Ibid.

[137]Calvin, *Institutes,* I.16.9.

[138]Feinberg et al., *Predestination and Free Will,* p. 32.

[139]Calvin, *Secret Providence,* pp. 281-82.

[140]Ibid., p. 282.

[141]Calvin, *Institutes,* I.17.13.

[142]Ibid., I.17.14.

[143]The case for the knowability of the future presented by middle knowledge proponents in chapter eight will not be presented again, but the same arguments would be made by proponents of this model.

[144]Feinberg et al., *Predestination and Free Will,* p. 167.

[145]Ibid., p. 168.

[146]Ibid., p. 32.

[147]Ibid., p. 34. Cf. also Helm, *Providence of God,* pp. 58-61.

[148]Helm, *Eternal God,* pp. 97-98.

[149]Ibid., p. 98.

[150]Ibid., p. 105.

[151]Ibid., p. 124.

[152]Calvin, *Institutes,* I.17.9.

[153]John H. Leith, *John Calvin's Doctrine of the Christian Life* (Louisville: Westminster John Knox, 1989), pp. 108-9.

[154]Calvin, *Secret Providence,* p. 237.

[155]Calvin, *Institutes,* I.16.3.

[156]Ibid., I.17.8.

[157]Calvin, *Secret Providence,* p. 237.

[158]Calvin, *Institutes,* I.17.9.

[159]Helm, *Providence of God,* pp. 113-14.

[160]Calvin, *Institutes,* I.16.2.

[161]Calvin, *Secret Providence,* p. 234.

[162]Calvin, *Institutes,* I.16.6.

[163]Calvin, *Secret Providence,* p. 236.

[164]Calvin, *Institutes,* I.16.2.

[165]Ibid.

[166]Helm, *Providence of God,* p. 117.

[167]Ibid., p. 123.

[168]Ibid., pp. 125-26.

[169]Ibid., p. 128.

[170]White, *Fall of a Sparrow,* p. 85.

[171]Ibid., pp. 89-90.

[172]Ibid., p. 126.

[173]Ibid., p. 128.

[174]Ibid.

[175]Ibid., pp. 128-29.

[176]In Vincent Brümmer, *What Are We Doing When We Pray? A Philosophical Enquiry* (London: SCM Press, 1984).

[177]Helm, *Providence of God,* pp. 147-51.

[178]Ibid., pp. 151-53.

[179]Calvin, *Secret Providence,* pp. 229-30.

[180]Ibid., p. 230.

[181]Calvin, *Institutes,* I.14.22.

[182]MacKay, *Open Mind,* p. 196.

[183]Calvin, *Secret Providence,* p. 236.

[184]Calvin, *Institutes,* I.17.3.

[185]Ibid., III.20.1.

[186]Ibid., III.20.2.

[187]Ibid., III.20.3.

[188]Ibid., III.20.44.

[189]Helm, *Providence of God,* pp. 154-55.

[190]Ibid., pp. 155-56.

[191]MacKay, *Open Mind,* p. 195.

[192]Ibid.

[193]Helm, *Providence of God,* p. 157.

[194]*City of God* V, 10, cited in Helm, *Providence of God,* p. 157.

[195]Helm, *Providence of God,* p. 158.

[196]Ibid., p. 160.

[197]Ibid., p. 159.

[198]Ibid.

[199]Calvin, *Institutes,* III.20.5.

[200]Ibid., III.20.15.

[201]Hazelton, *Providence,* p. 190.

[202]Calvin, *Institutes,* III.20.28.

[203]D. A. Carson, *A Call to Spiritual Reformation: Priorities from Paul and His Prayers* (Grand Rapids, Mich.: Baker, 1992; reprint, Leicester, U.K.: Inter-Varsity Press, 1992), p. 162.

[204]Ibid., p. 163.

[205]Ibid., p. 164.

[206]Ibid., p. 165.

[207]Harry Blamires, *The Will and the Way: A Study of Divine Providence and Vocation* (London:

SPCK, 1957), p. 36.

[208]Cf. Calvin, *Institutes,* I.18.3; III.24.17.

[209]Ibid., III.20.43.

[210]Helm, *Providence of God,* p. 153.

[211]Hazelton, *Providence,* pp. 193-94.

[212]Ibid., p. 194.

[213]Ibid.

[214]John Porteous, *Order and Grace: A Discussion of Prayer, Providence and Miracle* (London: James Clarke & Co., 1925), p. 149.

[215]Calvin, *Institutes,* III.20.2.

[216]Ibid., III.20.3.

[217]Ibid.

[218]Blamires, *Will and the Way,* p. 44.

[219]Ibid., p. 46.

[220]Calvin, *Institutes,* I.20.15.

Chapter 12: The Fatalist Model

[1]Brother Andrew and Susan De Vore Williams, *And God Changed His Mind Because His People Prayed* (1990; reprint, London: Marshall Pickering, 1991), p. 12.

[2]Roger Hazelton, *Providence: A Theme with Variations* (Nashville: Abingdon, 1956; reprint, London: SCM Press, 1958), p. 34.

[3]Ibid., p. 35.

[4]Cited by William Pollard, *Chance and Providence: God's Action in a World Governed by Scientific Law* (London: Faber & Faber, 1959), p. 124.

[5]G. C. Berkouwer, *The Providence of God,* trans. Lewis B. Smedes (Grand Rapids, Mich.: Eerdmans, 1952), p. 148.

[6]Ibid.

[7]Ibid., pp. 149-50.

[8]For instance, William Lane Craig states that Paul Helm believes "theological fatalism" (William Lane Craig, *Divine Foreknowledge and Human Freedom: The Coherence of Theism: Omniscience,* Brill's Studies in Intellectual History 19 [Leiden, The Netherlands: E. J. Brill, 1991], p. 26).

[9]Terence E. Fretheim, "The Repentance of God: A Key to Evaluating Old Testament God-Talk," *HBT* 10, no. 1 (June 1988): p. 65.

[10]John Martin Fischer, "Introduction: God and Freedom," in *God, Foreknowledge, and Freedom,* ed. John Martin Fischer (Stanford, Calif.: Stanford University Press, 1989), p. 12.

[11]Hazelton, *Providence,* p. 36.

[12]Ibid.

[13]Ibid., p. 37.

[14]Ibid., p. 35.

[15]Ibid., pp. 35-36.

[16]John Feinberg, Norman Geisler, Bruce Reichenbach and Clark Pinnock, *Predestination and Free Will: Four Views of Divine Sovereignty and Human Freedom,* ed. David Basinger and Randall Basinger (Downers Grove, Ill.: InterVarsity Press, 1986), p. 23.

[17]A. A. Long, *Hellenistic Philosophy: Stoics, Epicureans, Sceptics* (London: Duckworth, 1974), p. 164, cited in Benjamin Wirt Farley, *The Providence of God* (Grand Rapids, Mich.: Baker, 1988), p. 62.

[18]Peter R. Baelz, *Prayer and Providence: A Background Study. The Hulsean Lectures for 1966*

(London: SCM Press, 1968), p. 45, citing Epictetus, *Discourses*, 2.7.11ff., quoted in *Later Greek Religion*, ed. E. Bevan (London: 1927), p. 110.

[19]Ibid., citing Epictetus, *Discourses*, 2.16.41ff., in Bevan, *Later Greek Religion*, p. 111.

[20]Benjamin Wirt Farley, *The Providence of God* (Grand Rapids, Mich.: Baker, 1988), p. 62.

[21]Comments on the initial draft of this book, February 1999.

[22]Ibid., p. 104, citing Augustine, *The City of God* V, 9.

[23]T. J. Gorringe, *God's Theatre: A Theology of Providence* (London: SCM Press, 1991), p. 10, citing Augustine, *City of God* V, 9.

[24]*De Consolatione*, pp. 4, 6, cited in Gorringe, *God's Theatre*, p. 11.

[25]Gorringe, *God's Theatre*, p. 11.

[26]Aquinas, *ST*, Ia, q.116, a.3, cited in ibid.

[27]Allen Verhey, in the introduction to "Calvin's Treatise 'Against the Libertines,'" trans. Robert G. Wilkie and Allen Verhey," *CTJ* 15 (November 1980): 198, n. 40.

[28]Calvin, "Calvin's Treatise 'Against the Libertines,'" chap. 13, p. 207.

[29]John Calvin, *Institutes of the Christian Religion*, Library of Christian Classics 20, 21 (London: SCM Press, 1960), I.16.8.

[30]Karl Barth, *CD* III, *The Doctrine of Creation*, part 3, trans. G. W. Bromiley and R. J. Ehrlich, ed. G. W. Bromiley and T. F. Torrance (Edinburgh: T & T Clark, 1960), p. 113.

[31]Ibid., p. 116.

[32]Ibid., p. 162.

[33]Cited by Barth, *CD* III/3, pp. 162-63.

[34]This is well illustrated in a play by Euripides, *Alcestis* (cited by A. B. Bruce, *The Moral Order of the World in Ancient and Modern Thought* [London: Hodder & Stoughton, 1899], p. 102): "A bow of steel is hard to bend,/ And stern a proud man's will;/ But Fate, that shapeth every end,/ Is sterner, harder still;/ E'en God within the indented groove/ Of Fate's resolve Himself must move."

[35]Ibid., p. 150.

[36]W. P. Stephens, *The Theology of Huldrych Zwingli* (Oxford: Clarendon Press, 1986), p. 96.

[37]Ibid., p. 97.

[38]Ulrich Zwingli, *On Providence and Other Essays,* ed. Samuel Macauley Jackson and William John Hinke (Philadelphia: The Heidelberg Press, 1922; reprint, Durham, N.C.: Labyrinth, 1983), pp. 130-33.

[39]Ibid., pp. 156-57.

[40]Ibid., p. 177.

[41]Ibid., pp. 182-83.

[42]Ibid., pp. 227-28.

[43]Grace M. Jantzen, *God's World, God's Body* (London: Darton, Longman & Todd, 1984), p. 21, referencing Tertullian's *Against Praxeas*, p. 7.

[44]Ibid., p. 81.

[45]Ibid., p. 83.

[46]Ibid., p. 87.

[47]Ibid., p. 90.

[48]Ibid., p. 92.

[49]Ibid., pp. 94-96.

[50]Ibid., p. 127.

[51]Ibid., p. 149.

[52]Ibid., p. 150.

[53]Marcel Sarot takes note of this objection against the idea that the world is God's body but

avoids the complaint in the same way as Jantzen does. He concludes that his "modified Jant-zenian model of the world as the body of God not only enables us to hold that God is cor-poreal in the sense required by passibilism, but that it can be developed in such a way as to make it invulnerable to some of the most obvious objections," Marcel Sarot, *God, Passibility and Corporeality,* Studies in Philosophical Theology 6 (Kampen, The Netherlands: Kok Pharos, 1992), p. 242.

[54]Nancey Murphy, "I Cerebrate Myself," *Books and Culture,* January-February 1999, p. 24.

[55]Chapter six of John Searle's book, *Minds, Brains and Science* (Cambridge, Mass.: Harvard University Press, 1984).

[56]Searle, p. 26.

[57]Ibid., p. 86.

[58]Ibid., p. 87.

[59]Ibid.

[60]Ibid., p. 89.

[61]Ibid., p. 92.

[62]Ibid., p. 94.

[63]Ibid., p. 98.

[64]H. H. Farmer, *The World and God: A Study of Prayer, Providence and Miracle in Christian Experience,* 2nd ed. (London: Nisbet & Co., 1936), p. 142.

[65]Andrew, *And God Changed His Mind* (1990; reprint, London: Marshall Pickering, 1991), p. 11.

[66]Thomas Aquinas, *The Summa Contra Gentiles,* trans. The English Dominican Fathers (London: Burns Oates & Washbourne, 1923-1929), III.96.

[67]Ibid.

Chapter 13: A Middle Knowledge Calvinist Model of Providence

[1]This hierarchy among the creatures is consistently taught in Scripture. All creatures are valu-able to God who cares for them and should therefore be valuable to us, but we err when we make no value distinction between human beings (created in the image of God) and other creatures of God whose well-being is a part of our stewardship responsibility.

[2]As D. A. Carson observes, Joseph's statement "so it was not you who sent me here" is hyper-bolic. *Divine Sovereignty and Human Responsibility: Biblical Perspectives in Tension,* Mar-shalls Theological Library 7 (London: Marshall, Morgan and Scott, 1981), p. 10.

[3]Carson, *Divine Sovereignty,* p. 10, taking issue with G. C. Berkouwer.

[4]Gregory Boyd, *God at War: The Bible and Spiritual Conflict* (Downers Grove, Ill.: InterVar-sity Press, 1997).

[5]Cf. Clinton Arnold, *Powers of Darkness: Principalities and Powers in Paul's Letters* (Downers Grove, Ill.: InterVarsity Press, 1992), p. 101.

[6]Stephen Noll, *Angels of Light, Powers of Darkness: Thinking Biblically About Angels, Satan and Principalities* (Downers Grove, Ill.: InterVarsity Press, 1988), p. 106.

[7]Noll, p. 103; citing Gerhard von Rad in *TDNT,* 2:73-75.

[8]Noll, pp. 104-5.

[9]Ibid., p. 104.

[10]Arnold, *Powers,* p. 60.

[11]Sydney H. T. Page, *Powers of Evil: A Biblical Study of Satan and Demons* (Grand Rapids, Mich.: Baker, 1995), p. 76.

[12]Ibid, pp. 76-78.

[13]Keith Ferdinando, "Screwtape Revisited: Demonology Western, African and Biblical," In *The*

Unseen World: Christian Reflections on Angels, Demons and the Heavenly Realm, Tyndale House Studies (Grand Rapids, Mich.: Baker, 1996), pp. 124-25.

[14]Ibid., p. 123.

[15]Brother Andrew and Susan De Vore Williams, *And God Changed His Mind Because His People Prayed* (1990; reprint, London: Marshall Pickering, 1991), pp. 19-20.

[16]Commenting on the intent of Job's statement, H. H. Farmer notes that it was not a denial "that viewed from within the dimension of the temporal series, it was a human procreative act that 'gave,' and the activity of a diphtheric germ from a bad drain that 'took away.' The two statements do not contradict one another, for they are incommensurables, as relations in different dimensions are, and supremely so when one of the dimensions is that which stands over all other dimensional distinctions whatsoever, namely the dimension of God," See Farmer, *The World and God: A Study of Prayer, Providence and Miracle in Christian Experience,* 2nd ed. (London: Nisbet & Co., 1936), pp. 104-5.

[17]Noll, *Angels,* p. 106.

[18]John Calvin, *A Defence of the Secret Providence of God, by Which He Executes His Eternal Decrees: Being a Reply to the "Slanderous Reports" (Rom. iii.8) of a Certain Worthless Calumniator Directed Against the Secret Providence of God [Calvin's Calvinism* II], trans. Henry Cole (Geneva: 1558; trans. London: Sovereign Grace Union, 1927), p. 238.

[19]G. C. Berkouwer, *The Providence of God,* trans. Lewis B. Smedes (Kampen, The Netherlands: J. H. Kok, n.d.; reprint, Grand Rapids, Mich.: Eerdmans, 1952), p. 92.

[20]Cf. *What the Bible Says About God the Ruler* (Joplin, Mo.: College Press, 1984), pp. 188-89.

[21]This is a subject about which I have written elsewhere. "Can the Unevangelized Be Saved? A Review Article," *Didaskalia* 4, no. 2 (1993); "Salvation of the Unevangelized: A Position Paper Prepared for Delegates of the SEND International Council, 1996," an unpublished paper; "Divine Justice and Universal Grace: A Calvinistic Proposal," *Evangelical Review of Theology* 21, no. 1 (1997): 63-83; "The Universal Salvific Work of the Holy Spirit: Reducing the Scandal of Calvinism," a paper read at the Evangelical Theological Society, Jackson, Mississippi, November 22, 1996; and *Irenaeus on the Salvation of the Unevangelized,* ATLA Monograph Series, No. 31 (Metuchen, N.J: Scarecrow, 1993).

[22]E. Douglas Bebb, *God Does Intervene* (London: Epworth Press, 1954), p. 14.

[23]Alexander Balmain Bruce, *The Providential Order of the World* (London: Hodder & Stoughton, 1897), p. 259.

[24]Harry Blamires, *The Will and the Way: A Study of Divine Providence and Vocation* (London: SPCK, 1957), p. 43.

[25]John Boykin, *The Gospel of Coincidence: Is God in Control?* (Grand Rapids, Mich.: Zondervan, 1986), pp. 102-5.

[26]Ibid., p. 203.

[27]Berkouwer, *Providence of God,* p. 137.

[28]Ibid.

[29]Ibid., p. 140.

[30]A very fine exegetical demonstration of the clear teaching of these two points in Scripture is found in D. A. Carson's *Divine Sovereignty and Human Responsibility: Biblical Perspectives in Tension.* I agree with his conclusion that on the extensive biblical grounds that he examined, "notions of human freedom which entail absolute power to contrary" cannot be maintained (p. 209).

[31]Berkouwer, *Providence of God,* p. 98.

[32]Ibid., p. 127.

[33]Ibid., p. 141.

[34]D. M. MacKay, *Behind the Eye* (Oxford: Blackwell, 1991), p. 203.

[35]Jonathan Doye, Ian Goldby, Christina Line, Stephen Lloyd, Paul Shellard and David Tricker. "Contemporary Perspectives on Chance, Providence and Free Will: A Critique of Some Modern Authors," *SCB* 7 (1995): 125.

[36]Berkouwer, *Providence of God,* pp. 151-52.

[37]Ibid., p. 153.

[38]Ibid., p. 152.

[39]"And I think it must be allowed by all, that everything that is properly called a motive . . . has some sort and degree of tendency . . . to excite the will, previous to the effect or to the act of the will excited. This previous tendency of the motive is what I call the 'strength' of the motive. . . . And in this sense, I suppose, the will is always determined by the strongest motive" (Jonathan Edwards, *Freedom of the Will,* [1756], ed. P. Ramsey [New Haven, Conn.: Yale University Press, 1957], p. 142, as cited by Antony Flew [Antony Flew and Godfrey Vesey, *Agency and Necessity.* Great Debates in Philosophy (Oxford: Basil Blackwell, 1987), p. 63]).

[40]Feinberg, in *Predestination and Free Will,* p. 36.

[41]Austin Farrer's comments regarding God's providential use of the Assyrians are well said. "Isaiah was convinced that the Assyrian invasions were the scourge of God, a Father's correction of his sons' rebellion. But he knew that the Assyrians were not somnambulists under a divine hypnotism. The Assyrian was a rod in the hand of God's indignation, but he had no notion of being anything of the kind. His motives were acquisitive and political. . . . If we can make out a prophetic theory about the mechanism of the divine control, it lies in the openness of men's thoughts to pressures of which they are unaware. The Assyrian feels the force of the reasons for harsh action against Judaea; but the reasons might not have occurred to him, or an alternative use of his troops might have seemed more rewarding. The hearts of kings are in God's rule and governance; he turns them as it seems best to his godly wisdom," See Farrer, *Faith and Speculation: An Essay in Philosophical Theology: Containing the Deems Lectures 1964* (London: A. & C. Black, 1967; reprint, Edinburgh: T & T Clark, 1988), p. 61.

[42]Berkouwer, *Providence of God,* pp. 154-55.

[43]This is well argued by Gerard J. Hughes. God may *know* in 1992 that the proposition asserting that "Gerry Hughes will decide in 2000 to go to Scotland" is true. But what makes it true is that Hughes will decide this. "This ought not to be seen as some kind of retroactive causation on past truths, as though past truths were states of affairs, as it were 'things' that once past can no longer be changed. The connection between what is true and what I decide is logical not causal. My decision does not alter a past state of affairs, but logically determines what could truly have been said at some previous time," See Hughes, *The Nature of God,* Problems of Philosophy [London: Routledge, 1995], p. 77.

[44]W. S. Anglin is correct to assert that "Christian tradition is very strongly in favour of the thesis that God has complete, detailed knowledge of the future--for this, precisely, is the whole basis of prophecy," and that "to deny that God has complete foreknowledge—for any reason whatsoever (e.g., one's version of libertarianism seems to conflict with it)—is to make a radical departure from a number of very important religious traditions, including the one whose cornerstone is the prophet Jesus," This unlimited foreknowledge is something only God possesses (Is 41:22-23; 48:5; Dan 2:28, 45; Eccles 23:19-20; 39:19-20; Mt 26:34; Jn 14:27; Heb 4:12-13). W. S. Anglin, *Free Will and the Christian Faith* (Oxford: Clarendon Press, 1990), pp. 73-74. Francis Beckwith has a particularly interesting article on the philosophical problems posed to limited omniscience by the biblical test for a prophet, "Limited Omni-

science and the Test for a Prophet: A Brief Philosophical Analysis," *JETS* 36 no. 3 (September 1993): 357-62.

[45]David Basinger, "Middle Knowledge and Divine Control: Some Clarifications," *IJPR* 30 (1991): 130.

[46]Basinger, "Middle Knowledge," p. 138.

[47]John Feinberg rightly asks: "How can God *know*, even counterfactually, what *would* follow from anything else unless some form of determinism is correct?" ("God Ordains All Things," in *Predestination and Free Will: Four Views of Divine Sovereignty and Human Freedom*, ed. David Basinger and Randall Basinger (Downers Grove, Ill.: InterVarsity Press, 1986), p. 34.

[48]This point is made forcefully in William Hasker, *God, Time and Knowledge* (Ithaca, N.Y.: Cornell University Press, 1989), pp. 51-63.

[49]Anna Case-Winters, *God's Power: Traditional Understandings and Contemporary Challenges* (Louisville: Westminster John Knox, 1990), p. 69.

[50]David Basinger, "Can an Evangelical Christian Justifiably Deny God's Exhaustive Knowledge of the Future?" *CSR* 25, no. 2 (1995): 136. Cf. also David Basinger, "Simple Foreknowledge and Providential Control: A Response to Hunt," *FP* 10 no. 3 (July 1993): 421-27.

[51]Basinger, "Can an Evangelical Christian Justifiably Deny?" pp. 136-37.

[52]Cottrell, *God the Ruler*, p. 224.

[53]Ibid., p. 224.

[54]Ibid., p. 283. This is a response to Herman Bavinck's concerns about middle knowledge in *The Doctrine of God*, ed. and trans. William Hendriksen (Grand Rapids, Mich.: Eerdmans, 1951), p. 193.

[55]As Paul Helm says, God understands what it is like for a person to have had a birthday "ten days ago," See Helm, *Eternal God: A Study of God Without Time* (Oxford: Clarendon Press, 1988), p. 25.

[56]Paul Helm suggests that "the concept of foreknowledge applies not to a timeless knower's knowledge of certain events or actions, but to a temporal agent's recognition of timeless knowledge under certain temporal conditions" (Helm, *Eternal God*, p. 98).

[57]"The propositions are true now, but what the propositions are about has not yet occurred" (Helm, *Eternal God*, p. 117).

[58]Alvin Plantinga, *The Analytic Theist: An Alvin Plantinga Reader*, ed. James F. Sennett (Grand Rapids, Mich.: Eerdmans, 1998), p. 235.

[59]Alan G. Padgett, *God, Eternity and the Nature of Time* (New York: St. Martin's Press, 1992), pp. 125-37.

[60]Millard Erickson, *God the Father Almighty: A Contemporary Exploration of the Divine Attributes* (Grand Rapids, Mich.: Baker, 1998), pp. 134-40.

[61]Ibid., p. 134.

[62]Ibid., citing Thomas Morris, *Our Idea of God: An Introduction to Philosophical Theology* (Downers Grove, Ill.: InterVarsity Press, 1991), p. 138, and Ronald Nash, *The Concept of God: An Exploration of Contemporary Difficulties with the Attributes of God* (Grand Rapids, Mich.: Zondervan, 1983), p. 83.

[63]Erickson, *God the Father*, p. 138.

[64]Ibid., p. 139.

[65]Ibid.

[66]Ibid., p. 140.

[67]Ibid., pp. 276-77.

[68]Paul Helm, "The Impossibility of Divine Passibility," in *The Power and Weakness of God: Impassibility and Orthodoxy*, ed. Nigel M. De S. Cameron (Edinburgh: Rutherford House

Books, 1990), pp. 125-37.

[69]Erickson, *God the Father,* p. 161.

[70]Hendrikus Berkhof, *Christian Faith: An Introduction to the Study of the Faith,* rev. ed., trans. Sierd Woudstra (Nijkerk, The Netherlands: Uitgeverij G. F. Callenbach B. V., 1985; reprint, Grand Rapids, Mich.: Eerdmans, 1986), p. 141.

[71]Ibid., p. 142.

[72]Ibid., p. 223.

Chapter 14: A Middle Knowledge Calvinist Model of Prayer

[1]One fine study of prayer in the Gospels and Acts concludes that Luke-Acts "presents us with a bold double canvas of the early church in which the most significant redemptive-historical acts of God are portrayed as taking place in a context of prayer, revealed in advance to someone praying or—in roughly half the instances—actually cast as the Lord's response to his people's prayer," See M. M. B. Turner, "Prayer in the Gospels and Acts," in *Teach Us to Pray: Prayer in the Bible and the World,* ed. D. A. Carson (Grand Rapids, Mich.: Baker, 1990), p. 74.

[2]Harry Blamires, *The Will and the Way: A Study of Divine Providence and Vocation* (London: SPCK, 1957), p. 36.

[3]Commenting on Paul's words in Romans 1:10, David Peterson notes that "in expressing to the Father his godly desire to minister in Rome he acknowledges *his complete dependence on the will of God* for its fulfilment. Again in Rom 15:30-32, when Paul encourages his readers to join in earnest prayers for him, he adds the important proviso 'that by God's will I may come to you.' This does not introduce a note of uncertainty or doubt into prayer but is an acknowledgment that all things are in the hand of God. The apostle has devised plans that give him a strategy for accomplishing his God-given ministry (cf. Rom 1:11-15; 15:22-9) and he submits himself and his plans to the sovereign will of God through prayer. Thus prayer can express simultaneously *a specific appeal for God's help and a willingness to let God be God in answering the request!* Even when he is hindered from accomplishing his plans (Rom 1:13), he is encouraged to persevere in prayer for the fulfilment of an objective he believes to be entirely consistent with the revealed will of God" (David Peterson, "Prayer in Paul's Writings," in *Teach Us to Pray: Prayer in the Bible and the World,* ed. D. A. Carson [Grand Rapids, Mich.: Baker, 1990], pp. 89-90).

[4]Blamires, *Will and the Way,* p. 37.

[5]Ibid., p. 39.

[6]Turner, "Prayer in the Gospels and Acts," p. 81.

[7]Ibid.

[8]I note here just one possible reason for unanswered prayer that offers an interesting application of the Lord's Prayer. Harry Blamires suggests that few of us are spiritually mature enough to stand continual success. "God loves us too much to shower upon us, as a result of our prayers, the very circumstances that will more readily feed our pride, vanity, and self-dependence." In this way, God delivers us from temptation and does not lead us into evil and thus actually answers our prayer (Blamires, *Will and the Way,* p. 46).

[9]Keith Ward, *Divine Action* (London: Collins, 1990), p. 169.

[10]In this last regard, Keith Ward notices that there is a widely held view that prayer does not effect change in the world objectively but that it empowers the one who prays to do God's will more effectively. But, wisely, Ward observes that "if we can ask God to help and strengthen us, why should we not ask God to help others, since that is the ultimate focus of our concern in any case? If he can empower us in response to our prayers, so he could help

others by modifying the conditions which surround them, in response to our prayers" (Ward, *Divine Action,* p. 165).

[11]I affirm Vincent Brümmer's proposal that there are two presuppositions in impetratory prayer: (1) the things prayed for have what Peter Geach calls a "two-way contingency" (Geach, *God and the Soul* [London: Routledge & K. Paul, 1969], p. 87), that is, "it is neither impossible nor inevitable that God should bring them about"; and (2), the "prayer itself is a necessary but not a sufficient condition for God's doing what is asked" (Vincent Brümmer, *What Are We Doing When We Pray? A Philosophical Enquiry* [London: SCM Press, 1984], p. 30).

[12]Brümmer, *What Are We Doing,* p. 42.

[13]Cf., for instance, W. Bingham Hunter, commenting on a prayer that it will not rain on a birthday just two days hence. "In the case of our birthday petition: the previous month's weather, today's prayer and next week's party would all be going on simultaneously for God. To work in the future, God does not have to go back and adjust the past. He acts in eternity, where everything that happens chronologically in the universe's space/time history always 'is'" (W. Bingham Hunter, *The God Who Hears* [Downers Grove, Ill.: InterVarsity Press, 1986], p. 210, n. 1).

[14]Brümmer, *What Are We Doing,* p. 51.

[15]As B. M. Palmer put it, prayer "is not the cause which procures through its own efficiency, but merely the antecedent condition upon which a predetermined benefit is suspended. The purpose to give is, on Jehovah's part, sovereign and free; it is the spontaneous movement of His own gracious and loving will. Yet, in the exercise of the same sovereignty and goodness, He interposes the prayer of the creature as the channel through which His favor shall descend" (B. M. Palmer, *The Theology of Prayer* [Harrisonburg, Va.: Sprinkle Publications, 1980 reprint), p. 134; cited by Douglas F. Kelly, *If God Already Knows, Why Pray?* [Brentwood, Tenn.: Wolgemuth & Hyatt, 1989], p. 67).

[16]Paul Helm responds helpfully to this concern of Brümmer's, effectively defending the genuinely interpersonal nature of the relationship that exists between God the King and his praying subjects (Paul Helm, "Prayer and Providence," in *Christian Faith and Philosophical Theology: Essays in Honour of Vincent Brümmer Presented on the Occasion of the Twenty-fifth Anniversary of His Professorship in the Philosophy of Religion in the University of Utrecht,* ed. Gijsbert van den Brink, Luco J. van den Brom and Marcel Sarot [Kampen, The Netherlands: Kok Pharos Publishing House, 1992] pp. 103-15.) See also Paul Helm, *The Providence of God,* Contours of Christian Theology (Downers Grove, Ill.: InterVarsity Press, 1993), pp. 147-53. I appreciate his line of argument even though I am not committed to his acceptance of divine eternity as absolute timelessness.

[17]Helm, *Providence of God,* p. 157.

[18]*City of God,* V, 10; cited by Helm, *Providence of God,* p. 157.

[19]"God actually accepts the influence of our prayers in making up his mind . . . future events are not predetermined and fixed. If you believe that prayer changes things, my whole position is established. If you do not believe it does, you are far from biblical religion" ("God Limits His Knowledge," in *Predestination and Free Will: Four Views of Divine Sovereignty and Human Freedom,* ed. David Basinger and Randall Basinger [Downers Grove, Ill: InterVarsity Press, 1986], p. 152).

[20]Response to Clark Pinnock in *Predestination and Free Will,* p. 171.

[21]Sanders, *God Who Risks,* p. 270.

[22]Ibid.

[23]Ibid., citing Jonathan Edwards, "The Most High: A Prayer-Hearing God," in *Works of*

Jonathan Edwards, ed. Edward Hickman (The Banner of Truth Trust, 1974), 2:115-16 (emphasis is Sanders's).

[24]Sanders, *God Who Risks*, p. 271.

[25]Donald M. MacKay, *Science, Chance and Providence* (Oxford: Oxford University Press, 1978), p. 55.

[26]Ibid.

[27]Ibid., p. 60.

[28]Roger Hazelton, *Providence: A Theme with Variations* (Nashville: Abingdon, 1956; reprint, London: SCM Press, 1958), pp. 198-99.

[29]Ibid., p. 193.

[30]*Order and Grace: A Discussion of Prayer, Providence and Miracle* (London: James Clarke & Co., 1925), p. 149.

[31]H. H. Farmer, *The World and God: A Study of Prayer, Providence and Miracle in Christian Experience*, 2nd ed. (London: Nisbet & Co., 1936) p. 134.

[32]Ibid., p. 138.

[33]Ibid.

[34]Ibid., p. 141.

[35]Ibid., p. 264.

[36]Ibid., p. 265. A similar emphasis is made by Michael Murray and Kurt Meyers, as noted in my eighth chapter ("Ask and It Will Be Given to You," *RelS* 30 [1994]: 330).

[37]In Madurai, India, for instance, they frequently have long periods of drought. The local Council of Churches meets to pray for rain and "spectacular downpours of rain have occasionally been known more or less to follow this prayer," as we are told by T. J. Gorringe, *God's Theatre: A Theology of Providence* (London: SCM Press, 1991), p. 92.

[38]S. G. Hall, "The Prayer of the Church: What We Ask and How We Ask It," *ExpTim* 96, no. 3 (December 1984): 76.

[39]Ibid.

[40]I affirm William Lane Craig's argument that this "retrospective prayer" is not a case of backward causation. *The Only Wise God: The Compatibility of Divine Foreknowledge and Human Freedom* (Grand Rapids, Mich.: Baker, 1987), pp. 87-88. (See my presentation of Craig's argument in chapter eight.)

[41]I am uncomfortable with Donald M. MacKay's fascinating proposal that a distinction should be made between God-in-eternity and God-in-time, but it produces an interesting analysis of the sort of situation we are considering. He suggests that "the One whom we address in prayer meets us not as God-in-eternity but as God-in-time. . . . The logical standpoint valid for us in petitionary prayer is that of an agent, pleading (in time) with the all-powerful giver of all good for an outcome which from that standpoint is *not yet determined.* Yet as our earlier discussion has shown, none of this contradicts, nor is it contradicted by, what can be said in *retrospect,* as from the standpoint of God-in-eternity, to affirm his total sovereignty in the whole transaction" (*The Open Mind and Other Essays* [Leicester, U.K.: Inter-Varsity Press, 1988], p. 194). Similar ways of speaking of a dipolar model of God have been offered by John Polkinghorne (Polkinghorne, *Science and Providence* [London: SPCK, 1989], chap. 7), and John Houghton, "What Happens When We Pray?" *SCB* 7, no. 1 (1995): 14-15.

[42]Gary Thomas, "Doctors Who Pray," *CT,* January 6, 1997, p. 21.

[43]Cited in ibid., p. 22.

[44]Cited in ibid., p. 24.

[45]As H. D. McDonald observes, a problem with experiments to demonstrate that prayer does or does not work (e.g., praying for people in one wing of the hospital) is that it amounts to

tempting God. Since prayer is not automatic but still requires God to decide to act, it should not surprise us if he refused to participate in our experiment (H. D. McDonald, *The God Who Responds: How the Creator Relates to His Creation* [Cambridge: James Clarke & Co. Ltd., 1986], p. 127).

Bibliography

Adams, Marilyn McCord. "Is the Existence of God a 'Hard' Fact?" In *God, Foreknowledge, and Freedom,* edited by John Martin Fischer, pp. 74-85. Stanford, Calif.: Stanford University Press, 1989.

Adams, Marilyn McCord and Robert Merrihew Adams, eds. *The Problem of Evil.* Oxford Readings in Philosophy. Oxford: Oxford University Press, 1990.

Adams, Robert Merrihew. "Theodicy and Divine Intervention." In *The God Who Acts: Philosophical and Theological Explorations,* edited by Thomas F. Tracy, pp. 31-40. University Park: The Pennsylvania State University Press, 1994.

Alston, William P. "Divine Action: Shadow or Substance?" In *The God Who Acts: Philosophical and Theological Explorations,* edited by Thomas F. Tracy, pp. 41-62. University Park: The Pennsylvania State University Press, 1994.

———. "Divine and Human Action." In *Divine and Human Action: Essays in the Metaphysics of Theism,* edited by Thomas V. Morris, pp. 257-80. Ithaca: Cornell University Press, 1988.

———. "How to Think About Divine Action." In *Divine Action: Studies Inspired by the Philosophical Theology of Austin Farrer,* edited by Brian Hebblethwaite and Edward Henderson, pp. 51-70. Edinburgh: T & T Clark, 1990.

Anglin, W. S. *Free Will and the Christian Faith.* Oxford: Clarendon Press, 1990.

Aquinas, Thomas. *The Summa Contra Gentiles.* Translated by The English Dominican Fathers. London: Burns Oates & Washbourne, 1923-1929.

———. *The Summa Theologica.* Translated by The English Dominican Fathers. London: Burnes Oates & Washbourne, 1911-1925.

Armstrong, Brian G. *Calvinism and the Amyraut Heresy: Protestant Scholasticism and Humanism in Seventeenth-Century France.* Madison: The University of Wisconsin Press, 1969.

Arnold, Clinton. *Powers of Darkness: Principalities and Powers in Paul's Letters.* Downers Grove, Ill.: InterVarsity Press, 1992.

Baelz, Peter R. *Does God Answer Prayer?* London: Darton, Longman & Todd, 1982.

———. *Prayer and Providence: A Background Study.* The Hulsean Lectures for 1966. London: SCM Press, 1968.

Barbour, Ian G. "Time and Eternity." *CTNSB* 10, no. 2 (spring 1990): 25-27.

Barbour, Ian G. *Issues in Science and Religion.* New York: Prentice-Hall, 1966; reprint, New York: Harper & Row, 1971.

Barth, Karl. *Church Dogmatics.* Vol. III, Part 3, *The Doctrine of Creation.* Edited by G. W. Bromiley and T. F. Torrance. Translated by A. T. Mackay, T. H. L. Parker, Harold Knight, Henry A. Kennedy, John Marks. Zurich: Evangelischer Verlag A. G. Zollikon, 1951; reprint, Edinburgh: T & T Clark, 1961.

———. *Church Dogmatics.* Vol. III, Part 4, *The Doctrine of Creation.* Edited by G. W. Bromiley and T. F. Torrance. Translated by G. W. Bromiley and R. J. Ehrlich. Zurich: Evangelischer Verlag A. G. Zollikon, 1950; reprint, Edinburgh: T & T Clark, 1960.

———. *Church Dogmatics.* Vol. II, Part 1, *The Doctrine of God.* Edited by G. W. Bromiley and T. F. Torrance. Translated by T. H. L. Parker, W. B. Johnston, Harold Knight and J. L. M. Haire. Zurich: Evangelischer Verlag A. G. Zollikon, 1950; reprint, Edinburgh: T & T Clark, 1957.

Bartholomew, David J. *God of Chance.* London: SCM Press, 1984.

Basinger, David. "Can an Evangelical Christian Justifiably Deny God's Exhaustive Knowledge of the Future?" *CSR* 25, no. 2 (1995): 133-45.

————. "Divine Control and Human Freedom: Is Middle Knowledge the Answer?" *JETS* 36, no. 1 (March 1993): 55-64.

————. *Divine Power in Process Theism: A Philosophical Critique.* SUNY Series in Philosophy. Albany: State University of New York Press, 1988.

Basinger, David. *The Case for Freewill Theism: A Philosophical Assessment.* Downers Grove, Ill.: InterVarsity Press, 1996.

————. "Middle Knowledge and Divine Control: Some Clarifications." *IJPR* 30 (1991): 129-39.

————. "Simple Foreknowledge and Providential Control: A Response to Hunt." *FP* 10, no. 3 (July 1993): 421-27.

————. "Why Petition an Omnipotent, Omniscient, Wholly Good God?" *RelS* 19 (1983): 25-41.

Basinger, David and Randall Basinger. *Philosophy and Miracle: The Contemporary Debate.* Problems in Contemporary Philosophy, no. 2. Lewiston, N.Y.: Edwin Mellen, 1986.

Baugh, Steven M. "'Savior of All People': 1 Tim 4:10 in Context." *WTJ* 54 (1992): 331-40.

Bebb, E. Douglas. *God Does Intervene.* London: Epworth, 1954.

Beckwith, Francis J. "Limited Omniscience and the Test for a Prophet: A Brief Philosophical Analysis." *JETS* 36, no. 3 (September 1993): 357-62.

Berkhof, Hendrikus. *Christian Faith: An Introduction to the Study of the Faith.* Rev. ed. Translated by Sierd Woudstra. Nijkerk, The Netherlands: Uitgeverij G. F. Callenbach B. V., 1985; reprint, Grand Rapids, Mich.: Eerdmans, 1986.

Berkouwer, G. C. *The Providence of God.* Translated by Lewis B. Smedes. Kampen, The Netherlands: J. H. Kok, n.d.; reprint, Grand Rapids, Mich.: Eerdmans, 1952.

Billheimer, Paul E. *Destined for the Throne.* London: Christian Literature Crusade, 1975.

————. *Destined to Overcome.* Minneapolis: Bethany House, 1982; reprint, Eastbourne: Kingsway Publications, 1982.

Bilynskyj, Stephen. "What in the World Is God Doing?" In *The Logic of Rational Theism: Exploratory Essays,* edited by William Lane Craig and Mark S. McLeod, pp. 155-68. Lewiston, N.Y.: Edwin Mellen, 1990.

Blamires, Harry. *The Will and the Way: A Study of Divine Providence and Vocation.* London: SPCK, 1957.

Blocher, Henri. "Divine Immutability." In *The Power and Weakness of God: Impassibility and Orthodoxy,* edited by Nigel M. De S. Cameron, pp. 1-22. Edinburgh: Rutherford House Books, 1990.

Boros, Ladislaus. *Pain and Providence.* Translated by Edward Quinn. Mainz: Matthias-Grünewald-Verlag, 1965; reprint, London: Burns & Oates, 1966.

Boyd, Gregory A. *God at War: The Bible and Spiritual Conflict.* Downers Grove, Ill.: InterVarsity Press, 1997.

Boykin, John. *The Gospel of Coincidence: Is God in Control?* Grand Rapids, Mich.: Zondervan, 1986.

Brink, Gijsbert van den, Luco J. van den Brom and Marcel Sarot, eds. *Christian Faith and Philosophical Theology: Essays in Honour of Vincent Brümmer Presented on the Occasion of the Twenty-fifth Anniversary of His Professorship in the Philosophy of Religion in the University of Utrecht.* Kampen, The Netherlands: Kok Pharos, 1992.

Brother Andrew and Susan DeVore Williams. *And God Changed His Mind Because His People Prayed.* 1990; reprint, London: Marshall Pickering, 1991.

Bruce, Alexander Balmain. *The Providential Order of the World.* London: Hodder & Stoughton, 1897.

Brümmer, Vincent. *Speaking of a Personal God: An Essay in Philosophical Theology.* Cambridge: Cambridge University Press, 1992.

————. *What Are We Doing When We Pray? A Philosophical Enquiry.* London: SCM Press, 1984.

Bryant, Barry E. "Molina, Arminius, Plaifere, Goad, and Wesley on Human Free-Will, Divine Omniscience, and Middle Knowledge." *WesleyTJ* 27, no. 1-2 (spring-fall 1992): 93-103.

Calvin, John. "Calvin's Treatise 'Against the Libertines'; Introduction by Allen Verhey; Translation by Robert G. Wilkie and Allen Verhey." *CTJ* 15 (November 1980): 190-219.

———. *A Defence of the Secret Providence of God: By Which He Executes His Eternal Decrees: Being a Reply to the "Slanderous Reports" (Rom. iii.8) of a Certain Worthless Calumniator Directed Against the Secret Providence of God* [Calvin's Calvinism. Part II]. Translated by Henry Cole. Geneva: 1558; reprint, London: Sovereign Grace Union, 1927.

———. *Institutes of the Christian Religion.* The Library of Christian Classics, edited by John T. McNeill, trans. Ford Lewis Battles, no. 20, 21. London: SCM Press, 1960.

Cameron, Nigel M. de S., ed. *The Power and Weakness of God: Impassibility and Orthodoxy.* Scottish Bulletin of Evangelical Theology. Special Study, 4. Edinburgh: Rutherford House Books, 1990.

Carson, D. A. *A Call to Spiritual Reformation: Priorities from Paul and His Prayers.* Grand Rapids, Mich.: Baker, 1992; reprint, Leicester, U.K.: Inter-Varsity Press, 1992.

———. *Divine Sovereignty and Human Responsibility: Biblical Perspectives in Tension.* Marshalls Theological Library, 7. London: Marshall, Morgan and Scott, 1981.

———, ed. *Teach Us to Pray: Prayer in the Bible and the World.* Grand Rapids, Mich.: Baker, 1990.

Case-Winters, Anna. *God's Power: Traditional Understandings and Contemporary Challenges.* Louisville: Westminster John Knox, 1990.

Cashdollar, Charles D. "The Social Implications of the Doctrine of Divine Providence: A Nineteenth-Century Debate in American Theology." *HTR* 71, no. 3-4 (July-October 1978): 265-84.

Ciocchi, David M. "Reconciling Divine Sovereignty and Human Freedom." *JETS* 37, no. 3 (September 1994): 395-412.

Cobb, John B. Jr. and David Ray Griffin. *Process Theology: An Introductory Exposition.* Philadelphia: Westminster Press, 1976.

Cook, Robert R. "God, Middle Knowledge and Alternative Worlds." *EvQ* 62 (1990): 293-310.

Cooley, Phillip Allen. "Selected Models of the God-World Relationship in Twentieth Century Theology: Implications for a Contemporary Doctrine of Providence." Ph.D. dissertation, Southern Baptist Theological Seminary, December 1981.

Cottrell, Jack. *What the Bible Says About God the Ruler.* Joplin, Mo.: College Press, 1984.

Craig, William Lane. *Divine Foreknowledge and Human Freedom: The Coherence of Theism: Omniscience.* Brill's Studies in Intellectual History, 19. Leiden: E. J. Brill, 1991.

———. *The Only Wise God: The Compatibility of Divine Foreknowledge and Human Freedom.* Grand Rapids, Mich.: Baker, 1987.

———. *The Problem of Divine Foreknowledge and Future Contingents from Aristotle to Suarez.* Brill's Studies in Intellectual History 7. New York: E. J. Brill, 1988.

Crenshaw, James and Samuel Sandmel, eds. *The Divine Helmsman: Studies on God's Control of Human Events, Presented to Lou H. Silberman.* New York: Ktav Publishing House, 1980.

Davies, Horton. *The Vigilant God: Providence in the Thought of Augustine, Aquinas, Calvin and Barth.* New York: Peter Lang, 1992.

Dewar, Lindsay. *Does God Care?* London: Hodder & Stoughton, 1936.

Downey, Richard. *Divine Providence.* Treasury of the Faith 7. London: Burns Oates & Washbourne, 1928.

Doye, Jonathan, Ian Goldby, Christina Line, Stephen Lloyd, Paul Shellard and David Tricker. "Contemporary Perspectives on Chance, Providence and Free Will: A Critique of Some Modern Authors." *SCB* 7 (1995): 117-39.

Driedger, Sharon Doyle. "Prayer Power." *Macleans,* September 25, 1995, p. 41.

Drury, John. *Angels and Dirt: An Inquiry into Theology and Prayer.* London: Darton, Longman & Todd, 1972.

Duckro, Paul N. and Philip R. Magaletta. "The Effect of Prayer on Physical Health: Experimental Evidence." *JRHealth* 33, no. 3 (fall 1994): 211-19.

Erickson, Millard. *God the Father Almighty: A Contemporary Exploration of the Divine*

Attributes. Grand Rapids, Mich.: Baker, 1998.

Farley, Benjamin Wirt. *The Providence of God.* Grand Rapids, Mich.: Baker, 1988.

Farmer, H. H. *The World and God: A Study of Prayer, Providence and Miracle in Christian Experience.* 2nd ed. London: Nisbet & Co., 1936.

Farrelly, Dom M. John. *Predestination, Grace and Free Will.* London: Burns & Oates, 1964.

Farrer, Austin. *Faith and Speculation: An Essay in Philosophical Theology: Containing the Deems Lectures 1964.* London: A. & C. Black, 1967; reprint, Edinburgh: T & T Clark, 1988.

Feinberg, John, Norman Geisler, Bruce Reichenbach and Clark Pinnock. *Predestination and Free Will: Four Views of Divine Sovereignty and Human Freedom.* Edited by David Basinger and Randall Basinger. Downers Grove, Ill.: InterVarsity Press, 1986.

Ferré, Frederick. "Mapping the Logic of Models in Science and Theology." In *New Essays on Religious Language,* edited by Dallas M. High, pp. 54-96. New York: Oxford University Press, 1969.

Fischer, John Martin. "Freedom and Foreknowledge." In *God, Foreknowledge, and Freedom,* edited by John Martin Fischer, pp. 86-96. Stanford: Stanford University Press, 1989.

———, ed. *God, Foreknowledge and Freedom.* Stanford: Stanford University Press, 1989.

———. "Introduction: God and Freedom." In *God, Foreknowledge, and Freedom,* edited by John Martin Fischer, pp. 1-56. Stanford: Stanford University Press, 1989.

Flew, Antony and Godfrey Vesey. *Agency and Necessity.* Great Debates in Philosophy. Oxford: Basil Blackwell, 1987.

Flint, Thomas P. "Two Accounts of Providence." In *Divine and Human Action: Essays in the Metaphysics of Theism,* edited by Thomas V. Morris, pp. 147-81. Ithaca, N.Y.: Cornell University Press, 1988.

Forster, Peter R. "Providence and Prayer." In *Belief in Science and in Christian Life: The Relevance of Michael Polanyi's Thought for Christian Faith and Life,* edited by Thomas F. Torrance, pp. 108-32. Edinburgh: Hansel, 1980.

Forster, Peter R. "Divine Passibility and the Early Christian Doctrine of God." In *The Power and Weakness of God: Impassibility and Orthodoxy,* edited by Nigel M. De S. Cameron, pp. 23-51. Edinburgh: Rutherford House, 1990.

Forster, Roger T. and V. Paul Marston. *God's Strategy in Human History: God's Sovereignty and Man's Responsibility.* First British ed. Minneapolis: Bethany House, 1973; reprint, Crowborough, East Sussex: Highland Books, 1989.

Frame, John M. Review of *The Providence of God,* by Benjamin Wirt Farley. In *WTJ* 51 (fall 1989): 397-400.

Freddoso, Alfred J. "The 'Openness' of God: A Reply to William Hasker," 1996 [World Wide Web, home page].

———. "Medieval Aristotelianism and the Case Against Secondary Causation in Nature." In *Divine and Human Action: Essays in the Metaphysics of Theism,* edited by Thomas V. Morris, pp. 74-118. Ithaca, N.Y.: Cornell University Press, 1988.

Fretheim, Terence E. "Divine Foreknowledge, Divine Constancy, and the Rejection of Saul's Kingship." *Catholic Biblical Quarterly* 47, no. 4 (October 1985): 595-602.

———. "Prayer in the Old Testament: Creating Space in the World for God." In *A Primer in Prayer,* pp. 51-62. Philadelphia: Fortress, 1988.

———. "The Repentance of God: A Key to Evaluating Old Testament God-Talk." *HBT* 10, no. 1 (June 1988): 47-70.

———"Suffering God and Sovereign God in Exodus: A Collision of Images." *HBT* 11, no. 2 (December 1989): 31-56.

Gaiser, Frederick J. "Individual and Corporate Prayer in Old Testament Perspective." In *A Primer on Prayer,* edited by Paul R. Sponheim, pp. 9-22. Philadelphia: Fortress, 1988.

Garrigou-Lagrange, Reginald. *Providence* [La Providence et la confiance en Dieu]. Translated by Bede Rose. London: B. Herder, 1937.

Geach, P. T. "Omnipotence." *Ph* 48, no. 183 (January 1973): 7-20.

Geach, Peter T. *God and the Soul*. 1969; reprint, Bristol: Thoemmes Press, 1994.

———. *Providence and Evil*. Cambridge: Cambridge University Press, 1977.

Geisler, Norman. *Creating God in the Image of Man? The New "Open" View of God: Neotheism's Dangerous Drift*. Minneapolis: Bethany House, 1997.

———. "God Knows All Things." In *Predestination and Free Will: Four Views of Divine Sovereignty and Human Freedom*, edited by David Basinger and Randall Basinger, pp. 63-84. Downers Grove, Ill.: InterVarsity Press, 1986.

Gilkey, Langdon B. "The Concept of Providence in Contemporary Theology." *JR* 43, no. 3 (July 1963): 171-92.

———. *Reaping the Whirlwind: A Christian Interpretation of History*. New York: Seabury, 1976.

Gorringe, T. J. *God's Theatre: A Theology of Providence*. London: SCM Press, 1991.

Gregersen, Niels Henrik. "Providence in an Indeterministic World." *CTNSB* 14, no. 1 (winter 1994): 16-31.

Guagliardo, Vincent. "Nature and Miracle." *CTNSB* 10, no. 2 (spring 1990): 17- 20.

Habgood, John. "Discovering God in Action." In *In Search of Christianity*, edited by Tony Moss, pp. 108-20. London: Firethorn, 1986.

Hall, S. G. "The Prayer of the Church. What We Ask and How We Ask It." *The Expository Times* 96, no. 3 (December 1984): 73-77.

Harpur, Tom. *The Uncommon Touch: An Investigation of Spiritual Healing*. Toronto: McClelland and Stewart, 1994.

Hartman, Lance. "Does Prayer Change God's Mind?" *Discipleship*, no. 80 (1994): 36-41.

Hartshorne, Charles. *The Divine Relativity: A Social Conception of God*. New Haven, Conn.: Yale University Press, 1948.

Hasker, William. "Foreknowledge and Necessity." In *God, Foreknowledge and Freedom*, edited by John Martin Fischer, pp. 216-57. Stanford: Stanford University Press, 1989.

———. *God, Time, and Knowledge*. Ithaca, N.Y.: Cornell University Press, 1989.

———. "God the Creator of Good and Evil?" In *The God Who Acts: Philosophical and Theological Explorations*, edited by Thomas F. Tracy, pp. 137-46. University Park: Pennsylvania State University Press, 1994.

———. "The Openness of God." *CSR* 28, no. 1 (fall 1998): 111-23.

———. "Providence and Evil: Three Theories." *RelS* 28, no. 1 (March 1992): 91-105.

Hazelton, Roger. *Providence: A Theme with Variations*. Nashville: Abingdon, 1956; reprint, London: SCM Press, 1958.

Hebblethwaite, Brian and Edward Henderson, eds. *Divine Action: Studies Inspired by the Philosophical Theology of Austin Farrer*. Edinburgh: T & T Clark, 1990.

Helm, Paul. "Calvin (and Zwingli) on Divine Providence." *CTJ* 29 (November 1994): 388-405.

———. *Eternal God: A Study of God Without Time*. Oxford: Clarendon Press, 1988.

———. "The Impossibility of Divine Passibility." In *The Power and Weakness of God: Impassibility and Orthodoxy*, edited by Nigel M. De S. Cameron, pp. 119-40. Edinburgh: Rutherford House Books, 1990.

———. "Prayer and Providence." In *Christian Faith and Philosophical Theology: Essays in Honour of Vincent Brümmer Presented on the Occasion of the Twenty-fifth Anniversary of His Professorship in the Philosophy of Religion in the University of Utrecht*, eds. Gijsbert van den Brink, Luco J. van den Brom and Marcel Sarot, pp. 103-15. Kampen, The Netherlands: Kok Pharos, 1992.

———. *The Providence of God*. Contours of Christian Theology, edited by Gerald Bray. Downers Grove, Ill.: InterVarsity Press, 1993.

High, Dallas M., ed. *New Essays on Religious Language*. New York: Oxford University Press, 1969.

Hobson, George Hull Jr. "Towards a Doctrine of Providence: A Response to Contemporary Critiques." D.Phil Thesis, University of Oxford, 1989.

Hodgson, Peter C. and Robert H. King, eds. *Readings in Christian Theology*. London: SPCK,

1985.

Hoffmann, Joshua and Gary Rosenkrantz. "Hard and Soft Facts." In *God, Foreknowledge, and Freedom,* edited by John Martin Fischer, pp. 123-35. Stanford: Stanford University Press, 1989.

Houghton, John. "New Ideas of Chaos in Physics." *SCB* 1 (1989): 41-51.

———. "What Happens When We Pray." *SCB* 7 (1995): 3-20.

Hughes, Gerard J. *The Nature of God.* Problems of Philosophy, edited by Tim Crane and Jonathan Wolff. London: Routledge, 1995.

Hultgren, Arland J. "Expectations of Prayer in the New Testament." In *A Primer on Prayer,* edited by Paul R. Sponheim, pp. 23-35. Philadelphia: Fortress, 1988.

Hunt, David P. "Divine Providence and Simple Foreknowledge." *FP* 10, no. 3 (July 1993): 394-414.

———. "Prescience and Providence: A Reply to My Critics." *FP* 10, no. 3 (July 1993): 428-38.

Hunter, W. Bingham. *The God Who Hears.* Downers Grove, Ill.: InterVarsity Press, 1986.

Ivory, Thomas P. "The Teaching of John Henry Newman on the Doctrine of Prayer." *Ephimerides Theologicae Lovanienses* 52 (June 1976): 162-92.

Jantzen, Grace M. *God's World, God's Body.* London: Darton, Longman & Todd, 1984.

Kapitan, Tomis. "Providence, Foreknowledge, and Decision Procedures." *FP* 10, no. 3 (July 1993): 415-20.

Kaufman, Gordon D. "On the Meaning of 'Act of God.'" *HTR* 61, no. 2 (April 1968): 175-201.

Keller, Jack A. "On Providence and Prayer." *CC* 104, no. 32 (November 1987): 967-69.

Kelly, Douglas F. *If God Already Knows, Why Pray?* Brentwood, Tenn.: Wolgemuth & Hyatt, 1989.

De La Torre, Bartholomew R. *Thomas Buckingham and the Contingency of Futures: The Possibility of Human Freedom.* Publications in Medieval Studies, 25. Notre Dame, Ind.: University of Notre Dame Press, 1987.

Lane, Anthony N. S. "Did Calvin Believe in Free Will?" *VE* 12 (1981): 72-90.

———. *The Unseen World: Christian Reflections on Angels, Demons and the Heavenly Realm.* Edited by Anthony N. S. Lane. Tyndale House Studies. Grand Rapids, Mich.: Baker, 1996.

Langford, Michael J. *Providence.* London: SCM Press, 1981.

Leftow, Brian. *Time and Eternity.* Cornell Studies in the Philosophy of Religion, edited by William P. Alston. Ithaca, N.Y.: Cornell University Press, 1991.

Leith, John H. *John Calvin's Doctrine of the Christian Life.* Louisville: Westminster John Knox, 1989.

Levenson, Jon D. *Creation and the Persistence of Evil: The Jewish Drama of Divine Omnipotence.* 2nd ed. New York: Harper & Row, 1987; reprint, Princeton, N.J.: Princeton University Press, 1994.

Loughran, Thomas Joseph. "Theological Compatibilism." Ph.D. dissertation, University of Notre Dame, University Microfilms International, 1986.

Lucas, J. R. *Freedom and Grace.* London: SPCK, 1976.

———. *The Future: An Essay on God, Temporality and Truth.* Oxford: Basil Blackwell, 1989.

MacKay, Donald M. *The Open Mind and Other Essays.* Leicester, U.K.: Inter-Varsity Press, 1988.

———. *Science, Chance and Providence.* Oxford: Oxford University Press, 1978.

Mann, William E. "God's Freedom, Human Freedom, and God's Responsibility for Sin." In *Divine and Human Action: Essays in the Metaphysics of Theism,* edited by Thomas V. Morris, pp. 182-210. Ithaca, N.Y.: Cornell University Press, 1988.

Mavrodes, George I. "How Does God Know the Things He Knows?" In *Divine and Human Action,* edited by Thomas V. Morris, pp. 345-61. Ithaca, N.Y.: Cornell University Press, 1988.

McDonald, H. D. *The God Who Responds: How the Creator Relates to His Creation.* Cambridge: James Clarke & Co. Ltd., 1986.

McFague, Sallie. *Models of God: Theology for an Ecological, Nuclear Age.* London: SCM Press,

1987.

McKenzie, David. "Pannenberg on God and Freedom." *JR* 60, no. 3 (July 1980): 307-29.

McKim, Donald K. "The Puritan View of History or Providence Without and Within." *EvQ* 52 (1980): 215-37.

Molina, Luis de. *On Divine Foreknowledge (Part IV of the Concordia).* Translated by Alfred J. Freddoso. Ithaca, N.Y.: Cornell University Press, 1988.

Morris, Thomas V., ed. *The Concept of God.* Oxford Readings in Philosophy. Oxford: Oxford University Press, 1987.

————, ed. *Divine and Human Action: Essays in the Metaphysics of Theism.* Ithaca, N.Y.: Cornell University Press, 1988.

Moss, Tony, ed. *In Search of Christianity.* London: Firethorn, 1986.

Muller, Richard A. *God, Creation and Providence in the Thought of Jacob Arminius: Sources and Directions of Scholastic Protestantism in the Era of Early Orthodoxy.* Grand Rapids, Mich.: Baker, 1991.

Murphy, Nancey. "Does Prayer Make a Difference?" In *Cosmos as Creation: Theology and Science in Consonance,* edited by Ted Peters, pp. 235-45. Nashville: Abingdon, 1989.

————. "Of Miracles." *CTNSB* 10, no. 2 (spring 1990): 15-16.

Murray, Michael J. and Kurt Meyers. "Ask and It Will Be Given to You." *RelS* 30 (1994): 311-30.

Musser, Donald W. and Joseph L. Price, eds. *The Whirlwind in Culture.* Bloomington, Ind.: Meyer Stone Books, 1988.

Nee To-Sheng (Watchman Nee). *Sit, Walk, Stand.* 4th ed. Bombay: Gospel Literature Service, 1957; reprint, London: Victory Press, 1962.

————. *What Shall This Man Do?* London: Victory Press, 1961.

Nelson, Peter. *God's Control Over the Universe: Providence and Judgment in Relation to Modern Science.* Caithness, U.K.: Whittles Publishing, 1992.

Noll, Stephen. *Angels of Light, Powers of Darkness: Thinking Biblically About Angels, Satan and Principalities.* Downers Grove, Ill.: InterVarsity Press, 1988.

Oden, Thomas C. *The Transforming Power of Grace.* Nashville: Abingdon, 1993.

Ogden, Schubert M. *The Reality of God and Other Essays.* London: SCM Press, 1967.

Outler, Albert C. *Who Trusts in God: Musings on the Meaning of Providence.* New York: Oxford University Press, 1968.

Owen, Huw Parri. *Christian Theism: A Study in Its Basic Principles.* Edinburgh: T & T Clark, 1984.

Padgett, Alan G. *God, Eternity and the Nature of Time.* New York: St. Martin's Press, 1992.

Page, Sydney H. T. *Powers of Evil: A Biblical Study of Satan and Demons.* Grand Rapids, Mich.: Baker, 1995.

Pannenberg, Wolfhart. "Providence, God, and Eschatology." In *The Whirlwind in Culture,* edited by Donald W. Musser and Joseph L. Price, pp. 171-82. Bloomington, Ind.: Meyer Stone Books, 1988.

————. *Systematic Theology.* Translated by Geoffrey W. Bromiley. Göttingen: Vandenhoeck & Ruprecht, 1989-1991; reprint, Grand Rapids, Mich.: Eerdmans, 1991-1994.

Partee, Charles. "Predestination in Aquinas and Calvin." *RefRev* 32, no. 1 (fall 1978): 14-22.

Peacocke, Arthur R. "Theology and Science Today." In *Cosmos As Creation: Theology and Science in Consonance,* edited by Ted Peters, pp. 28-43. Nashville: Abingdon, 1989.

Peters, Ted. "Cosmos As Creation." In *Cosmos As Creation: Theology and Science in Consonance,* edited by Ted Peters, pp. 45-113. Nashville: Abingdon, 1989.

————, ed. *Cosmos As Creation: Theology and Science in Consonance.* Nashville: Abingdon, 1989.

Peterson, David G. "Prayer in Paul's Writings." In *Teach Us to Pray: Prayer in the Bible and the World,* edited by D. A. Carson, pp. 84-101. Grand Rapids, Mich.: Baker, 1990.

Phillips, D. Z. *The Concept of Prayer.* London: Routledge and Kegan Paul, 1965.

Pike, Nelson. "Divine Omniscience and Voluntary Action." *PhRev* 74 (1965): 27-46.

————. "Divine Omniscience and Voluntary Action." In *God, Foreknowledge, and Freedom,* edited by John Martin Fischer, pp. 57-73. Stanford: Stanford University Press, 1989.

Pinnock, Clark, Richard Rice, John Sanders, William Hasker and David Basinger. *The Openness of God: A Biblical Challenge to the Traditional Understanding of God.* Downers Grove, Ill.: InterVarsity Press, 1994.

Pinnock, Clark H. and Robert C. Brow. *Unbounded Love: A Good News Theology for the 21st Century.* Downers Grove, Ill.: InterVarsity Press, 1994.

Pittenger, Norman. *God's Way with Men: A Study of the Relationship Between God and Man in Providence, "Miracle," and Prayer.* The Library of Practical Theology, edited by Martin Thornton. London: Hodder & Stoughton, 1969.

————. *The Lure of Divine Love: Human Experience and Christian Faith in a Process Perspective.* New York: Pilgrim, 1979.

————. *Process-Thought and Christian Faith.* Digswell Place, U.K.: James Nisbet & Co., 1968.

Plantinga, Alvin C. *God, Freedom, and Evil.* 1974; reprint, Grand Rapids, Mich.: Eerdmans, 1980.

Polkinghorne, John. "Can a Scientist Pray?" *Col* 26, no. 1 (1994): 2-10.

————. "God's Action in the World: 1990 J. K. Russell Fellowship Lecture." *CTNSB* 10, no. 2 (spring 1990): 1-7.

————. "A Note on Chaotic Dynamics." *SCB* 1, no. 2 (1989): 123-27.

————. *Science and Providence: God's Interaction with the World.* London: SPCK, 1989.

————. "Setting the Problem." *CTNSB* 10, no. 2 (spring 1990): 8-12.

————. *The Way the World Is: The Christian Perspective of a Scientist.* London: SPCK, 1983.

Pollard, William G. *Chance and Providence: God's Action in a World Governed by Scientific Law.* London: Faber & Faber, 1959.

Pope, Hugh, O.P. *The Teaching of St. Augustine on Prayer and the Contemplative Life: A Translation of Various Passages from the Saint's Sermons and Other Writings.* London: Burnes Oates and Washbourne Ltd., 1935.

Porteous, John. *Order and Grace: A Discussion of Prayer, Providence and Miracle.* London: James Clarke & Co., 1925.

Ramsey, Ian T. *Models for Divine Activity.* London: SCM Press, 1973.

Reines, Alvin J. "Maimonides' Concepts of Providence and Theodicy." *HUCA* 43 (1972): 169-206.

Rice, Richard. *God's Foreknowledge and Man's Free Will.* Rev. ed. Minneapolis: Bethany House, 1985.

Richmond, Patrick. "Divine Providence and Limits on Liberty," January 8, 1996 [Student Essay at the University of Oxford].

Sanders, John. *The God Who Risks: A Theology of Providence.* Downers Grove, Ill.: InterVarsity Press, 1998.

Sarot, Marcel. *God, Possibility and Corporeality.* Studies in Philosophical Theology 6. Kampen, The Netherlands: Kok Pharos Publishing House, 1992.

————. "Omnipotence and Self-Limitation." In *Christian Faith and Philosophical Theology: Essays in Honour of Vincent Brümmer Presented on the Occasion of the Twenty-fifth Anniversary of His Professorship in the Philosophy of Religion in the University of Utrecht,* edited by Gijsbert Van Den Brink, Luco J. Van Den Brom and Marcel Sarot, pp. 172-85. Kampen, The Netherlands: Kok Pharos, 1992.

Schilling, S. Paul. "Chance and Order in Science and Theology." *TToday* 47, no. 4 (January 1991): 365-76.

De Schrijver, Georges. "Religion and Cosmology At the End of the 20th Century." *CTNSB* 14, no. 1 (winter 1994): 1-15.

Searle, John. *Minds, Brains and Science.* Cambridge, Mass.: Harvard University Press, 1984.

Sennett, James F., ed. *The Analytic Theist: An Alvin Plantinga Reader.* Grand Rapids, Mich.: Eerdmans, 1998.

Sharples, R. W. "Nemesius of Emesa and Some Theories of Divine Providence." *VC* 37 (1983): 141-56.

Sontag, Frederick. "Does Omnipotence Necessarily Entail Omniscience?" *JETS* 34, no. 4

(December 1991): 505-8.

Sponheim, Paul R. "The God of Prayer." In *A Primer on Prayer,* edited by Paul R. Sponheim, pp. 63-76. Philadelphia: Fortress, 1988.

————, ed. *A Primer on Prayer.* Philadelphia: Fortress, 1988.

Stephens, W. P. *The Theology of Huldrych Zwingli.* Oxford: Clarendon Press, 1986.

Stirling, Andrew. "The Spirit, the Church and the Transformation of South Africa." *Faith Today,* March-April 1995, 74-76.

Stump, Eleonore. "Petitionary Prayer." *APQ* 16, no. 2 (April 1979): 81-91.

————. "Providence and the Problem of Evil." In *Christian Philosophy,* edited by Thomas P. Flint, pp. 51-91. Notre Dame, Ind.: University of Notre Dame Press, 1990.

Stump, Eleonore and Norman Kretzmann. "Eternity." In *The Concept of God,* edited by Thomas V. Morris, pp. 219-52. Oxford: Oxford University Press, 1987.

Sturch, Richard. *The New Deism: Divine Intervention and the Human Condition.* Bristol: The Bristol Press, 1990.

Suchocki, Marjorie. "A Process Theology of Prayer." *AJTP* 2 (May 1981).

Swinburne, Richard. *The Christian God.* Oxford: Clarendon Press, 1994.

Tanner, Kathryn E. "Human Freedom, Human Sin, and God the Creator." In *The God Who Acts: Philosophical and Theological Explorations,* edited by Thomas F. Tracy, pp. 111-35. University Park: Pennsylvania State University Press, 1994.

Thomas, Gary. "Doctors Who Pray." *CT,* January 6, 1997, pp. 20-30.

Thomas, Owen. "Recent Thought on Divine Agency." In *Divine Action: Studies Inspired by the Philosophical Theology of Austin Farrer,* eds. Brian Hebble-thwaite and Edward Henderson, pp. 35-50. Edinburgh: T & T Clark, 1990.

Tillett, Wilbur Fisk. *Providence, Prayer and Power: Studies in the Philosophy, Psychology and Dynamics of the Christian Religion.* Nashville: Cokesbury Press, 1926.

Torrance, Thomas F., ed. *Belief in Science and in Christian Life: The Relevance of Michael Polanyi's Thought for Christian Faith and Life.* Edinburgh: Hansel Press, 1980.

Tracy, Thomas. "Narrative Theology and the Acts of God." In *Divine Action: Studies Inspired by the Philosophical Theology of Austin Farrer,* eds. Brian Hebble-thwaite and Edward Henderson, pp. 173-96. Edinburgh: T & T Clark, 1990.

Tracy, Thomas F. "Divine Action, Created Causes, and Human Freedom." In *The God Who Acts: Philosophical and Theological Explorations,* edited by Thomas F. Tracy, pp. 77-102. University Park: Pennsylvania State University Press, 1994.

————. *God, Action, and Embodiment.* Grand Rapids, Mich.: Eerdmans, 1984.

————, ed. *The God Who Acts: Philosophical and Theological Explorations.* University Park: Pennsylvania State University Press, 1994.

Tupper, E. Frank. "The Bethlehem Massacre--Christology Against Providence." *RevExp* 88 (1991): 399-418.

————. "The Providence of God in Christological Perspective." *RevExp* 82 (fall 1985): 579-95.

Turner, M. M. B. "Prayer in the Gospels and Acts." In *Teach Us to Pray: Prayer in the Bible and the World,* edited by D. A. Carson, pp. 58-83. Grand Rapids, Mich.: Baker, 1990.

van Inwagen, Peter. *An Essay on Free Will.* Oxford: Oxford University Press, 1983.

————. "The Place of Chance in a World Sustained by God." In *Divine and Human Action: Essays in the Metaphysics of Theism,* edited by Thomas V. Morris, pp. 211-35. Ithaca, N.Y.: Cornell University Press, 1988.

VanderMolen, Ronald J. "Providence As Mystery, Providence as Revelation: Puritan and Anglican Modifications of John Calvin's Doctrine of Providence." *CH* 47 (1978): 27-47.

Ward, Keith. *Divine Action.* London: Collins, 1990.

————. *Rational Theology and the Creativity of God.* Oxford: Basil Blackwell, 1982.

Weaver, J. Denny. "Conrad Grebel's Developing Sense of Deity." *MQR* 52, no. 3 (July 1978): 199-213.

White, Vernon. *The Fall of a Sparrow: The Concept of Special Divine Action.* Exeter: Paternoster Press, 1985.

Widerker, David. "Two Forms of Fatalism." In *God, Foreknowledge, and Freedom,* edited by John Martin Fischer, pp. 97-110. Stanford: Stanford University Press, 1989.

Wiles, Maurice. "Divine Action: Some Moral Considerations." In *The God Who Acts: Philosophical and Theological Explorations,* edited by Thomas F. Tracy, pp. 13-29. University Park: Pennsylvania State University Press, 1994.

————. *God's Action in the World: The Bampton Lectures for 1986.* London: SCM Press, 1986.

Witt, William. 23 March 1996 [E-mail message].

Wright, John. "Creation and Providence." *CTNSB* 10, no. 2 (spring 1990): 13-14.

Young, Robert. "Petitioning God." *APQ* 11, no. 3 (July 1974): 193-201.

Zemach, Eddy and David Widerker. "Facts, Freedom, and Foreknowledge." In *God, Foreknowledge, and Freedom,* edited by John Martin Fischer, pp. 111-22. Stanford: Stanford University Press, 1989.

Zwingli, Ulrich. *On Providence and Other Essays.* Edited by Samuel Macauley Jackson and William John Hinke. Philadelphia: Heidelberg Press, 1922; reprint, Durham, N.C.: Labyrinth, 1983.

Index of Names

Page numbers in bold type indicate that special attention has been given to the subject.

Index of Subjects

accident. *See* chance
agency, divine and human. *See* causation, divine and human
Alternate Service Book, Anglican, 19
Arminianism, 155
Barthian model, 179, **206-31**, 364, 394 n. 76
  critique of, by the middle knowledge Calvinist model, 317, 343
  critique of, by the openness model, 109, 227
critique of, by the redemptive intervention model, 138, 393 n. 51
Book of Common Prayer, Anglican, 19
butterfly effect, 94
Calvinist model, 99, 155, 179, **232-70**, 274-75, 276-77, 364
  critique of, by the Barthian model, 208, 210-11, 214, 229
  critique of, by the church dominion model, 126
  critique of, by the fatalist model, 282
  critique of, by the middle knowledge Calvinist model, 294, 300, 302, 305, 309, 317-19, 324-27, 330
  critique of, by the Molinist model, 157, 170-71
  critique of, by the openness model, 77, 89, 99, 102, 109, 135
  critique of, by the

redemptive intervention model, 135-36, 137, 138-39, 141, 148
  critique of, by the Thomist model, 187
case study of the abducted missionaries, 26
  in the Barthian model, 229-31
  in the Calvinist model, 266-70
  in the church dominion model, 129-31
  in the fatalist model, 284-85
  in the middle knowledge Calvinist model, 332-36, 345-47, 359-62
  in the Molinist model, 174-77
  in the openness model, 113-18
  in the process model, 68-70
  in the redemptive intervention model, 149-52
  in the semi-deist model, 49-51
  in the Thomist model, 202-5
causation, divine and human, 365-67
  in the Barthian model, 208-10, **212-18**, 220
  in the Calvinist model, 234-41, 243-48, 250-52, 256-65
  in the church dominion model, 124, 127
  in the fatalist model, 274-79
  in the middle knowledge Calvinist model, 291-92, 295, 298, 300-307, 323, 331-32, 338-47, 354-59, 405 n. 41
  in the Molinist model, 155, 164,

168-71
  in the openness model, 78, 82, **91-95**, 97
  in the process model, 54-63
  in the redemptive intervention model, 137-38, 141, 142, 144-46
  in the semi-deist model, 33-37, 38-42
  in the Thomist model, 168, **179-90**, 192, 197, 198, 199
chance
  in the Calvinist model, 237-38, 242, 247, 256-58
  in the fatalist model, 274
  in the middle knowledge Calvinist model, 306-9
  in the openness model, 78-79, 85, 94, 96
  in the process model, 63
  in the redemptive intervention model, 142
  in the Thomist model, 195
change of mind or plans by God. *See* repentance, divine
chaos theory, 94, 300
church dominion model, 101, **119-31**, 272, 363
  critique of, by the Calvinist model, 262
  critique of, by the middle knowledge Calvinist model, 297, 301-2
compatibilism, 73, 184-90, 191-93, 243, 246, 253, 282, 305, 311, 313, 365
concurrence. *See* causation, divine and human
continuism, 46

continuous creation, providence as
  in the Calvinist model, 236
  in the process model, 60
  in the semi-deist model, 42
corporate prayer. *See* prayer, by groups
Cyrus, 39, 89, 136, 144, 145
decree, divine. *See* plan of God
deism, 365. *See* semi-deist model
demons. *See* Satan and the demonic
determinism/indeterminism. 366-67
  in the Barthian model, 212-13
  in the Calvinist model, **243-48**, 249-50, 255, 258-59, 260, 274-75, 276-77
  in the fatalist model, 272-79, 281-84
  in the middle knowledge Calvinist model, 299, 310-14, 316, 317, 342
  in the Molinist model, 156, 166
  in the openness model, 84, 85, 96
  in the redemptive intervention model, 134, 135, 137, 138, 141, 148
  in the Thomist model, 180, 184-88
election, 365-67
  in the Barthian model, 207-8, 210, 215-16, 221
  in the Calvinist model, 252
  in the fatalist model, 279
  in the middle knowledge Calvinist model, 312, 346-47, 357
  in the Molinist